The Study and Teaching
of International Relations

The Study and Teaching of International Relations

A Perspective on Mid-Career Education

Edited by R.C. Kent and G.P. Nielsson

Frances Pinter (Publishers) Ltd., London
Nichols Publishing Co., New York

First Published in Great Britain in 1980 by
Frances Pinter (Publishers) Limited
5 Dryden Street, London WC2E 9NW

ISBN 0 903804 52 2

Published in the U.S.A. in 1979 by
Nichols Publishing Company
Post Office Box 96
New York, N.Y. 10024

Library of Congress Cataloging in Publication Data

Main entry under title:
The Study & teaching of international relations
1. International relations – Study and teaching
2. International relations – Study and teaching
(Continuing education) I. Kent, R.C. II. Nielsson, G.P.
JX1291 S775 1979   327'.07   79-1906
ISBN 0 89397 057 3

Typeset by Anne Joshua Associates, Oxford

Printed in Great Britain by A. Wheaton & Co. Ltd., Exeter

To Dr. Ross N. Berkes

whose commitment was the life-blood of the School of International Relations for almost three decades.

Contents

Foreword   *J. N. Rosenau*

Introduction   *Randolph C. Kent and   Gunnar P. Nielsson*

Acknowledgements

The editors are aware of the many people who have played roles in this unique academic experiment, the United Kingdom Graduate Program of the School of International Relations, University of Southern California. Amongst these, we would like to acknowledge Cdr. Hammond M. Rolph (USN, Ret.), deputy director of USC's School of International Relations, who has always guided us through the maze of academic administration with such care, wit and consideration.

We would also like to acknowledge Mrs. Luda Spilewsky for her attention to detail and her care for the students both in Los Angeles and in London.

We would like to thank the Graduate School and the School of International Relations of the University of Southern California for the significant support which they have provided for the program in general and this book in particular. We would like to thank many people, in London and in Los Angeles, for their support; but to name everyone and to explain the contributions they made would require another book. Our gratitude, however, to members of the "Core Faculty" must not go unmentioned, as well as our gratitude to Dr. John Schutz, Dr. Rebecca Dixon, Mr. Nelson Horn and Professor Susan Strange.

We would also like to use this opportunity to thank two other people. The challenges and the satisfaction of directing the UK program and writing and editing this book could never have been enjoyed without the support we received from our wives. Valerie and Bobbie may we thank you.

Randolph C. Kent
Gunnar P. Nielsson

Foreword

James N. Rosenau

This is a coherent collection of essays by colleagues who have shared a unique experience and who have extended themselves to share the valuable lessons of that experience with a wider audience. All of them participated, in one way or another and at one time or another, in the overseas graduate programs of the School of International Relations at the University of Southern California. In so doing they were constantly working at the cutting edge of change in world affairs. As scholars with disciplinary commitments and as educators dedicated to providing suitable training for mid-career students, their collective experiences and reflections offer a rich source of insights into both the dilemmas of international relations (IR) and the growth of IR as a serious and practical field of intellectual inquiry.

A central theme pervading all the ensuing essays involves the convergence of the study and practice of international relations. As the world gets smaller and increasingly interdependent, as socio-economic issues become ever more salient on the world's agenda, the training of practitioners in the field emerges as a crucial and urgent task for those institutions that offer programs in public affairs. No longer is the practice of IR confined to the conduct of diplomacy, the provision of consular services, or the formulation and implementation of military strategy. Today world affairs are also sustained in corporations, in trade unions, in banks, in universities, and in a host of other private, nongovernmental or supragovernmental agencies, with the result that a vast array of organizational roles have been, so to speak, transnationalized. That is, to the long-established responsibilities that have conventionally defined leadership positions in the private sector have been added a new set of obligations and opportunities pertaining to the international consequences of performance in the positions. Many corporate managers, bank officers, union officials, university administrators, religious leaders, and scientific specialists — to mention only a few of the more obvious roles — are now transnationalized. They now make decisions on behalf of their organizations or professional commitments that can have worldwide ramifications. This being so, it is plainly incumbent upon those who study and teach IP to supplement their long-established curricula and courses with materials and emphases that will enable these newly transnationalized, mid-career role occupants to retool, to acquire the sensitivities and information necessary to the creative performance of their new and expanding responsibilities.

As Director of USC's School of International Relations during three of the ten years of experience assessed in these essays, I can testify that the problems of reshaping curricula and mounting a dynamic mid-career program are both extraordinarily difficult and profoundly exciting. At stake is nothing less than the challenge of making the modern university immediately relevant to the needs of a rapidly changing world, and doing so in the context of ongoing intellectual assumptions and administrative procedures that were designed for an earlier, less complex era — not a no-win situation, but seemingly not conducive to much more than the circumstance of you-win-a-few-lose-a-few.

Among the most difficult problems involved in the building of a viable IR mid-career program are those that derive from the age and experience of the students it is designed to serve. These are not young people just out of college, but rather more advanced persons in their thirties and forties who had had one or another kind of intensive experience in world affairs. Thus the established techniques and procedures for evoking and sustaining the interests of students do not obtain. The interest and motivation are there, and the problem is to satiate them, to provide a training that has immediate relevance as well as a long-term perspective. The problem lies in the combination of these dimensions. The mid-career student, having been constantly in touch with the practical and day-to-day world, is likely to be impatient with the scholarly approach that seeks larger, long-term contexts in which to put the immediate situations. The scholar tends to look for the general pattern; the mid-career student tends to be interested in the particular circumstance; and this difference can serve as either a creative tension that enlivens a graduate program or a terrible mismatch that undermines it. A number of the ensuing chapters make it clear, at least to me, that the programs described here neither avoided nor yielded to this problem, that high standards of intellectual excellence were maintained even as allowance was made for the special concerns of the students, that the tensions between general and particular knowledge were used constructively, enabling the faculty and students to learn from each other.

In reading these essays one is also impressed with the concern for the depth as well as the breadth that underlay the curriculum. Six fields of inquiry – methodology, foreign policy analysis, international organization, international political economy, area and regional studies, and military strategy – comprised the core of the program and each of them were developed to such a fine point that they stand alone as separate and distinct fields even as they also mesh into a coherent program. Arguments about how IR should be divided into sub-fields abound, and there is of course no single, right way of subdividing, but it seems evident from Chapters 1–7 and 9–15 that those responsible for the USC programs in England devoted long and successful hours working out a scheme for subdivision that can be readily justified on both intellectual and pedagogical grounds.

For understandable reasons, none of the authors step back to assess the program for which they worked so diligently as one of the indicators of the changing face of world affairs. But from a transnational viewpoint, from the perspective of a shrinking world in which the activities and lives of individuals are shaped and altered by persons or circumstances in other lands, that is exactly what the scholars who sustained the USC program were doing. They not only trained transnational actors; they were transnational actors, key links in the chain whereby information about and conceptions of the international system get diffused throughout the system. The more complex international life becomes, the more do educational institutions emerge as vital sources of knowledge through which both private organizations and public agencies keep their personnel abreast of the changing environment in which they must function. As is clearly evident in the introduction, no one foresaw at the outset of the USC program in 1966 that it would come to play such an important role in the large world affairs community of London. But that did happen, partly because able people worked long and hard to make it happen, but perhaps mainly because a widening gap fostered by the changing world scene was there to be filled. If USC had not done it, some other university would have. The need for the retraining of individuals with transnational responsibilities in the ways of diplomacy, military strategy, and international political economy was too pressing to ignore, and it is surely significant, at least symbolically, that the gap was filled by a university from far off California, innocent with respect to the norms and procedures of British higher education, but also anxious to serve its self-defined mission as a contributor to international education. USC's central administrators did not always appreciate the tasks their people in IR had acquired for them, and often they failed to provide budgetary and moral support when it was urgently needed, but they were also so distant from the London scene that they allowed the program to unfold with a minimum of bureaucratic regulation. None of the British universities in London undertook the task because their established norms and procedures inhibited recognition of the need, much less efforts to fill it. So the job fell to a remote institution with a small IR school eager to expand its horizons. The result was truly transnational: an American institution with a largely British faculty training students from a variety of countries to be sensitive to the circumstances and conditions of the world's mounting interdependence.

I have long felt that there may well be other national capitals with large world affairs communities where the same changing circumstances have also created a need for a mid-career master's program that is both acute and unmet. And for a while I had the vision that the USC's School of International Relations might capitalize on its London experience and inaugurate similar programs on a global scale. Some preliminary discussions in 1978-1979 with counterparts in Australia and India, for example, affirmed that the gaps existed in Canberra and New Delhi and that efforts to fill it in those capitals might well be undertaken.

With a year's hindsight, however, it is clear that the vision of USC performing this role was ill-founded. Not only has its School of International Relations fallen on hard times, but further discussions have also revealed that, no matter how worthy the intensions, any proposal from any U.S. university to launch such a program would be greeted in many of the world's capitals as another instance of American imperialism. And this is perhaps as it should be. My original vision was obviously unrealistic. Clearly no single university can possibly do the job, and it was only the aspirations of a newly appointed Director (since resigned) to contributing a global discipline that allowed the vision to flourish in the first place.

But the idea was unreaslistic not because it smacked of imperialism (such impulses did not, I believe, underlie the vision). Rather in retrospect it appears inappropriate because it runs counter to the dynamics of trans-nationalization. Virtually by definition, these involve decentralization of the mechanisms and institutions through which the changes wrought by mounting interdependence are absorbed. The gap will have to be filled in a variety of ways by a variety of educational organizations in a variety of lands. That this will happen seems unquestionable. The need for mid–career retraining in IR is likely to grow on a global scale and thereby foster efforts to remedy it. And as that happens, the pioneering efforts described and assessed in these essays will surely serve as a valuable guide to the problems that will be encountered and to viable means of solving them.

Introduction

Randolph Kent and Gunnar Nielsson

The development of international relations as an academic discipline and the approaches used to teach that discipline to a mid-career student clientele are the two major themes which have guided us in writing this book. The book is based upon experiences gained from conducting an American graduate program in international relations for mid-career students in the United Kingdom since 1966.

For all the strengths and weaknesses of the University of Southern California's U.K. Program, we probably have engendered more conceptual coherence than most international relations programs and we have catered to a clientele that, over the years, has emerged as distinctly different from the conventional graduate student body found in British and American universities.

The instructors who have constituted the U.K. Program's "core faculty" during the last decade have each contributed original essays dealing with developmental perspectives of the major fields that comprise international relations studies as well as essays about their classroom experiences of presenting their various subjects to mid-career students. The editors, in addition to being core faculty contributors in two fields of concentration, provide accounts of the developments of the "teaching paradigm" which have come to characterize the curriculum structure of the U.K. Program during the decade they have served as program directors, Nielsson from 1969 to 1975 and Kent from 1975 to 1979.

To us, the introspection about our joint experiences suggests two levels of readership. The first is the beginning graduate student of international relations in general and the mid-career students who undertake programs such as ours in particular. We believe this book presents a suitable introductory overview to the professional study of interantional relations because it covers the basic issues about alternative approaches to the subject as a social science in both a comprehensive and coherent manner.

The second level of readership are those who, in one way or another, are involved in the rapidly expanding practice of mid-career education: instructors, university administrators, program planners as well as educational specialists. While we, ourselves, do not pretend to be pedagogical experts, we believe our experiences over nearly one and a half decades enables us to offer an interesting and useful case study in mid-career education.

The mid-career student

Viewing our subject in the widest possible perspective, the environment within which conventional higher education developed has been sustained, and has gained credibility in society is rapidly changing. The conventional student body has consisted of young people moving directly from twelve years of primary and secondary education on to four years of full time college and university education. Although a small proportion of them proceed to several years' advanced professional education, for most of them, at the age of 22 or 23, completing a bachelor's degree has been viewed as the exit visa from schooling.

Two converging trends of change are upsetting this conventional educational environment. In the first place, the constant change in post-industrial societies and the expanded leisure time accompanying increasing affluence have combined to create new attitudes toward higher education. More and more people have come to view formal education as a key source of adaptation, "retooling" and personal renewal for middle age and older age groups in the population. Educational planners have introduced the concepts of "continuing education" and even "permanent education" to capture the characteristics of the new practices whereby middle-aged professional people renew their formal educational efforts as a way of being responsive to constantly changing working conditions; whereby middle aged women seek new compensations for the "empty nest syndrome"; and whereby retired people finish a life-long ambition to complete an academic degree at a more leisurely pace.

The impact of this change in attitudes and practices has already begun to be felt, especially in undergraduate college and university studies. It has been estimated that 4.5 million out of the 11 million persons attending higher educational institutions in the United States are part time students. Some educational experts have forecast that, by the end of the 1980s, more than one half of American university students will be "mature returnees" over 35 years of age.

The second discernible trend has been the decline of the size of the conventional student body. This is explained in terms of changing demographic patterns in economically advanced societies and, to some degree, a reflection of increased disillusion with university education by young people because of the apparent lack of direct correspondence between academic achievement and enhanced career opportunities. Yet, many universities and colleges do not appear ready to undertake the adaptations in their administrative, curricula and pedagogical practices necessary to meet these changing operating conditions and, hence, to ensure their survival as institutions relevant to society as a whole. For example, the design of application forms and procedures is far removed from the characteristics of the mature returnees' life experiences; there is little or no provision for specialized guidance counseling for older students; few institutions are willing to experiment with giving academic credits for experiential learning; no attention is paid to the need for special remedial training to equip the older students with the study skills they lack after 15 to 20 years' absence from formal schooling; and few faculties have engaged in rethinking and consequent retooling in their teaching practices in order to be more responsive to the different needs of the new student clientele.

This broad characterization of major changes in the American higher education environment provides the general context within which we present the experiences we have gained from conducting a graduate program in international relations for mid-career students. However, the reader should be cautioned that we are not suggesting that our thoughts on mid-career education are in any sense comprehensive or definitive. What we are suggesting is that our experiences over fourteen years have led us to certain conclusions about our particular sort of clientele; that our conclusions have resulted from the tests and transitions of a vibrant program; and that, in preparing this volume, we hope that those involved in the burgeoning field of mid-career education, be they administrators, academicians, or educational specialists, will benefit from our particular experiences.

During the first ten years of the U.K. Program, most of the mid-career students were American military personnel and civilian employees of U.S. government agencies stationed overseas. Since 1975, the composition of the student body has changed significantly. In the early 1970s, a serious decline in what had been the program's traditional student body developed because of reductions of U.S. forces and, especially, the closing of several military headquarters in and around the London area. This situation led to the decision to take the program out into "the open market," so to speak, with the hope of interesting members of the diplomatic corps and the business community of London in becoming involved in a masters degree program. The result has been a remarkable transformation of the student clientele. For ten years, we had dealt with a culturally homogeneous group. During the last four years, the student body has become very heterogeneous, as the program had to adjust to the educational backgrounds, the cultural identities and perspectives of diplomatic officers from 43 different states (representing developed Eastern and Western states as well as the less developed Third and Fourth World states). Moreover, business personnel from more than 40 multinational enterprises, mostly American, with offices in the London area joined the program.

Hence, in our discussions throughout this book, when we refer to our mid-career students, we mean the military officers, diplomats and corporate executives who, in one way or another, are professionally affected as practitioners by the fluctuations and transitions of the international environment. In their own right, our students are experts in international relations professions that run the gamut from intelligence analysis and weapon systems maintenance to Eurodollar dealings and diplomatic procedures.

The development of such a diverse mid-career student body has presented yet another challenge for the program in terms of how to ensure unity and coherence in our approach to teaching international relations as an academic subject. In a general educational perspective, this type of student clientele has forced us to face such basic questions as: 1) How do we break down the fixed assumptions, the rigidity of views characteristic of older students? 2) How do we relate theories and models found in the academic discipline to the accumulated experiences of more mature students? 3) How do we broach the increasingly sophisticated social science methodologies to students who only too often shied away from mathematics because of poor performance in introductory courses in quantitative analyses twenty years ago? 4) How do we help a student "retool" in basic learning skills in order to think conceptually and to write graduate level research papers? 5) How can we cope with the need to introduce complex theoretical approaches when the students' historical understanding, let alone political science background are, at best, weak and mostly non-existent? 6) How do we satisfy the seasoned international practitioners who joined the program expecting it to be an extension of their professional experiences plus a survey of current events and are then confronted with an academic approach that emphasizes the need to generate new ways to think about world politics, to adapt to new analytical tools and to pose new problems and questions about the future? These are the type of educational conditions and issues which we have had to face in our fourteen years' experiences with graduate level teaching of international relations to a transnational, mid-career student clientele in an overseas environment.

One generalization which our joint experiences have taught us is that there is clearly a difference between teaching mid-career students and conventional graduate students coming straight from the ranks of high school and then undergraduate university studies to graduate school. We were not overtly conscious of the differences when the program was established. The differences and their constituent elements emerged as we gained experience over the years and became more explicit as we decided to assemble our thoughts for publication in this book. Generally speaking, the distinction between the mid-career student and the conventional graduate student is not one of quality in either direction. It principally entails levels of trade offs. The conventional graduate student approaches his or her education with a relatively higher degree of receptivity. This is not to suggest that cynicism or naivete or sophistication is common to one type of student and not the other. It is to suggest that, no matter how worldly the conventional student, when compared to the mid-career student, he or she uses educational experiences to form concepts views and opinions. To be part of this formative process is certainly a rewarding experience for most academicians. To watch a student savour a wide variety of contending ideas, to be both mediator and arbitor of concepts, to guide the development of opinions are the benefits of dealing with what we have called the conventional graduate student.

And yet, in this same vein, the conventional graduate student can challenge his or her instructor only within the parameters that the instructor has initially established. The feedback process, the learing experience for the instructor, in other words, is limited to the framework which the immediate educational process has determined. This is in contradistinction to the mid-career student. Most often, here is a student who approaches education with relatively fixed attitudes and beliefs, who knows what he or she wants to learn about and who can draw from perceived realities based on personal experiences to challenge or to confirm an instructor's ideas. In this sense, mid-career education is a dialogue, a meeting point of the practical and the academic.

While such conditions appear to undermine the rewards offered by teaching conventional graduate students, there are other rewards involved in teaching mid-career students. There is the reward of immediate feedback drawn from practical experience, the reward from implanting new ideas in reinvigorated soil which may be translated into practice quickly; there is the reward from establishing dialogues between the practitioner and the academician. But such rewards demand different approaches to teaching in order to kindle the dialogue and utilize the students' experiences as part of the teaching techniques in the classroom context. This is an area in which educationalists need to devote their expertise in the future in order to provide academicians in general with the pedagogical fruits of systematic enquiries which can serve as guidelines for improvements in teaching mid-career students. The accounts of our experiences which follows should only be considered a special case study within the general context of responsiveness to the changing environment in higher education.

The development of the United Kingdom Program in international relations

For any university which contemplates establishing an academic program overseas as an international branch of its home campus activities, the ideal model must surely be the ability to transplant geographically its home campus working conditions. The international branch would be an exact replica, but on a smaller scale, of the academic unit on campus. In its teaching dimension, such an ideal model would involve a steady rotation of the faculty who would gain international experience, would be able to conduct research in the field and would establish regular and long-lasting professional contacts with foreign academic colleagues which might blossom into an exchange relationship whereby foreign academicians would guest-teach on a regular rotation basis on the home campus and thereby bring about a continuous transnational linkage. All of these faculty activities would take place as part of a regular semester teaching load, on regular salary plus transportation costs covered without encroaching on accumulation of sabbatical leave time. While a major portion of the student body might be recruited overseas, the ideal model overseas program would provide the home campus students the opportunity to complete part of their education in an international environment taking courses which were an integral part of the university's regular curriculum and taught by regular home campus faculty.

In its research dimension, the ideal model international branch would provide access to research facilities for faculty and students equal to those prevailing on the home campus. Advanced graduate students could complete all or substantial parts of the field research in connection with thesis and dissertation requirements in this international program setting. Faculty could plan research projects which could be conducted there; in fact, joint research projects with international faculty might be justified by and be contracted for on the basis of the available foreign research facilities.

In its administrative dimension, the ideal model international branch would have established adequate office facilities and staff to provide efficient services giving support to all the teaching and research activities marking a vibrant educational enterprise. Finally, the financial dimension would be characterized by a self-sustaining budget with tuition income sufficient to cover all costs of the international program, including an overhead cost constribution to the home campus' general budget and, in very good fiscal years, an additional contribution to the home campus sponsoring academic unit to be used for new student financial aid, augmenting library resources and other such worthwhile endeavors.

From such dreams are decisions made to engage in experiments with international programs. The ideal model characteristics constituted explicit and implicit objectives to be realized when, in 1964, the University of Southern California accepted the invitation from the American Air Force in Europe to establish the first graduate programs for its personnel stationed there. As part of this experiment in part-time student, graduate education during off-duty hours, U.S.C.'s School of International Relations established a program in the United Kingdom in 1966.

With the hindsights and accumulated experiences of fourteen years, the most appropriate way to characterize the operation of the U.K. Program is that of a parasitic existence, working on the peripheries of two major organizations — the military and the university — whose primary functions did not allow for a great deal of attention to be paid to graduate education for part-time mid-career students. For the first decade, the governing conditions were a series of crises in a struggle for survival which was manifested by constant tension between maintaining academic standards and financial viability.

The U.K. Program was established with the expectation that it would be financially self-sustaining on the basis of tuition income — with military personnel using their individual Veteran's Administration allowance for education — augmented by logistical support from the Air Force in the form of office and classroom facilities, purchase of library materials and covering transcontinental travel expenses for faculty and administrative staff. By the fifth year of the program's existence, the Air Force contract was cancelled because they felt that tuition costs were too high. The U.S. Navy headquarters in London gave us a new and different contract (and the international relations program was introduced in West Germany sponsored contractually by the U.S. Army). Subsequently, the logistical support provisions have been reduced to office facilities only with the program budget assuming the cost of transportation, library purchases and rental of classrooms, all of which added strains on the budget.

More significantly, assignments of military personnel overseas became increasingly volatile as the armed forces were subjected to reductions of forces, resulting in major reorganization of bases and internal changes in the composition of units. The consequence for the U.K. Program was that the initial bases and headquarter stations became insufficient sources from which to recruit the number of new students necessary to cover the costs of the program. In response, by 1969, the U.K. Program began a process of "base proliferation" which lasted six years. A teaching center was established in Upper Heyford near Oxford which lasted until 1973. In 1973 another teaching center was established in a U.S. Government communication center in Harrogate, Yorkshire, which lasted until 1976. In 1973, without an Air Force contract, but legitimised as a program for U.S. military personnel by the Navy contract, we established an independent teaching center in a village college on the outskirts of Cambridge, equidistant from four Air Force bases from which the program has attracted students to make it viable to this day.

The consequences of base proliferation for the conduct of the program was considerable geographical dispersal and an expansion of the size of the student body to such an extent that the teaching loads could not be covered by rotating faculty from the home campus. The use of locally hired faculty, which in the early days had been minimal to augment the home campus faculty, gradually expanded to the point that, by the mid-1970s, the composition of the faculty had changed to consist of the program director as the "continuity person" from campus plus predominantly British faculty teaching on a part time basis with occasional guest-teaching by home campus faculty, mostly during summer sessions. While to the outsider this development could appear as a clear case of educational imperialist expansion by design, the changes were really the result of scrambling for financial viability on the periphery of major organizations which were under severe pressure to reduce their operations in Europe. As the School's Director of Special Programs, Ross N. Berkes, so aptly characterized this development: "Survival for us has been like jumping from sinking life-boats — and dragging the crippled crafts along so long as they were still afloat."

As mentioned earlier, by 1975 a major decision was made to expand the student body by trying to attract diplomats and corporate executives from multinational enterprises with offices in the London area. The success of this venture has changed the composition of the London teaching center student body to the point where military personnel comprise only one quarter of the mid-career students there. This new, heterogeneous student clientele in London and the independent teaching center in Cambridge have provided the U.K. Program with a degree of stability during the last three years which it has not had before. However, it is probably premature to create expectations of long term security for the program considering the past behavior pattern of continuous crises of survival.

Maintaining academic standards has meant a struggle to gain credibility with the faculty and administrative officials on the home campus for whom an overseas program is considered a peripheral activity which can quickly become a drain on university resources rather than an asset in the form of enriching the students' education with the experiences gained from international residence as part of completing a degree program.

The key issue has been the decision to operate the U.K. Program as a directly integrated part of the School's graduate curriculum rather than establishing it as a special degree or certificate program sponsored by the School of International Relations. The consequence is that the U.K. Program must comply with all academic standards in every respect while being conducted in a very different educational environment.

One of the constituent elements in maintaining academic standards has been to comply with admission requirements. While there has been no problem for a majority of applicants, the mid-career students do present significant differences compared with more conventional graduate students. We are dealing with applicants who have been away from formal schooling for ten to twenty years and who now present us with the criteria of seasoned professional maturity and seriousness of commitment as counterbalance to overcoming a checkered undergraduate transcript. Furthermore, everybody who applies struggle over the requirement of obtaining a satisfactory score on the Graduate Record Examination. Designed for completion at the time an undergraduate student reaches the senior year, middle-aged applicants suffer because they are rusty on the techniques of objective exam-taking as well as being rusty on the basic elements of quantiative analysis. In its verbal segment, the GRE's are designed with situational references to middle class American experience which too often create hardships for foreign applicants and American minority students.

To be responsive to these special conditions, a great deal of emphasis is placed on several personal interviews with the administrative director as well as the academic director for every applicant to the U.K. Program. Furthermore, the university's Graduate School has allowed a certain quota of applicants – between 10 and 20 percent – to be admitted in Special

Student Status based on the recommendation of the resident director and the home campus School director of special programs. That status allows the student to complete up to three of the eight courses required for the M.A. degree while retakes of the Graduate Record Examination are completed and a special admission status screening is done in which the coursework performance is taken into consideration. A regular mid-point formal screening process has been added through which the resident director and the local core faculty review the performance standard of each individual student. Hence, the quality of the student body, from admission to completion, is the subject of constant monitoring and screening to ensure a stringent adherence to standards necessary to maintain credibility with the university's Graduate School.

The quality of teaching is another important element also constantly evaluated to assure that the U.K. Program maintains academic standards similar to those on the home campus. A student input in the form of regular systematized evaluation of each course is one source of confirmation that teaching standards are kept high. the director of the program has always been a practicing international relations academician which assures constant monitoring of instructor quality. Over the years, a regular core faculty, consisting of established British academicians in the discipline of international relations, have been vitally important in developing excellence in teaching both by their individual contributions and by serving as referees in selecting new faculty members. Several of the core faculty members have guest-taught on the home campus which has provided a channel of mutual understanding and assessment concerning the quality of teaching. The expectation of regularly rotating home campus faculty involvement has not materialized to the extent hoped for initially. (Neither has the sustained interest in studying abroad by graduate students from the home campus materialized to the extent expected.) After the initial enthusiasm, many of the regular faculty have found teaching overseas too disruptive to both their private family lives and to their demands for continuous management of research programs on campus. However, at least one faculty member teaches in either the U.K. or the German programs every year and they provide another important source of validation that education standards are maintained. Finally, the School's Director of Special Programs chairs the oral examination of every M.A. candidate in the program during his bi-annual official visits which serve as a constant check on the quality of the faculty.

The provision of adequate study and research facilities is yet another constituent element in maintaining academic standards. It has involved the establishment of a regular textbook acquisition operation, the purchase of a sizeable library collection of general core reference materials, the arrangement of access to local university and research institute libraries and writing special overview pamphlets on available research facilities in the districts where the U.K. Program has had teaching centers. Program responsiveness to the demands for access to the tools of learning has progressed to the point that a special full time staff member is assigned to the role as "resource person" to assist the students in this respect. While it could not be claimed that the research facilities in international relations studies available to the U.K. Program students and faculty match those on the home campus, every effort has been made to meet the problem of part-time students working in a foreign environment and, in the London area, it approaches the functional equivalent of access to published resources maintained by the university campus in Los Angeles.

Careful attention is also paid to maintaining a student-faculty ratio which assures the small-group learning process of a graduate program. In spite of cost factors, whenever an introductory core course enrollment reaches around twenty students, it is divided into two sections. In general, the average class size in most of the courses is between 8 and 12 students.

For part-time, mid-career students, constant counseling is especially important. It is a tribute to the core faculty, who teach on a part-time basis, that they have provided excellent counseling in connection with their individual courses, while the director provides the necessary longer-term guidance and counseling about progression through the entire program.

Hence, maintaining academic standards has involved a process of constant monitoring and inspections by responsible officials in the U.K. as well as on the home campus. To convince doubting university officials that part-time, mid-career students could indeed comply with the strenuous requirements of the general study loads as well as specific research projects expected in a good graduate program, the School of International Relations mandated a professor from a different academic unit to conduct a systematic enquiry of the U.K. Program's standards. After a two months' visit to the U.K. Program and three months' study of comparable factors on the home campus, the final report, issued in December, 1969, concluded that the U.K. Program, ". . . is unquestionably of high academic quality and undoubtedly meets and surpasses the minimum standards of the Graduate School." Subsequently, representatives from the Graduate School made annual inspection visits during the early 1970s and, in 1975, all the European programs were inspected by the re-accreditation team of the Western Association of Schools and Colleges in order to be included as an integral part of the curriculum within an accredited university.

However, the stark reality of conducting an international educational program often differs considerably from the ideal model expectations which motivate universities to engage in such experiments. In spite of a general commitment to add international dimensions to the educational opportunities in major universities, the specific international programs often tend to become disputed stepchildren in a family preoccupied by its primary tasks of ensuring satisfaction of pressing needs on the home campus. Operating on the edge of the sword of educational quality and financial viability, maintaining an international program demands an intense, continuous commitment and immense resourcefullness by the responsible officials directly involved which can lead to unintended consequences in the struggle for survival.

Lest the reader should have concluded that the efforts have been futile and the outcome completely negative, let us hasten to add that the U.K. Program has evolved into a fine international relations program that has acquired a respectable reputation in academic circles in the United Kingdom as well as among the faculty in the university's Schol of International Relations. Working with a group of international relations specialists associated with John Burton's Centre for the Analysis of Conflict, the emerging British core faculty and the U.K. Program directors have co-operated since 1970 to establish a curriculum structure which is both comprehensive in scope and coherent in approach. The fact that the program directors have had a relatively high degree of flexibility in selection of local faculty and the fact that the British core faculty, in teaching for the U.K. Program, have been freed from the constraints of adjusting their activities within the established traditions of settled academic units in their respective "home" institutions, combined to provide the right conditions for experimentations in the development of the program which have led to the emergence of a "teaching paradigm" based on the world society analytical framework.

Overviews of both theoretical approaches to international relations studies and of social science methodologies with stress on the need to subject "the facts" to analyses based on competing theories leading to alternative explanations have become the hallmark of the basic core courses. Applying contending theoretical approaches to global-scope analytical topics such as strategy and conflict analysis, international co-operation and integration and foreign policy analysis comprise a second core element of the curriculum. Elective courses on regional international relations and special topics courses complete the characteristics of the existing program curriculum structure. By careful sequencing of the coursework, we believe we have succeeded in establishing a uniquely well-integrated approach to teaching international relations.

The strengths and weaknesses of our approach and the experiences of applying it to a special student clientele are subject to the reader's judgment upon a review of the discussions which follow in the rest of this book.

Introductory overview of the content of the book

This book is organized into three major parts. In Part I, the core reference literature used in teaching international relations in the U.K. Program is reviewed. Our experiences as teachers of mid-career students comprise the subject of Part II and student reactions to our teaching is presented in Part III.

The purpose of Part I, Developments in International Relations Studies, is to provide a general review of the core reference literature in various fields of concentration found within this academic discipline. We do not pretend that these reviews represent a comprehensive and exhaustive account of each field of concentration. Rather, the intention is to discuss key developments which each contributor views as centrally related to teaching his subject in the U.K. Program.

A broad developmental perspective of international relations as a social science is presented by Little in Chapter I. The main thesis concerns the pattern of development of international relations studies in the twentieth century. Within the general context of a movement from philosophy to differentiated social sciences, international relations was initially reformist and prescriptive in outlook and based on historical explanations methodologically. The idealist, reformist stage was displaced after the Second World War by the "Realist" power politics approach identified with the writings of Morgenthau. The more recent developments such as the rise of the behavioral movement, the introduction of systems theory and the state-centric versus the transnational and world society approaches are discussed in greater detail. Little concluded that the proliferation of theoretical approaches and research techniques have established many equally important and overlapping lines of cleavage, the co-existence of which makes international relations a complex, but exciting new academic discipline.

The so-called "great debates" about methodological issues are the subject of Mitchell's review in Chapter II. He analyzes the strength and weaknesses of the "classical" (traditionalist) approach which dominated in the 1940s and 1950s; the behavioral approach of the 1960s; and the post-behavioral approach of the 1970s. While the debates have been concerned with the "how" rather than the "what" of international relations studies, the expanded scope of the issues by the increased attention paid to general philosophy of science questions seems to have made that distinction less and less meaningful. The issues have also involved a persistent attack on the methodological weaknesses of a state-centric approach which have results in suggested alternatives such as the issues area approach, the world society approach and the social class approach characterizing the structural theories of the peace researchers.

The introduction of strategic studies as an academic field of specialization in university curricula is a relatively recent development, Groom observes in his review of strategy and conflict analysis literature in Chapter III. Strategic studies have tended to be public policy oriented and "value promotive" with a great power bias. A basic problem is that there is no adequate conceptual framework for the analysis of "grand strategy"; i.e., at the level where military, economic and political factors converge. Groom concludes that there is a trend toward putting the field in a broader perspective as more theory-oriented strategic analysts return to a concern with first principles such as the nature of conflict, the causes and functions of conflict and its dynamics of exacerbation and abatement. It seems likely that the focus of the recent literature on decision-making processes in connection with procurement policy formulation, the role of the military–industrial complex in industrialized states, and the sociological attributes and political roles of the military in less developing states will lead to an incorporation of strategic studies and conflict analysis into the political sociology of the world society approach.

In Chapter IV, Taylor reviews the development of international institutions in terms of the problems of, and the prospects for, developing a working constitution in international society. Since the First World War, studies of the role of international institutions have been characterized by four phases. First, and coinciding with the existence of the League of Nations, international institutions were viewed as instruments of state policies. Subsequently, they were viewed as actors with the capacity to define positions on international issues and, then, as "effectors" capable of bringing about changes in the environment within which they operate (the integrative developments of regional institutions such as the European Communities were viewed as "effectors"). Most recently, the roles of international institutions are viewed as that of potential "controllers" in issues areas where the individual states seem unable to control the situations; e.g., policies on developing seabed resources and other issue areas which reflect the general condition of complex interdependence.

Harrod develops the thesis, in Chapter V, that the current phenomenal rise of international political economy studies is the response to certain developments since the end of the Second World War. These developments have called into question the adequacy of the hitherto predominant liberal–capitalist theories of international economics with their emphasis on principles of commodity exchanges, comparative advantages and econometric modelling based upon such principles. He views the emergence of less developing states, the growth in size and scope of operation by multinational enterprises, the energy supply crisis, and the slow-down in growth of the industrial states as key factors in the shift in focus toward greater concern with, and incorporation of, political variables in theories purporting to explain economic behavior. The establishment of "development economics," the emergence of dependency theories and greater recognition of interdependence in the world economy are manifestations of the new political economy emphasis. By adding issues of equitable distribution (and severe maldistribution) to issues of efficient production, it becomes clear that an international political economy approach must include politics, diplomacy and the struggle for power.

The development of various approaches to foreign policy analysis is the subject of Chapter VI. The main issue, according to Kent, is how to reconcile the differences in emphasis between the phenotypic approach of studying how a particular state formulates foreign policies on particular issues and the genotypic approach of focusing on a general analysis of how states function as a specie in the international system. In his review, Kent shows that the development of new approaches to foreign policy analysis has made this field of concentration more sophisticated. Studies based on a "process orientation" have been improved since the decision-making approach was introduced by Snyder *et al.* as a significant challenge to the more simplistic Realist, rational-actor approach. It has led to more careful scrutiny of the psychological, organizational, cybernetic and sociological variables involved in policy-making processes. Kent also reviews the more recent development of comparative studies of foreign policy which includes attempts to verify a relationship between patterns of state attributes and external behavior as well as Rosenau's challenging linkage politics framework which attempts to break down the level of analysis problem according to which previous studies of state behavior had been divided.

Finally, in Chapter VII, Nielsson provides an overview of the studies of regional international relations. His thesis is that there exists a basic epistemological and methodological incompatibility between the configurative approach followed in area studies programs and the empirical theoretical approach to international relations studies. He presents an analysis of the main characteristics of American area studies programs as they have evolved over the last three decades in order to demonstrate the prevalence of the configurative approach. In addition, he argues, the development of a theory-guided approach to regional studies has also been hampered by the fact that most of the newer theories have been global in scope. In his review of the theory literature on regional interantional relations, Nielsson discerned three basic categories; the regionalism and world order approach, regional integration theories and the regional subsystem approach. The most recent conceptual frameworks, which treat regions as global subsystems, had introduced a comparative dimension, but they suffer from a lack of methodological refinement.

Teaching the various international relations subjects to mid-career students is the focus of Part II. It is organized in the same topical sequence as Part I and includes a discussion of how the different subjects are presented and developed in the courses. We shall dispense here with more specific characterizations of each chapter, similar to the introductory overview of the chapters in Part I. Instead, we shall review the major points raised by the authors concerning teaching international relations in general, the sociological attributes an intellectual predispositions of the mid-career student clientele, and the instructors' experiences in teaching this particular type of students.

The review of the U.K. Program's curriculum structure, presented in the beginning of Part II, clearly demonstrates the "teaching paradigm" which has come to characterize the program, with its emphasis on a conceptual approach both in the formal theory course and the analytical topics course, plus the exposure to the requirements of rigorous social scientific methodology. The diversity and disparity of theories and methodologies reveal the insecurity that generally haunts academics teaching the subject of international relations as an independent academic discipline. The world society approach provides an especially provocative challenge to the attempt by "mainstream" state-centric, power politics theorists to establish well defined boundaries by which the independence of the discipline is supposed to be marked. The problem of defining boundaries remains a constant source of insecurity and disputes for all teachers of international relations and it stands in clear contradistinction to the equally persistent pre-occupation with unity within the discipline. The effect on teaching international relations is that students must be prepared to accept contentions about fundamental principles and to live with the confusion created by the need to evaluate the same "realities" with different and often competing theoretical and methodological lenses.

There is agreement among the authors that what differentiates midcareer students from conventional graduate students is that they represent the epitome of professional transnationals. They have already traveled the globe widely. They work in large, complex bureaucracies with world-wide connections — whether public organizations such as foreign ministries and military forces or private organizations such as large, multinational enterprises. Hence, their professional reference worlds are characterized by hierarchical authority relations and specific issue and policy directive behavior patterns. From an academic perspective, the mid-career students enter their graduate studies with extremely diverse backgrounds both in terms of undergraduate degree specializations and professional experiences. Generally in their mid-thirties when entering the program, the mid-career students have had their first formal educational experiences during the Cold War period when security issues were of paramount significance in studying world politics.

In terms of intellectual predispositions, mid-career students are extremely pragmatic. They are concerned with direct, immediate experiences, with power, with strategies of determination to win in conflict situations. When pursuing an advanced graduate degree, they judge educational objectives by what is perceived to be useful for their present professional positions. Their professional expertises often work as "blinkers" to an appreciation of the more broad-scope approaches to international relations studies. They have a tendency to overlook the significance of value preferences in social choice situations and, from their experiences with clear-cut authority relations in their daily professional lives, their attitudes toward decision-making processes are relatively impervious to the effects of long-term systemic forces. They have a penchant for order and organization due to their professional environments often manifested by their relative intolerance of ambiguity. Mid-career students' professional experiences are frequently augmented by paying great attention to the mass media as sources of additional information and interpretations of major events in the world around them. Initially, mid-career students are mostly oriented toward a rather mechanical learning process. They view the theory courses as a "right of passage" to proceed to coursework they perceive as more concerned with the specific substantive realities of world politics; but they will accept a new conceptual and methodological "box of tools" if those tools are shown to be directly applicable to analysis of issues which relate to their work experiences.

Compared to teaching conventional graduate students, who have no or very little practical professional experience, the mid-career student clientele confronts the instructor with a combination of diverse past formal educational backgrounds and at least a decade of practical professional experiences in subject areas where the instructor has none. In such a context, rather than trying to compete with the students' practical experiences in international relations, the primary purposes of the U.K. Program has been to offer competing theoretical views of the world as bases of explanation. In other words, to persuade the students to accept the complex and ambiguous "reality" that different theoretical and methodological perspectives represent different codifications of the same "facts" and to inculcate a frame of mind that accepts the need to evaluate specific issues through multiple paradigmatic approaches in order to create awareness of alternative explanations. Such an educational objective requires a commitment to a learning process that involves expanding the scope of enquiry and deepening of understanding rather than mechanical accumulation of facts about a set reality. It has been our experience that the professional training, the previous political experiences and long term cultural socialization comprise formidable barriers to the successful achievement of our primary educational objective. The search for parsimonious empirical theories, stimulating conceptual frameworks and verified empirical generalizations about recurrent patterns of behavior are likely to be dismissed as irrelevant pursuits preserved for "ivory tower" academicians. In teaching pragmatic mid-career students, we have tried to break down such barriers gradually by accepting that most of them begin their venture into methodology course requirements by single case studies — initially viewing the more sophisticated methodologies as too esoteric. Sometimes we have been successful in using mass media analyses as common points of departure for a reexamination of particular issues through different theoretical perspectives. In other cases, the multi-cultural composition of the members of a particular class have been used as starting points for developing specific national interest perspectives on common foreign policy issues, an interesting way to demonstrate the problem of ethnocentric bias in the study of international relations. This incremental approach has been accepted as necessary stepping stones in the learning process. Through constant coordination of core course instruction, through students' experiences with conducting an advance "mini-thesis" research project, and through the review program preceding the final comprehensive examinations, we hope that students are led toward the preferred outcome of an increased theoretical and methodological sophistication in the analysis of the discipline. The specific characteristics of this learning process, as each instructor has experienced them, are the subject of Chapters VIII through XV in this book.

In part III, the students' reactions to the U.K. Program are discussed in different contexts. Responses by graduates to a general survey about the program experiences as a whole are presented in Chapter XVII. While some aspects were criticized, the major features of the U.K. Program were strongly supported. In their evaluations of the teaching approach, the curriculum structure and the academic administration, the respondents stressed the high quality of instruction and the comprehensiveness and coherence of the approach to international relations studies which characterize the presently structured curriculum. Key courses were identified in terms of degrees of difficulties, relevance to the "real world" (as they perceived it) and degree of enjoyment. The survey established that completion of the program had had a significant impact on subsequent career developments for one third of the graduates.

In the different context of a single graduate's perspective, in Chapter XVIII Pieragostini presents his reaction to the alternative conceptual frameworks introduced in the core courses. He focusses the discussion on the differences among the traditionalist power theorists, the state-centric empiricist behavioralists and the world society approach.

In Chapter XVIII Sandole discusses the impact of one instructor's teaching on students' attitudes. He has measured degrees of attitude changes among students in nine classes on three different core course subjects which he has taught over a four year period. He then provides interpretative explanations of the reasons for discernible patterns of changes from Realist to "Non-Realist" attitudes toward international relations.

PART I

DEVELOPMENTS IN INTERNATIONAL RELATIONS STUDIES

CHAPTER 1

The Evolution of International Relations as a Social Science

Richard Little

In the origins of Western thought, a fundamental distinction can be found between history and philosophy. The historian studied the constant flow of events precipitated by human interaction and attempted to explain the relationship between the events using a narrative account. The philosopher, on the other hand, made a search for the unchanging aspects of human experience. It was from these philosophical roots that contemporary natural and social science evolved.

The study of international relations, however, has traditionally been studied as history. Only in the twentieth century has there been a move to identify international relations as a social science. As a social science, therefore, international relations has rather distinctive antecedents. In this chapter I shall try to trace these antecedents by contrasting the development of international relations with social science.

The emergence of the social sciences

It can be argued, as Woodworth does, that the social sciences are as "old as the inquiring self-conscious mind of man". (1) In making this argument, it is assumed that the social sciences have grown out of an awareness by the individual of his or her relationship to the environment, followed by a desire to understand this relationship. We are all, according to this line of argument, incipient social scientists. In terms of recorded thought, the contemporary social scientist can certainly trace his or her roots back to the early Greeks, whose philosophers pondered at length upon man's relationship to the environment. Aristotle, for example, concluded that because of the capacity for rational argument and action, man has become not only a social but also a political animal and it is this characteristic which distinguishes man from the other creatures of nature. Subsequent

1

philosophers, informed by this line of thought, have, as a consequence, always found it necessary to explore the political dimension of human behaviour.

For philosophers in the past then, there was an intimate connection between the study of politics and the study of society. The demarcations which have grown up between disciplines — with sociology, for example, being separated from politics — are a fairly recent phenomenon. From the time of the early Greeks until at least the seventeenth century, philosophers were engaged in what Rickman calls an 'undifferentiated search for knowledge' and philosophy was equated with the sum total of scientific knowledge; there was not even a sharp distinction drawn between the naural and social sciences. (2) It should not be concluded, however, that when in the hands of the philosophers the social sciences were part of a "universal science" and possessed of a coherence which has in more recent times, with the emergence of separate disciplines, been completely lost. This is not quite the case; knowledge has always been compartmentalized — but it is true that there was, before the emergence of independent disciplines, what Schumpeter identifies as a "compound of sciences". The "compound" rested on the assumption that the natural and the social world was governed by a set of universal laws which the philosopher could discover by a deductive or rational process of thought.

Knowledge, however, has followed the line of an exponential curve and the "compound" survived only until the onset of the scientific revolution when the knowledge curve began its dramatic vertical sweep. At that point, Schumpeter argues, the "compound broke to pieces as the exigencies of the division of labour asserted themselves". (3) Progress was made as individual scientists came to concentrate on narrow avenues of knowledge and so, first in the natural sciences and then later in the social sciences, knowledge began to expand on the basis of independent disciplines. With this development, it has become increasingly clear that the individual is no longer the repository of all knowledge; knowledge is a commodity to which the individual only has access through the medium of the written word. Knowledge resides in what Popper calls the "third world", separate from a common physical world and the divergent mental world which are the possession of each individual. (4) The distinctive quality of this knowledge, or so it came to be thought, was that its status as knowledge was dependent upon empirical observation. Knowledge which could not be verified by observation came to be down-graded as metaphysical.

After the emergence of separate disciplines in the natural sciences, philosophers continued to hold sway over the undifferentiated social sciences. But these philosophers were closely in touch with the remarkable developments taking place in the natural sciences. Seventeenth-century philosophers such as Hobbes and Descartes endeavoured to develop a view of man and his relationship to the environment which was compatible with the contemporary image of the physical world as expounded, for example, by Galileo and Harvey. They used the successful ideas derived from the natural sciences as models for the social sciences. Subsequently, with the very rapid growth of knowledge it became increasingly difficult for philosophers to keep track of the research done by natural scientists and, according to Toulmin, as a consequence, philosophers began to rely on outdated views of how natural scientists were depicting the world. (5) With the passage of time, philosophy came to be identified with metaphysics and a sharp distinction was established between "philosophical" and "scientific" understanding.

Inevitably, therefore, the status of philosophy as the fountainhead of knowledge began to decline. There was a growing faith amongst those who wished to develop an understanding of human behaviour in what has come to be known as positivism, that is, the view that the procedures of the physical sciences are the only available model for acquiring reliable knowledge. (6) These developments made it only a matter of time before the social sciences would also split away from philosophy and follow in the wake of the natural sciences.

By the eighteenth century, the cleavages between philosophy and the social sciences were already becoming evident. Economics emerged at this time as an independent social science, separate from its philosophical origins, on the one hand, and its long association with *oeconomia*, or household management, on the other. There was an attempt by the neophyte economists to identify behavioural laws which would describe economic activity in any social context. (7) During the nineteenth century, further fragmentation took place and the modern foundations of psychology, sociology and anthropology were laid down. In all cases the influence of positivism was strong and there was a powerful desire to emulate the natural sciences which had made such huge intellectual strides since they had established their own identities. Indeed Comte used the term "social physics" before finally settling on the term "sociology" to describe the "science" of social phenomena which he was so anxious to develop. Progress, therefore, was associated with the establishment of autonomous disciplines which would proceed using the methods adopted by the natural scientists. These early days of the newly emerging social sciences were ones of optimism and there were few doubts that the social sciences would be able to keep pace with the progress being made in the natural sciences. Of course, not everyone interested in the study of human behaviour welcomed this development. Many social scientists preferred to maintain the link with philosophy, believing that human behaviour is not amenable to analysis on the basis of scientific method. They insisted that the reflective method of the philosopher was more appropriate to the study of human behaviour than the systematic empiricism of the natural scientist.

Philosophy and the emergence of international relations

Although it is perhaps easy to overdraw this picture of the social sciences, one by one developing a sense of independence and breaking away from philosophy — and certainly, as we shall show, there have been other ways of characterising their development — it does correctly give the general impression that they emerged from a common source and on the basis of a similar process. This picture, however, contrasts sharply with the general view of how international relations came into existence as a separate discipline. The majority of the social sciences have developed on the basis of a rich philosophical tradition. Sociology, anthropology, economics, psychology and political science all have important philosophical antecedents. But past philosophers, as both Wight and Lijphart have pointed out, failed to develop any sustained body of thought about relations among states. (8) Lijphart has argued, however, that it would be wrong to say that there is no philosophical literature in this field. Although scattered and cursory, philosophers have had something to say about international relations.

There is, however, some dispute amongst international relations specialists about the degree of diversity which this literature displays. Lijphart, for example, insists that the literature can be associated with a single, distinctive view of the world. According to Lijphart, philosophers depicted international relations in terms of sovereign states interacting in an anarchical international system on the basis of a balance of power. This assessment of the philosophical literature has, however, been contested by Bull, who asserts that it is possible to identify three quite separate philosophical approaches to the analysis of international relations. (9) He associates the approach identified by Lijphart with Hobbes who believed that states always stood in a "posture of warre" because of the absence of any international sovereign. But he contrasts this view with that presented by Grotius who contested the Hobbesian view, arguing that states are in practice constrained by the existence of international laws. This position reflects a belief which can be traced back to Aristotle: that men, because

4

they are rational thinking beings, will voluntarily subscribe and submit to rules since it is only on the basis of rules that order can be established. Finally, Bull identifies an approach associated with the views of Kant. According to Kant, while it may be true (as Hobbes suggests), that the interests of states are basically in conflict, it is also true that the interests of individuals are essentially in harmony. It is, therefore, the existence of states, argues Kant, which prevents the realization of these common interests.

With the rise of positivism and the use of a systematic form of investigation, social scientists endeavoured to confront and resolve many of the age-old controversies debated in the past by philosophers. However, despite existence of contrasting views of international relations these have failed in the past to generate the kind of philosophical debate which provided the bedrock upon which most of the social sciences were built. The spirit of inquiry and controversy with which most social sciences were imbued when they were initiated did not, therefore, extend to international relations.

The reformist phase of international relations

The emergence of international relations as an independent discipline came not as a challenge to the sovereignty of philosophy and an attempt to resolve on-going philosophical debate, but as a response to real world events. Appalled by the carnage of the First World War, academics accepted a responsibility to identify factors which would promote peace in the future. It was from this basis that international relations was established. The new discipline was, therefore, initially reformist and prescriptive in outlook. Those responsible for instigating the new discipline held to the common belief, inherent in a Hobbesian view of the world, that war had occurred in the past because of the way that the international system had been organised. For many, the guidelines for change were embodied in the provisions for peace which President Wilson laid down during the First World War in his Fourteen Points. It was believed necessary, for example, to redraw political boundaries so that nations and states coincided, and to establish an international organisation which would provide a forum wherein the nation-states could work out their disagreements by debate rather than by violence. (10)

The new discipline was established, therefore, with the primary task of resolving the persistent problem of war; and the problem was not defined in terms of a limited understanding of the phenomenon of war, but rather in terms of the difficulties associated with bringing about change. The response to this difficulty as Thompson has pointed out was an upsurge of interest in international law and international organizations. (11) After the First World War, the vast majority of academics in the United States with an interest in the field of international relations were working in one of these two areas. Moreover, these academics were not concerned with empirical investigations of the conditions under which law and organisations had worked successfully in the past; they were preoccupied primarily with technical and procedural questions. It was assumed, therefore, that provided the necessary changes were introduced, peace would follow automatically.

This essentially pragmatic approach which prevailed when international relations was first established is clearly very different from the orientation which characterised the initial phase of the mainstream social sciences. The difference is even reflected in the titles used to designate the disciplines. "Psychology", "anthropology", "sociology", "economics" and "politics" are all labels which are neutral in terms of time and space. They do not commit the scholar to look at human behaviour in a particular area, in a particular era. The titles given to the various social sciences lack historical specificity and this historical bias reinforces the idea that when the disciplines were established there was a conscious desire to follow in the direction set by natural sciences: there was to be a search for general laws which would cut across the barriers of time and space. In practice, there has been a tendency for the social sciences to be both time specific and ethnocentric but this failure does not serve to invalidate the original aim. If there had been any intention of attempting to follow in the tracks laid down by the established social sciences, then the study of international relations ought to have ended up with a designation such as "interpolymetrics" or "macropolitics" to emphasise that the discipline was not concerned with the "here and now" but the "what has and always will be".

Although it may appear that this point is either trivial or facetious, the fact remains that the discipline associated with the subject matter of international relations had never attracted a title which has won universal approval. In the words of one critic, for example, the application of the term international relations to a discipline which purports to study relations among states, is "superficial and inaccurate and, therefore, misleading". (12) These strictures are directed at the use made of the word "international", a term coined in the nineteenth century by Jeremy Bentham and denoting activity "among nations". (13) As any first-year textbook is quick to point out, however, the political units which interact in the global arena are rarely coterminous with nations. Nor would the term "inter-state relations" help, since the state can be considered a

6

tolerably recent phenomenon and such a title would exclude any study of the interaction among polities which do not constitute states. It can, of course, be argued that this demand for semantic precision is pedantic since words almost invariably acquire connotations which extend far beyond what they originally denote. At the same time, however, the importance and relevance of such a dispute over semantics should not be allowed to obscure the essential point that international relations was established initially with the objective of generating ideas about law and organisation which would be applied by decision-makers in their endeavour to avoid war; it was not concerned with uncovering laws which would assist in the comprehension of an infinitely complex reality. Because the objective of the discipline was instrumental rather than investigatory, academics in this area never made any serious attempt to develop a neologism comparable with those employed by the established social sciences.

History and the emergence of international relations

By the twentieth century, although it was being discovered, painfully or otherwise, that progress in understanding human behaviour was much more difficult to achieve than had been predicted by those under the influence of nineteenth-century optimism, a commitment persisted to the aim of making the world intelligible by identifying valid generalisations and on the basis of these generalisations forming "scientific" laws and theories in the manner of the natural sciences. The discrepancy between this approach and the approach being adapted by specialists in international relations, however, did not reflect any innate arrogance but rather the persuasive influence of a very different tradition or mode of thought. The difference can be identified even in terms of intellectual origins. Thus while social sciences such as sociology and politics can trace their lineage back to Plato and Aristotle who can clearly be identified as philosophers, international relations looks backwards to Thucydides who was not only a philosopher but also an historian. (14)

The nature of the distinction between philosophy and history is contentious, but as Bock has shown very clearly, it is possible to trace the divide between history and philosophy to the early Greeks. The Greeks drew a distinction between the search for "laws and processes of social change" — a task which can be associated with the philosopher — and the establishment of a "record of change" — a task associated with the historian. In more formal terms, the distinction between philosophy and history reflected for the Greeks a "division of human experience into natural and accidental categories". (15) Such a division has persisted until the present day. It is evident, for example, in A. J. P. Taylor's discussion of the origins of the Second World War. "Wars", stipulates Taylor, "are very much like road accidents. They have a general cause and particular causes at the same time." The general cause of every road accident can be attributed to the "invention of the internal combustion engine"; but at the same time, there are particular causes; "excessive speed, drunkeness, faulty brakes, [and] bad road surface". (16) In the case of war "international anarchy" provides the general cause, while the particular causes are the idiosyncratic, contingent events which precede the outbreak of war.

Taylor then goes on to attack the idea of using general causes to explain events in international relations; the "defect" in using "international anarchy", for example, as an explanation of war is that "since it explains everything, it explains nothing". In fact, Taylor has picked something of a strawman to attack in order to make his point, for while philosophers have considered that "international anarchy" provides a necessary pre-condition of war, it has not been considered to constitute a sufficient condition to explain the advent of war. At the very least, the balance of power is also introduced as an explanatory variable to account for the existence of both war and peace in international relations. Despite this caveat, Taylor's analysis does serve to illustrate the gulf which has traditionally existed between philosophers and historians: philosophers have always searched for the unchanging factors which underlie the human condition while historians have striven to provide specific explanations of particular events.

The historian, by inclination, therefore, is predisposed to dispute determinism. There is a dislike of what is sometimes called "philosophies of history" − attempts to discern overarching patterns and trends in history. For the historian, history unfolds on the basis of contingent events and not on the basis of a predetermined plan. Popper dubs such philosophies of history as "historicism" and has delivered a stinging critique of all attempts to depict the course of history as predetermined. (17) There is no doubt, however, that early social scientists, Marx, for example, were very attracted to the idea of developing a philosophy of history which would thereby allow the social scientist to describe the future course of society. Historians are inherently sceptical of such endeavours and when pushed to the extreme argue, to the contrary, that history can be described in terms of, and is determined by, the actions of a limited number of important historical individuals. This line of argument was seen to be particularly persuasive in the area of diplomatic history. For the historian, to understand and explain the invasion of Russia by France in

8

1812, for example, it is only necessary to identify how Napolean perceived the situation and identify the grounds for his perception. Once this is done, then the action becomes perfectly comprehensible.

International relations has traditionally been studied from this perspective, with war and peace described and explained in terms of the motives and actions of the major decision-makers. For the international historian, history was determined by Castlereagh and Metternich, by Palmerston and Bismarck. Even in more recent times, a similar mode of analysis can be identified; for example, the Second World War, according to Taylor, was brought about by the opportunism of Hitler. The historian therefore decries the search for overarching laws; the historian insists that the mode of explanation found in the natural sciences is inappropriate as a model for explanations of historical events. History can only be examined as a sequence of contingent events and it requires a narrative account as a consequence. A major element of this account will be, of course, the idiosyncratic motivations of the actors who precipitate the events. The historian, therefore, has developed a very different kind of explanation to the one favoured by positivists in other areas of social science. (18)

It was on the basis of historical explanation, however, that the new discipline of international relations was established; and this tradition is very different to the philosophical foundation from which the mainstream social sciences emerged. It meant, for example, that the new specialists in international relations felt under no compunction to search for general laws which could describe and explain the action of states. In line with the diplomatic historian it was assumed that the future course of events was neither predetermined nor beyond the control of decision-makers; instead it was accepted that the course of history would unfold on the basis of deliberate actions taken by the key decision-makers.

In addition, the new specialist also assumed that the orientation of all decision-makers in international relations had changed. In the past it had always been in the interest of decision-makers under certain circumstances to foment war. As a consequence, war had been a recurrent feature of international relations. But it was now believed that because of the horror of the First World War the viewpoint of decision-makers in all states had changed. War had been demonstrated to be disfunctional for all parties: victors and vanquished alike. As a consequence, academics proceeded on the assumption that decison-makers in all states would be willing to resolve disputes by peaceful means. It followed, therefore, that the most important task for the academic was to develop ideas about techniques, procedures and institutions which could help states to reach accommodation when they disagreed. International law and international organizations appeared at that time to represent the most important sources of peaceful change available at the inter-state level and it was in those areas that academics concentrated their attention.

This approach, however, implicitly rested upon the assumption which had traditionally been made by diplomatic historians: that the course of events taken in international relations could be understood and explained in terms of the motives of the statesmen operating in the international arena. There was little or no allowance made for the idea that an international event such as war might represent the unintended consequence of interactions amongst states and that an explanation for the behaviour of states should not therefore be sought in terms of the motives of the statesmen involved, but rather in terms of the nature and configuration of the participating states. A logical consequence of this line of argument is, of course, that war may ensue no matter how good the intentions of the participating statesmen. When international relations was initiated as a discipline, however, academics eschewed this apparently deterministic idea and were predisposed to accept the more voluntaristic form of analysis associated with diplomatic history from which could be derived the potentially optimistic conclusion that war may be avoided provided that decision-makers are motivated to avoid war.

In the years following the First World War, specialists in the study of international relations persisted in their attempt to develop mechanisms of peaceful change. With the passage of time, however, their endeavours became increasingly remote from events which were actually taking place in the international arena. The hope that decision-makers would be motivated to use international law and international organisations to resolve their disagreements was not realised and, as a consequence, it became progressively more unrealistic to work on the assumption that war would be avoided because decision-makers were motivated to maintain peaceful relations. However, with few exceptions, there was little inclination within the newly formed discipline to extend the field of study to include an examination of war and conflict. (19)

To a large extent this failure to change direction can be explained by institutional and professional inertia, but it is also possible to point to a degree of ethnocentrism within the discipline which encouraged a kind of intellectual myopia. In this connection, it should be noted that international relations was first established as an independent discipline within the United States and Great Britain. Both can be described as *status quo* countries which did not consider that there was any need for fundamental change in the international arena. Both countries, therefore, were likely to benefit from a world where order and change were determined on the basis

10

of international law and international organisations. Ethnocentrism influenced the thinking of the academics in these two countries to the extent that they failed to appreciate that decision-makers in other countries still considered war as a rational policy to pursue. Most of these Anglo-American academics did not take sufficiently into account the fact that not everyone experienced their own revulsion of war. As a consequence, they persisted in their examination of modes of peaceful change while international events proceeded along a different course, leading to the outbreak of the Second World War.

The realist phase of international relations

With the benefit of hindsight, the first phase in the development of international relations has been dubbed not so much as one of reformism but of idealism, a period of wishful thinking when academics looked at how reality "ought to be" rather than "how it is". One of the first expressions of this viewpoint is found in *The Twenty Years' Crisis* written at the end of the 1930s by E. H. Carr, an English historian with a special interest in international relations. Carr conceived of international relations as a science and argued, moreover, that the subject was passing through the same initial stages which the more mature sciences had experienced. For Carr, international relations, like all sciences, had come into existence to satisfy a particular purpose: medical science was designed to deal with sickness, and engineering arose from the desire to build bridges; in the case of international relations, the purpose was to "cure the sickness of the body politic". Carr then suggested that during the early stages of scientific development, "the element of wish or purpose is overwhelmingly strong" and as a consequence this phase is characterised as "utopian". The alchemist, for example, is depicted as a utopian thinker who did not stop to inquire "whether the properties of lead were such as to make it transmutable into gold". It was, therefore, "only when the visionary project ended in failure that the investigators were prompted to apply their thoughts to an examination of the 'facts' ". (20)

Carr saw himself as the harbinger of change in the study of international relations — a realist — who was prepared to examine the "facts" about international relations and to move the discipline beyond the "visions" which had been described by the early "idealists". With the outbreak of the Second World War and the collapse of the plans to preserve peace, Carr's line of argument proved very persuasive and his description of the discipline moving from a utopian phase to one of realism was widely accepted. In retrospect, however, it can be seen that his description involves a misrepresentation. The misrepresentation centres on Carr's claim that the realist, unlike the idealist, examined "the facts". As Carr himself demonstrated very effectively in a subsequent work, "facts" do not exist except in so far as they form part of an interpretation. As he puts it "a fact is like a sack — it won't stand up till you've put something in it". (21) Facts, therefore, only come into existence when an analyst develops an interpretation of reality. Using this line of logic, it follows that the alchemist was no more of a utopian or less of a scientist than a modern chemist. The alchemist simply operated on the basis of a different interpretation of the "facts". And similarly, the idealists were no more or less utopian than the realists; they also simply interpreted their "facts" from a different perspective.

The perspective adopted by the realists finds its most authoritative expression in Hans J. Morgenthau's *Politics Among Nations*, perhaps the single most influential work produced since the inception of the discipline. Morgenthau, a European *émigré* to the United States, is normally identified as the founder of the realist school of thought in international relations, although in fact he only gave expression to a line of thought which can be traced back to Thucydides. However, although there are others, who have expressed very similar ideas, it was Morgenthau who was seized upon and used to provide a new direction for the discipline. In contrast to the idealists who held to the voluntaristic idea that it was possible, if decision-makers were so desired, to develop and maintain peaceful relations amongst states. Morgenthau and his fellow realists clung to the deterministic notion that the behaviour of states is governed by certain unalterable laws and attempt to operate against these laws will never succeed. These laws, according to Morgenthau are "impervious to our preferences" and it follows, therefore, that "men will challenge them at the risk of failure". (22) At the heart of Morgenthau's thesis is the assumption that "statesmen think and act in terms of interest defined as power". In other words, states only act to maintain or enhance their power position; power, for Morgenthau, represents the most important explanatory concept in international politics and on the basis of this concept, it is possible to "bring order and meaning to a mass of phenomena which without it would remain disconnected and unintelligible".

As already indicated, there is nothing new about Morgenthau's thesis. The realist position can be traced back to Thucydides who argued, as an historian, that behind all the reasons given for the outbreak of the Peloponnesian War lay the "unalterable" factor of power. (23) International historians continue to cling to the idea that power constitutes the concept which can best order and explain the complex of material with which they have to deal. Charles Mee, for example, in his analysis of the Potsdam Conference, held in 1946, which was to set the scene for the Cold War, rejects the wide variety of theories advanced to explain the breakdown of relations between the United States and the Soviet Union. Each explanation is flawed, he argues, by the "assumption that men sought peace only to be overwhelmed by forces beyond their control". Mee insists that the record of the Potsdam Conference will not support this "comforting view of good intentions thwarted by irresistible forces". He advances, instead, the purely realist view that the conference "exhibits three men who were intent upon increasing the power of their countries and of themselves and who perceived that they could enhance their position more certainly in a world of discord than of tranquility". (24)

Interpretations of this kind have the virtue of making explanations of events in international relations both dramatic and remarkably straightforward. For this very reason, Rothstein has argued that Morgenthau's thesis proved to be very attractive to decision-makers as well as to academics not only because it could be readily grasped, but also because it confirmed their intuitive notion of how the world operated. (25) Thus Morgenthau has been habitually associated with a rather stark and somewhat simplistic view of pure "power politics", although in point of fact, this represents an over-simplification of his position for it fails to take account of his observations about an "ineluctable tension" between the dictates of power and those of moral command, and also his belief that power politics is not incompatible with the emergence of world government. A power political or realist interpretation of international relations, therefore, is only straightforward if these complicating factors are omitted. Such complications, however, are frequently glossed over generally in order to highlight the difference between realism and idealism.

Although a proper appreciation of Morgenthau's position would require an exegesis of these complicating factors, such an exegesis is not necessary for an understanding of Morgenthau's role in the development of international relations as an independent discipline. The importance of realism in general and Morgenthau in particular arises from the stress laid upon the need for theory in order to understand international events. By accepting this line of argument, the discipline began to move in the direction taken earlier by social scientists in other disciplines and it is not surprising to find by social scientists in other disciplines and it is not surprising to find Morgenthau asserting, therefore, that by developing a theory, it becomes possible to conceive of international relations in terms of an "autonomous sphere of action and understanding apart from other spheres, such as economics". It can be inferred very clearly from the realists, as a consequence, that to emerge as an independent discipline, international relations requires an independent theoretical framework.

The emergence of behaviouralism in social science

It is ironic that at the very time when international relations was beginning to come of age as an *independent* social science, there was a powerful movement developing in other areas of social science committed to eliminating the boundaries which had been established between the disciplines over the previous hundred years. There was a growing feeling that these lines of demarcation were not so much boundaries as barriers which were proving to be insurmountable, preventing social scientists from communicating with each other. As a consequence, economists, for example, were considered to be developing theories about economic behaviour which failed to take account of, and on occasions ran contrary to, the findings of psychologists. At least to some social scientists, therefore, it seemed imperative to establish an approach which would demolish the barriers which were perceived to be separating disciplines and stultifying the development of the social sciences. These advocates of an interdisciplinary approach came to be known as behaviouralists and by the late 1940s a "behavioural movement" had been launched.

In essence, the behaviouralists wished to identify some means of transcending the established disciplines. Not surprisingly they looked first to the natural sciences for guidance and it seemed apparent that underlying the disparate areas of knowledge in the natural sciences, providing a unifying factor, was the use of scientific method. Behaviouralists, therefore, quickly established that the application of scientific method should constitute the *sine qua non* for all behavioural research. Although this insistence on the application of scientific method proved uncontentious for the more established social sciences, such as economics and psychology, in sociology, anthropology and political science, the association of behaviouralism with scientific method precipitated a split within these disciplines between behaviouralists and anti-behaviouralists. The reason for this was because many academics in these fields continued to favour a reflective philosophical mode of analysis and were strongly opposed to a "positivist" approach to knowledge. In practice, therefore, behaviouralism, as a movement, proved more effective in terms of splitting the existing disciplines than drawing the different disciplines together.

As well as being committed to the use of scientific method, the newly emerged behaviouralists were also united by an unwillingness to operate within the constraints of the established theoretical frameworks which had

14

in the past served to give some cohesion and unity to the existing social sciences; behaviouralists came to consider these frameworks as "unscientific". Marxism and functionalism constituted the two major albeit opposing theoretical positions available to social scientists at that time and each had acquired staunch supporters from all disciplines. Moreover, because they represented sharply contrasting views of man and society, they tended to serve as the basis for many key debates found within the divergent disciplines which made up the social sciences. (26) At first sight both Marxism and functionalism appear to provide useful potential theoretical frameworks on which to base research. Under the influence of philosophers such as Popper, however, behaviouralists started to depict such frameworks as unscientific on the grounds that they represent closed systems of thought, closed because they are not amenable to falsification subsequent to empirical investigation.

The early behaviouralists were firmly convinced that many of the divisions of opinion found in social science could be resolved by empirical investigation. They were critical of the reflective approach favoured by some social scientists, and the use of *ad hoc* examples to illustrate theoretical ideas in preference to systematic investigation of reality. For the behaviouralist, the major task was to go into the real world and find out what was actually happening. The "traditionalist", for example, would know "from experience" that the willingness to take risks varies and he might speculate as to the reasons for the variation but the behaviouralist would want to find some means of measuring the variation, so that individuals could be callibrated along a dimension of risk — having achieved a measure of risk-taking, the behaviouralist would then endeavour to discover factors which influence risk-taking. For example, if the behaviouralist found that factors such as age, sex or social background affected the willingness to take risks, these would be considered important findings.

Within a comparatively few years, on the basis of this kind of research, it was possible to put together an inventory of "scientific findings" about human behaviour drawn from the work of behaviouralists operating in the various social sciences. It seemed as if behaviouralism had quickly come of age, however, with the publication of these findings came a barrage of criticism. These criticisms were not only from anti-behaviouralists but also from social scientists who favoured the use of scientific method; both groups argued essentially that the findings were either "banal" or so atomistic and fragmented that they gave no sense of cumulative knowledge. (27) It was argued that behaviouralism had spawned findings without generating theory which could order and explain the findings.

The criticism from those who favoured the use of scientific method reflected the existence of a major long-standing division amongst social scientists. On one side of the dividing line there are, and have always been, social scientists who believe that it is the behaviour of the individual which constitutes the legitimate focus of attention for the social scientist. Explanations, therefore, must always be formulated from the standpoint of the individual. Advocates of this school of thought are referred to as methodological individualists. On the other side of the fence are the holists or collectivists. Social scientists of this persuasion believe that individuals are intimately linked into social systems, such as the family, a firm, or a factory, and that their behaviour is fundamentally affected by the characteristics of the system in which they operate.

Social scientists, therefore, should be searching for properties of the systems in which individuals operate. For example, an holistic statement would take the form that as organisations grow in size, they develop increasingly hierarchical structures. This statement reflects the holistic belief that systems display behavioural properties, independent of the individuals who operate within the system. Explanations must, as a consequence, be sought at the level of the system and not at the level of the individuals who comprise the system. Methodological individualists strongly contest this idea and insist that systems do not exist, except as a collectivity of individuals. (28) Explanations must, therefore, be grounded at the level of the individuals. So, the example about organisations given above is, at best, incomplete for the methodological individualist because it is operating at the level of systematic abstractions. It must be reduced to the level of individual behaviour. Only then is there a satisfactory description and explanation of the situation.

Some of the criticism levelled against the behaviouralist came, therefore, from social scientists who felt that behaviouralism had ignored the macro-level or system aspects of individual behaviour. Moreover (according to the holist), the fragmented nature of behavioural findings was inevitable, because the behaviouralist ignored the critical importance of the systems in which individuals operate. It is perhaps not surprising that some of the most stinging criticism against the behaviouralists came from Marxists and functionalists who both accept the need for thoughts. (Although Marxists were also quick to point out that the behaviouralists tended to have a distinct functionalist, *status quo* bias.)

Philosophers of science have traditionally argued that science developed only when it moved away from attempts to get holistic explanations of the natural world. As a consequence, they have always been sceptical of the efforts in social science to develop explanations, putatively scientific, which are holistic. However, after the Second world War, a body of scientists, began to develop an area of thought under the title of General Systems Theory, which argued that as a consequence of anti-holism amongst natural scientists, science is now completely fragmented, lacking any sense of integration. This body of thinkers argued that the notion of a *system* could be used to reintegrate scientific knowledge. They stipulated first, that anything can be conceived of as a system, that is, a set of related parts: an atom consists of a set of related parts; an organism consists of a set of related parts; the weather can be conceived as a set of interrelated parts. More important, they argued that there are a limited set of principles which govern all systems. It was on the basis of these principles that they intended to reintegrate scientific knowledge.

The general systems theorists did not, however, stop at the natural world. They insisted that there are man-made systems and that these are also embraced by the same set of limited principles which govern the natural world. Now, of course, many social scientists who favoured an holistic approach found this an immensely exciting idea and so, after the Second World War, as the ideas of the General Systems Theorists became known to social scientists, so the conception of a systems approach gained currency in social science. Although equated with behaviouralism, because of its emphasis on scientific method, systems-thinking brought the old debate between holism and methodological individualism back to the centre of the stage.

The emergence of behaviouralism in international relations

Although the early realists moved international relations away from the historical mode of explanation which had implicitly continued to influence the idealists after the inception of the discipline, they were unalterably opposed to the discipline developing a behavioural perspective. Morgenthau, for example, like many social scientists, simply did not believe that the scientific method of investigation can be applied to the analysis of human behaviour. He compared the international relations specialist to a portrait painter who can, on the basis of training and inborn skills, reveal all the essential features of international relations. The analysis of human behaviour for Morgenthau is a question for interpretive skill, using known laws of human behaviour; it is not a question of scientific investigation. Morgenthau's frame of reference, his laws of human behaviour, reflect in fact a closed and therefore deterministic mode of thought. For example, Morgenthau's central proposition, that: "statesmen think and act in terms of interest defined as power" admits no exception and therefore allows for no variation. It constitutes a high-level proposition – a general theory — which is an anathema to the behaviouralist who believes that investigation must start with the variation which can be found in all human behaviour. (29)

Given the dominance of the realists' position and the widespread belief that Morgenthau had provided an adequate explanation of international relations, it is not surprising to find that behaviouralism made a slow start in the study of international relations. It was only in the mid-fifties that behaviouralists began to emerge in international relations. It was also to be expected that because of the opposition by realists to behaviouralism that the behaviouralists should be seen as establishing a second school of thought in opposition to the realists (or "traditionalists" as they later came to be called). At that time, the disjunction between the two schools of thought appeared to be absolute. The difference between realism and behaviouralism is evident when their respective approaches to decision-making are compared.

When analysing decision-making in international relations, Morgenthau worked from the premise that decision-makers are completely rational. His thesis rests upon the notion of rationality and he has, as a consequence, difficulty in dealing with situations where decision-makers appear to have acted irrationally. In the latest edition of *Politics Among Nations*, for example, he accepts that the involvement by the United States in Vietnam may only be explainable by reference to a "coherent theory of irrationality" but he insists that such a situation must be defined in terms of a "pathology" of international relations and no attempt is made to account for such behaviour within his theory. (30) Richard Snyder, on the other hand, who was one of the first behaviouralists to venture into this area argued that state actions flow not from an objective, rational evaluation of any situation but rather from the decision-maker's subjective definition of the situation. (31) The task of the analyst, therefore, is to identify and explain the factors which precipitate divergent definitions. A wide variety of factors, ranging from the personality of the decision-makers through to their standard operating procedures can affect this definition and Snyder hoped that having made a check list of the pertinent factors, it would be possible on the basis of a large number of case studies to build up empirical generalisations relating these factors through to variations which occur in the way decision-makers define any given situation. In practice, there have been, as yet, insufficient case studies to make such generalisations and there is some scepticism if progress can be made in this direction. As doubts were being experienced in this area, systems theory emerged out of the scene and appeared to open a more promising line of investigation.

The development of a systems approach in international relations is normally associated with Morton A. Kaplan. Although there were other scholars such as McClelland who recognised the importance of the systems approach at an earlier date, it was with the publication of *System and Process in International Politics* that the significance of a systems approach was generally acknowledged. (32) From the start, Kaplan insisted that only by employing a systems approach could international relations develop as a social science and his interest centred not on specific interactions among states, but rather on "model behaviour within a particular kind of international system". As dictated by the systems approach, therefore, Kaplan was advocating that the explanation for state behaviour be moved from the level of the individual decision-maker and up to the level of the international system.

In contrast to Morgenthau, and the realists in general, who argued that the fundamental characteristics of international relations are unchanging, Kaplan boldly asserted that the characteristic behaviour of international "actors" – not states, which are historically specific entities – can undergo major transformations and that it was the task of the international relations specialist to develop models of international systems which would generate an explanation of these divergent patterns of behaviour. Kaplan was, in other words, making a strong plea for a move away from a preoccupation with events in contemporary international relations and towards a theoretical concern with the way in which the structure of the international system can affect the constituent members of that system. As if to reinforce this plan, Kaplan chose not to delve into the past in order to identify periods where the characteristic behaviour of international actors could be shown to differ. Instead while accepting that history can be depicted as the laboratory of international relations, he set up purely theoretical models of different international systems. Although two of these models drew upon knowledge of the past, the other models include features which have never been observed to exist; these features served to emphasise the central thesis that the model behaviour of actors in any international system will be affected by the structure of that system.

Kaplan's work has subsequently run into a great deal of criticism, but it is important to acknowledge that he did pioneer a much more theoretical approach to the discipline and in doing so he provided a clear indication of the benefits to be derived from working to develop an alternative to the historical mode of explanation. The criticism has been primarily on the grounds that Kaplan's models emerge as closed systems, similar in form to Morgenthau's conception of the international system, and just as Morgenthau is unable to explain deviant behaviour, so Kaplan is unable to explain the process whereby systems are transformed. (33) Nevertheless, Kaplan did successfully draw attention to the importance of examining transformations in the international system. He broke the historical spell which had been cast by Morgenthau.

Transformations in the international system and the study of international relations

Kaplan's plea for a theoretical study of system transformation coincided with the realisation by many scholars — both behavioural and traditional — together with many decision-makers that dramatic changes were occurring in the contemporary world which were precipitating major transformations in the international system. From the end of the Second World War, for example, it was evident that it was no longer adequate to discuss the security of the state in terms of a balance of power. It appeared that this time-honoured mechanism had given way to a global division between two competing blocs which affected relations through the international system. Bipolarity had superseded the balance of power and — at least in Kaplan's formulation — such a development constituted a transformation in the relations among states. But even before the ramifications of bipolarity had been fully assimilated, technology precipitated another critical development with the introduction of intercontinental ballistic missiles. The conception of nuclear deterrence came of age and Americans immediately recognised that future wars could potentially result in the desolation of the United States. For the Russians, and indeed most Europeans, this did not represent a new phenomenon, but for Americans, who had grown accustomed to the idea of inviolable security afforded by their continent's hitherto impregnable position, the idea of direct and devastating attack proved revelatory. In the words of one scholar, the state had been rendered "permeable"; the hard shell of territoriality had been stripped away, and he forecast — although he was to recant some years later — the end of the state system. (34) Other scholars, more sanguine, and hopefully more prescient, argued to the contrary that the event ushered in a new age of peace into great power relationships. (35)

Not surprisingly, strategic studies blossomed and flourished during this period when defence planners were having to revise radically and with increasing frequency the strategic doctrine designed to maintain the security of the state. Not all scholars appreciated this concern with the "wages of war" and this whole school of thought has been subjected to some withering attacks; but as the dilemma which new arms technology poses for security persists so also does the interest and concern with strategic studies. (36)

To many observers, however, the emergence of nuclear deterrence seemed to ossify the structure of the international system. Moreover, because the conflict between the two blocs associated with the East and the West was aparently so deep-seated, reflecting fundamental ideological differences as well as a power confrtonation, it appeared superficially that the cleavage had permeated every aspect of international relations. It took a perceptive theorist to draw attention to the failure of bipolarity to explain much of what was going on in the world: that this was not more apparent was only because of the continuing preoccupation with great power relations – a legacy of realism. Regional subsystems, however, were displaying an internal dynamic unaffected by the division between the Soviet Union and the United States and, moreover, because of this "discontinuity", as the "super powers" developed interests in these regions it was becoming apparent that both super powers were establishing sets of interests which were neither coherent nor compatible. (37)

Nowhere was this phenomenon more clearly displayed than in Western Europe where, after the Second World War, the United States rapidly developed a complex of competing interests. One of these interests – encouraging economic collaboration in Europe – came to fruition with the founding of the European Economic Community. Academics saw the community as initiating a unique experiment in international co-operation opening up the possibility of major transformation at the regional level, and establishing a new area of study for the specialist in international relations. Although interest in the process of integration at the international level had been given serious attention by isolated scholars for many years, it was only with the establishment of the European Community that the discipline as a whole turned its attention to the phenomenon and within a very short space of time, integration emerged as a significant area of concern. As Deutsch demonstrated very clearly, however, there was nothing intrinsically new about the process of integration since it was on this basis that most European states had come into existence. It would seem, therefore, that the new-found interest was generated primarily by the emergence of the European Community which could serve as a laboratory for social scientists. (38)

On the face of it, the formation of the European Community posed a major challenge to the dominance of the state-centric approach which has traditionally dominated the study of international relations. The approach, closely associated with realism, is often identified with a "billiard-ball" model, which depicts the international system in terms of interactions among a set of cohesive independent actors all operating on the basis of rational principles, designed to maintain the autonomy of the state. In

21

practice, the emergence of the European Community left the "billiard-ball" model largely unscathed because realists were able to see the Community as a potential "super-state" — which did indeed represent the hope of some early advocates.

Nevertheless, since 1950, the billard-ball model has come under increasing attack. One source of attack came from academics with a special interest in international relations who had begun to play an active role in the formulation of American foreign policy and who had become increasingly conscious as a consequence of the mismatch between the assumptions built into the billiard-ball model and their own experiences. What they observed, within the process of policy formulation in the United States, was a set of competing bureaucracies, each with their own set of values and interests; policy was the product of the interaction amongst these bureaucracies. (39) At the same time, they were also made aware of the range of pressure groups, beyond the government circle, which also affected the direction taken by foreign policy. From this perspective, foreign policy formulation appeared not as a rational response to changes in the external environment, but more akin to the process whereby domestic policy is made. The net result was a growing interest in foreign policy analysis and it has now become a separate field of study. As Americans became increasingly conscious of "mistakes" being made in American foreign policy, particularly the débâcle in Vietnam, it was to foreign policy analysis that they turned for an explanation. Here, if anywhere, seemed to lie the source of Morgenthau's "pathology" of international relations.

While foreign policy analysis certainly added a complicating factor to the analysis of international relations, it still worked essentially within a framework which assumed the states are independent autonomous actors. By the 1960s, however, analysts were beginning to have severe reservations about whether events within the contemporary international system could be accommodated within such a framework. Rosenau, in particular, began to point to the way the boundaries between states were becoming increasingly blurred. (40) Activities in one state could frequently only be explained by reference to activities in another state. This phenomenon was particularly apparent in economics where decisions designed to deal with a problem in one state, had ripple effects which lapped over the boundary of the state and began to affect activity in other states. (41) But this interlocking of economic systems was also affecting the political decision-making process. Rosenau endeavoured to characterise this phenomenon as linkage politics, but, partially because decision-makers began to discuss linkage in a different context, it became more generally described in terms of transnational politics and interdependence. Intimately associated with the phenomenon of interdependence was the phenomenal growth of non-state actors, ranging from international terrorist groups through to the world bank. Indeed, so dramatic did all these developments begin to appear that for a period academics were almost seduced by the idea that the state was about to be overwhelmed by the process of interdependence and that the international system would succumb to new forms of global organization with the multinational co-operation being advanced as a likely contender. There were, however, plenty of realists around only too ready to douche any such speculation and cogently argue that states were unlikely to abrogate either their power or their authority. As a consequence, it is still widely accepted that for the moment, whatever new phenomena emerges within the international system, can be safely accommodated within a state-orientated framework.

The current state of the discipline

The impression may now mistakenly have been given of international relations as a rather fickle discipline, moving from subject to subject in such a way as to keep pace with changes in the world. But this is not the case, although it is true that the horizons of the discipline have been steadily expanding. Starting with a central interest in international law and international organisation, the range of interest within the discipline has been constantly enlarged during the twentieth century. Thus although the discipline has now been extended to embrace the study of interdependence, this was not done at the expense of other subjects already established such as strategic studies. Other subjects have continued to grow and evolve. At the same time, however, it must be acknowledged that there is an element of fashion, or topicality, within the discipline and general interest in any particular subject or approach does tend to wax and wane.

The proliferation of approaches and research techniques constitutes one of the most distinctive features of international relations at the present time. Alker, for example, has identified twelve different schools of thought currently operating in the United States and when attention is turned to Europe, the number increases. (42) The growth in approaches, however, does not tell us anything about the growth of knowledge and understanding in the discipline. Not surprisingly on this issue there are clear differences of opinion, primarily because there are epistemological differences about what is meant by growth of knowledge. On the one hand, it is argued that there is a growth of knowledge when the level of information about a subject is extended. Those favouring an historical approach tend to be inclined to this position. There is, therefore, always an element of excitement when a new set of foreign office archives are opened up; although the excitement is tempered by past experiences which suggests that the new archives are unlikely to contain any dramatic revelations. Behaviouralists, on the other hand, influenced by the epistemology of the natural scientist, are loath to admit that knowledge accumulates on the basis of increasing information. For them, knowledge only increases when a new level of theoretical understanding has been achieved. The general conclusion reached by a group of eminent social scientists at a symposium devoted to this question was that no accumulation has as yet taken place. (43) Some, however, were encouraged by the proliferation of approaches and methodological techniques employed within the discipline, seeing this as a necessary preliminary to the growth of knowledge.

Conclusion

In the mid-sixties, it was common to talk about a Great Debate in international relations. The "Debate" was between "behaviouralists" such as Kaplan and "traditionalists" such as Morgenthau and Bull. One school advocated, and the other deplored, the use of scientific method. Although, of course, there was some substance to this debate, in many ways it failed to pay sufficient attention to other "debates" which were equally important within the discipline. It was assumed that this debate took precedence and that all other debates were subsumed under the "great" methodological divide.

Now that the dust has begun to settle and it is possible to look at this debate in the context of earlier and later debates, it becomes clear that it was quite erroneous to think of the discipline divided along a single cleavage. As the discipline has grown and matured, it is apparent that, over time, a whole series of debates have been superimposed one on top of the other and the discipline has, as a consequence, become increasingly diverse and complex.

So, although the "traditionalists" and "behaviouralists" were divided on how to study international relations, they were agreed on the need to make general propositions about international relations. They must, therefore, be distinguished on the one hand, from the narrative historian who wishes to develop explanations of idiosyncratic events and the Marxist historian, on the other, who believes that there are historical epochs which are identified by changes in the mode of economic production.

By the same token, the division between the behaviouralist and the traditionalist tells us nothing about the normative position of a scholar: whether it is believed, for example, that the current international order is just or unjust, or even whether this is a question which ought to be asked by the international relations specialist. There is, needless to say, a fundamental division of opinion on these questions. In this chapter, I have endeavoured to chart the evolution of the discipline of the twentieth century where the narrative historical approach was generally accepted.

During the first half of the twentieth century, this mode of analysis persisted and was predominant within the discipline. At the same time, throughout this period, as Wolfers observed in a very perceptive article, the idea of a "multi-state system composed of entities of strikingly similar character and behaviour appeared realistic to observers and analysts alike". (44) The discipline, therefore, had a unity of focus and method.

Since 1950, however, the discipline has undergone dramatic changes. It has been infused by the notion of social science. As a consequence, it has inherited all the debates and conflicts which exist in the social sciences. These conflicts, moreover, do not converge along a single cleavage line. Scholars divided by the cleavage line defined by one debate are likely to find themselves united on another. Paradoxically, therefore, although from one perspective, the discipline can appear very divisive because it is riddled with so many debates, from another perspective, the large number of cross-cutting cleavages established by the debates can have an integrative effect. Both these perspectives are true and it is this fact, more than any other, which distinguishes the natural and the social sciences as areas of knowledge. In the natural sciences, in every discipline there is universal consensus on the core areas of knowledge. No such consensus exists in the social sciences.

As international relations has evolved as a social science, therefore, it has lost the unity of focus possessed when the subject was viewed only as diplomatic history, but as the subject has become more diverse in terms of method and approach, it has gained in terms of the intellectual challenge it poses for students of the discipline.

References

1. Robert S. Woodworth, *Contemporary Schools of Psychology*, London, Methuen & Co., 1964, p. 3.
2. H. P. Rickman, *Understanding and the Human Studies*, London, Heinemann, 1967, p. 1.
3. J. Schumpeter, *History of Economic Analysis*, New York, OUP, 1959.
4. See Karl R. Popper, *Objective Knowledge: An Evolutionary Approach*, Oxford, Clarendon Press, 1972, where he discusses at length his ideas about World 1, World 2 and World 3.
5. S. Toulmin, *Human Understanding*, Princeton, PUP, 1972.
6. The association of positivism with the methods of the natural sciences was first

7. The search for "general laws" is a characteristically "positivist" conception of what science involves. Many social scientists believe that such laws cannot be found in the social world. However, economists have managed better than any other discipline to derive what approximates to general laws. See W. H. Riker, "The Future of a Science of Politics", *American Behavioural Scientist*, 21, 1977, 11–38.

8. See M. Wight, "Why is there no International Theory" in H. Butterfield & M. Wight (eds), *Diplomatic Investigations: Essays in the Theory of International Politics*, London, Allen & Unwin; and A. Lijphart, "The Structure of the Theoretical Revolution in International Relations", *International Studies Quarterly*, 18, 1974, 41–74.

9. H. Bull, *The Anarchical Society*, London, Macmillan, 1977.

10. See Alfred M. de Zayas, *Nemesis at Potsdam*, London, Routledge, 1977, where the failure to implement Wilson's principles is discussed.

11. See K. W. Thompson, *Realism and the Crisis of World Politics*, Princeton, PUP, 1960.

12. John A. Lukacs, *The Last European War*, London, Routledge & Kegan Paul, 1977.

13. See H. Suganami, "A Note on the Origin of the word 'International' ", *British Journal of International Studies*, 4, 1978, 226–32.

14. For a discussion of the importance of the historical method in Thucydides' thinking, see Richard D. Sears, "Thucydides and the Scientific Approach to International Politics", *Australian Journal of Politics and History*, 23, 1977, 28–40.

15. Kenneth E. Bock, *The Acceptance of Histories: Towards a Perspective for Social Science*, California University, Publications in Sociology and Social Institutions, 1956.

16. A. J. P. Taylor, *The Origins of the Second World War*, London, Hamilton, 1963, pp. 102–3.

17. Karl R. Popper, *The Poverty of Historicism*, London, Routledge & Kegan Paul, 1957.

18. This account of historical method might be said to be over-simplified, for a much more sophisticated account, written by someone who believes that the study of international relations can only proceed on the basis of this method. See Charles Reynolds, *Theory and Explanation in International Politics*, London, Martin Robertson, 1973.

19. Although international relations was dominated by an "idealist" approach during the inter-war years, there were alternative approaches in existence. See W. T. R. Fox, "Pluralism, the Science of Politics and the World System", *World Politics*, 27, 1974–5, 597–611, who discusses the work of Charles E. Merriam during the period.

20. E. H. Carr, *The Twenty Years' Crisis*, London, MacMillan, 1939.

21. E. H. Carr, *What is History?*, Harmondsworth, Pelican, 1964, p. 11.

22. H. J. Morgenthau, *Politics Among Nations*, 5th edn, New York, Alfred A. Knopf, 1972, p. 4.

23. But note that Sears (n. 14) denies that realism can be traced back to Thucydides.

24. Charles L. Mee, *Meeting at Potsdam*, London, Deutsch, 1974, p. xiii.

25. R. L. Rothstein, "On the Costs of Realism", *Political Science Quarterly*, 87, 1972, 347–62.

26. For a discussion of Marxism and functionalism, see W. G. Runciman, *Social Science and Political Theory*, Cambridge, CUP, 1965.

27. For an account of behavioural findings, see B. Berelson and G. A. Steiner, *Human Behaviour, An Inventory of Scientific Findings*, New York, Hariott Brace, 1964. For an analysis of the criticisms, see R. L. Ackoff and F. E. Emery, *On Purposeful Systems*, London, Tavistock Publications, 1972.

28. See the discussion amongst social scientists in J. O'Neill, ed., *Modes of Individualism and Collectivism*, London, 1973.
29. See, for example, Fred N. Kerlinger, *Foundations of Behavioural Research*, New York, Holt, Rinehart & Winston Inc., 1964, who discusses the issue in his chapter on variance.
30. Morgenthau (n. 22), p. vii.
31. R. C. Snyder, "A Decision-Making Approach to the study of Political Phenomena" in R. Young, ed., *Approaches to the Study of Politics*, Evanston, Northwestern UP, 1958.
32. C. A. McClelland, "Systems and History in international relations", *General Systems Yearbook*, 3, 1958, 221–47.
33. See, for example, R. Pettman, *Human Behaviour and World Politics*, London, Macmillan, 1975.
34. John H. Herz, *International Poltiics in the Atomic Age*, New York, Columbia UP, 1959; and "The Territorial State Revisited" in J. N. Rosenau, *International Politics and Foreign Policy*, New York, Free Press, 1969, revised edn.
35. See, for example, F. H. Hinsley, *Power and the Pursuit of Peace*, Cambridge, CUP, 1963.
36. See, for example, Philip E. Green, *Deadly Logic*, Columbus, Ohio, State University Press, 1966.
37. Oran R. Young, "Political Discontinuities in the International System", *World Politics*, 20, 1968, 369–92.
38. Karl W. Deutsch, *et al., Political Community and the North Atlantic Area*, Princeton, PUP, 1957.
39. See, for example, Morton H. Halperin, *Bureaucratic Politics and Foreign Policy*, Washington, The Brookings Institute, 1974.
40. See J. N. Rosenau, ed., *Linkage Politics*, New York, Free Press, 1969.
41. See Richard N. Cooper, *The Economics of Interdepence*, New York, 1968.
42. Bruce M. Russett, "Methodological and Theoretical Schools in International Relations" in *Design for International Relations Research: Scope, Theory, Methods and Relevance*, ed., Norman D. Palmer, Philadelphia, American Academy of Political and Social Sciences, 1970.
43. J. N. Rosenau, ed., *In Search of Global Patterns*, New York, Free Press, 1976.
44. A. Wolfers, *Discord and Collaboration*, Baltimore, John Hopkins Press, 1962, p. 4.

CHAPTER 2

Analysing the "Great Debates": Teaching Methodology in a Decade of Change

C. R. Mitchell

Any graduate level course in international relations methodology taught during the past decade has had to confront and overcome a major pedagogical problem, the product of a unique period in the development of international relations as a field of study. During this time (roughly from the early 1960s to the mid-1970s), the subject matter to be conveyed in a methodology course has undergone a series of significant upheavals, necessitating a far from superficial review of the philosophical presuppositions underlying the analysis of international relations as a candidate member of the "social sciences". As the period from the early nineteen-sixties advanced, it became increasingly (and to some eyes, distressingly) necessary to dwell upon philosophical fundamentals of the discipline, before proceeding to consider either practical research techniques, or the substantive findings that have arisen from the employment of such techniques.

The changes that have taken place in the general philosophical debate since the early 1960s have been many and varied, ranging from disputes about the suitability of humanistic subject matter for the methodology of the natural sciences, to debates about the nature of the relationship between the observer and what is being observed in a given field. In such a complex and inevitable multi-dimensional development, simple classification schemes should normally be shunned, save as a preliminary ordering device. None the less, it is possible to distinguish three very broad schools of thought within the general debate about the bases of the social sciences in general, and international relations in particular, namely, the "classical"; the "behavioural" (or "scientific"); and the "post-behavioural" (or paradigmatic). These broad schools, or movements, in the political sciences have numerous aspects, but each can be regarded both as proposing a particular mode of research, and as a basis for defining and increasing the level

28

of acceptable "knowledge" about a given subject matter. Their existence cannot be ignored in any course concerning the "how" of a discipline as opposed to the "what"; and their differences inevitably form the basis of fruitful inquiry when we consider the bases upon which the search for sure knowledge of international structures, processes and behaviour must be sought. The remainder of this paper sketches some of the essential features of each of these research modes, and some of the problems they give rise to for students of international relations methodology.

A. COMPETING RESEARCH MODES

It is repeating the obvious to begin with the point that the 1960s in international relations saw a series of rapid changes in the methodological assumptions that underlay the study of the discipline – indeed, in the ideas held by scholars of the nature of the discipline they practised. A series of "great" – if, to some eyes, somewhat fruitless – debates occurred during the 1960s and continued on into the 1970s, so that international relations students rapidly became familiar with the arguments and counter-arguments of the "classicists" and the "behaviouralists", and later with those of the "behaviouralists" and the "post-behaviouralists". Apart from a healthy wariness of such dichotomous classification schemes (which usually obscure more than they reveal), students on methodology courses in the mid-1960s also learned that they had been spared a previous "great debate" between "idealists" and "realists", the echoes of which had died down, at least in the United Kingdom, by 1965. However, by that date most courses on methodology almost inevitably plunged headlong into the debate between classicists and behaviouralists. Bull's assault upon the shortcomings of the behavioural approach to international relations and his plea for a return to classicism, was first published in 1966, (1) and while the debate between idealist and realist had been mainly about whether international relations studies should be prescriptive or descriptive, that between classicists and behaviouralists concerned question of which approach was appropriate for analysing the subject matter of international relations.

The debate thus involved fundamental questions of philosophy and method, including the nature of explanation and of discovery and the logic of proof. At the time, it was characterised as the difference between the historian and the scientist, and whose approach was more appropriate, given the subject matter of international relations especially its lack of a statistically significant number of sufficiently similar cases and its apparent resistance to anything save the most misleading quantification.

By the end of the 1960s, this particular debate was fairly standard material in courses on methodology, and one Canadian scholar described how he provided his students with copies of Bull's original article and Kaplan's reply, with instructions to join in the debate in one of their own term papers. (2) However, by this time the situation had been further complicated by the emergence of a substantial body of criticism of behaviouralism itself, criticism that was levelled both at its practical results and its philosophical shortcomings.

The post-behaviouralist school, the emergence of which can for convenience be dated from the 1968 meeting of the American Political Science Association at which David Easton delivered his personal renunciation of the behavioural movement in political science he had helped to found two decades previously, (3) condemned behaviouralism, again on the methodological grounds. On this occasion, the basic criticism was not that the philosophy and methods of the natural sciences could hardly be applied to international relations because of profound differences between the natural and social worlds. Rather, it was that behaviouralism as a movement had fundamentally mistaken the nature of the scientific enterprise and its philosophical foundations, and was applying an outdated, positivist concept of scientific analysis, no longer philosophically speaking tenable.

In many ways, parts of this post-behavioural critique of using "the scientific approach" to international relations were far more damaging to the behaviouralist approach than were the stictures of the classicists, although classical criticism still continued into the 1970s, the so-called "post-behavioural era". However, for international relations students confronted with the task of understanding the philosophical and methodological assumptions upon which their discipline was based, the eruption of this new set of arguments into an area already characterised by subtle (and less-subtle) differences of opinion about "significant" and "valid" research methods (and hence about "findings"), complicated still further an already complex subject; and made a not intrinsically fascinating aspect of an international relations programme even less attractive.

The nature of this impact can be judged by briefly exploring some of the details of the changing methodological assumptions of the past decade in international relations.

B. BEHAVIOURAL METHODOLOGY

As we mentioned above, whereas the debate between idealist and realist largely revolved about the question of the purpose of research, or of "why", that between the classicist and the behaviouralist mainly concerned method, or of "how". One of the major features of the so-called behavioural revolution in international relations which began in the late 1950s and had reached the United Kingdom in the early 1960s, was the behaviouralists' self-conscious scrutiny of the philosophical assumptions underlying efforts to analyse the subject matter of international relations. To this was allied a concern for the actual methods and techniques through which a fundamentally "scientific" philosophy was to be put into effect in the day-to-day business of research. The behaviouralists' call was for a systematic and rigorous approach to analysing international relations, an approach that would avoid all the perceived shortcomings of historically based attempts to build up a systematic body of empirically tested theory about individual, group, state and system behaviour in the field of international politics.

(i) The behavioural critique

The behavioural approach contained both a methodological challenge to the traditional study of international relations, and a critique of what were seen as the latter's methodological shortcomings. Behavioural criticisms of conventional attempts to understand the nature of international relationships covered a wide spectrum, but the major critique was that classical methodology was both lacking in rigour, and essentially non-cumulative. Implicit also in behavioural arguments against traditional international relations scholarship was its relatively narrow scope and its concentration upon international politics as a unique aspect of the social world. This traditional tendency, it was argued, cut off international relations studies from insights and theories derived from other disciplines, such as sociology or social psychology and limited severely the universe from which examples could be drawn, comparisons made, and patterns of behaviour or interaction elucidated. The behavioural approach did not deny the uniqueness of international political phenomena. However, while admitting that all phenomena are unique in some aspects, it also emphasised that phenomena previously treated as wholly disparate might, if re-examined, show interesting commonalities.

The most succinct statement of the behavioural approach to the study of politics remains Easton's paper published in 1967. (4) The rebuttal of

Bull's counter-reformation in international relations that most clearly summarises the behaviouralist position in the mid-1960s is Singer's contribution to the 1967 (5) symposium on "contending approaches" to international studies. Both papers reflect the behaviouralist impatience with classical insistence upon the shifting and imprecise nature of their common subject matter, and the need to rely upon experience and intuitive understanding in any attempt to analyse the course of international relations. Both papers implicitly criticise past use of imprecise concepts which are non-operationalised (and hence not measurable); of relationships which are vague and are stated to hold under some circumstances, yet not in others; and of arguments taking the form of the caricature, viz. "All Indians always walk in single file; I know; the one I saw did". Less immediately striking, but equally salient, is the criticism of the lack of any steady cumualtion of theory, of any gradual but unmistakable accretion of tested and (in some cases) discarded hypotheses, building into a body of accepted and predictive theory about aspects of the field.

The loudness of the debate, and the strength of accusation and counter-accusation between the contending approaches, tended to obscure the point that, while there were major differences between the two schools of thought, there were a number of important similarities. Some of these we will discuss below when dealing with the post-behavioural challenge to behaviouralism, but here it is appropriate to mention that many classicists and behaviouralists shared a belief in the possibility and existence of general theories. While behaviouralists were self-consciously searching for one, those employing the historical approach to analysis as Hempel (6) has pointed out used general theories (often implicitly) when they sought to explain any event or series of human actions. Similarly, both classicists and behaviouralists could justly be regarded as operating broadly within an empiricist tradition, both in what they regarded as suitable evidence for thesis or hypothesis and in their assumption that objective knowledge about the nature of the international system and international behaviour could, in principle, be acquired, even if the process was long, drawn out and difficult. The realist position had been generally accepted within the field, and most classicists would probably have agreed with Easton's rubric that "ethical evaluation and empirical explanation involve two different kinds of proposition that . . . should be kept analytically distinct. . . ." (7) The differences lay in how, and with what degree of accuracy, objective knowledge could be acquired, and by what sure methods. The major behaviouralist criticism of those employing classical methods of analysis was not that they failed to be basically empirical, but that they failed to be openly, systematically and self-consciously empirical.

(ii) The behavioural effort

From the methodological point of view, the 1960s could be regarded as the time when behaviouralist scholars attempted to illustrate through their own researches the benefits to be gained for international relations through a rigorous, "scientific" approach. Illustrative examples of the benefits — and perils — of "the scientific approach" in international relations abounded, and could be used in the teaching of courses on methodology as examples of the manner in which Gurr's five stages of problemation, specification, operationalisation, data collection and interpretation (8) could be rigorously implemented in the search for comparative and cumulative knowledge.

The value of such work in illustrating the ramifications of the behavioural insistence upon clear, operational definitions of concepts, measurement wherever possible and relevant, and clearly stated, falsifiable hypotheses building from an old theory or towards a new one, was considerable. It was possible to use Singer's paper on alliance aggregation and war as an example of the need for careful definitions of even such familiar terms as "war", and also of the manner in which a sociological theory involving cross-cutting allegiance could be logically extended, and then applied to international society. (9) In dealing with the experimental tradition in the sciences, it was possible to turn to the range of what Banks has called "analogue analysis" in international relations; (10) on the one hand utilising Guetzkow's large-scale model building endeavours of the Inter-Nation Simulation project, (11) while at the other extreme using the "stripped down" conflict situations of Game Theory or the rather more complex experimental studies of negotiating behaviour recently summarised by Druckman, (12) as examples of studies that controlled some factors in the research design, while allowing other variables to vary. Similarly, the advantages and problems of observer participation in on-going interactions, together with the methodological problems of observer-effects and of systematic and reliable recording (familiar to anthropologists), could be illustrated by Alger's work on the United Nations (13) and by an increasing volume of literature on problem-solving workshops, particularly those conducted by Burton (14) and Doob. (15) Again, the problems of eliciting new data by survey and interview methods could be exemplified by reference to the behavioural interest in the foreign policy decision-making process, a use that increased after the results of the "polls" themselves became a significant in-put into the decision-making processes of several countries. As part of this last tendency, the systematic use of various forms of content analysis at the level of individual decision-makers also illustrated one possible way in which intuition and hunch could be improved in the analysis of the (changing) attitudes and perceptions of decision-makers; Holsti's pioneering efforts in this direction offers useful insights into what could be done with such techniques. (16)

However, the most obvious impact of the behavioural revolution in international relations was a mounting attempt to avoid the anecdotal, and instead to test out propositions against as large a universe of data as possible. If "general" propositions and theories were to be tested for their "generalisability" then the data against which the tests should be made had to be drawn from widely different places and times. This conception lay at the root of a number of large-scale, aggregate data projects, the results of which began to appear in the literature of the late 1960s. Such projects were massive and expensive, involving both comparative analysis of structure and behaviour, and trend analysis, to test out propositions held in the best natural science traditions, to be universal in space and time. Rummel's DON (Dimensionality of Nations) project was an effort to apply his conception of field theory to a social system of separate and independent states, necessitating the collection and analysis of large amounts of structural and behavioural data for nearly 100 nation-state units. By contrast, Singer and Small concentrated upon gathering data on war and the structure of the international system from 1815 to 1965 in order to be able to test out the general applicability of both traditional "balance of power" theories and other hypotheses stemming from the classical literature itself. The Yale Political Data Program resembled the DON project in some aspects, but developed from Deutsch and Russett's shared interest in the processes of integration, and bore the imprint of this interest in the way in which data were defined and gathered. In addition to such aggregate projects, a movement that might best be described as "systematised history" also began to produce research findings to illustrate other behaviouralist efforts at developing a cumulative body of knowledge. Probably the best known of this movement were the events-data studies, now proliferating but originally inspired by McClelland's WEIS project.* Both of these projects originated in efforts to study international crises and in a typically behavioural desire to discover – if possible – common or repetitive patterns in the structure of such phenomena; and both, in rather different ways, could be seen as resulting from efforts to

---

*(World Event Interaction Survey) which sought to classify the interactions of states, and the Stanford studies of international crises, which involved the systematic use of content analysis to measure psychological variables – and their impact on policy decisions – at times of high tension and threat.

apply behavioural tenets of rigour and cumulation to similar aspects of the field.

A final significant development in this behavioural "revolution" was that the research findings of the projects outlined above, and many others, began to find their way into the discipline as the central subject matter of textbooks. These had been notably absent for a period, and the tendency was to replace older, traditional textbooks with new editions, to produce new, short, introductory works, or to rely on books of readings to introduce students both to the main outlines of the field, and to work being carried out "on the frontiers". This situation began to change, first with the production of Holsti's pioneering effort in 1967, (17) and later with Sullivan's text, which constitutes a comprehensive review and consolidation of the work of members of "the behavioural persuasion" in international relations scholarship over the last ten or fifteen years. (18)

The research work itself, and the textbooks based upon it, do not merely illustrate the advantages of adopting a behavioural approach to analysis. They also point to some of the drawbacks of using this approach, drawbacks which show few signs, at present, of being overcome. There are many of these, but we could perhaps mention four that seem particularly serious:

(a) An increasing tendency to let available research techniques dictate the kinds of research problems that are pursued rather than the other way around. Importance tends to be sacrificed to contemporary "research-ability".

(b) Allied to the above, a behaviouralist tendency towards narrowing down research problems to questions that are answerable by rigorous, scientific research methods, thus resulting (at present) in the production of numerous, precisely carried out but isolated research reports, which remain specialised answers to specialised questions. As opposed to stated behaviouralist objectives, their research practice has not produced a tendency towards the cumulative development of integrated theory; Guetzkow's "islands of theory" have shown few signs of growing, or linking to form new continents of knowledge.

(c) The fact that the behavioural approach, by its demands for rigour and accuracy, requires that too much is excluded from study (or that, many variables are held constant in order to deal with those that vary). The result is that those aspects of international relations rigorously analysed are divorced from the complex interacting reality of politics and diplomacy. In other words, the phrase "All other things being equal" implies *so many* other things being equal which seldom or never are, that its application in academic analysis removes research findings from any practical value in dealing with situations likely to be encountered in reality.

(d) While the behavioural approach has had a healthy impact upon previous tendencies towards mono-causality and deterministic theory, the changed emphasis on multiple causality and probabilistic theories awaits successful validation and practical applications.

C. POST–BEHAVIOURAL METHODOLOGY

These critical points, and many others, have all been made by classicists in their counter-attack upon what they regard as the pretensions of behavioural analysis. However, the main assault on the use of the behavioural approach in international relations (and in political science in general) has come from another quarter. Furthermore this attack was significant for the whole enterprise of trying to develop an accepted body of objective knowledge about international relationships; and, because it was again based upon philosophical and methodological grounds, it provided yet another set of problems for students attempting to understand the epistemology and methods of their field of chosen study.

(i) The post-behavioural critique

In a curious way, the anti-behavioural wave of criticism that manifested itself within the general political science discipline in the late 1960s contained within it many of the arguments and attitudes which would have been familiar to a proponent of the "idealist" position in international relations in the first of the "great debates" we have discussed above. Common to both movements was an emphasis on the importance of values in research, both in the purposes for which research was undertaken; and in the underlying (and often unstated) valued premises of the researcher himself. Similarly, the post-behavioural call for relevance in research echoed the aims of the idealist school in international relations to improve international society, especially to avoid wars and conflict, and to direct intellectual endeavour to these ends.*

Again, the post-behaviouralists' impatience with the apparent caution

*The so-called "peace research" movement in international studies could also be regarded as a late flowering of the idealist school, although many of the movement's value premises would have seemed strange to proponents of world government or international federalism, or a global system of law and institutions.

of behaviouralists in becoming involved in the "brute realities of politics" in favour of abstraction, and irrelevant findings concealed in esoteric language, mirrors both idealist and classicist criticism of a major effect of the behavioural movement on the study of international relations. Finally, the idealist desire to use intellectual endeavour to bring about (desirable) change is matched, by the post-behavioural charge that, by its concentration on a description and analysis of what is, the behavioural approach purveys "an ideology of empirical conservation", possibly modified by an inclination towards incremental change. (19) The news that accurately describing a world as it exists is necessarily an inherently conservative action might come as a surprise to those familiar with Marx's description of nineteenth-century capitalism or – at a lower level – Baker's description of the slave trade in the Sudan in the 1860s. (Although the important methodological point that one's values do help to determine which of the multitudinous aspects of reality one selects for description should not be ignored.) However, the general tenor of the post-behaviouralists' criticism, that one's social and political purpose should direct one's research efforts, rather than the other way around, constitute a major criticism of the behaviouralists' implicit position regarding the value of empirical knowledge of the world for its own sake.

A more far-reaching criticism contained in some post-behavioural attacks upon "the pretensions of the so-called social scientific approach" lay in the argument that all knowledge was essentially subjective, and at base any statement about the world (whether regarded as "empirical" or "normative") was an ideological statement. A corollary of this argument was that, to evaluate the worth of any research, one had to be familiar with the values of those carrying it out, because such values could not but affect the kind of questions posed and the kind of findings achieved. Research could only be assessed within some framework of values, for knowing about the world was essentially an internal, subjective matter. Hence, by arguing that the questions, findings and applications of research are all socially conditioned, post-behaviouralists tended also to attack the possibility of any form of objective knowledge about the world – that is, knowledge that stands in some sense apart from the values, socially determined beliefs, preferences and expectations of the observer, and which could be agreed upon by any observer, no matter what his intellectual, social or ideological background.

This particular aspect of the post-behavioural critique has been strongly attacked by many scholars, both practising political scientists and philosophers of science, who take issue with the argument that there can be no objectively true facts, and its corollary that one cannot distinguish between correct and incorrect propositions. Landau, for example, while agreeing that what any researcher perceives is highly "theory laden", "field determined" and often the result of the social situation of the observer, nevertheless insists that anti-behaviouralists are wrong in their denial of the possibility of external criteria to test the validity of observations or hypotheses. (20) The crucial point is that, in their attacks on the positivist philosophy that lies at the back of behaviouralism, the "epistemological relativists" are caught in a trap of their own making. If their arguments about the ideological-cum-social foundations of statements is accepted, then, unless their own argument is itself afforded a special status, there is no way in which it can be tested for validity, or be regarded as a more accurate description of the world than any other statement. By adopting such a line of argument, and by abolishing external criteria of validation, anti-behaviouralists find themselves confronting the logical impasse of Mannheim's Paradox. (21)

Arguing that a limited form of objective knowledge is possible is not, however, to argue that values do not affect the way in which behaviouralists have carried out research during the last decade. The manner in which experience is categorised and ordered in our own minds; the concepts that we use to label and describe selected aspects of the world; and the rules that are formulated to separate off certain classes of entities from others, are all highly subjective, and may be individually or socially determined (or — more likely in the scholastic world — determined by the intellectual traditions of a particular discipline). These aspects, as any thoughtful behaviouralist would admit, all form part of the highly *subjective* side of the behavioural effort, leaving the checking of hypothesised relationships between concepts and categories to agreed rules which constitute the *objective* side of the enterprise. That behaviouralists themselves admit to an element of subjectivity in analysis helps to explain the impact of another methodological input into international relations which occurred in the late 1960s. This input focused attention on arguments about the possibility of cumulative, as well as objective knowledge about the social world; led to renewed doubts about the use and validity of studying international relations within the behavioural framework; and resulted from the gradual osmosis into political science and international relations of Kuhn's ideas on "scientific revolutions" and the nature of paradigms. (22)

(ii) "Paradigms" in international relations

Apart from the resurgence of "historicism", the behavioural approach to studying international relations has also had to contend with the argument,

38

originally put forward by Kuhn, that the process of developing knowledge within a discipline consists not of a gradual growth, but of a series of stages, each quite distinct from the others, and each dominated by a particular frame of assumptions, or "paradigm", which renders knowledge in one period incommensurate with knowledge in another. The periods themselves are separated by "revolutions" in thought, which change the shape of the discipline, its fundamental assumptions about the world it is dealing with, and the kinds of questions that can be meaningfully asked and answered. Although Kuhn has now abandoned some of the more extreme aspects of his theory, (23)* the application of his original formulation to a field such as political science and international relations has come close to making research findings in that field a mere procession of momentary fads, without any independent empirical justification, possibility of self-correction, or opportunity for cumulative growth of improvement. Within a Kuhnian framework, what passes for knowledge becomes "paradigm-dependent" and in no sense "objective".

The adoption of a Kuhnian element into post-behavioural criticisms of behavioural methodology raised a series of new challenges to behavioural researchers in political science. For example, one of the functions of a dominant paradigm was stated to be the selection of important problems to be resolved − in other words, the structuring of the field research and its boundaries − and it was easy to link this argument with the post-behaviouralist charge that behavioural political science had concentrated upon the trivial or the irrelevant because of the inadequacy of their paradigm. Again, it was argued that the behaviouralists' vaunted claim to "scientific objectivity" rested upon a fundamental misapprehension about the foundations of knowledge, which always depended upon a prior set of untestable and subjective assumptions regarding the nature of the world, and the findings it was possible to make about that world.

These characteristics of Kuhn's "paradigmatic" approach to the growth of disciplines appeared initially to make a significant contribution to explaining the generally confused methodological state of political science itself, and even to bring some order into the "great debates" of international relations. If one accepted Kuhn's argument about dominant or competing paradigms, or about pre-paradigm stages, it became possible to deal with the widely different approaches to analysis that existed in the field of political studies, by arguing that these were the end products of widely different sets of starting assumptions about the fundamentals of

*Even in its initial formulation, it was never quite clear whether *The Structure of Scientific Revolutions* was intended to be an historical account of how the natural sciences developed, or a contribution to the philosophy of science itself.

the field of study. As Holt and Turner argued in an early paper, paradigms contain a number of basic elements which form a framework giving direction to a field of study and distinguishing one paradigm from another. Important elements include:

(a) A conceptual element establishing the basic units of which reality is deemed to consist; concepts (such as force, power, status or conflict) are judged by their utility in developing theories, not by any truth or falsehood.

(b) A theoretical element, involving a linking together of concepts in a deductive structure of propositions, some of which (at least) are amenable to empirical verification/falsification.

(c) An interpretive element, setting out rules for establishing when the prediction derived from theoretical formulations are correct or incorrect.

(d) A selective element (mentioned above, identifying relevant questions that can be asked within the limits of paradigm, and those which cannot even be considered within its confines. (For example, a state-centric paradigm in international relations makes it difficult to consider international class problems, except in terms of hierarchies of state units). (24)

Putting the argument in a slightly different way, in Charles Taylor's phrase, (25) the major function of a paradigm is to point to "crucial dimensions of explanation". In other words, paradigms indicate criteria for starting to look for answers to questions; where (the level of analysis); at which particular units (individuals, decisions, markets, classes, states, alliances); and how (means of distinguishing relevant from irrelevant information). In this sense, paradigms are essentially selection devices, the choice of phenomena to be analysed being made from among an almost infinite universe of phenomena-to-be-explained, and phenomena to do the explaining. For example, in attempting to account for the rise of "McCarthy-ism" in the United States, different paradigms would point research efforts in the direction of individuals' psychological conditions; interest group conflict within U.S. domestic politics; the clash of party and personality within the U.S. legislative branch; and U.S.-Soviet relations in the late 1940s and early 1950s.

In more formal terms, we are arguing here that, far from being wholly new ways of conceptualising an external world within an observer (i.e. being an *internal creation* of an observer which he may then be able to share with others), paradigms are different ways of recognising and (more important) classifying a limited number of phenomena from a potentially limitless universe of phenomena and occurrences. The result is to leave out of consideration many other aspects of a complex and unlimited reality that can form the central foci of other, competing paradigms. Practically speaking, the process involves picking out and labelling particular phenomena* to serve as basic building blocks for the development of theoretical assertions about the nature of a small part of the referent world.† The process (often referred to as conceptualisation")‡ also further involves the selection of attributes or characteristics of the selected units of analysis. Again, there are an almost infinite number of unit qualities available for investigation, given that any unit of analysis — particularly in the social world — is essentially a multi-attribute phenomenon that can be classified along any number of dimensions. (Consider the number of different ways in which a human individual — or a human decision — can be distinguished from another individual or another decision.)

Finally, a paradigm will direct attention to the kinds of (repetitive) relationships postulated to exist between the attributes of the selected units of analysis, and indicate those which (if they exist) are salient in explaining the changes in the nature of units of analysis (that is their structural or behavioural attributes). In this fashion, a paradigm focuses attention on a particular level of analysis, that is to say different units and unit-attributes in order to explain a problem which is also, to some degree, determined by the paradigm. (For example, in studying voting behaviour, one paradigm will direct attention to attitudes and learning processes rather than body temperature or EEG readings, while another will focus attention upon social structure and class loyalty, and yet another on family background and intra-familial relationships.) However, we should note that in this formulation of a paradigmatic approach, there still remains an element of external checking which can be regarded as a form of objectivity. While the selection of the concepts (units and attributes) via classification (inclusion and exclusion), and the proposal of relationships of a particular type are all observer-determined (subjective), the procedures for establishing whether the units *do* all share other attributes

*Rapaport refers to this process and its attendant difficulties as "the problem of recognition". (26)

†Note that the labels used to describe classified phenomena are — by the nature of language itself — often highly value-laden, so that, even at this primary stage of conceptualisation values are involved in a dual fashion; in deciding (i) what classification scheme to employ; and (ii) what to label the resultant categories.

‡"Conceptualisation" can, in this sense, be regarded as a preliminary act of classification into units of analysis sharing some quality that enables them to be classified as a group. As Gurr points out, there is, potentially, an infinite number of such units in the social world, ranging from classes, ethnic groups, decisions, elections, alliances, and policies to the familiar state units of international studies. (27)

and whether the relationships between attributes *do* exist are independent of the observer (objective).

(iii) The search for a dominant paradigm

The practical implications of the introduction of a paradigmatic approach into international relations methodology were that a number of voices were raised in criticising behavioural scholars on another set of grounds; namely that they had dismally failed to break away from the predominant (and misleading) paradigm in international relations, and that, for all their insistence upon the methodological differences between themselves and classical scholars, both schools were really operating within a common strait jacket of assumptions about the nature of international relations. Moreover, this conceptual strait jacket prevented them from selecting the more interesting and relevant aspects of international society, and satis-factorily explaining pressing current problems neglected by behavioural research − indeed, not amenable to analysis within that movement's chosen framework.

While not being particularly clear about whether the traditional paradigm had always been inadequate to explain critical aspects of inter-national relations, or whether the world had changed so radically as to render that paradigm thoroughly misleading, many post-behavioural critics of the international relations methodology dominating the 1960s argued that all the so-called behavioural revolution had accomplished was to formalise, and make more rigorous research that remained funda-mentally based upon an unchanged set of assumptions about the nature of the field, its crucial units of analysis and their salient attributes, and the kinds of relationships which promised the most powerful explanations of "key" problems of international relations. Burton had begun this "challenge to orthodoxy" in the United Kingdom in the mid-1960s, (28) but it was most systematically presented by Handelsman *et al.*, who emphasised that the quantitative work resulting from the behavioural revolution in international relations was state-centric, assumed a rationality of decision-making behaviour based upon criteria of power maximisation and non-interdependence of preference functions, made a sharp distinction between international and domestic politics, and concen-trated upon competitive relationships between the chosen units of analysis. (29) To this might be added the assumption that international society was dominated by scarcity and constant sum relationships, which resulted in patterns of bargaining behaviour over the distribution of a limited amount of each valued commodity or position; and that political relationships between state units were the dominant dimensions in any explanation of the crucial problems of the field.

In many ways, the relative inadequacy of the dominant framework for developing theory in international relations has been recognised (or re-recognised) for a number of years, at least from the time that Wolfers (30) had enquired about the nature of the actors in international politics and Deutsch had led the effort to apply a systems approach to international society. (31) As the 1960s drew on into the 1970s, two major responses to such criticisms became discernible. The first was to make minor modifications to the assumptions of the dominant, state-centric paradigm (or "billiard-ball model" as it was sometimes affectionately known). On the one hand such modifications introduced other forms of "international actors" to add to the traditional state-as-unit-of-analysis, such as the international organisation, or the multinational corporation; and on the other modifications attempted to break down the conventional distinction between the domestic and the international, while retaining the state as the fundamental unit of analysis. This latter effort led to the introduction of such concepts as "the penetrated system", (32) or an attempt to develop a bridging field of "linkage politics", (33) or to concentrate upon the analysis of "transnational systems". (34)

The alternative response was more radical, and even more confusing for students coming "cold" to the study of international relations theory and methodology. This was the effort to develop wholly new "paradigms" to direct analysis in the field: those which rejected the traditional assumptions of both classicists and behaviouralists (no matter what techniques of research both used), and those which sought to develop a starting framework that pointed to different conceptualisations, units of analysis, types of relationship and problem areas from those conventionally deemed to be the concern of international studies. One such framework was proposed by Handelsman et al. at the end of their critique of quantitative behavioural research. When discussing an "emerging alternative paradigm" (35) they advocated the adoption of a "world policy process framework", where the basic unit of analysis was "the issue". Even though they argued that the framework emphasised the need to consider subnational, national and transnational actors simultaneously, their effort revealed implicitly how difficult it was to free oneself totally of the assumptions of the state-centric paradigm.

An alternative approach was provided by the Burtonian school in the United Kingdom, which attempted to develop a "world society" approach to a field of international studies, much more broadly defined, with "the system" as the basic unit of analysis, and the characteristics of relationships existing between sub-systems* as the main means for explaining unit behaviour. (36) Finally, a Scandinavian school of peace research developed a paradigm (later taken up by West German scholars such as Senghaas) (37) which also ignored the traditional state-as-unit-of-analysis approach, and posited instead a framework consisting of a Centre and a Periphery (both involving different and non-contiguous areas of the globe) and the various kinds of flows (material, energy, people and information) and relationships existing between these basic units. (38) Partly because the emphasis of this framework was on economic relationships between (and within) units, partly because of its resemblance to classical Marxist analysis transferred to a global level, and partly because of the shift in popular interests to problems arising from relations between the developed and the underdeveloped countries, this particular paradigm has attracted considerable attention, and resulted in not a little research of considerable quality. Thus, the Centre–Periphery paradigm currently exists alongside a number of other new frameworks, as well as the more traditional state-centric paradigm.

D. THE PRESENT SITUATION

The end result of this methodological *furore* is a situation of some confusion for students and teachers of epistemology and research techniques in the field of international relations. In brief, three competing schools of thought coexist uneasily, and from time to time engage in direct, furious debate over the fundamentals of their chosen discipline.† An oversimple view might lead one to the conclusion that the three schools are geographically based, or at least have their strongest adherents in particular academic regions. The behavioural approach seems undoubtedly to have had its major impact in North America; the classical approach remains the backbone of international studies in the United Kingdom — with some notable exceptions — while the critical post-behavioural is most apparent in Scandinavia and in West Germany, where it has been fed by ideas emanating from the Frankfurt School of Sociological Theory, and by what appears to be a recent, but rather general German rejection of positivist philosophy. At the present time, no synthesis appears to be emerging from

*For example, relationships may be characterised as more or less legitimised, more or less interdependent, or more or less dominant or egalitarian.

†See, for example, the recent series of articles by Landau, Rudner, Braybrooke and Lindblom in the *American Political Science Review*; and the account of the methodological assault on the assumptions of peace research contained in the *Journal of Conflict Resolution*.

44

the dialectic between the classical thesis, and the behavioural antithesis which so rapidly became overtaken by its own post-behavioural antithesis. Hence, courses on methodology have to cope with this tripartite division in some way, and make the subject intelligible to those taking them. The difficulties are considerable, but, at least, the times are interesting.

References

1. H. Bull, "International Relations: The Case for the Classical Approach", *World Politics*, April 1966.
2. James Eayrs, personal communication.
3. D. Easton, "The New Revolution in Political Science", *American Political Science Review*, December 1969.
4. D. Easton, "The Current Meaning of Behaviouralism" in J. C. Charlesworth (ed.), *Contemporary Political Analysis* (New York, Free Press, 1967).
5. J. D. Singer, "The Incompleat Theorist: Insight Without Evidence" in K. Knorr and J. N. Rosenau (eds), *Contending Approaches to International Relations* (Princeton, N.J., Princeton University Press, 1969).
6. C. G. Hempel, "Explanation in Science and History" in R. G. Colodny (ed.), *Frontiers of Science and Philosophy* (London, Allen & Unwin, 1962).
7. D. Easton, "The New Revolution in Political Science", *American Political Science Review*, December 1969.
8. T. R. Gurr, *Polimetrics* (Englewood Cliffs, N.J., Prentice Hall, 1972).
9. J. D. Singer and M. Small, "Alliance Aggregation and the On-set of War" in J. D. Singer (ed.), *Quantitative International Politics* (New York, Free Press, 1968).
10. M. H. Banks, "Conflict: Behavioural Approaches" (London, Centre for the Analysis of Conflict (Mimeo), 1969).
11. H. Guetzkow *et al.*, *Simulation in International Relations* (Englewood Cliffs, N.J., Prentice Hall, 1963).
12. D. Druckman, *Human Factors in International Negotiations* (Beverly Hills, Sage Pubs., 1973).
13. C. F. Alger, "Inter Action and Negotiation in a Committee of the U.N. General Assembly", *Papers of the Peace Research Society (International)*, 1966.
14. J. W. Burton, *Conflict and Communication* (London, Macmillan, 1969).
15. L. W. Doob (ed.), *Resolving Conflict in Africa: The Fermeda Workshop* (New Haven, Yale University Press, 1970).
16. O. R. Holsti, "The Belief System and National Images: A Case Study", *Journal of Conflict Resolution*, VI, 1962.
17. K. J. Holsti, *International Politics: A Framework for Analysis* (Englewood Cliffs, N.J., Prentice Hall, 1967).
18. M. P. Sullivan, *International Relations: Theories and Evidence* (Englewood Cliffs, N.J., Prentice Hall, 1976).
19. D. Easton, "The New Revolution in Political Science", *American Political Science Review*, December 1969.
20. M. Landau, "Comment: On Objectivity", *American Political Science Review*, September 1972.
21. M. Landau, *Political Theory and Political Science* (New York, Macmillan, 1972).
22. T. Kuhn, *The Structure of Scientific Revolutions* (Chicago, Univ. of Chicago Press, 1962).
23. T. Kuhn, Postscript to *The Structure of Scientific Revolutions* (Chicago, Univ. of Chicago Press, 2nd edn.).
24. R. T. Holt and J. M. Richardson, "Competing Paradigms in Comparative Politics"

in R. T. Holt and J. E. Turner (eds), *The Methodology of Comparative Research* (New York, Free Press, 1970).

25. C. Taylor, "Neutrality in Political Science" in P. Laslett and W. G. Runciman (eds), *Philosophy, Politics and Society* 3rd edn (Oxford, Basil Blackwell, 1967).

26. A. Rappoport, "Various Meanings of Theory", *American Political Science Review*.

27. T. R. Gurr, *Polimetrics*, p. 37 (Englewood Cliff, N.J., Prentice Hall, 1972)

28. J. W. Burton, *International Relations: A General Theory* (Cambridge, Cambridge Univ. Press, 1965).

29. J. R. Handelsman, J. A. Vasquez, M. K. O'Leary and W. D. Coplin, *Color it Morgenthau* (Syracuse, Prince Research Studies Paper No. 11, Maxwell School, Syracuse University).

30. A. Wolfers, "The Actors in International Politics" in *Discord and Collaboration* (Baltimore, Johns Hopkins Press, 1962).

31. K. W. Deutsch, *The Nerves of Government* (New York, Free Press, 1963).

32. A. M. Scott, *The Revolution in Statecraft: Informal Penetration* (New York, Random House, 1965).

33. J. N. Rosenau (ed.), *Linkage Politics* (New York, Free Press, 1969).

34. R. O. Keohane and J. S. Nye (eds), *Transnational Relations and World Politics* (Cambridge, Mass., Harvard Univ. Press, 1971).

35. J. R. Handelsman *et al.*, *Color it Morgenthau* (Syracuse, Prince Research Studies Paper No. 11, Maxwell School, Syracuse Univ.).

36. J. W. Burton, *World Society* (Cambridge, Cambridge Univ. Press, 1973).

37. D. Senghaas, "Conflict Formations in Contemporary International Society", *Journal of Peace Research*, 1973, p. 163.

38. J. Galtung, "A Structural Theory of Imperialism", *Journal of Peace Research*, 1972 (2), p. 81.

CHAPTER 3

Strategy: The Evolution of the Field

A. J. R. Groom

It is only in recent years that "strategy", "strategic studies", "strategic aspects of international relations" or "peace and security", to give but a selection of course titles, have been taught in universities. Nevertheless, such courses are now a normal component of undergraduate degrees in international relations or politics. Postgraduate students can pursue Masters degrees in the subject separately or in the context of an international relations or politics degree and, of course, it is possible to pursue a doctorate in the field. Thus it appears that over the last twenty years there has been a tremendous growth of interest in strategy in academic circles: for not only are there students and teachers but a rash of research institutes has also sprung up around the world. (1) However, it should be borne in mind that the growth in academic activity strikes the eye in part because the growth started from a low level of interest. The total amount of teaching and research in the field is still not that great — and the development has been uneven both in its distribution around the world as well intellectually.

If we trace the development of strategy in its geographical distribution it is evident that, as an academic subject, it first came to the forefront in English language universities particularly in Britain and the United States. It is now to be found in university systems throughout the developed world including the U.S.S.R. and Japan. However, it does not appear to be widely taught in universities in the third-world countries (with some exceptions such as India). Nevertheless, the massive flow of arms to the third world has begun to stimulate academic discussion in countries such as Iran and is giving rise to teaching and research institutes in the field of strategy.

However, the geographical distribution of the countries in which work in the field can be found is not the only source of unevenness. This can also be seen in the content of research and teaching.

On the whole research has been politically *engagé*. It has been undertaken either at the direct request of or in order to influence decision-makers whether on the *status quo* or revolutionary sides of the barricades. Relatively short-term questions of use to practitioners have been its prime concern and it has, to a surprising degree, eschewed conceptual questions. Thus its intellectual standing leaves something to be desired due to the absense of a well-developed body of theory and to the active concern with current events since without empirical theory research on current events is essentially speculative in nature. There is nothing as practical as a good theory! In some Western countries, particularly the United States, the role of university strategists in government-inspired research has brought with it the risk of a serious corruption of traditional Western academic values of freedom and independence. Government-inspired research is often subject to political parameters which cannot be questioned. Such a situation frequently prevails in non-Western countries. Of course these objections do not arise when the government promotes its own "in house" research but only when government-inspired research pervades the university where traditionally such parameters are anathema and where the pursuit of knowledge aspires to be universal in spirit. Strategists are, however, not the only scholars to succumb to the siren calls of govenrment. The topicality of much research has spilled over into the university teaching of strategy where it takes the form of an analysis of current events, often from a particular political standpoint.

Whether as researchers or teachers, strategists tend to take sides – they are value promoting rather than value controlled in their endeavours in the sense of being concerned with what their values tell them "ought to be". In their desire to achieve their goals they are sometimes negligent of what is or they may be inclined to let an "is" imply an "ought". More fundamentally we do not know what "is" since strategists have not yet arrived at an empirically based theory. While value-free social science is a chimera, a more rigorously value-controlled strategic theory is a necessity which is sadly lacking. This is the principal weakness of strategy at its present stage of development. However, this rather unhappy state of affairs is beginning to change. Strategy, as we shall argue below, is beginning to move in the direction of political sociology due to its growing concern with revolutionary war, the military–industrial complex and the findings of cognate areas of the social sciences. In this strategy is sharing in the general tendency for the social sciences to begin to regain that unity of conception and method that characterised them a century ago.

While strategy is a new subject there is, paradoxically, an old literature.

In its contemporary form strategy has been a university subject for twenty years, but strategic questions have exercised the minds of political and social philosophers and practitioners over the centuries, even back to classical antiquity in Greece and in China. (2) Strategy is an integral part of social and political thought without which such thought would be incomplete. Strategy, broadly conceived, is concerned with the mechanisms of power politics, that is, the ways and means whereby an actor can be induced or coerced into actions which it would not otherwise undertake since the criteria for its actions are not acceptable to it. Power politics can exist at any level and in any sphere of human relations and wherever it exists strategy is relevant.

Of course power politics rarely appear in a pure state — the war between Rome and Carthage being a dramatic exception. Rather, social relations can be situated on a spectrum between the "ideal types" of power politics and legitimised politics. Any particular transaction can be located on the spectrum according to the degree to which the action is based upon criteria fully acceptable to the participant and in his "perfect knowledge" of the particular situation. Strategy deals with those social relations which fall more towards the power politics end of the spectrum.

Strategy, as it is taught in universities and pursued in research institutes, is not as broadly conceived as this. It is more concerned with the sharp end of power politics — with war, with armaments, with revolution, with "terrorists". This is a matter of convenience since jurists presumably study power politics as they analyse the problems of law and order in domestic society and psychologists, sociologists and anthropolotists are concerned with the modalities of coercion at different levels. This points to a grave *lacuna* in the literature: nowhere is strategy treated as a whole. The task is, of course, daunting in the extreme but *prima facie* deterrence, to take but one example, has structural similarities whether it is between parent and child, deviant and the law and the United States and the Soviet Union. There is little if any transfer of findings from one area of strategy to another and strategy as presently constituted in universities and research institutes is the worse for it. In part this explains the paucity of conceptual thinking in strategy.

To the military man strategy is usually thought of in juxtaposition with tactics — the former being the macro-element of generalship and conception of battle and the latter being the micro-element of execution. These subjects have been taught in military academies through the centuries but, with notable exceptions such as von Clausewitz's *On War*, (3) they have made little impact on political and social thought and practice. This is because they have been conceived as being essentially technical in nature —

for example, the use of the tank on the battlefield. It is also due to the philosophy assiduously cultivated by the generals that war is a matter for the generals. In other words, strategic factors dominate and may even determine political factors in warfare. This doctrine has, until relatively recently, been particularly strong in the United States. It is, however, noticeably less strong in the British and French tradition due to their colonial experiences and it is totally absent where the Clausewitzian dictum of "war is the continuation of politics by other means" has held sway, namely in the thought of Marxist strategists such as Lenin and Mao and their successors, disciples and strategists. For them political decisions must dictate the use and form of coercion employed even at the tactical level and it is one of the functions of political officers to ensure that this is so. Political goals prevail over military *desiderata* at all levels. War (and tactics) is too important to be left to the generals, as Clemenceau pointed out. This view has now been accepted almost universally as the result of wars of national liberation, guerrilla tactics and terrorism. Thus tactics and the art of generalship are grist to the strategist's mill in so far as they have political repercussions. Rarely, however, are questions purely military.

Given the ubiquity of strategy in the terms that it has been described it is not surprising that it found its way, under a different rubric, into courses in international relations when they first began to be taught in the years following the First world War. At a time when the focus was centred upon the League of Nations, there was much consideration given to the requirements for, mechanics of and experience with collective security, sanctions, disarmament and alliances – all topics later to find a home in strategy courses and on which a considerable literature appeared in the inter-war period. The rise of Hitler took the focus away from such "League of Nations" subjects as collective security and disarmament and, with the Second World War, it settled on the conduct of the war. This gave a tremendous fillip to armchair strategists the world over, since information was readily available through the media and the issues were such that not only were they clear to all but they involved all. Moreover, the armchair strategists, like their leaders, quickly came to realise that it was not only a question of generalship in the field but of what Churchill called "Grand Strategy" – that area where military, economic, political and psychological factors came together in an amalgam on which the fate of whole societies depended. The literature on the Second World War, which seems to be never-ending at both the popular and the scholarly level, attests to the degree of interest the subject has evolved. The war ended and a new era opened with the dropping of two atomic bombs on Japan in 1945.

Grand strategy in the Second World War and the advent of nuclear weapons secured a separate place for strategy in the context of courses on international relations but, curiously, this did not occur until the mid-fifties. The dropping of the bomb stimulated a relatively short-lived and often ill-informed debate between those who saw the atomic bomb merely as a "bigger bang" and those who argued that it had changed radically the nature of inter-state relations. Thereafter silence reigned until the testing of the hydrogen bomb and the growth of the Soviet Union's nuclear capability stimulated thought on the relationship between deterrence and defence and the implications — political and military — of mutual deterrence. The literature emerged and the courses, degrees and research institutes sprang into being.

For the best part of a decade the nuclear literature burgeoned; then it faded away almost as quickly as it had emerged. Perhaps the reason for this was first the pressing need to explore the political, military and technological complexities of the nuclear world and then the realisation that no adequate conceptual framework for the study of strategy in this domain existed. Thee was consensus on the desirability for a second strike force in a situation of mutual deterrence but no definite answers were forthcoming to questions concerning how many weapons were enough to deter — and against whom in which circumstances, the tactical use of nuclear weapons, massive retaliation or graduated deterrence, conventional war in the nuclear shadow and the like. It was easy and in a macabre way fun to write scenarios, but the assumptions on which such scenarios were based could be neither confirmed nor refuted with any degree of assurance on the basis of empirical theory. Thus when the options had been spelled out in their grand lines there was little point in haggling over or even pursuing details. The literature on nuclear deterrence theory dried up, although lately it is showing signs of revival as it becomes more evident that there is a real possibility of horizontal nuclear proliferation. (4) Such an event may well give rise to a new surge of nuclear deterrence 'theorising', or to put it more realistically "speculation", since its conceptual framework seems unlikely to be any more firmly based than before.

In the meantime in other areas of strategy some conceptual studies were being undertaken. The frequent failure of the colonial powers to prevail in colonial, neo-colonial or hegemonial confrontations brought in its wake the study of revolutionary war, guerrilla tactics and terrorism. (5) This is one area where there has been a notable contribution from third-world writers, both theoreticians and practitioners or in many cases theoretician-practitioners. (6) Western thinking on the same subject was for a period markedly inferior because it reflected Western policy which was to react to challenges to authority militarily rather than trying to understand them sociologically. Only when this policy had patently failed did a serious conceptual literature emerge first in France, then in Britain and finally in the United States.

The area of Western strength (and its Achilles heel) has been in building up military capabilities. This is also increasingly true of the Soviet Union. Since both the United States and the Soviet Union are manifestly capable of developing and producing advanced weapons systems of literally amazing performance characteristics, and in prodigious quantities, it might be thought that they could rest comfortably on their laurels safe in the knowledge of mutual deterrence and their ability to police their respective zones of influence. But while the super powers have established *détente* between themselves on a basis of mutual deterrence, their policing power has declined despite their technological genius and awesome military capabilities. The eviction of the Soviet Union from Egypt and the United States from Indo-China illustrates the Achilles heel: superior military capabilities are not always or easily translatable into utilisable military force in particular instances. The strong can be muscle-bound. (7) Strategists are only slowly coming to grips with such phenomena since it requires a fundamental reappraisal of the role of force in power politics, an evaluation of the effectiveness of different forms of coercive activity in a variety of situations and a reconceptualisation of the relationship between military and non-military factors. Such a reappraisal requires that strategists who have advised or written from the viewpoint of the super powers make a reluctant and painful admission that in some instances they were wrong not merely at the level of implementation but also in their basic conceptual framework.

Such a reappraisal has had little effect on the arms race, although expanded defence budgets and technological innovation have given rise to an interest in decision-making. This has led to the application of operations research techniques, such as systems analysis, to defence procurement. More generally, there has been a concern with the ramifications of a military–industrial complex. Such a complex is an inevitable concomitant of large defence budgets, massive procurement and great technological innovation. It has given rise to the accusation that the corporate, military, political and bureaucratic élites with a vested interest in such a complex have deliberately fostered the growth of tension and subverted the democratic will in order to further their sectional interests to the detriment of the general good and of peace. However, other decision-making theories and empirical studies suggest that there is no cohesian and control in the military–industrial complex and more generally in government and, therefore, there can be no plot. The relevant question is not "Who governs?" but "Is government possible?". The frightening answer is not that the military–industrial complex is controlled by wicked self-serving élites but that it is not subject to control at all and that it is by no means certain that it is amenable to control. (8)

Such problems only exist in the major arms-producing countries, although other problems of civil–military relations arise in all countries (since very few countries maintain no armed forces). Issues concerning civil–military relations are universal in time. Indeed, they raise some of the fundamental political questions: "Who are the guards and who guards the guards?" While much of the interest in civil–military relations has been concerned with third-world countries, due to their proclivity for military regimes, the problem is an ever-present one for developed countries as well, as the debate over conscription, challenges to authority in all spheres and outright rebellion (as in Northern Ireland) indicate. The return of defeated imperial armies to societies which have scant respect or even a role for the military and in which, in the eyes of the military, permissiveness and subversion are rampant, does not auger well for smooth civil–military relations. Fortunately, military sociologists have already started work describing the military – its personnel, its mores and its values. (9)

Defence procurement in the quantities of recent years has brought renewed interest in one of the oldest topics in strategy – the arms race, disarmament and arms control – theorising about which dates back to the beginning of the twentieth century. Starting from simple and sometimes accurate notions of the "merchants of death", the literature quickly came to embrace the mathematical models of Lewis Richardson. (10) The "merchants of death" can be found in modern guise in the colossal arms sales by the big four – Britain, France, the U.S.A. and the U.S.S.R. – to the third world and the mathematicians have a haven in several journals. (11) More recently, studies of the arms race have concentrated on the action-reaction model and the domestic process models of procurement. (12) In the action-reaction model, a perceived threat induces a state to procure additional weapons systems or to develop new ones which in its turn gives rise to a reaction by a second state which thereby brings a further response thus creating the arms race spiral. The domestic processes model, on the other hand, suggests that procurement may be due less to international factors than to national factors such as bureaucratic processes, technological innovation and the general strategic requirement to keep an arms industry in being as well as to vested interests and general economic considerations. Of course, an arms race could begin in the action–reaction mode and continue in that of the domestic processes model. Clearly, the arms race is the starting point for studies concerned with disarmament and arms control. Few studies have yet given adequate attention to the implications of an arms race primarily caused by domestic processes for arms control and disarmament.

Modern efforts to secure disarmament or arms control stretch back to the Hague Conferences of 1899 and 1907. The approach to disarmament, where genuine and not merely "cosmetic", has often been of an idealistic nature since, to be successful, disarmament requires there to be a change in the nature of relations — power politics giving way to legitimised politics. Too often, however, writers and politicians alike have been content to imagine schemes for the organisation of a disarmed world; (13) too rarely have they been prepared to analyse the political as opposed to the organisational process by which such a world could be reached. It is not surprising that attempts at arms control have been more successful. The purpose of arms control — to give a system of power politics greater stability — is less ambitious and its realisation is likely to be more immediate, but even in this case there is a distressing unwillingness to integrate attempts at arms control with analyses of the arms race.

Arms control negotiations are an important element in foreign policy — at least for the super powers. Thus the circle is complete. "Grand strategy", "power politics", "high politics" — the epitome of foreign policy as traditionally conceived — all have their strategic element. International relations, to name but one discipline, would be lacking without the strategic element. Yet it is difficult to pretend that the strategic element is properly integrated conceptually into the study of international relations. The modalities of power politics are well covered in the literature but there is little written about the manner in which and the reasons why a system of power relationships can change into legitimised relationships of the contry. Nor does the literature in international relations reflect findings about strategic questions at other systems levels. Clearly, as international relations embraces both legitimised and power politics as well as extending to many non-state actors and different levels of analysis, in short, there is a need for a new conceptual framework. Within such a framework the study of strategy will remain important.

In the foregoing paragraphs some timorous suggestions regarding the likely future developments in the field of strategy have been made. It is now germane to the discussion to assert them in a forthright and hopefully coherent manner and also to suggest ways in which strategy ought to develop.

54

While the study of strategy was confined to staff colleges, and when it was primarily the concern of the military, then considerations of force capability and "worst case" analysis predominated. The military sought to get as close as possible to that chimeric goal of absolute security and, in consequence, were concerned with how to prepare for the worst and what to do if it should materialise. Moreover, it was assumed that capability was both a good indicator of intentions and readily utilisable so that a comparison of capabilities was a good predictor of outcomes. The reaction to such a *Realpolitik* approach was an idealist-rationalist one in the shape of proposals for disarmament and institutional mechanisms for dealing with disputes. These traditional approaches still exist, but they no longer dominate the field, since on the one hand capabilities are clearly not always good predictors of intentions or outcomes and, on the other hand, the panaceas of the idealist-rationalist approach have not succeeded in creating the necessary consensus for their success. Moreover, the relationship between the super powers has been more characterised by "deterrence" than "defence" — an historical change which emphasises the communality of the problems of power politics at various levels since in domestic society "deterrence" is also a dominating notion.

"Defence" (for these purposes it subsumes the notion of offence) seeks to deprive a target actor *manu militari* of its ability to take independent actions. "Deterrence" is the taking of actions or the making of threats designed to so structure the environment of a target actor that it will choose the option favoured by the deterrer. The relationship is psychological rather than physical and the aim is to influence rather than to destroy the target's ability to take independent decisions. Since every power in the world is vulnerable to nuclear attack by at least one other power, there is, literally and analytically, no real defence at many levels of conflict. Hence the post-war concern with deterrence in super power relationships. Equally, the emphasis has shifted from simple analyses of capabilities to the decision-making process relating capabilities and intentions in a situation of deterrence. It is no longer merely a question of who has the big battalions but of what is a credible threat to a particular target on a particular issue at a particular time. The structure of deterrence which gives rise to the credibility of a threat is the same at all levels of social relationships, namely, the interaction of what is at stake, the sanction and the likelihood of its application.

Considerations such as these point to a return to first principles. What is the nature of conflict? What are its causes? What are its functions? How is it exacerbated or abated, settled or resolved? Such questions are the domain of the contemporary conflict researcher. He delves not only into the macabre world of the strategic nuclear balance between the super powers but also into conflict at all levels using the insights, findings and methodology of a variety of sciences in an effort to fuse them into an adisciplinary whole. Some strategists are moving in a convergent direction when they question the axioms of power politics, since such axioms are not always reliable either as an empirical description or as a prescriptin. But power politics is an important part of reality which needs to be described and explained. When is coercive capability utilisable? Against whom? By whom? In what circumstances? Or, more fundamentally, when does a situation of legitimised relations lose its legitimacy? How? Why? Conversely, when does a system of power politics lose its sting and gradually change its nature? Is it a fortuitous question or are there factors that we can identify and manipulate? These are questions of interest both to the strategist and the conflict researcher.

Strategy is moving towards sociology. Indeed, with conflict studies, it forms part of political sociology. The psychology of deterrence, the sociology of the decision-making process, the civil–military complex, the role of the military in societies of diverse kinds, conflict and co-operation at all levels have broken down the technical barriers of the subject. A technical analysis of the strategic balance makes no sense on its own. It needs to be put into a political and conceptual context. It is part of a multi-faceted phenomenon — conflict — about which we know little save that such technical analyses need to be allied to basic studies on such fundamental issues as the nature of authority — when it is acceptable, when it is not — or the importance of role behaviour. In short, strategy is beginning to find its place in the political sociology of world society. The strategist is slowly learning to vary his unit of analysis: no longer does he content himself with state actors and formally organised military bodies. He is learning to vary his level of analysis so that findings from conflicts at other levels, such as communal or industrial conflict, are utilised and the effects of such conflicts on other levels of analysis, including inter-state relations — his traditional area of concern — are taken into consideration. Moreover, the strategist, like other social scientists, is beginning to move beyond notions of discipline and even inter-disciplinarity to adisciplinarity where problems are grouped under new rubrics — development, identity, authority, conflict, integration and the like — in an attempt to see them as a whole regardless of level or unit of analysis and methodological or disciplinary orgins.

Social scientists are concerned with patterns of behaviour. They are concerned with the political process in a variety of systems of transactions, that is to say the manner in which demands for change arise, the ways in which they are articulated, the options available and their selection, the response chosen and the feedback resulting from its application and in the explanation and prediction of such phenomena. In this sense, social science is finding the unity it lost a century ago. If the concern with decision-making, that is motivation, process and the structures to which this process gives rise — politics in short — is a common denominator of the social sciences, the criteria on which this process is based is not common to all systems of transactions. The criteria can range from those that are entirely acceptable to the actors — a fully legitimised process — to those that are imposed by some actors upon other actors — a system of power politics — by way of a system that acts as a constraint on some actors and favours others without the "underdogs" being fully aware of it — a system characterised by structural violence. These are, of course, ideal types not found in the real world. However, in the real world it is not difficult to ascertain the general position at which a particular transaction lies on a spectrum between power and legitimised politics. Moreover, we can plot the ebb and flow between these two poles. In such a situation, the strategist has a central role to play for his domain is the modalities of power politics, the "whys" and "wherefores" of transactions that fall towards the power end of the spectrum. He is concerned with what happens in systems in which the decision-making process functions on the basis of criteria imposed by some actors on others, how this state of affairs arises, how it works and how it changes. Clearly, the strategist with an international relations background will give his greatest attention to systems in which large organised groups such as states employ or threaten to employ overt violence in war, but the context of such studies is beginning to be greater, and should be greater, embracing studies and findings using other actors at and across other levels of analysis in an adisciplinary framework. The strategist is entering unaccustomed fields: he needs to display, at the intellectual level, that exemplary vigour and valour attributed to the heroes of his past on the field of battle.

References

1. For a survey of the literature in the field see the author's chapter on Strategy in A. J. R. Groom and C. R. Mitchell (eds), *International Relations Theory: A Critical Bibliography*, London, Frances Pinter, 1978.
2. See Sun Tzu, *The Art of War*, London, Oxford University Press, 1963, trans. S. B. Griffith; Thucydides, *History of the Peloponnesian War*, London, Dent's Everyman Library No. 455, trans. Richard Crawley.
3. Karl von Clausewitz, *On War*, ed. and trans. Michael Howard and Peter Paret, Princeton, Princeton University Press, 1976.
4. See for example, Richard Rosecrance, "Strategic Deterrence Reconsidered",

Adelphi Paper No. 116, London, International Institute for Strategic Studies, 1975.

5. See Chalmers Johnson, *Revolutionary Change*, Boston, Little, Brown, 1966; Henry Eckstein (ed.), *Internal War*, London, Macmillan, 1964 and A. J. R. Groom, "Coming to Terms with Terrorism", *British Journal of International Studies*, forthcoming 1978.

6. See, for example, Che Guevara, *Guerrilla Warfare*, London, Pelican, 1969; Mao Tse-tung, *Basic Tactics*, New York, Praeger, 1966; A. H. Nasution, *Fundamentals of Guerrilla Warfare*, London, Pall Mall, 1965; and, on the counter-insurgency non-third world side, Frank Kitson, *Low Intensity Operations*, London, Faber, 1971 and Sir Robert Thompson, *Defeating Communist Insurgency*, London, Chatto & Windus, 1967.

7. For an elaboration of the argument see A. J. R. Groom, "After 1984: Ten Disturbing Trends", *Osterreichische Zeitschrift für Aussenpolitik*, Vol. 17, No. 3, 1977.

8. See Chapter Two in A. J. R. Groom, *Strategy in the Modern World* (forthcoming).

9. See the several volumes edited by Morris Janowitz and Jacques van Doorn.

10. *Statistics of Deadly Quarrels*, London, Stevens, 1960; *Arms and Insecurity*, London, Stevens, 1960.

11. Notably the *Journal of Conflict Resolution*.

12. See Colin S. Gray, "The Arms Race Phenomenon", *World Politics*, January 1971 and "The Urge to Compete: Rationales for Arms Racing", *World Politics*, January 1974.

13. See G. Clark and L. B. Sohn, *World Government through World Law*, Cambridge, Harvard University Press, 1966.

CHAPTER 4

The Development of Theory of International Organisation: The Four Phases of Writing

Paul Taylor

In this chapter it is argued that the literature on international organisation in this century can be organised conveniently into four main phases of development, though elements from each phase have survived to the present. It is argued that the study of international organisation focuses upon the problems of international government, as understood in each phase, though there is no agreement among scholars about the form which this should take. Each of the phases reveals a characteristic relationship between international institutions and international society, and between structures and processes at the international level. Each implies a different view of the ideal form of international society, and corresponding bases of order between states. Concentration upon characteristic relationships between institutions and society in the succeeding phases allows a coherent arrangement of contemporary writings, and encourages an examination of the forces of order in international society which is related to, but not limited by, thinking about order within the state.

The first characteristic of the subject of international organisation is that it is concerned with the development of formal structures in international society. The main examples of formal structures are of course international institutions which are created by agreement of the participating actors and which are given permanent offices and institutional arrangements. Their founders may be either governments, in which case they are conventionally called Inter-Governmental Organisations (IGOs), or private groups of individuals, in which case they are called International Non-Governmental Organisations (INGOs). Estimates indicate that there are about 200 IGOs and just under 2,000 INGOs, though the precise figures vary with the criteria used to determine essential characteristics. (1) The most international elements in these institutions are undoubtedly the permanent offices or the secretariats in that they exist and function entirely in international society, whereas state representatives and governments have a role at both the national and international level. This characteristic of international institutions as the only full-time members of international society means that the student of international organisation, in contrast with the student of other branches of international relations, has less need to justify the distinctive character of his subject by reference to a special methodology. In particular he has less need to distinguish himself from the historian or the lawyer, and to attach himself consciously to the social sciences. The object of study possesses a central feature of essentially international importance which is itself sufficiently distinctive to justify its inclusion in the field of international relations. The point is not that students of international organisation have not used new social science methods — they do so increasingly — but rather than methodological tests need not be applied to distinguish it as a branch of international relations.

The subject of international organisation must also include the wide range of processes which feed into the formal structures, and which reflect the increasing range of interaction between states. The structures represented by the institutions are seen as channels which affect or modify in some sense the processes which link them with states and with each other. They are nodes of formal organisation imposed upon a matrix of informal processes. We call the latter international organisation, too, if they show observable patterns and regularities. The subject of international organisation has, therefore, come to include two interrelated elements called, first, international institutions, and second — using the same term — international organisation. It should be stressed that not all interactions between states (processes) are of concern to the student of international organisation: they are of interest only if they are relevant to questions concerning the power and authority of international institutions or if they are in fact, or potentially, predictable, routine and orderly, and have therefore become a relatively fixed feature of international society. The student of international organisation is therefore concerned with processes in international society from a perspective which is rather different from that, say, of the foreign policy analyst. The student of foreign policy presumably focuses upon factors which explain policy outputs from the state, whilst the international organisation student is concerned first with the ways in which international institutions and organisation are utilised successfully as instruments of, and constraints upon, national policies and objectives, and secondly with international organisation and institutions as indications of a growing international order, that is, of a strengthening consensus about appropriate rules of procedure and management in the international system.

It seems to this writer that the ultimate purpose of enquiry into international organisation is to trace the development of international government in the broadest sense; it concerns, in other words, the possible emergence in relations between institutions and international society of a wide range of agreed procedures for the peaceful reconciliation of conflicting interests, for the management of common concerns, and the promotion of peaceful change, which are accepted by major actors, states or individuals. It is, of course, not the case that all students of international organisation are supporters of such developments, but they all want to know how far they have gone. It is also not the case that there is any clear view about the form of these arrangements as might be expected given the wide range of views about the nature of interest, and the way in which interests might be related to institutions in a stable system. The task of the student of international organisation has been seen variously as one of understanding the government, as we have defined it, of a decentralised community of nation-states, or of a collectivity of inter-penetrated national systems, or of a world which is organised primarily along functional lines. Interests have been viewed as essentially pluralist (*Gesselschaft*) or harmonious (*Gemeinschaft*), as the condition of stability, and institutions as ideally fragmented, thus posing problems of co-ordination, or as ideally centralised (in reflecting political aims), thus posing the problem of the fragmentation of particular functions. But among these various permutations of interest and institutions there are a number of recurrent questions concerning, for instance, the nature of authority, or community or legitimacy. And students of international organisation are continuously tempted to discover among the changing world which they analyse and explain an ideal arrangement for the times, which could be called a constitution for the new international society. They are tempted to stand back from their attempt to understand to assert − having, they think, understood - that this is how it ought to be. It is these concerns, presumably, which underline the continuing close relationship between this branch of international relations and the student of government and of law, not just international law.

It follows from this concern with possible constitutional arrangements, however oblique or critical this might be, that the development of the broad lines of the theory of international organisation is about different ways of relating international institutions to international society.

International organisation theory reflects different views about the role of institutions which are normally ignored in writings about government within the state. In large part this is concerned with relationships between structure and process in international society — institutions and organisations as we have defined them. In this international organisation has often drawn upon accounts of the development of institutions within the state, but it has also had to bear in mind the possibility of the emergence of new forms of stable society-institutional relationships.

One of the conclusions reached by Haas in 1970, for instance, was, in effect, that the constitution of international society, although concerned with similar central questions such as legitimacy and authority, could be fundamentally different in its institutional-societal relationships from that found within any one of the existing states. (2) He argued, in developing Lindberg's and Scheingold's ideas, that the pattern of authority-legitimacy transfer could vary according to whether the emerging system (Europe) was dominated by functional arrangements, or moved towards the model of the regional super-state, or combined existing states with high levels of functional interdependence. As yet the four main phases through which students of international organisation have passed since the beginning of the twentieth century have been distinguished more by characteristic questions than by accepted answers. However, they do at least reveal changing assumptions about the potential role of international institutions in international society, and about the broad shape of the imminent international constitution.

The four phases of relationships between international institutions and society are now discussed briefly as an introduction to a more detailed discussion later in this chapter. From the vantage point of the late seventies it is possible to distinguish a first phase of writing about international organisation which shows a sharp contradiction between those who, on the one hand, insisted that international institutions were no more than *instruments* of state policy, and on the other, those who took a highly normative, prescriptive approach, and discussed ideal arrangements such as international courts or arbitration tribunals. This period may be conveniently labelled the dichotomous phase. Though these types of writings are still produced, the dichotomous pattern dominated the inter-war years and earlier.

In a second phase, institutions were seen as *actors* having the capacity to define a position in relation to a proposed action. They were thought to develop an experience of their own, and a will to achieve a set of preferred goals, although the resources available to them to do so were rather limited and mainly involved the prestige and reputation of individual international civil servants: they did what they could, on the sufferance of the dominant state actors, though the range of tasks with which international institutions were concerned was consistently expanded in this period. This attitude is reflected in many writings since the Second World War, but it was dominant in the 1950s. However, it should be noted that the concept of actor, though it may now be recognised in theorising in the earlier period, did not become current terminology until the 1960s. (3)

In a third stage of international organisation writing, international institutions were given a more active role than that which is implied in the concept of actor. They were more frequently seen as capable of effecting changes in their environment, and, because of this, may be conveniently labelled *effectors*. Much of the writing about integration theory in Western Europe, for instance, was concerned to examine the ways in which "supranational" institutions made decisions and used their resources of power and authority to carry them out. The observation was now more frequently made that such institutions could be instrumental in changing policies or structures. Institutions outside Western Europe, too, were examined for symptoms of "supranationalism".

The fourth phase is one of recent origin in the mid-1970s, and is therefore inevitably set out in a somewhat tentative way in this essay. The main features of the writing in this phase are an increasing concern with international institutions as potential or actual *controllers* of areas of international society, which governments are unable to control by themselves or in alliance with each other. There is an international realm, it is felt, in which both institutions and governments are seen to have an interest but which can only be controlled effectively at the international level.

It is here, of course, that theorising about international organisation has become closest to theorising about relations between governments and people and their affairs within the state. International society is seen not exclusively, as hitherto, as a product of interaction between national societies, but also as embracing a distinctive society which might be better labelled a transnational society, possessed of its own institutions and providing the framework for its own *world politics*. In the economic realm, as Miriam Camps has said, the suggestion is of an incipient, closed industrial world economy, which is imposing itself upon an international economy dominated by interactions between national economies. (4) This phase is essentially a development from the very high level of interactions between some states in such areas as trade and information exchange which developed particularly rapidly through the 1960s, (5) when there was concern with international institutions as effectors.

The four successive phases of writing on international organisation in this century reveal, therefore, four different views on relationships between institutions and society. The earlier relationships are, however, also to be found in the later phases: they dominate in the one to which they are attributed but are not exclusively found there. One reason for this is that there are differences between perceived characteristics of international organisations in various regions, and between them and organisations at the universal level. Although major research may appear to be focused upon concepts which suggest increasing control over international society, this does not indicate that most institutions are obtaining such power. It suggests only that leading scholars have questioned whether some institutions might not be developing in this way, in some regions, or in relation to some functions, regionally or at the universal level. These changes in the concerns of theorists do not therefore necessarily reflect any general tendency at the governmental level in international society towards increasing order or disorder; most institutions are probably still best viewed as either instruments or actors. Some characteristic empirical and theoretical concerns of scholars in each of the four phases of writing are now considered.

Institutions as instruments of state policy and as imminent world government

The characteristic of international society stressed in this dichotomous phase was that it was dominated by states and by the idea that states retained the right to decide whether international institutions should act. The focus is upon IGOs. The institution was seen to be an agent of states, acting only in so far as they agreed and not as defining and pursuing its own policies. The archetypal voting procedure, it was accepted, was the liberum veto, or the rule of unanimity; states could, at the extreme, prevent any action if they dissented or otherwise refused its application to themselves. This view was reflected in the early days of the League in the form of the secretariat under Secretary-General Eric Drummond, which stressed traditional administrative service functions rather than attempting to play an initiating, more active role, as was encouraged in the United Nations by Article 99 and followed particularly by Dag Hammarskjold.

The first reaction to this view was that co-operation among sovereign states within framework institutions was the proper form of international government. Edmund C. Mower illustrates this approach in his book called *International Government*, (6) published in 1931. Arthur Salter also stressed the primary importance of institutions as frameworks for co-operation between the national governmental agencies in his book

Recovery, published in 1932. His view of international organisation as a kind of residual category, doing only what was left to them by the states, is illustrated in his argument about the ways of achieving economic recovery. He wrote that the "National Economic Council needs to the extent to which economic life is international to be related to the similar institutions of other countries, and for this purpose a World Economic Council is required, drawing its membership from National Councils, and associated with the League of Nations . . ." But "standing behind them all, the Central Government [of states], the only ultimate guardian of the public interest, because it is the only one whose authority is drawn from the public itself, must watch, intervening if necessary". (7) Quite a number of scholars and public figures took this "realist", minimalist view of international organisation. (8)

Stress upon co-operation between sovereign states as the basic feature of international government was, however, part of a debate with other students of international organisation who have since been placed among the ranks of the so-called "idealists", one of whose leading figures was Norman Angell. These scholars were responsible for a second, idealistic/prescriptive theme in this period, which saw in international organisation a potential world government; they stressed the potential for change, and improvement in international society. It is difficult to weigh the strengths of one side of an argument within a scholarly community, particularly some fifty years later, but a study of the literature of the 1920s and 1930s has left this writer with the impression that the realists, even then, were considerably more numerous and influential than has been suggested, in particular by E. H. Carr and N. Spykman. (9) Hans Morgenthau was someone who managed after the Second World War to write more attractively and originally in the realist vein and rightly obtained great recognition, but he was the latest example of a number of realists and not the revolutionary spirit which he is sometimes thought to be.

In fact in the study of international organisation, and quite possibly international relations in general, it could be argued that the realist school had been dominant throughout. In writings about the League of Nations Sir Frederick Pollock argued that that institution was no more than "a concert of independent powers", (10) as did Alfred Zimmern (11) and such statesmen as Lord Curzon. (12) Against this it was argued that the League was a super-state in the making (13) or that there should be a federation of peace-loving states "now". The latter proposal, usually attributed to Clarence Streit, (14) was criticised again in favour of sensible co-operation between sovereign states which should acquire "the habit of framing military and economic policy without regard for the needs and interests of other countries", by E. H. Carr in his *Conditions of Peace* in 1942. (15) Leonard Woolf was also concerned in his writings on international government at the end of the First World War to stress the importance of recognising the sovereignty of states. (16) But this is not to deny that Woolf's writing, and *inter alia* that of Rappard (17) and Angell (18) frequently showed evidence of confidence, despite the difficulties recognised by others as "reality", in an emerging community of states within which international government would emerge. It was sometimes perhaps over-idealistic and much too optimistic in its expectations of radical change in the modes of inter-state relations; but the output of idealistic prescriptive writing was in part a reaction against the stress by so many on the impossibility of bringing about any fundamental change in the main features of the political terrain. Yet it should be pointed out that much of the writing on international organisation in this phase was intended as a contribution to the debate about the settlement at the end of the First World War, and that the functionalist writings of David Mitrany, though beginning to appear in the early 1930s, did not attract much attention until the 1940s.

The main theories reflected in writings during this phase of relationships between international institutions and society may now be briefly set out as follows: institutions were seen by a significant number of international organisation scholars to be merely agents or instruments of governments; some idealists saw them as embryo forms of international community, but they were not usually thought capable then of making an impact of their own on public policy; they were frequently seen as too remote from public attention, and as channels of private or secret diplomacy; and they were thought by realists, who may well have been dominant, to be properly controlled by states exercising a veto. Significantly, a considerable body of writing on the main features of international law emerged during this period, but such writings frequently tended to be concerned with questions such as the acquisition of a legal personality by international institutions (often denied) or on the development of procedures by which states could organise their affairs, even on such basic questions as the rules of debate in plenary meetings, within their framework.

Institutions as actors

The second phase was dominated by writings which inquired into the ability of international institutions (again, in the main, IGOs) to modify the policies discussed within institutional frameworks by governments.

The institution was seen to be developing a mind of its own, a fund of experience and information, and the will — and the opportunity — to do what it could. But it was not seen as generating major initiatives or as having any major impact upon its environment in either the policy outputs or structures of the states. It was an amender, a modifier, an interpreter — an actor almost in the strict sense — rather than a creator or initiator. States are still seen as the masters, and the national interest remained the staple diet.

At least one international institution, the International Labour Organisation, had begun to show some of these qualities under a particularly active leader, Albert Thomas, in the inter-war period, and there were some indications that the Secretary-General of the League had come to play a more effective role than that envisaged for him in the Covenant. (19) But in the first years after the end of the Second World War scholars began increasingly to perceive institutions as actors and this led to a great flowering of research in the 1950s which can be usefully related to this idea. The two institutions which represented the new style of institution particularly well early on were the Organisation of European Economic Co-operation, with its strong co-ordinating role in the distribution among Western European states of Marshall Aid funds, and the Secretary-General of the United Nations, who was now formally encouraged by Article 99 of the Charter to adopt the role of international diplomat, and to represent the international interest as forcibly as he could. Dag Hammarskjold was, of course, the Secretary-General who was most active in using these opportunities. (20)

The idea of actor, as has been pointed out, implies an interpretation and modification of policies. It was natural therefore for scholars to become interested in the ways in which national policies could be amended within international institutions, and to study the effects of these amendments, or occasionally, their lack of effect. Accordingly the new role of international officials in multilateral diplomacy, from the United Nations to the North Atlantic Treaty Organisation, the OEEC and the Council of Europe, was examined more closely than hitherto using an increasing range of methodology. The effects of multilateral diplomacy in the United Nations and elsewhere were explored and its symptoms in voting patterns in international assemblies, block building, and voting procedure were analysed. (21) There was also a further investigation, and considerable refinement, of the concept of a security system and consideration of the contribution of international institutions in various types of system. (22) Such concepts as preventive diplomacy and permissive enforcement were added to the traditional though now critically

67

re-examined concepts of collective security, (23) the concert system and the balance of power. The UN Emergency Force in the Middle East and the Korean involvement greatly stimulated such concerns. Any bibliography from one of the general texts on international organisation from this period contains references to the increasing range of literature on these various themes.

The character of the prevailing attitude among scholars about the relationship between international institutions and international society is indeed indicated in the fact that this was the period of large, general accounts of the development of international organisation such as those by Inis Claude, Cheever and Haviland, Stephen Goodspeed, Clyde Eagleton and Leyland Goodrich. (24) Why were such accounts written then and why have few appeared since? The main reason is that their authors saw the development of international organisation as lying essentially in the manageable central theme of the strengthening of the traditional community of states with the assistance of a novel creature, a hand-maiden of the emerging international order, called international institutions. They did not doubt that it would be much the same as the old order – the same but better. Their task was assisted by two fortuitous circumstances: first, that the theme could be appropriately handled by a historical and descriptive methodology and their skills are well fitted to this kind of task. They were not to be daunted by the new methodology of behaviouralism. Secondly, the range of international organisation which existed seemed manageable and capable of being encompassed in the covers of one book. They were insightful, realistic and not unaware of the awful dangers, some new, some old, of international politics.

But they were cautiously optimistic: the community of states was seen as being capable of transforming "swords into ploughshares" and developments in international organisation were thought to point in this direction. The view of international institutions as actors in the sense employed in this essay is logically consistent with their view that international government was basically a matter of an improved ordering of relations between states with the assistance of enlightened international institutions. There were a number of other factors, though, which helped, amongst which, perhaps, historical circumstances should be mentioned. The United Nations achieved apparent success in Korea and at Suez; the United States and its allies dominated the UN General Assembly, itself an encouraging factor, though perhaps unconsciously appreciated, for these mainly American scholars; and after the death of Stalin in 1953 there was a discernible improvement in East–West relations.

In later phases of international organisation theorising scholars were deterred from writing general accounts of their subject by an increasing uncertainty about the direction of development of international society. In the sixties and seventies doubts increased about the likelihood of the existing states surviving as the dominant actors; there were a number of alternative visions of the future world, emanating mainly from the United States, ranging from neo-functionalist supranationalism to transnational inter-penetration. There was also the increasingly apparent paradox which scholars in the area of international organisation found themselves reluctant to examine: the view that more powerful international institutions had emerged had to be set against the appearance of more intractable problems in international society such as the North-South, rich–poor disagreements, the increasing concentration upon regional trading blocs and, of course, the spread of nuclear weapons. Assertions of world society had to be set against the blossoming of dependency theory. Furthermore, international institutions became so numerous and various in their purpose and character that it became increasingly difficult to select a useful number of them to illustrate a coherent general theme such as the earlier one of the emerging community of states. The new methodology which appeared in the wake of the behavioural revolution was also conducive towards the fragmenting of any overall picture of the subject: what differing truths could the various tools produce?

International institutions as effectors

In this phase, which was mainly the 1960s into the early 1970s, institutions, particularly at the regional level, were examined closely by leading scholars for symptoms of their achieving an impact upon their environment in the structures and policies of the states. They were in other words seen as possibly effecting changes which were in some way part of a process of international integration. The changing circumstances which permitted such institutions to emerge were of course also examined as they had been in the cases of earlier pahses. However, in this later phase scholars began to inquire into the capacity of institutions to obtain goals even in the face of opposition from particular member governments; sometimes they were seen to act directly upon people and individuals within the state in defiance of governments' intentions, and NGOs were given much more attention. States were no longer confidently accepted as the irreducible actors, and links between institutions and elements within the state were more frequently stressed.

Although the foundation of this approach may be found in the 1950s, particularly in Ernst Haas's writing on the European Coal and Steel

Community, (25) the major part of the contributions were associated with the emergence of the European Communities in the 1960s. (26) Haas became the leader of an influential school of theorists of international organisation called neo-functionalists, who specialised in integration theory. Others who have been members of this rather loosely knit school included Leon Lindberg, Joseph Nye, Stuart Scheingold, J. P. Sewell, Lawrence Scheinman and Karl Kaiser. Their theories have been widely discussed and analysed, and it would be superfluous to attempt a further detailed analysis here. But perhaps the main points should be outlined: the theory was developed from the functionalist ideas of David Mitrany, particularly his *A Working Peace System*; (27) it is gradualist, in that it sees international integration as moving from areas of lesser salience to areas of higher salience; it is concerned with the understanding of the processes by which a single political system could emerge between two or more previously separate political systems, particularly at the regional level; and it detected and described various subordinate economic, political and social processes, such as *spillover*, which it was thought would move interantional integration from one level to the next. (28)

These concerns are reflected in the wide range of detailed studies undertaken by the integration theorists. The major influence upon the methodology and choice of subject, apart from functionalism, seems to this writer generally to be the new tools of behaviouralism, theories of pluralism and interest group politics, and also, though this intellectual debt usually goes unacknowledged, decision-making theories, as represented in the work of Snyder, Bruck and Sapin. (29) The neo-functionalists are very much concerned with aspects of decision-making such as how the international institutions came to make decisions about specific areas previously reserved to the state, and about how and why such decisions are accepted or rejected by the actors to whom they are directed, be they governments or other actors.

Such decision-making concerns as the significance of changing perceptions and the range of informal constraints and pressures on decision-makers recur in neo-functionalism. In studying these they are concerned centrally with bureaucrats and other people in key institutional settings who are thought to mirror changing perceptions of channels of responsibility, and in Scheinman's term, push forward the "inter-penetration of bureaucracies". (30) National bureaucrats are seen to be changed in their perception of appropriate ways of solving problems, particularly those created by existing integration, so that they increasingly consult partners in other bureaucracies, including the international institution, and increasingly support decisions which further integration. They perceive new paths of responsibility which sometimes extend outside states. In addition the neo-functionalists are concerned with modes of bargaining, and with perceptions of the salience of various interests and in evaluating the extent to which responsibility in more salient areas is transferred to the new international institutions. Various concepts of neo-functionalism such as *politicisation* and *incremental decision-making* are also readily deduceable from writings of the decision-making theorists. The neo-functionalist debt to decision-making theory is hardly surprising since it is well fitted to the task of breaking open institutions so that their actual decision-making procedures, as opposed to formal stipulations, together with related constraints and pressures can be examined, and adjustments detected as integration proceeds.

The neo-functionalist view of institutions as *effectors* does not of course imply that they are seen as exercising arbitrary power. The conditions in which they can define and obtain goals, and the limitations upon this ability, are also a crucial part of their study. But it now seems generally agreed that they failed to make sufficient allowance in their theories for the determination of people and some politicians to retain control over their own affairs; states were more resistant to integration than they had thought. Charles De Gaulle, the late President of France, was peculiarly difficult to assimilate into the theory, and that led to a number of modifications, and an increasing complexity, in the theory. Neo-functionalist writings were drastically reduced in frequency after 1970. There was a failure to assimilate the various factors which seemed to restrain processes of integration, particularly in Europe, and which restrained the process of transferring powers to the "supranational" international institutions. Their role as effectors was seen to be restricted by the lack of supportive influences in political and economic/social circumstances, both among the governments and at other levels of the state.

The neo-functionalists' concern with institutions as *effectors* relating to actors and structures within the state was very much linked with apparent developments in the European Communities, and led them to stress an understanding of decision-making in international institutions and its interaction with decision-making at the national level. This concern with decision-making was also reflected in the interests of scholars who focused upon non-regional institutions which dealt mainly with governments at the world level. The feeling that institutions in themselves might in some circumstances be able to take decisions to effect changes in areas of importance to the state led these scholars to ask a question which had previously been thought critical only at the national level: who governs? Cox and Jacobson's book (31) was very much in the tradition of

Dahl's classic inquiry into American politics of the late 1950s, which in turn followed from works such as C. Wright Mill's *The Power Elite* (1957) and Floyd Hunter's *Community Power Structures* (1953). (32)

Cox and Jacobson were interested in the use of power, influence and authority within international institutions, as had been Dahl in an American city, and they deduced a category of actors (brokers, initiators, controllers and vetoers) (33) and a typology of decisions, as well as a rather simplistic account of the environment in which the institutions acted, to help explain this. The application of this framework to specific institutions by contributors suggests a wide range of powers and authority in international institutions. One, the International Monetary Fund, emerges as possessing both power and authority which it can exercise on member governments in certain circumstances, as an effector. (34) There are various combinations of permanent staff and coalitions of member states which possess power and authority, but sometimes staff, the institution proper, can wield considerable power in itself.

The work of Karl Deutsch and his followers should also be considered here, although some of his writing dates from an earlier phase, the 1950s. His work concentrates upon the patterns of transactions among states (he and his followers are sometimes called transactionalists) and he sees in such changing patterns one indicator of the level of community among the peoples in those states. (35) The more transactions, and the more balanced and responsive they are, the higher the level of community, and the greater the chance of settling disputes without violence, of achieving a security community. Deutsch has been very concerned with the development of nations, and with the various indications of this particular example of community, rather than with the detailed operation of international institutions. (36) This is a point made by Leon Lindberg. (37) He argues, however, that the permanence and stability of institutions, be they international or national, depends critically upon the attainment of appropriate support in a community of values and attitudes, which is reflected in transactions. He concentrates, however, on the *process* side of international organisation, on the achievement of regular, routine and predictable flows around and into the international institutions. His concern is with the circumstances in which institutions can act as effectors, rather than upon the internal operation of institutions. A further characteristic of this phase of writing on international organisation is also illustrated by his writing; he assumes that organisations may cut across national frontiers and are capable of penetration deep into states, and are not, as is the case in earlier phases, mainly a matter of intra-governmental contacts. Indeed Professor Deutsch's work, together with the rediscovery of the functionalism of

David Mitrany, was one of the major incentives towards the focusing of academic attention in this phase upon the growth of non-governmental international organisations.

Institutions as controllers

As has been pointed out the features of this phase, the current one, are as yet barely discernible. But it is possible to detect a growing interest among scholars, as reflected in their view of international organisation, in the development of international institutions which are in the process of capturing a functional territory from member states. (38) As the states are dependent upon the rewards produced by the exercise of these functions they allow a kind of independence of control to the institutions. It is not suggested that states are believed to be becoming superfluous or that international institutions in general are becoming more powerful, but rather that there is an area of activity which is identified as specifically international, or transnational, and which is controlled internationally or transnationally. Some of these areas are of rather low salience, and it should be noted that there is no necessary direct link between the increasing number of controlling institutions and the abandonment of the sovereignty of states.

The perception that such developments are actual or imminent in areas of rather higher salience, however, is inspired by the problems of control posed for national governments, acting separately, by the very high level of interdependence, particularly in the economic field, which has appeared in some areas of the world. Morse and others have discussed these problems which generally seem to push towards the creation of competent institutions with powers commensurate with the necessary control function at the appropriate global or regional level. (39) The need is, it is thought, for institutions to be set up which can regulate the international monetary system, or the international trading system, at that level (usually the global one) at which this goal can be obtained. States would be consulted, and could well exercise a general supervisory mandate over the institution, but the implication is that such institutions would have the kind of day-to-day control function previously exercised only by rather technical low politics institutions such as those responsible for air safety or reporting or controlling the spread of disease. The new institutions would, however, be acting in more salient areas like money and trade.

Within the broad field of interdependence theory has emerged a sub-field, which focuses upon relations across national frontiers between non-governmental actors, called transnationalism. NGOs became a primary focus. One of the major pioneering works in this area was that of Keohane and Nye. (40) The theory has something in common with functionalism in that it deals with non-governmental international organisations and owes a considerable intellectual debt to that theory, but its focus is different in that it is not concerned with understanding the implications of such organisations for integration processes, but more with how they affect the foreign policy working of states. The implication is that that process has been fundamentally altered in that it now has to deal with semi- or wholly autonomous non-state political systems which include sections previously within their own jurisdiction. The problems of control already mentioned are an aspect of this fundamental alteration.

The transnational organisations which more than any other both reflect and stimulate the heightened interdependence which sustains transnationalism are, of course, multinational business enterprises. The character of this non-governmental organisation provides a major incentive towards the setting up of institutions through which they be controlled. But there are other examples, some of a more traditional sort, such as the Ford Foundation or the Roman Catholic Church. And there are a number of less structured organisations which are being established such as transnational trade unions and associations of specialists, businessmen and others with interests found in many countries. It is apparent that many of these organisations themselves generate forces towards the setting up of matching control organisations in which governments may also have an interest but which they cannot control. The best example of this perhaps is the growth of multinational business and one of its consequences in the parallel pressures towards the growth of multinational trade union organisations. This is in fact an indication of one of the distinctive features of international organisation in this phase: that the transnational domain is capable of producing forces which generate organisations which relate mainly to itself. Multinational business, however, is also one of the forces which has helped indirectly to sustain the power and authority of more traditional inter-governmental organisations such as the IMF, by acting as channels for the movement of large sums of money between national centres and amplifying the problem of monetary stability. This may be one of the forces which has moved these more traditional organisations towards the concept of the controller, in the eyes of some writers.

It is obvious that much of this is speculative and in any case seems to relate to a relatively small area of international organisation. Yet it is about an area which is of critical importance to the modern state, and which sharpens the curiosity of scholars about the form of the state in coming years. It is obvious too that although there is a great deal of writing about specific empirical areas such as the multinational business corporation or foreign policy making in a period of high interdependence, the theory is very underdeveloped. In fact it is probably best described as a pre-paradigm rather than a pre-theory. It presents an impression of a different view of the world, in which international organisation has a very different role from its earlier ones, but the number of falsifiable hypotheses of any kind of predictive value is rather small. It is also the case that the development or apparent development of these more powerful institutions may appear to be hard to reconcile with the continuation of some of the traditional problems of international society, and indeed the amplification of some of them such as the differences between the rich and the poor countries. This is perhaps one of the central paradoxes of international organisation: that a strengthening of scholarly concern with the forces of order is matched by a continuing concern with the divisive elements in international society. And at the present time this paradox is associated with the beginnings of a reaction against concepts of increasing interdependence by those who seem more impressed with an increasing statism and pluralism in international society. There is here a neat parallel with the early phase of writing on international organisation: now realism is found in the reaction to what is held to be a prevailing orthodoxy of idealism about such questions as interdependence, whereas in the first phase idealism seemed to be more a reaction to the then prevailing realism.

These then are the major phases of theorising in international organisation to date. There has clearly been considerable development in the subject through these phases, both in terms of methodology and in terms of foci of interest, but as was explained earlier, the central theme, the one to which scholars regularly return, is that of the manner of the government of international society. It seems to this student, however, that scholars have responded to empirical developments with a range of theories, pre-theories and paradigms, which suggest a movement away from the decentralised international community of states towards a more interpenetrated system with some potential for the consolidation of the mechanisms for control in international institutions at the regional and, occasionally, at the global level. We must not, however, underestimate the potential of the realist backlash.

References

1. See Michael Wallace and J. David Singer, "Intergovernmental Organization in the Global System, 1815-1904: A Quantitative Description", *International Organization*, Vol. XXIV, No. 2, Spring 1970; and Kjell Skjelsback, "The

Growth of International Non-governmental Organizations in the Twentieth Century" in Robert O. Keohane and Joseph S. Nye, Jr, *Transnational Relations in World Politics*, Harvard University Press, Cambridge, Mass., pp. 70–92.

2. Ernst B. Haas, "The Study of Regional Integration: Reflections on the Joy and Anguish of Pre-theorizing", *International Organization*, Vol. XXIV, No. 4, Autumn 1970, p. 634.

3. See use of concept of actor in Carol Ann Cosgrove and K. Twitchett, *The New International Actors: the UN and the EEC*, London, Macmillan, 1970, particularly their Part One, pp. 11–49.

4. Miriam Camps, *"First World" Relationships: the role of the OECD*, Paris, Atlantic Institute for International Affairs; New York, Council on Foreign Relations, December 1975. Atlantic Papers, 2/1975, pp. 50–1.

5. See, for example, Peter J. Katzenstein, "International Interdependence: Some long-term trends and recent changes", *International Organization*, Vol. 29, No. 4, autumn 1975, pp. 1021–34.

6. Edmund C. Mower, *International Government*, Boston, Mass., D. C. Heath & Co., 1931, esp. pp. 398–405.

7. Sir Arthur Salter, K.C.B., *Recovery: The Second Effort*, London, Bell & Sons, 1932, p. 221.

8. See in this context Inis Claude Jr's account of changes in voting procedures in international institutions in his *Swords into Plowshares*, University of London Press (3rd edition), 1965, pp. 111–37.

9. E. H. Carr, *The Twenty Years' Crisis, 1919–1939*, London, Macmillan, 1962.

10. Sir Frederick Pollock, *League of Nations* (2nd edition), 1922, p. 97.

11. Sir Alfred Zimmern, *The League of Nations and the Rule of Law 1918–1935*, London, Macmillan, 1936.

12. Lord Curzon, quoted in Mower, op. cit., p. 400.

13. David Jayne Hill, *The Problem of a World Court: the story of an unrealized American idea*, New York, Longmans, 1927.

14. See Clarence Streit, *Union Now with Britain*, Harper, New York and London, 1941.

15. E. H. Carr, *Conditions of Peace*, New York, Macmillan, 1942, p. 96.

16. L. S. Woolf, *The Framework of a Lasting Peace*, London, Allen & Unwin, 1917, p. 92.

17. William Emmanuel Rappard, *The Quest for Peace Since the World War*, Cambridge, Mass., Harvard University Press, 1940.

18. See Norman Angell, *The Great Illusion – Now* (1938 edition), Harmondsworth, 1938.

19. See Edward J. Phelan, *Yes and Albert Thomas*, New York, Columbia University Press, 1949; F. P. Walters, *A History of the League of Nations*, London, Oxford University Press, 1952, especailly Chapters 5 and 7.

20. See Leon Gordenker, *The UN Secretary-General and the Maintenance of Peace*, New York, Columbia University Press, 1967.

21. See Chadwick F. Alger, "Personal Contact in Intergovernmental Organizations", in Herbert C. Kelman (ed.), *International Behaviour*, New York, Holt, Rinehart & Winston, Inc., 1965. See also References in Alger, loc. cit., p. 546.

22. See Ernst B. Haas, "Types of Collective Security: An Examination of Operational Concepts", *The American Political Science Review*, March 1955, Vol. XLIX, No. 5, pp. 40–62.

23. See Howard C. Johnson and Gerhart Niemeyer, "Collective Security: The Validity of an Ideal", *International Organization*, Vol. VIII, No. 1, February 1954.

24. Inis Claude Jr, *Swords into Plowshares*, University of London Press (3rd edition), 1965 (1st edition, 1956); Clyde Eagleton, *International Government*, New

York, Ronald Press, 1948 (revised edition); Leyland M. Goodrich, *The United Nations in a Changing World*, New York, Crowell, 1959; Daniel S. Cheever and Henry Field Haviland, *Organizing for Peace: International Organizations in World Affairs*, London, Stevens, 1954; Stephen Goodspeed, *The Nature and Function of International Organization*, New York, Oxford University Press, 1964.

25. Ernst B. Haas, *The Uniting of Europe: Political, Social and Economic Forces*, Stanford, Stanford University Press (2nd edition), 1968.
26. See bibliography on theories of regional integration in Leon N. Lindberg and Stuart A. Scheingold, *Regional Integration: Theory and Research*, Cambridge, Mass., Harvard University Press, 1971, pp. 428-33.
27. David Mitrany, *A Working Peace System*, London, Royal Institute of International Affairs, 1943.
28. See R. J. Harrison, "Neofunctionalism" in Paul Taylor and A. J. R. Groom (eds), *International Organization: A Conceptual Approach*, London, Frances Pinter, 1978, pp. 253-69.
29. R. Snyder, H. W. Bruck and B. Sapin, *Decision-making as an Approach to the Study of International Politics*, Princeton, Princeton University Press, 1954.
30. Lawrence Scheinman, "some Preliminary Noteson Bureaucratic Relationships in the European Economic Community", *International Organization*, Vol. XX, No. 4, Autumn 1966, pp. 750-74.
31. Robert W. Cox and Harold K. Jacobson, *et al.*, *The Anatomy of Influence: Decision-making in International Organization*, New Haven, Yale University Press, 1974.
32. See Robert A. Dahl, *Who Governs?*, New Haven, Yale University Press, 1961; C. Wright Mill, *The Power Elite*, New York, Oxford University Press, 1957; Floyd Hunter, *Community Power Structures*, Chapel Hill, University of North Carolina Press, 1953.
33. Cox and Jacobson, loc. cit., p. 12.
34. Susan Strange, "IMF: Monetary Managers" in Cox and Jacobson *et al.*, loc. cit., pp. 263-97.
35. See the excellent account of aspects of Deutsch's work by Donal Puchala in his "Integration and Disintegration in France–German Relations, 1954-1965", *International Organization*, Vol. XXIV, No. 2, Spring 1970. See also Karl W. Deutsch, *Political Community and the North Atlantic Area*, Princeton University Press, 1957.
36. See Karl W. Deutsch, *Nationalism and Social Communication*, Cambridge, Mass., MIT Press, 1963 and 1966.
37. Leon N. Lindberg, "Political Integration as a Multidimensional Phenomenon Requiring Multivariable Measurement", *International Organization*, World Peace Foundation, Vol. XXIV, No. 4, Autumn 1970, p. 656.
38. See Ernst B. Haas, "An International 'Scientific Society'?" in Geoffrey L. Goodwin and Andrew Linklater (eds), *New Dimensions of World Politics*, London, Croom Helm, 1975, pp. 73-85.
39. Edward L. Morse, "The Transformation of Foreign Policies and Modernization, Interdependence and Externalization", *World Politics*, XXII, April 1970.
40. See Robert O. Keohane and J. S. Nye, Jr (eds), *Transnational Relations and World Politics*, Cambridge, Mass., Harvard University Press, 1970 and 1971; Robert O. Keohane and Joseph S. Nye, Jr, *Power and Interdependence: World Politics in Transition*, Boston, Brown, Little & Co., 1977.

CHAPTER 5

The Evolution of the Subject of International Political Economy 1967–1977: with Special Emphasis on the Impact on Mid-Career Education

Jeff Harrod

Fifteen years ago students specialising in international relations would normally have had to be content with courses entitled "International Economics" or "Foreign Trade Theory" to satisfy their need for an economic dimension of international relations. Now they will most likely find "International Political Economy" as an integral part of any international relations undergraduate or graduate programme. It is therefore difficult to discuss changes *within* the subject; instead the objects of analysis must be the trends and forces which have precipitated this new subject and how they have influenced the subject's form and content.

The emphases and structure of the discussion which follows were designed for the express purpose of considering the developments in the field of international relations and political economy in relation to the teaching of mid-career students. Thus, for example, the events which have occurred in contemporary world history which have assisted the emergence of the new subject have been given emphasis because discussions at the lectures yield more questions based on these events, which many students have lived through, than questions arising from intra-disciplinary and intellectual developments. This is merely to note that this paper has been written for a specific purpose and should not be considered as a free-standing, independent account of a disciplinary development as the latter would have resulted in a different emphasis and structure.*

---

*Such an account of the developments would require a detailed and chronological review of the literature which has not been attempted here.

The basic development: the emergence of international political economy

The title "International Political Economy" is symbolic in that it implies a *rapprochement* between economics and politics and indicates a narrowing of the artificial gap between them. From an historical perspective the division within the discipline of economics between economics and political economy developed most rapidly in the 1920s and 1930s. Three basic reasons for this development may be identified; the desire of younger economists to escape from the ideas of nineteenth-century liberalism, which incorporated within it a political philosophy as well as a distinct economic policy; the desire to use the relatively new mass of statistics being published by governments; and the impact of the logical positivist school of philosophy. The result was the establishment of a positivist, empirical branch of economics in opposition to the theoretical or ideological and policy-oriented mainstream.

International relations, itself suffering from the confrontation of the realists and idealists, originally opted to follow the positivist school into technical international economics as a background for discussion of international relations. In the 1950s and 1960s students of international relations were then equipped by writers such as Kindelberger, Meade and Samuelson, (1) to know the logic and supposed effects of the comparative cost (free trade) dynamic, the self-regulatory mechanisms in balance of payments and the advantages of fixed exchange rates and so on. Occasionally within the framework of an international economics course students would be exposed to the approach of a "traditional" economist concerned with the problems of a "just international economic order". (2) But such approaches were decried as lacking in modernity and scientific precision and died with their exponents.

In fact, the traditional approach, with its broader political and philosophical aspects, was closer to international political economy which began to emerge in the form of courses entitled "International Economic Relations", "The Politics of International Economic Relations" and "Economic Analysis for International Relations". Although this emergence is the subject of the subsequent sections of this paper it is necessary to note here that the development was based upon a new intellectual legitimacy; it became legitimate to seek answers to international economic phenomena, not only in terms of self-regulating market forces, or in rational economic behaviour of economic man, but in terms of power, whether based on economic, psychological, or military coercion. For those who have studied international economics Becket provides a particularly vivid example of the differences in approach and the different questions raised by international economics and international political economy:

> No doubt the hoariest theory in international trade is that of comparative advantage first expounded by David Ricardo in the early 19th century. Ricardo pointed out through a neat arithmetical demonstration that even though one country produced its goods more economically (in terms of labour time) than the goods of another country, there still would be gains from trade if the disadvantaged country traded the good in which it had a comparative advantage (less of a disadvantage). To illustrate this Ricardo constructed a two-country, two-good "model" which students of economics have learned by rote for generations. Even if Portugal can produce both wine and cloth cheaper than England, if England has a comparative advantage in cloth production it still will be mutually advantageous for the two countries to trade, Portugal sending wine to England and England sending cloth to Portugal. This as a matter of fact was an accurate picture of the actual trade between England and Portugal. The theory was impeccable within its assumptions, but the historical development of the actual trade had little to do with any arithmetic demonstration. It happened that Portugal was developing a substantial textile industry behind protectionist barriers. By superior force the British imposed upon Portugal the Treaty of Methuen in 1705 which opened up the Portuguese market to British textiles. The Portuguese industry was ruined and Portugal remained a producer of agricultural products. (3)

In this case the concern of economics for demonstrating the *advantages* of specialisation caused it to disregard the power which created the conditions or at least a different type of surplus. It also chose to ignore the power inherent in one kind of production — industrial — over another — agricultural. Ideally, political economy is concerned with just these omissions as well as with the relationship between power and economy: it permits the Lasswellian political question of "Who gets what, when, why and how?" to be asked and to be answered without being confined to a consideration of the nature of economic man. It became permissible to examine political man, who, it is thought, has a greater degree of voluntary action, in the search for the answers to these fundamental questions. The emergence of this new legitimacy and hence new subject is based, first, upon historic developments which have an impact in the field of international economics and, secondly, upon intellectual developments which required that conventional subject and disciplinary boundaries be broken.

80

Historic developments affecting international economics

Out of many developments which have affected ideas and approaches in economics, four can be singled out as being of major importance. First, the emergence into popular consciousness of the less developed countries as distinct states and power entities with economic demands and complaints; secondly, the growth in size and operation of the transnational corporation; thirdly, the rise in oil prices and the general fears of raw material and energy shortages; and fourthly, the decline in economic growth and increase in inflation in the industrial countries.

The first development was probably the most important. What appeared to be the sudden emergence of a large number of poor countries not only altered perceptions of the world economy within international economics but also resulted in a new branch of economics subsequently known as development economics. Before the 1960s the less developed countries were mostly colonies and their needs and views of the world economy were unheard except through the intermediary of the metropolitan powers. The policies of these powers towards the economic place of colonies, especially as to the need for continued development of colonial ancilliary production of raw materials and semi-manufactures for use in the industrial countries, were generally accepted. There was little investigation into domestic or international causes of world poverty and no consideration at all of the world mal-distribution of income.

The opposition of the United States to directly administered colonies, the gradual weakening of the hold of European powers over their colonies and ex-colonies and the presence of the United Nations meant that by the early 1960s the demands of the newly independent states began to be heard – reaching a crescendo in 1964 with the first United Nations Conference on Trade and Development (UNCTAD). The UNCTAD Conference was the first concerted and political attack on the hallowed principle in international economics that "trade was an engine of growth". The conference marked the beginning of a rethinking of economic concepts and the final stage of the search for a restatement of existing international economic orthodoxy. Thus, for example, the arguments of the economic causes of imperialism of the 1920s re-emerged and Hobson, Lenin and Frank (4) eventually had to be placed alongside Kindelberger, Harbler and Johnson (5) and international politics was brought back into international economics.

The emergence of the less developed countries also brought with it a new instrument of state foreign policy which was economic in nature. Economic aid created "development diplomacy" and with it the need to examine the interplay between industrialisation and economic assistance and strategy, hegemony and influence. International capital transfers by non-state entities could still be considered in their pure economic form but state grants and loans and their distribution were so blatantly governed by non-economic factors that economists were increasingly confined to stating what "should be" while political scientists started to look at what "is" and "why". (6)

The second historic development — the growth of the transnational corporation — had been a long-time phenomenon which emerged into the consciousness of scholars and commentators only when it became so large that it could not be politically ignored and then it met with political opposition. Starting in the mid-1950s the activities of the transnational corporation began to raise the political questions relating to the nature of sovereignty, penetration of state political systems, the nature of extra-national power and finally in the 1970s the political effects of changing the location of the world industrial production. These issues seemed to make the narrow discussion of the economic advantages or disadvantages of foreign direct investment less than adequate. It was not only in the third world that these issues were raised: De Gaulle argued that the entry of the United Kingdom to the European Economic Community was a United States "Trojan horse" filled with IBM executives who, implanted in Europe, would prevent the emergence of Europe as a world force.

But it was in the third world that nationalism emerged as a counter-ideology to world economic integration based upon direct capital flows and trade. Nationalisation of foreign companies was an overtly political response to what economists had liked to contain as an economic phenomenon. The literature surrounding the transnational corporation could not ignore these issues and so it became, essentially, a literature of international political economy where the economics and mathematics of international capital transfers had to merge with cultural, social, technological and political issues. (7)

By the time the rise in oil prices came in the early 1970s, the subject of international political economy was sufficiently established to provide a forum for the discussion of the politics of energy and raw materials. Economists could note that oil-producing countries were simply pursuing a successful cartel policy of receiving a high price by restricting supply for an inelastic demand curve. But whether the cartel could persist was an international political question. The power inherent in domination of markets or supplies of key commodities and the control of key currencies began to be incorporated with economic analysis.

The end of the era of sustained economic growth in industrial countries is the final development which promoted the growth and interest in international political economy. For those who have enjoyed it, economic growth has been seen as part of the natural order, an order which permitted the yearly division of growth amongst competing groups in such a manner that relative political and social tranquility was sustained. But it now seems that the existing systems of distribution have been positive-sum games which became zero-sum games under conditions of minimal or zero growth. One result has been inflation, which in turn has resulted in the search for an international demon, or at least a search at the international level for inflationary causes. (8) The interconnections between foreign economic policy, the international economy, the ways of organising domestic economies and international conflict, demand the competences of an international political economist, and will in turn, create a demand for him to break fresh fields in search for new approaches.

These historic developments innovated, promoted and sustained some intellectual developments and discoveries important to the emergence of international political economy.

Developments within international economics

Given that at the beginning of the period under discussion international political economy was only weakly established as a subject, developments which have affected its growth and acceptance have been within the field of economics, in international relations, itself, and in the philosophy of science. Six of these have been distinguished for discussion: (i) the discovery of the long-term decline in the terms of trade for developing countries; (ii) the criticisms of the comparative cost dynamic; (iii) the statement and refinement of dependency theory; (iv) the creation of the discipline of development economics; (v) the development within the field of international relations of interest in regional studies, linkage politics, transnational relations, interdependence; and (vi) the beginnings of the collapse of positivism and empiricism in the social sciences.

The first three of these are intimately connected and each provided inputs for the other which resulted in a massive and direct challenge to the positivist school of international economics. Paradoxically (or not so for its advocates), it was an empirical approach which sowed the seed for the collapse of economic orthodoxy. In the early 1960s, Eugene Staley working with statistics gathered by the General Agreement of Tariffs and Trade discovered that in terms of the goods they exported the developing countries were paying increasingly more for the industrial goods they purchased from industrial countries. Coupled with British Board of Trade

Statistics these showed a 75-year decline to the detriment of primary product producing countries. These and other studies were used by Raoul Prebisch and Hans Singer to make a frontal attack on the idea that trade would lead to industrial growth. Prebisch, moulding this idea into the UNCTAD conference of 1964, provided a jamboree for international political economists at which previously economic concepts were now discussed in the framework of political north–south confrontation. The inevitable result was that the prescriptions demanded for the trade situation caused an examination of the intellectual basis of previous policies and prompted the second development mentioned above, the re-examination of the comparative cost dynamic and, with it, all the institutional and technical structures of free trade. If, for example, free trade was not a dynamic at all but merely a justification for the nineteenth-century use of British sea power and the continued dominance of British manufactures then what place did the dynamic of comparative cost have in history and in the future?

The essential process involved here was the beginning of a more rigorous investigation of the "givens" of international economics which unleashed in turn a critical wave which traditional international economics was not equipped to counter. If the existing nature of production and exchange between Britain and Portugal, as in the Ricardo example, were not taken as given then it was necessary to know why Britain produced cotton textiles and Portugal did not. The answer, it seemed, lay in politics, or at least in diplomacy and coercion based upon economic objectives. Likewise, "investment capital seeks maximisation and chooses on this basis from a number of given investment climates" would be the orthodox statement of the dynamic of capital flows. But if investors or the governments of investors were influential in the creation of a "given" investment climate then maximisation would depend on the international and domestic politics surrounding the use of power to create or change investment climates. These questions of politics and hegemony required a broader analysis than that found within economics, and cast doubt on the utility of economic analysis which now appeared to be over-refined abstractions for the purpose of theoretical elegance.

The challenge to these givens and to free trade orthodoxy in turn paved the way for new perceptions of the world economy. Inevitably it had to be an oppositional one, a mirror image to previous perceptions. Thus the Centre-Periphery model of the world economy is the complete counter to previous doctrines; trade is not an engine of growth, less developed countries did not occur but were created by the policies and dynamics of trade and investment, the dynamic of the world economy is not free trade and maximisations within accepted rules, but domination politically and exploitation economically. (9) Economists suddenly found themselves seeking by empiricists' methods to prove or disprove a perception which had to a large extent been deductively produced. But a strong and refined oppositional model, regardless of its essential viability, had the greatest impact within the subject for it meant that the research scholar. and teacher had to consider a different perception. In short, there existed a forceful goad to non-habitual perception.

The fourth influence was in the emergence of a new branch of economics, that of development economics. First attempts made at examining the factors relating to development, whether defined as industrialisation or as *per capita* income growth, proceeded on the basis of existing concepts in economics, and principally on the isolation of economic rationale, the assumptions of equilibrium theories, and economic man maximising on material basis. These proved inadequate for as Belshaw very early pointed out: "There is a need for a wider, if less tidy, approach by economists, which draws on the resources of other social sciences or applied arts — anthropology, sociology, political science, education, law or public administration — and sets economic motivation, not austerely apart but in its proper place in complex systems of responses, beliefs, organisations and institutions." (10) But the consideration, use and integration of all these factors in an "untidy" approach made an empirical and positivist approach virtually impossible within development economics. It had to become the political economy of development (even though, in fact, the name has not changed) and this meant that scholars interested in international aspects of development were also pushed in that direction.

Developments within international relations also affected the development of international political economy, principally in a manner which supported and sustained its growth. The growth of regional studies which required a multi-disciplinary approach to any particular region emphasised the politics of economic relations. Students and scholars in regional studies, in viewing the region in totality, were required to place the interrelatedness of politics, economics and culture in a key position. The growing interest in political linkages outside of diplomacy between nations, the concepts of transnational relations and world society and the emergence of an "interdependency" literature required scholars of international relations and international economics to resort to each other's fields of specialisations in order to improve their analysis and satisfy political and intellectual demands. (11) Thus Keohane and Nye ask, as one of two major questions addressed in their book on *Power and*

Interdependence, (12) "What are the major features of world politics when interdependence, particularly economic interdependence, is extensive?" Whether or not the value-judgement inherent in the concept of inter-dependence is accepted it is clear that economic relations have been accepted at least in some important cases, as the basis for international politics.

At the deepest philosophical and intellectual level perhaps the most pervasive of developments in the creation of international political economy was the decline of the hold of positivism in economics. Like most philosophies, modern logical positivism was excessively simplified in order to fit social, cultural and political environments. It began to mean a general "scientific" approach, which in turn was defined as an absence of an over-riding theoretical perspective, an emphasis on data and observation, on inductive method, on methodology and a concentration on the functioning of parts rather than wholes. In modern terminology it meant the micro-investigation of a single variable regardless of the theoretical viability of the whole system. It also provided a convenient scholarly form of avoiding confrontation, "isms" and ideology.

In mid-twentieth-century scholarship it became evident that there was an inverse ratio between the degree of prestige and acclaim for the products of scholarship and the degree of positivism they exhibited; the more data filled, the more fact producing the subject, the greater prestige support and money it received. But because such positivist methodologies tend to neglect the sea for a larger symmetry amongst various phenomena the greater the use of positivist methods the greater the possibility of intellectual reaction to it. The result has been that those subjects most successful in adopting positivist methods rapidly reached a zenith of social acclaim and then declined through internal schisms and fragmentation. They would then be replaced by other subjects on the upward curve of data production. So it has been since the 1920s that economics replaced law and was in turn replaced by sociology in perceived importance as each in turn accepted and pursued positivist methods.

Economics came to the fore through claiming to be governed by the positivist aphorism that cognitive statements, those which could be proved true or false, were the mainstay of the discipline, as opposed to the emotive statements of religion, ethics or politics. The scientific economists could then distinguish themselves from both the nineteenth-century liberals and Marxists but, ironically, they were left with the largely deduc-tively produced tenets of early economics as the pointers for areas of empirical investigation, making conflict between the two inevitable. A further problem was that they lost the unifying force of the liberal philosophy's objective of a free society. Its replacement — the temporal and quantifiable goal of economic growth — did not provide sufficient cohesion to prevent fragmentation within the discipline.

The impact of the intellectual and historic events already described coupled with the prescriptive failures and predictive weakness of economics resulted in increasing defections and fragmentation beginning in the early 1960s. It was then that Departments of Economics became Departments of Political Economy, and international political economy became something different from international economics. Positivist economists found refuge in econometrics and in an artificially quantifiable world existing within the milliards of binary responses of regression analysis. Sociology then became the new empirical social science.

The change in economics naturally affected international economics, but the emergence of international political economy was assisted by its, albeit tenuous, associations with international relations. International relations, like psychology, had great difficulty in becoming entirely positivist, although some scholars certainly did their best. The need to take cognisance of the competing world views held by the world's élites and the difficulty of applying positivist methods to inter-state (13) relations meant that international political economy could find a relatively neutral niche within international relations programmes.

This is not to suggest that international political economy rejects positivism, but rather that the contents of the subject as evolved makes it more difficult to adopt a micro, fragmented approach. Nor does it suggest that there have not been international economic scholars who did not always insist on a political economy approach and consistently put the words "politics of" before the cherished notions of economics. (14) That the subject has emerged in its current form is a vindication of their approach and a testimony to their persistence.

Current problems within the subject of international political economy

The newness of the subject and the continuing intellectual challenges have meant that there has not yet developed a "mainstream" of knowledge and approaches in teaching the subject. As the subject is partly the product of the ethical and political turmoil which confront many areas of scholarship it is possible that, unlike previous experiences with new subjects as, for example, international organisation after 1949, such a mainstream will not develop. Although it is early to predict, the forces analysed above mitigate against the development of a single text which is widely used either as a source of wisdom or in a heuristic fashion as a counterpoise to classroom teaching in the manner of Claude's *Swords into Ploughshares* in international organisation and Morgenthau's *Politics Among Nations* in international relations.

It is difficult for the subject to be concentrated, as in the past, around the processes and dynamics, without considering objectives. International economics could be about production and distribution of production and the latter is essentially political. Two problems confront any attempts to avoid the issue of the objectives of power, of linkages or of organisational or regional arrangements in the world economy. The first is that about 80 per cent of the world production is consumed by 15 per cent of the world population. The second is that the dependence school of political economists have succeeded in the wide dissemination of their analysis which posits that this maldistribution has been deliberately caused by those who control the world economy and that it continues to be operated in a fashion to accrue benefits disproportionately to the pockets of a minority. These force discussions of results, objectives and justice rather than structure, process and strategies for the maintenance of the *status quo*.

The subject is then at the centre of an intellectual and moral pressure to answer questions which previous generations of scholars have been able to ignore, ensconced as they were in the warm shrouds of the legitimacy of positivism. There is now a growing acceptance that international political economy is concerned with power; Kindleberger, for example, in his book *Power and Money* takes his economics and applies it to a layman's view of what international relations is, namely, nation-states, sovereignty, diplomacy and a struggle for power. But the fit is uneasy for his application of the power analysis to the specific area of economics brings him close to having to answer the question which realists themselves traditionally refused to answer, namely power for what purpose? When they did reply they normally merely restated their contention that power was sought for its own sake.

Two divisions begin to develop within the teaching of the subject. The first relies heavily on some of the dependence theory and examines power processes within the interplay between economics and politics and overtly states that the dynamic is the attempt to maximise wealth and retain privilege — a materialist struggle for power. The second concentrates on a more economic process approach examining the political impact of economic policy coupled with a descriptive approach to competing world views of the world economy. International political economy is not only about politics; it is a political subject and no intellectual apology is necessary in stating that whether this division in the subject becomes sharper or merges into an acceptable synthesis will depend not on scholarship but on the political environment in which that scholarship is situated.

References

1. C. P. Kindelberger, *International Economics*, Homewood, Ill., 1968 (4th edn); J. E. Meade, *The Balance of Payments*, London, 1951 (1st edn); P. A. Samuelson, *Economics: An Introductory Analysis*, New York, 1965 (6th edn).
2. See, for example, W. Ropke, *International Order and Economic Integration*, Dordrecht, 1969.
3. I. J. Becket, "The World Economy: Short on Change", *Risk* (World Council of Churches), Vol. III, No. 1 and 2, 1967, fn p. 20.
4. J. A. Hobson, *Imperialism: A Study*, London, 1938 (3rd edn); V. I. Lenin, "Imperialism, The Highest Stage of Capitalism – A Popular Outline", in *Selected Works*, Vol. 5, 1936, pp. 3–123; A. G. Frank, *Capitalism and Underdevelopment in Latin America*, Harmondsworth, 1971.
5. See, for example, Kindleberger, op. cit.; G. Harberler, *International Trade*, New York, 1936; H. G. Johnson, *Money, Trade and Economic Growth*, New York, 1962.
6. See, for example, Mason, *Foreign Aid and Foreign Policy*, New York, 1964; T. Hayter, *Aid as Imperialism*, Harmondsworth, 1971.
7. See, for example, R. Vernon, *Sovereignty at Bay*, London, 1971; H. Stevenson, *The Coming Clash: The Impact of the International Corporation on the Nation State*, London, 1971; Barnett and Muller, *The Global Reach: Power of the Multinational Corporation*, New York, 1978.
8. Some of these points are elaborated further in R. W. Cox, J. Harrod and others, *Future Industrial Relations: An Interim Report*, Geneva, 1972.
9. These views and the theory are expounded by such authors as A. G. Frank, op. cit.; R. Stavenhagen, *Sept Thèse Erronées sur l'Amerique Latin*, Paris, 1972; D. Goulet, *The Cruel Choice*, New York, 1971.
10. H. Belshaw, "Economic Development as an Operational Problem", *Civilisations*, Vol. II, No. 2, 1952, pp. 159–60 as quoted in L. Shannon *Underdeveloped Areas*, New York, 1957. For a further discussion of this approach see J. Harrod, *Trade Union Foreign Policy*, New York, 1972, pp. 18–21.
11. A discussion of these developments are found in J. Harrod, "Transnational Power", *London Yearbook of World Affairs*, 1976, Vol. 30, pp. 97–115.
12. Keohane and J. Nyp, *Power and Interdependence: World Politics in Transition*, Boston, 1977.
13. See S. Strange, "International Economics and International Relations: A Case of Mutual Neglect", *International Affairs*, Vol. 46, April 1970 and the discussion in J. Harrod, "International Relations, Perceptions and Neo-Realism", *London Yearbook of World Affairs*, 1977, Vol. 31, pp. 289–305.
14. In particular G. Myrdal, *An International Economy*, London, 1955 and subsequent work and S. Strange, as for example "The Politics of International Currencies", *World Politics*, Vol. 23, January, 1971, pp. 216–31.

CHAPTER 6

Foreign Policy Analysis: Search for Coherence in a Multifaceted Field

Randolph Kent

Foreign policy analysis concerns "the hows and whys" of state behaviour. Yet even this simple and perhaps self-evident definition belies the complexity of two fundamental and interrelated issues so crucial for an understanding of the field's evolution: the objective of the analyst and his level of analysis.

The study of state behaviour incorporates a vast panoply of considerations, any of which may be important depending upon what the analyst seeks to understand. The analyst might be interested in determining the impact of non-governmental actors such as multinational corporations upon the behaviour of states, or he might be interested to explore the ways co-operation between and amongst elements of national bureaucracies affect the actions of states. He might wish to consider the effectiveness of communication flows in the Soviet Union prior to and during the Cuban missile crisis of 1962, or he might wish to assess the coalition tendencies of states in general during times of relative stability or crisis. However, no matter which particular area of interest he chooses, the analyst is ultimately opting for one of two possible objectives.

The analyst will either seek to explain how states, as a specie of global actors, function within the international system, or, alternatively, he will seek to explain how the particular characteristics of a particular state within that specie function. The differing objectives are important and basic. By necessity, the analyst who seeks to explain the "hows and whys" of state behaviour from the perspective of states as a specie of actors will assume, seek and stress commonalities of behaviour patterns. He will attempt to deal with the specie of states as a *genotype*. The analyst who looks towards the unique characteristics of a particular state or group of states, by definition, assumes, seeks and stresses uniqueness as the source

90

of explanations of state behaviour. As opposed to *genotypic* knowledge, the latter pursues *phenotypic* knowledge. (1)

Intricately tied to the question of the analyst's objective is the issue of the most appropriate level of analysis from which to investigate the "hows and whys" of state behaviour. The analyst, wishing to understand state behaviour from what has been called the most all-encompassing perspective, could approach the subject on the level of the international system. Having chosen that level of analysis, he might agree with J. D. Singer that the international system is indeed one of the most "promising points of focus", enabling the observer "to examine international relations in the whole, with a comprehensiveness that is of necessity lost when our focus is shifted to a lower and more partial level". (2) Yet, as the quest for genotypic knowledge tends to emphasise the commonalities of characteristics, so, too, does the international system level of analysis tend to over-homogenise the components of the system, leaving "little room for divergence in the behaviour of our parts". (3)

Alternatively, the analyst can approach his investigation of state behaviour by focusing upon a particular state or group of states. His search for understanding the hows and whys of state actions might uncover rich details and intricate facts which could well serve to explain the behaviour of the particular state units under focus. Here, however, the analyst is faced with the problem that the nation-state level of analysis could lead to "a marked exaggeration of the differences among our sub-systemic actors". (4) In other words, by focusing upon the nation-state level, the analyst risks two hazards. In the first place, he will have no reliable evidence that the factors affecting the policies of one state or one set of states can be used as factors to explain the policies of other sets of states or states in general. In the second place, the analyst, by concentrating principally upon a component of the system, cannot be sure that there were not more global systemic factors affecting the policies of his particular nation-state which were missed by his lower level of analysis.

The objective — either genotypic or phenotypic knowledge — and the levels of analysis problem — either the international system or the nation-state — clearly poses a dilemma for the analyst of state behaviour. Not only do differing objectives and levels of analysis proceed from differing conceptual assumptions, but they also present the all-too-evident problem that, whatever route the analyst chooses, his investigations will be significantly restricted by the conceptual boundaries of that route.

To seek understanding about the hows and whys of state behaviour from the international system perspective might generate one type of knowledge about the actions of states. However, the analyst, beginning from the system perspective always has to contend with the challenge that he has grossly distorted critical variables. He might explain, for example, the 1815 Quadruple Alliance as further evidence of state tendencies to form coalitions to preserve balances of power, but his explanation ignores the important evidence that the key state in that coalition, Great Britain, *only* joined because of the unyielding insistence of two men, Viscount Castlereagh and the Duke of Wellington.

Must one, therefore, conclude that to understand the development of coalitions of states, one must first understand the "personality variables" of men such as Castlereagh and Wellington for all coalitions over time? On the other hand, in dealing with the interactions of states at the international system level, can one ignore the fact that state actions ultimately are the products of decision-making processes *within* states? Can one perhaps assume that those processes leading to foreign policy acts all are bounded by certain common characteristics? Or are the decision-making processes of states so tied, for example, to the idiosyncracies of decision-makers that any search for common patterns of processes amongst states would be a futile quest? Or is the issue, as Arnold Wolfers contends, one of knowing *when* "to descend below the high level of abstraction". (5)

According to Wolfers, the movement from one level of analysis to another depends upon a distinction between acts of compulsion and non-compulsion in the international system. This distinction is determined by the degree of serious external danger threatening the state. Aggressive action by one state which leads to the loss of territory by another state might be a good example of compulsion. Wolfers believes that an "empirical study would validate the hypothesis . . . that almost any nation which has suffered a loss of territory or has been subjected to discrimination will, when its power permits, takes some action to redress its grievances . . . regardless of the personal characteristics of its leaders or the peculiarities of its national culture". (6)

Alternatively when the conditions of non-compulsion exist, when the state does not face serious external threat but the state still reflects "dissatisfaction with the *status quo*", then "it would be a mistake to ignore the impact of the individual or national differences on the behaviour of states". (7)

Although Wolfers's suggestion may be criticised as over-simplistic, one must recognise the extraordinary difficulty of his goal, namely, to propose a reconciliation between the differing levels of analysis which will lend coherence to a variety of approaches to the study of state behaviour.

Of any single theme in the field of foreign policy analysis, it is this very search for an appropriate means of coherently incorporating varying levels of analysis that marks most poignantly the field's evolution: the attempt to reconcile the overhomogenised view of the international system perspective with the distortions of uniqueness which emerge from concentrations upon single states as actors; the attempt to deal with the state through a single unitary actor approach while recognising that ultimately the actions of states originate in a labyrinth of domestic processes no less complicated than the very thought processes of decision-makers themselves.

In outlining the evolution of foreign policy analysis, and hence in seeking coherence in a multifaceted field, one is only too aware that few clear-cut answers to very basic problems have been posited. Since the mid-1950s, when foreign policy analysis evolved as a distinct field within the international relations discipline, there certainly has been no satisfying reconciliation of the perspectives at either end of the levels-of-analysis spectrum. Yet this seemingly frustrating conclusion must be off-set by two important qualifications.

The first qualification is that the past two decades have at least witnessed an airing of these fundamental problems, which in and of itself is a fact worth noting. Of the two underlying themes in this discussion concerning the field's evolution, the first is principally devoted to this airing, the emergence of contending approaches into the full glare of the academic arena. However, this retrospective overview of foreign policy analysis is not undertaken merely to dwell upon complexities which have haunted the field's evolution. Rather it is undertaken to suggest that increased sophistication has been brought to bear upon the debate and to emphasise that the debate has not been allowed to fester but instead has generated a challenging inter-disciplinary dynamic of its own.

The second qualification, and the second theme of this discussion is that, despite the fundamental and unresolved contradictions implicit in differing objectives of analysts and levels of analysis, new approaches to the study of foreign policy have emerged. What will later be described as linkage politics and comparative study of foreign policy, to name just two, do not necessarily suggest the paths towards conceptual reconciliation of contending approaches, but they do mark important new points on the wide spectrum of approaches to the study of foreign policy.

Finally, in the subsequent discussion, the reader should be forewarned that, since this author is principally concerned with genotypic knowledge about states, his assessment of the field's evolution will be from the perspective of the development of tools with which to analyse states as a specie.

The evolution of the process orientation

So much of international relations has been fundamentally a response to or a reaction against the conceptions and implications of the Realist paradigm, or the "power-oriented", "billiard-ball" analysis of international politics. The Realists, viewing the state as the predominant actor in global politics but pleading the futility of penetrating internal processes of the state system, represent the quintessence of over-homogenised analysis. The Realist case rests upon the assumption that the actions of men and states result from an unrelenting attempt to expand or preserve power; that power, therefore, is *the* explanatory factor in international politics. Tied to this deterministic power orientation are three further assumptions: that in preserving or expanding power, state actions are responses solely to the external power configuration of other states; that state actions emanate from a unified and power-motivated decision-making élite; that the decision-making process is "rational" to the extent that it is predictable in purpose (e.g. extending or maintaining power) and goal maximising in operation.

In what Pettman has called "an unambiguous blow in the behavioural revolt against the externally oriented, deterministic and reified approach to state performance", (8) Richard Snyder and associates in 1954 attempted to construct a universally applicable model of decision-making from which the domestic as well as external determinants of foreign policies could be assessed. Employing a range of social science disciplines, such as social psychology and organisational theory, Snyder sought to relate the perceptions, images and information flows of decision-makers to and from their environments, and, in so doing, sought to reflect the relationship and interactions between external and domestic factors impinging upon states' policies.

The Snyder model generated substantial criticism, but nevertheless, it represents a seminal work in the international relations discipline for at least two reasons. In the first place, whatever work had been done in other disciplines on decision-making processes prior to Snyder *et al.*, that monograph was original in the context of international politics, and emanating from that effort was, for all intents and purposes, the sub-field of foreign policy analysis in the form in which it is generally accepted today. (9)

Secondly, there seems little doubt that, as Snyder later maintained, four fundamental features of the early monograph have "endured" and influenced in one way or another the vast majority of contributions in foreign policy analysis. These features are that foreign policy analysis (i) must take into account the decision-makers' perceptions of their environment, (ii) should consider the decisional context as a set of intervening variables, (iii) must explore the structures and methods by which units responsible for decision-making arrive at decisions, and (iv) must bring the tools of other social sciences into the study of individual and group decision-making.

These four fundamental and "enduring" features can be seen to have dramatically affected the wealth of domestic process-oriented literature which has emerged since 1954 and certainly over the past decade. Of the four, perhaps the last — the need to incorporate the tools of other social sciences into the study of decision-making processes — has proven the key by which the first three have led to sophisticated penetration of the billiard-ball conception of state behaviour.

While they all interrelate in the context of foreign policy analysis, these "tools of other social sciences" can be separated into four categories: (i) psychological, (ii) organisational, (iii) cybernetic and (iv) sociological approaches to the study of decision-making.

Psychological approaches involve at least three analytical dimensions: (i) psychological assessment of individual leaders, (10) (ii) psychological analysis of individuals in terms of attitudes, perceptions and images, (11) (iii) social psychological analysis of individuals in groups, groups interactions, and group dynamics. (12)

Contrary to the Realists' assumptions of unicausality and rationality, the more psychologically oriented analysts of foreign policy have determined that such factors as ideology and belief systems are important variables in explaining foreign policy choices, (13) that the processing of information upon which decisions are dependent is restricted by cognitive limitations, (14) and that group dynamics often stymie the perception of alternatives in a decision-making situation. (15)

In other words, psychological assessments of decision-making processes lead to several alternative suggestions about the ways foreign policies are formulated. There is a high probability, for example, that input from the foreign policy environment into the decision-making process has a significant chance to be misperceived, misinterpreted or ignored unless that input fits the cognitive expectations of decision-makers. (16) Fundamental changes in decision-makers' conceptions are slow in occurring because of the cognitive consistency mechanisms which protect the decision-maker from seeking alternatives. (17) When groups, e.g. a Cabinet or an inter-departmental meeting, seek to interpret information and make choices, the likelihood of considering broad or sweeping alternatives is significantly eroded by the dynamics of what one writer has called the "groupthink syndrome". (18) All of these examples reflect on the general competences of states and suggest a potentially valuable proposition that, from a psychological perspective, state processes are only incrementally responsive to changing stimuli from the foreign policy environment. (19)

The organisational orientation of foreign policy analysis incorporates attempts to chart the sources of inputs and outputs to and from the decision-making unit, (20) to describe as well as to model the sequential steps leading to a decision, (21) and to test certain general assumptions about organisational and administrative behaviour in a foreign policy context. (22) These efforts extend from the abstract to the specific case study, from the decision-making unit under crisis conditions to units in non-crisis situations. (23)

The very fact that decision-making units require different procedures to respond to crisis and non-crisis situations is important, (24) but that the organisational structure often is incapable of adjusting to these different conditions is a statement of even greater consequence. (25) As opposed to the perspective of a rational, goal maximising and responsive actor, the state, viewed from organisational theory, comprises not a single, adaptive entity, but rather a set of competing, contending and, on occasion, semi-autonomous sub-systems. (26) Organisational characteristics, such as the need for standard operating procedures, the need to factor organisational problems to appropriate sub-components, the need for highly focused concentration upon organisational survival, all channel the efforts of organisations into fulfilling limited objectives in routine ways. Organisational analysis of foreign policy machinery unveils a picture of systems and their component parts, limited in their sensitivity, protective of their particular domains, and restrictive in their operations. While psychological theory posits the view that decision-makers tend to view foreign policy acts of *other* states as essentially purposeful and holistic, (27) organisational theory posits the view that foreign policies are frequently unco-ordinated, disjointed and "satisficing" acts that flow from the various sub-units involved directly or indirectly in the foreign policy process. (28)

The cybernetic orientation to the analysis of foreign policy reflects Snyder's specific concern for the communication patterns and information flows in decision-making units. Transposing Norbert Wiener's approach (29) to systems in general onto the system of the nation-state, the cybernetic-oriented analyst seeks to trace inputs and outputs to, through and from the foreign policy system. A system's characteristics, such as the need to maintain equilibrium ("homeostasis"), its capacity to receive, process, and respond to information ("requisite variables", "feedback mechanisms", etc.), the need to screen out noise, disorder, ambiguity, randomness and uncertainty ("entropy", "negentropy") (30) are used to identify the responsiveness, learning capacities, and decisional patterns of the foreign policy process. (31)

In many respects the conclusions of the cybernetic analyst parallel many of the conclusions mentioned under the heading of psychological approaches. Certainly the Realist assumptions of rational decision-making processes cannot be sustained from the cybernetic vantage point. Where the Realist would assume that decision-makers weigh a wide range of alternatives in making a decision, the cybernetic analyst assumes that the decision-making system is attuned to receiving only a limited set of information and to reacting to that information in a way that again is limited by "pre-programmed" responses. Major changes in systems occur at times when there is a "systemic collapse", or, a systems overload. In other words, the machinery of foreign policy-making will continue to screen out information to which it is not programmed and will respond to information to which it is programmed until the screening and responding mechanisms can no longer cope with the input. Perhaps, in the American foreign policy context, an example might be the evolution of the containment policy, where that policy was maintained despite changes in the foreign policy environment (input) until the "Vietnam overload" of the late 1960s. From a cybernetic perspective, one could suggest that major and fundamental shifts in policies are dependent on or must await such systemic collapses.

Like the psychological, organisational and cybernetic approaches, the sociological approach to foreign policy analysis is conceptually interrelated and overlaps in one way or another with at least one of the other approaches. The purpose of the sociological approach is to detach institutionalised foreign policy from assumptions of uniqueness and to seek patterns of general application and potential empirical testability. In the context of this last point, David Easton's *A Systems Analysis of Political Life* (32) symbolises the potential of the "sociological approach" and represents a landmark in what Snyder had earlier called the need for exploring the "internal setting" affecting the decision-making process.

For the purpose of foreign policy analysis, sociology provides a partial means to deal with the cultural and societal diversity of the domestic origins of international action. In one sense, the approach's bounds are limitless, incorporating all work which reflects diversity and commonality of societies. However, our concern is with the environment in which decisional inputs and outputs and decisions, themselves, take place. Thus, the characteristics of one society to accept "open bargaining" as part of the political process of decision-making as opposed to closed bargaining is an example. (33) The backgrounds and affiliations of political élites, the sources of interest groups, societal fears, stereotyping, etc., all are critical issues in determining influences which affect decisions. (34)

The themes of commonality and diversity which emerge from the sociological perspective again eschew the over-homogenised view of the Realists while meeting, to some extent, Singer's criticisms of over-concentration upon uniqueness. Sociological approaches do indeed raise the spectrum of cultural differences, but also open the way to attempts to measure how such differences (e.g. pluralistic versus non-pluralistic societal structures) affect the types of foreign policy acts of differing types of states.

New doors or closed doors

That state behaviour can be understood by analysing the domestic decision-making processes of states is a level of analysis which has many detractors, not least of whom has been J. D. Singer who wrote not long ago that "not all of us, of course, will find (the decision-making approach's) inapplicability a major loss; considering the criticism which has been levelled at the decision-making approach, and the failure of most of us to attempt its application, one might conclude that it is no loss at all". (35) Even Wolfers, in suggesting ways that both the international system and state processes approach might be compatible, concludes that the latter is really relevant only when the observer wishes to explore deviations from the general patterns of state behaviour. (36)

Both analysts imply that primary concentration upon domestic processes is a pit of frustration. Having taken the plunge, the observer will fall into an endless search for the motives of decision-makers and similarly elusive data. Singer emphasises that the investigation of processes is a diversion into phenomenological issues when in fact there *is* a "real world" in which nations' actions can be accurately and systematically explained. Wolfers maintains that, except for deviant behaviour, state processes must begin with two fundamental assumptions which, in essence, equate and transpose general characteristics of states on to decision-makers: that men acting for states place "exceedingly high value on the so-called possessions of the nation" and that there are " 'general traits of human nature' which are likely to operate with particular strength in men who hold positions of authority and national responsibility". (37) Thus, in essence, Wolfers suggests that, under normal circumstances, to know the national interest of the state is to know the motivation of state decision-makers who guide state actions.

Neither Singer nor Wolfers, however, reflects the full scope or the full potential of the process orientation of foreign policy analysis. Singer disregards the possibility that states' processes, like states themselves, might have observable and identifiable patterns, and Wolfers proceeds from assumptions which do little more than suggest that states act, and hence state leaders act, for reasons of national interest. What in fact have emerged out of the process orientation of foreign policy analysis to date are points of analysis and potential hypotheses far more fundamental than either have conceded.

When compared with the Realists' holistic, unified and rational interpretation of state actions, which held such sway through the mid-1950s, the past two decades have witnessed a major change in the approaches and tools to analyse foreign policy. Yet foreign policy analysis, as a field within the IR discipline, still has to contend with Singer's critique and Wolfers's search for balance. Have all the new approaches to the processes of foreign policy done anything to open up doors to more sophisticated, genotypic knowledge about state behaviour? Or, do the necessary variables demanded by such process approaches still bar the way towards generalised knowledge and still maintain a closed door onto the objectives of the international system level of analysis?

The answer, like so many answers in the discipline, is complex and not clear. There is no doubt that new paradigmatic perspectives concerning the processes of state behaviour have emerged over the past few decades. Both Allison (38) and Steinbruner, (39) for example, have suggested the importance of approaches which contradict the assumptions of the Realist paradigm. However, where Allison sees the "reality" of the foreign policy process being explained from traditional (realist) as well as alternative (e.g. organisational) perspectives, Steinbruner asserts that the bulk of new investigations (e.g. psychological, organisational, cybernetic) spell a decrease in relevance of the rational, realist approach to an understanding of a substantial portion of the state policy process.

Still, despite such contending and contentious paradigmatic perspectives, Snyder's 1954 concern with the processes of foreign policy has at least opened the door to focusing upon *general patterns* of foreign policy processes. The "billiard ball" has been penetrated and the path towards useful generalisations has been made more evident. By way of closing this discussion, it might be appropriate to suggest examples of some potentially important pre-theoretical considerations:

1. Foreign policy acts of a state are frequently contradictory and disjointed, as might be suggested in #2, but for reasons suggested in #3 are rarely seen to be;
2. A state probably does not function as a unified goal-seeking actor in

the international system, but rather the state might be viewed as a set of sub-systems, each contending, competing, overlapping, with other sub-systems within and outside the state, and each seeking to pursue formally or informally limited objectives through or outside the official machinery of the state;

3. Due to limitations arising out of cognitive, group and organisational processes, members of one sub-system will tend to assess the acts of another sub-system in the light of the limited objectives of the former and will perceive the acts of the latter as consistent, essentially holistic, and purposeful;

4. Since members within all sub-systems of all states are affected by cognitive, group and organisational effects, one might assume that there are certain commonalities of state processes which affect the behaviour of states in general;

5. One consequence of effects suggested by #3 and #4, might be that the intentions of foreign policy acts of one state are frequently misperceived by other state actors in the international system, and that, therefore, many actions of states are generated by such misperceptions;

6. A further consequence suggested by #3 and #4, is that state actions are essentially limited to the established perceptions, procedures and routines of individuals and organisations which recommend and implement foreign policy acts;

7. A third consequence could be that states' foreign policy acts are only modified, or, significantly depart from continuity, when there is a fundamental and overwhelming challenge to the established perceptions, procedures and routines of individuals and organisations which recommend and implement foreign policy acts.

Perhaps the single most important point about the evolution of the process orientation of foreign policy analysis has been the conscious attempt to probe variables which could lead to genotypic knowledge about the processes of state behaviour. Yet, while the field has made marked headway in this regard, one is still faced with Singer's fundamental point that the process orientation does not aid the observer in explaining the actions of states from that most fruitful and all-encompassing focal point: the international system level of analysis. Even if Singer were to concede the validity of the generalisations mentioned above, it is clear that they do not necessarily add greater understanding about "such phenomena as the creation and dissolution of coalitions, [or] the frequency and duration of specific power configurations . . .". (40)

Foreign policy analysis as attribute patterns

What so obviously has been and continues to be required is what Rosenau has called the need "to probe the 'internal influences on external behaviour' ". (41) In other words, though process concerns have generated a variety of potential pre-theoretical considerations, there is an all too apparent gap in the field, between these processes and the external actions of states. How does one "link" characteristics of domestic processes with the actions undertaken by states in their external or foreign policy environments?

Since the mid-1960s, such concerns generated a trend amongst a variety of foreign policy analysts who sought to explore the degree to which differences in state structures and environments could account for types of foreign policy acts of states. The explorations assumed that differences in state structures could account for differences in policy acts; but, unlike those studies which stressed the uniqueness of individual states' structures, the explorations by analysts such as Rosenau, assumed that state differences could also be classified into certain identifiable typologies.

Furthermore, it was felt that typologies of state structures in and of themselves merely perpetuated the conventional lack of differentiation between types of *issues* which affected states, and therefore shed little light upon the ways different external issues affect different domestic processes and vice versa. By categorising types of issues, the observer could be aided in the task of identifying the interactions, interdependencies and interrelatedness amongst actors within, across and between boundaries. Hence, by typologising issues as well, the artificial barrier between the study of states' domestic politics (national orientation) and states' international politics (foreign policy orientation) would disappear as concentration would be focused upon more "realistic" interactive and transactive processes comprising foreign policy acts.

Common to all such analytic endeavours emerging out of the 1960s was the conscious search for typologies, categorisations, or, what we shall call "attribute patterns". For our purposes, "attributes" can be defined "as anything that describes the make-up of a nation, differentiating one state from another in terms of political, social, economic, or, as some might argue, psychological characteristics". (42) By "attribute patterns" we are suggesting that even particular characteristics which distinguish one state from another can be categorised into "types" which might reveal a pattern for comparing the activities of different kinds of states.

In resorting to such forms of categorisation, analysts have sought to identify two basic features of state behaviour: (i) the types of variables in the domestic process which account for the types of actions undertaken officially by states or affect, through informal means, the foreign policy actions or environments of states; and (ii) the types of structural character- istics of states, issues and capabilities and goals (means–ends) that correlate with certain types of foreign policy acts.

The attribute orientation of foreign policy analysis is predominantly concerned with the "hows" rather than the "whys" of internal–external patterns of behaviour. This is not to say that the focus upon attribute pat- terns precludes investigation of the "whys", but rather the assessment of "whys" are deferred until meaningful correlations can offer focus for causal investigations.

Linkage politics

Certainly one attribute oriented approach of significance is that of "link- age politics" which in one basic sense can be viewed as exposing the inherent problems in determining what we have referred to as the types of variables in the domestic process which might account for the types of actions undertaken officially by states or affect through informal means the foreign policy actions or environments of states.

Linkage politics, as a term in the field of foreign policy analysis, is most closely identified with the pre-theoretical considerations of James Rosenau. Like Snyder's 1954 model of foreign policy processes, Rosenau's linkage conception has generated severe criticism because of its extensive and frequently ill-defined variables (3888!). (43) Yet like Singer's model, Rosenau's is seminal, not for what it proves, but for the perspectives and suggestions which it raises. Rosenau has constructed a complex framework which attempts to set forth types of domestic variables which impact upon types of external issues and vice versa. Twenty-four aspects of any indivi- dual "polity" (state) are singled out as being potential contributors or reci- pients of inputs or outputs to and from at least six sub-environments (e.g. the contiguous environment, the resources environment). And while an understanding of the framework would deserve far greater explication, for our purposes the framework's importance rests upon what it seeks in general to achieve.

According to Rosenau, the framework attempts to prevent "perpetuation of the analytical gap between comparative and international politics" (44) by eliminating the distinction between national and international politics. Secondly, the various polity variables reflect an attempt to prevent focusing only on "manifest linkages", and instead to direct the analyst's attention to a variety of "unfamiliar and latent linkages" between components of the polity and the polity's environment. Thirdly, "the polity side of the framework should greatly inhibit the tendency to treat national governments as having undifferentiated internal environments and thus to rely on the national interest as an explanation of international behaviour". Fourthly, the sub-environmental side of the framework "should substantially curb the tendency to regard politics as having undifferentiated external environments". Fifthly, the framework makes the distinction between direct and indirect linkage phenomena. This distinction allows for two further sets of important considerations: on the one hand, direct (purposeful) output and input reflect stimuli not only to and from governments but also to and from non-governmental actors, e.g. multinational corporations, as well. On the other hand, it also attempts to account for unintentional (non-purposeful) phenomena between and amongst components of domestic systems and their environments.

While the framework has not led to a significant body of replication or testing, there is little doubt that it was at the forefront of a wide variety of literature seeking to assess state actions in terms of the multiplicity of domestic variables impacting upon and responding to issues in the policy environment. Perhaps the most obvious examples to which one might turn are many of the works concerned with states' roles in issues such as ecology and international economic relations. Furthermore, one can point to works by authors such as Deutsch, who has investigated "linkage sub-systems" located within the states and directly linked to the external environment, and other authors who have attempted to unravel linkage networks in specific regional contexts. (45)

Linkage politics, like foreign policy analysis in general, has not as yet generated acceptable theories about the behaviour of states, but at this early stage, linkage analysts have at least pointed to pre-theoretical concerns that would seem to reflect much more acceptable bases for dealing with the complexities of states' "hows and whys". Not only does it proffer perspectives from which to consider the domestic–external interaction process, but it also emphasises the possibility of generalising about such interactive processes for states as a genotype.

Comparative study of foreign policy

The distinction between comparative study of foreign policy and linkage politics is small and arguably even non-existent. Yet to the extent that the latter has certain conceptual foundations which arose independently of the former, it perhaps deserved the separate assessment it has been given. The two, however, share the same intellectual paradigm, the same fundamental methodological orientation, and certainly the same concern for determining the attribute patterns of state behaviour.

For our purposes three approaches to the comparative study of foreign policy should be mentioned: interaction analysis; comparative attributes analysis, and internal–external behaviour correlations. The distinctions, it should be made clear, are essentially for convenience; for it is a happy circumstance that in this particular area of foreign policy analysis, there is a healthy overlap and interactive process which frequently have merged the three into a unidirectional blend. Interaction analysis specifically concerns the types of events which take place between and amongst states. Using McClelland's WEIS (World Event Interaction Survey) project as an example, one sees the attempts to correlate amounts and types of co-operation and/ or conflict between and amongst states with the amounts and types of identifiable acts occurring between one state and another. Events are less important as individual acts, and more important as components of "streams of events" or "event flows" which reflect the patterns of state behaviour over time. (46) The significance of methods such as WEIS is that the state and its acts are brought beyond the realm of individual uniqueness to higher levels of generalisations which are testable and not time bound.

Interaction analysis and comparative attribute analysis are both concerned with patterns over time. However, the principal focus of the comparative attribute approach is with correlations of state actions and state structures. Rummel, for example, in the DON (Dimensionality of Nations) project has sought to assess characteristics such as states' economic development, size, and politics in terms of foreign policy behaviour. (47) Comparative attribute analysis has stimulated a variety of projects similar to DON, and certainly has been subjected to the scientifically important process of replication. Its development also has been marked by attempts to combine comparative attribute analysis with interaction analysis. For example, Salmore and Hermann have employed categories from WEIS to test for correlations between types of state structure (e.g. size, development) and type of state behaviour. (48)

Similar to the previous approaches, internal–external behaviour correlations are concerned with attribute patterns over time. The first two, however, are less concerned with the interrelationship between domestic behaviour and external behaviour, and far more involved with either the characteristics of foreign policy acts, themselves, or the state attributes which correlate with foreign policy acts. This third category is principally oriented towards correlating domestic behaviour of states with states' external behaviour. For example, the generally accepted "political wisdom" that international conflict is often generated by state leaders to dampen domestic unrest has been the subject of considerable testing by analysts. Research into the patterns of domestic behaviour and external behaviour has led to significant modifications of what had been the previously accepted "wisdom". (49)

Yet, while the methodologies of these three approaches to the comparative study of foreign policy are sophisticated and while certain correlations are frequently intriguing, the contribution which these approaches have made to an understanding of state behaviour remains an open question. McGowan feels that, despite the relative youth of this aspect of foreign policy analysis, considerable progress has been made:

> We have learned something about the causes and consequences of foreign policy behaviour, although with varying degree of confidence in our knowledge. But more basically, we have learned that a complete social phenomenon can be accounted for by a number of types of independent variables. We have learned that concepts comprising both independent and dependent variables can be operationalized and validly measured, and that analysis using these measurements can lead to generalizations applicable across different political systems. (50)

However, in the final analysis, McGowan's hopes still must be tempered by the fact that the comparative study of foreign policy has not arrived at any cohesive, all-inclusive pre-theoretical conceptions to explain state behaviour. Rather, comparative study of foreign policy, like all the endeavours subsumed under the heading of *Foreign Policy Analysis As Attribute Patterns*, has refocused many analysts' attention, has added new research points on the levels of analysis spectrum of foreign policy analysis, has shown the potential usefulness of the methodological tools of social science, and has derived intriguing sets of correlations about a host of foreign policy actions.

Coherence in a multifaceted field

"But no theory" must seem to the reader the leitmotif of the discussion as a whole. Trekking through the field of foreign policy analysis as both process and attribute patterns, the reader has stumbled upon this or similar phrases throughout. And if the lack of developed theory has characterised the excursion, so, too, have the unresolved issues of analysts' objectives and levels of analysis. Added to the difficulties are the multiplicity of possible routes, each seeming to head towards different and unconnected destinations. Thus, the reader must wonder whether, in this lively but seemingly disjointed field, there is any coherence at all.

We would like to suggest that there is. Coherence emerges from the predominant interest of many analysts to seek genotypic knowledge about the "hows and whys" of state behaviour; it emerges with the predisposition of such analysts to seek general patterns of states' processes as well as states' attributes.

Singer's disenchantment with the process orientation of foreign policy analysis reflects a concern that analysts could not generate useful generalisations, when in retrospect it would now seem that the potential for meaningful generalisations do indeed exist. Wolfers's assumptions about the limited applicability of the process orientation also seems misguided, since in a complex world, the perception of compulsion or non-compulsion depends upon the actors within and across state boundaries who are affected by the distinction. Hence, the process orientation is necessary to avoid the simplification which Wolfers's views might suggest.

But more important than just fending off critics, what actual offerings have the intellectual movements in the field proffered? We would suggest, briefly, two: (i) a change in paradigmatic perspective, and (ii) a foundation upon which to build knowledge.

The paradigmatic perspective which the field offers is one in which the responsive capabilities of states have been totally reassessed. The rational state-as-actor model of the Realists has been challenged by the analytic perspectives of an emerging multi-disciplinary assessment, which finds the variables of state processes far more complex and far less rational than traditionally assumed. Furthermore, by concentrating upon the general dimensions, or variables within the processes of states, analysts have greater opportunity to move away from the holistic conception of states and to witness the dimensions of internal–external interactive processes by viewing the forces at play from the perspective of issue-areas.

A further important dimension of the evolution of foreign policy analysis, one which also can be incorporated under the heading of paradigmatic changes, is that state behaviour can be treated systemically without falling into the trap of over-homogenisation. While process patterns have begun to unravel variables within the polity, attribute patterns have begun to assess correlations between such variables and the types of actions undertaken by states. In other words, the shifting paradigmatic perspective of the foreign policy analyst has not only challenged the responsive capability of the state as an actor in international affairs, it has also brought into question the very boundaries of statehood.

There is in the international relations discipline a type of academic escape clause which concedes that, though theories have not emerged, a foundation upon which to build knowledge has. As a general qualifier, it is also relevant to the field of foreign policy analysis. No theories, *per se* have developed but foreign policy analysts can at least comfort themselves with the knowledge that methodologies have been introduced and analytical focal points have emerged which demonstrate the potential for more social scientific approaches to the study of state behaviour. Where two decades ago the prospect of generalising about the types and motives for transactions between and amongst states was treated as an impossible task, an increasing body of foreign policy analysts are accepting the possibility that variables of processes and attribute patterns are susceptible to observation and can be categorised for purposes of genotypic knowledge.

We cannot as yet say, for example, why nations form and dissolve alliances, but we can suggest the conditions under which types of nations will seek to build or dismantle coalitions. (51) In itself, this is progress, for such suggestions emerge from a clear, testable and replicable set of propositions which the antecedents of foreign policy analysis, such as the Realist school, had so blatantly lacked.

As a concluding point in this discussion of foreign policy analysis, we would mention the relationship between process and attribute patterns — the two themes in our assessment of the field. The latter, attribute patterns, might be regarded as generating the "hows" of state behaviour. The analyst who seeks to characterise state actions along the lines of issues, state and behaviour types, does more than delve into a world of compelling correlations; he also supplies those analysts concerned with process patterns with points of departure into the "whys" of state actions. To investigate correlations between structural attributes and coalition tendencies is important in and of itself, but understanding depends upon investigation into "why" the components of the state system tend to respond in the ways such correlations suggest. In the same way that the attribute-oriented analyst feeds departure points to the analyst involved in process patterns, the latter supplies the former with more sophisticated variables upon which to base correlational studies.

As described, the field of foreign policy analysis might appear systematic and coherent. Such a conclusion unfortunately is more wishful than real. The fact is that the field encompasses, in one sense, elements of both disorder and direction: disorder being the natural product of differing objectives and levels of analysis; direction resulting from the particular perspectives offered by those in the field who attempt genotypic investigations in a social scientific manner.

References

1. For further discussion of *phenotypic* and *genotypic* knowledge, see: J. N. Rosenau, "Comparing Foreign Policies: Why, What, How" in *Comparing Foreign Policies: Theories, Findings and Methods*, J. N. Rosenau (editor), Sage Publications, Los Angeles, 1974.
2. J. D. Singer, "The Level of Analysis Problem in International Relations", p. 22 in J. N. Rosenau, *International Politics and Foreign Policy*, Free Press, New York, 1969.
3. Ibid., #2, p. 23.
4. Ibid., #2, p. 24.
5. Arnold Wolfers, *Discord and Collaboration: Essays on International Politics*, Johns Hopkins University Press, London, 1975, p. 19.
6. Ibid., #5, p. 18.
7. Ibid., #5, p. 19.
8. Ralph Pettman, *Human Behaviour and World Politics*, Macmillan Press Ltd., London, 1975, p. 33.
9. This refers to the "decision-making" orientation, using insights of individual and social psychology as well as sociology, to enable one to understand the output process of foreign policy.
10. A. L. George and J. L. George, *Woodrow Wilson and Colonel House: A Personality Study*, John Day, New York (1956).
11. E.g. J. De Rivera, *The Psychological Dimensions of Foreign Policy*, Merrill, Columbus, Ohio, 1968.
12. E.g. B. E. Collins and H. Guetzkow, *A Special Psychology of Group Processes for Decision Making*, John Wiley, New York, 1964.
13. E.g. Ole Holsti, "Cognitive Dynamics and Images of the Enemy: Dulles and Russia" in D. Finlay, O. Holsti and R. Fagen, *Enemies in Politics*, Rand McNally, Chicago, 1967.
14. E.g. L. Festinger, *A Theory of Cognitive Dissonance*, Harper & Row, New York, 1957.
15. E.g. D. Pruitt, "Conclusions: Toward an Understanding of Choice Shifts in Group Discussion", *Journal of Personality and Social Psychology*, 1971, #20, pp. 495–510.
16. E.g. G. H. Snyder and P. Diesing, *Conflict among Nations*, Princeton University Press, New Jersey, 1977. In particular, see: Chapter IV on Information Processing.
17. E.g. L. Festinger, as above, #14.
18. I. L. Janis, *Victims of Groupthink*, Houghton Mifflin, Boston, 1972.
19. In this regard, the evolving attitudes of US elites towards Vietnam during the 1960s and early 1970s might prove a fruitful investigation. An example of such research is O. R. Holsti and J. N. Rosenau, "The Meaning of Vietnam: Belief Systems of American Leaders", April 1977 (manuscript unpublished at the time of this author's writing).
20. E.g. R. Snyder, H. Bruck and B. Sapin (eds.), *Foreign Policy Decision Making*, Free Press, New York, 1962.
21. E.g. K. Deutsch, *The Nerves of Government*, Free Press, New York, 1966.
22. E.g. D. P. Warwick, M. Meade and T. Reed, *A Theory of Public Bureaucracy*, Harvard University Press, Cambridge, Massachusetts, 1975.
23. D. Braybrooke and Charles Lindblom in *A Strategy of Decision* (Free Press, New York, 1970) focus upon the non-crisis process of policy evaluation; whereas G. Paige in *The Korean Decision: June 24–30* (Free Press, New York, 1968) is concerned with the process of crisis response.
24. See: introductory chapter in C. F. Hermann's *Crises in Foreign Policy*, The Bobbs-Merill Company, Inc., New York, 1969.

25. E.g. G. Allison, *Essence of Decision: Explaining the Cuban Missile Crisis*, Little, Brown, Boston, 1971.
26. Ibid., #25.
27. This view of the way decision-makers seek to determine "causation" in the acts of others is linked to the social-psychological approach known as "attribution theory".
28. See the principle of "disjointed incrementalism" in D. Braybrooke and Charles Lindblom, *A Strategy of Decision*, Free Press, New York, 1970.
29. N. Weiner, *Cybernetics*, John Wiley, New York, 1948.
30. For an interesting discussion on "entropy" and "negentropy", see: D. Singer, "System Stability and Transformation: A Global System Approach", *British Journal of International Studies*, Volume #3, Number #3, October 1977.
31. See: J. Steinbruner, *The Cybernetic Theory of Decision*, Princeton University Press, Princeton, New Jersey, 1974.
32. D. Easton, *A Systems Analysis of Political Life*, John Wiley & Sons, Inc., New York, 1965.
33. H. A. Kissinger, "Domestic Structure and Foreign Policy" in J. N. Rosenau (editor), *International Politics and Foreign Policy*, Free Press, New York, 1969.
34. H. C. Kelman, "Patterns of Personal Involvement in the National System: A Social Psychological Analysis of Political Legitimacy" in J. N. Rosenau (editor), *International Politics and Foreign Policy*, Free Press, New York, 1969.
35. Ibid., #2, p. 25.
36. Wolfers, op. cit., p. 14.
37. Wolfers, op. cit., p. 13.
38. G. Allison, *Essence of Decision: Explaining the Cuban Missile Crisis*, Little, Brown, Boston, 1971.
39. J. Steinbruner, *The Cybernetic Theory of Decision*, Princeton University Press, Princeton, New Jersey, 1974.
40. Ibid., #2, p. 22.
41. J. N. Rosenau, "Pre-Theories and Theories of Foreign Policy" in R. B. Farrell (editor), *Approaches to Comparative and International Politics*, Northwestern University Press, Evanston, 1966, p. 27.
42. M. P. Sullivan, *International Relations: Theories and Evidence*, Prentice Hall, Inc., Englewood Cliffs, N.J., 1976.
43. Rosenau's "linkage framework" can be found in his "The Components of a Linkage Framework" in his edited work *Linkage Politics*, Free Press, New York, 1969. Some constructive criticism of Rosenau's linkage framework can be found in J. Frankel, *Contemporary International Theory and the Behaviour of States*, Oxford University Press, London, 1973, p. 43 and in R. Pettman, *Human Behaviour and World Politics*, Macmillan Press Ltd., London, 1975.
44. This quote and subsequent quotes in this paragraph are from J. N. Rosenau, *Linkage Politics*, Free Press, New York, 1969, pp. 53ff.
45. An interesting array of linkage explorations, including a sample of K. Deutsch's investigations, can be found in J. N. Rosenau's *Linkage Politics*.
46. See: R. G. Sherwin, *WEIS Project Final Report*, School of International Relations University of Southern California (ARPA Contract N00014-67-A-0269-0004).
47. R. J. Rummell, "Indicators of Cross-National and International Patterns", *American Political Science Review*, #63 (March 1969), pp. 127-47.
48. S. A. Salmore and C. F. Hermann, "The Effect of Size, Development and Accountability on Foreign Policy", *Peace Research Society Papers*, 14 (1970), pp. 27-8.
49. See, for example, foreign policy behaviour and domestic conflict in P. J. McGowan and H. B. Shapiro, *The Comparative Study of Foreign Policy: A*

Survey of Scientific Findings, Sage Publications, London, 1973, pp. 79–83, 198–9.

50. Ibid., #49, p. 224.
51. See, for example, M. East, S. Salmore and C. F. Hermann, *Why Nations Act: Theoretical Perspectives for Comparative Foreign Policy Studies*, Sage Publications, London, 1978.

CHAPTER 7

Area Studies and the Regional International Subsystem

Gunnar Nielsson

Introduction

While the adoption of explicated conceptual frameworks as guides to teaching and research has gained considerable acceptability within the global-scope subfields of international relations, as demonstrated in the preceeding chapters, it has been extremely difficult to develop a theory-guided approach to regional international relations.

The theme pursued in this chapter is that the differences between the area studies approach and international relations theories have been so great that, within the academic discipline in general, regional studies is the subfield which has suffered the most from an intense and direct confrontation between the traditional and the behavioral orientations.

The development of the analysis of this theme proceeds from a general review of the composition of area studies programs in American universities, in order to sustain the argument that they are dominated by a configurative approach, to a selective review of the theory oriented literature about regional international relations. The analysis is strongly influenced by the author's bias in favor of the need to develop an empirical theory of rational international relations which will facilitate future systematic, comparative research and teachings.

The area studies approach

One of the major developments in American universities has been the near-exponential growth since the end of World War II of area studies programs in non-Western world areas. The expansion of interest in non-Western areas rose sharply for a number of reasons. The United States had had new direct experiences in the Pacific and North African regions as part of the

111

military campaigns in the 1940's. The pre-war university curricula had been parochial in their focus on the Western democratic political systems, but the crisis in European democracies, reflected in the rise to international significance of authoritarian and totalitarian systems in Asia and Europe, demonstrated the limitations of such a parochial approach. The emergence of new states from old colonies turned increased attention to what became known as "Third World" areas. Much of the intellectual efforts at describing and explaining developments within and among the new, non-Western states were undertaken with the ideological bias that they would follow a path to political democratization similar to that of the Western World. This ideological orientation was reinforced by the generally non-aligned new states of Africa and Asia and the "older" states of Latin America. The Cold War conditions were especially significant as an impetus for expansion of non-Western area studies in the United States, given its new role as a global superpower and the leader of the democratic Western bloc in a bi-polarized world conflict. Finally, in the narrower perspective of American political science, that profession was undergoing significant changes manifested by a shift in emphasis toward broad-scope enquiries into processes of political change and development which challenged the predominantly institutionalist emphases of the past. (1)

As a result of this reorientation, non-Western area studies mushroomed in American universities. A crude indicator of the enormous expansion of non-Western area studies is U.S. government funding of research projects. Between 1949 and 1963, 3,196 research projects were initiated through government funding: 386 on Africa, 529 on Latin America, 381 on the Peoples Republic of China, and 1900 projects on the USSR. The Kennedy Administration was especially active in promoting this expansion. It funded the initiation of 1,279 research projects between 1961 and 1963 which represents 40 percent of the postwar research projects in area studies sponsored by the U.S. government until 1963. In addition, 140 area studies research projects had been initiated and funded by American private foundations. The impact on American universities is perhaps indicated by the fact that graduate level language and area studies programs expanded from 62 to 153 between 1954 and 1964. (2)

While the expansion of such programs came to a halt in the late 1960's and early 1970's, the result of the growth of non-Western area studies is dramatically represented by findings produced by Richard D. Lambert's comprehensive survey in 1970-71 of area studies in the United States, sponsored by the Social Science Research Council and published by the American Academy of Political and Social Sciences with the title *Language and Area Studies Review*. (3) In preparing the survey, Lambert identified a total of 13,139 area studies specialists, 620 area studies programs in American universities and colleges, and 7,177 students specializing in area studies in the academic year 1970-71. Lambert's remarkably comprehensive and thorough study is based on responses to questionaires from 5,618 specialists (51.1 percent of the total contacted), 286 program directors (on the basis of which he identified 312 area studies programs subjected to careful analysis), and 3,242 students specializing in area studies (42.5 percent of the total number of the 1970-71 student specialists).

The geographical distribution of area studies shown in Table I establishes that Asian studies has the largest number of area specialists, university courses and programs. (5) Latin American and Eastern European area studies are the next largest, each accounting for approximately 20 percent in each category. Middle East and African area studies are the smallest programs, while Oceanian area studies consist of a minuscule proportion of the total area studies specialists. It is interesting to observe here that Western European area studies were excluded from the survey because it was impossible to establish workable parameters for selection of representative members in the three categories. Western European traditions and contemporary affairs have become part of the general reference world of American scholarship in every academic discipline to such an extent that it is no longer feasible to discern sufficiently distinct characteristics in university curricula to include it as a separate world area. At a recent Conference of Europeanists, one speaker complained that it was generally assumed in American universities that an introductory course in Western civilization qualifies a person to be considered familiarized with the Western European region. (6)

The basic theoretical assumption upon which area studies are based is that geography and culture are the key factors to consider in order to describe and explain behavior. Hence, only a configurative approach (7) can capture the contextual complexity and nuances which characterize attributes and behavior of social, economic and political systems. A configurative approach must be the point of departure in any study of the great variety of responses by single national, cultural communities to the apparently similar socio-economic and political characteristics of the socalled modernization process. In contrast to the discipline generalists' assumption of the existence of global-scope patterns of behavior, most area studies specialists assume that ideographic differences among diverse culture groupings characterize international relations far more than global recurrent patterns. (8) Furthermore, such differences can best be described and explained through an *empathetic understanding* of particular "cultural

113

Table I. DISTRIBUTION OF AREA STUDIES SPECIALISTS, COURSES AND ACADEMIC PROGRAMS BY WORLD AREAS

World Areas:	Total		Asia		Latin America		Eastern Europe		Middle East		Africa		Oceania	
	Total	%	Total	%	Total	%	Total	%	Total	%	Total	%	Total	%
Area Studies Specialists	5,618	100	2,265	40.3	983	17.5	946	16.8	711	12.7	689	12.3	24	0.4
Area Studies courses	8,885	100	2,879	32.4	2,275	25.6	1,889	21.3	1,252	14.1	590	6.6	–	–
Area Studies Programs	203	100	76	37.4	41	20.2	41	20.2	29	14.3	16	7.9	–	–

Source: *The Lambert Study*. See reference 4.

imperatives" which are viewed as the basic dynamic force underlying political behavior.

Consequently, the analytical tools to be brought to bear are not the general theories and rigorous scientific methodologies of the discipline generalists, but intensive case studies which can unearth sources of explanation based on insights into the complex texture of situational contexts. Intensive language training, and concentrated studies of cultural, anthropolitical, geographical, historical, sociological, economic and political factors pertaining to a particular culture group are the avenues through which area studies competence is achieved.

It follows, then, that the key feature in acquiring knowledge organized through an area studies program is its multi-disciplinary composition. According to Lambert's review, the area studies specialists were identified with nineteen different academic disciplines grouped into the following eight categories: (9)

1 – *Humanities*: Art, Drama, Music, Philosophy and Religion
2 - *Language Related*: Language and Literature, and Linguistics
3 – *Historical*: History and Archeology
4 – *Social Sciences*: Geography, Anthropology, Demography, Economics, Political Science, Psychology, Sociology, Criminology and Urban Studies
5 – *Education*
6 – *Applied and Professional*: Natural Sciences, Engineering, Business, Architecture, Communication, Law, Health, Military Science, Social Work, Public Administration and Agriculture
7 – *Area Studies General*
8 – *Nondisciplinary*

Table II shows the general academic discipline distribution of area specialists and by specific world areas. The first generalization this overview allows is that practically all the area specialists belong to an established academic discipline. The small category of non-disciplinary specialists are comprised of researchers working outside of academia. Less than four percent of the area specialists are identified in the general area studies category.

A second important generalization this distributive overview supports is that, while area studies specialists nominally represent a wide variety of academic disciplines; they are, in reality, concentrated in a few "core" disciplines. The twelve separate disciplines found in the categories of education and applied and professional disciplines account for no more than 6.5 percent of the total. The overwhelming majority of area studies specialists have disciplinary competences in history, the humanities and

Table II. DISTRIBUTION OF AREA STUDIES SPECIALISTS BY ACADEMIC DISCIPLINE AND BY WORLD AREAS IN PERCENTAGES

World Areas: Academic Disciplines:	Total		Asia	Latin America	Eastern Europe	Middle East	Africa	Oceania
	Total	%	%	%	%	%	%	%
History	1,508	26.8	26.6	24.1	36.9	25.9	19.6	4.2
Language and Literature	792	14.1	11.4	13.3	22.7	18.4	8.1	–
Humanities	315	5.6	8.9	1.3	1.6	9.3	2.9	–
Subtotal of "core" Disciplines	2,615	46.5	46.9	38.7	61.2	53.6	30.6	4.2
Social Sciences	2,229	39.7	39.0	48.0	28.4	27.0	56.6	91.7
Applied and Professional	206	3.7	2.7	6.2	2.9	3.5	4.5	–
Nondisciplinary	208	3.7	4.5	2.9	3.0	3.4	4.1	–
General Area Studies	204	3.6	3.6	1.6	3.1	10.3	0.7	–
Education	156	2.8	3.3	2.6	1.5	2.3	3.5	–
Total	5,618	100.0	100.0	100.0	100.0	100.0	100.0	100.0

Source: *The Lambert Study.* See reference 10.

the social sciences. These three categories were listed by 86.2 percent or 4,844 of the respondents in the survey.

Languages and literature, the humanities and history comprise the core of the configurationist approach to area studies. Combined, they account for 46.5 percent of the area specialists' academic disciplines and 61.8 percent of courses taught in area programs. (11) Of these three categories, history is by far the most important single academic discipline in area studies. As Lambert observed:

> History remains the center of area studies both in terms of specific disciplinary courses and in terms of the way other disciplinary courses are organized. It also tends to serve as the entry discipline through which a college or university initiates its studies of an area. Area history is taught in more programs than is any other discipline. National or regional units are, after all, sensible units for historical analysis, although they may not be for many of the other disciplines. (12)

The major proportion of history courses in area studies programs cover the pre-modern periods; i.e., prior to the nineteenth century. Only a small proportion of the history courses cover the classical period while 64 percent of the courses deal with the periods between the classical period and the end of the eighteenth century. Only 13 percent are recent period history, comparative and economic history courses accounted for only 2.0 percent while general-scope history courses represented 17 percent of the total.

Language and literature and linguistics represent another of the cornerstones in area studies programs. In the configurationist approach, language fluency and familiarity with literary traditions are viewed as important prerequisites for developing an empathetic understanding of a particular culture group. The significance of these disciplines is underscored by the fact that they account for 30.2 percent of all area program coursework. (13) Among the area specialists, 80 percent were competent in at least one foreign language and 35 percent were polylingual.

The humanities represent the smallest proportion of the area specialists and coursework among the core disciplines with 5.6 percent of the specialists and 9.5 percent of area program coursework. Philosophy and religion are the two most important disciplines within the humanities and they are heavily influenced by the classical civilization approach in the liberal arts curricula. In fact, these "substantive" humanities, linked up with classical literature, form an extension into modern area studies programs of the Oriental and Hebraic classical civilization studies. That the Orientalist tradition still remains strong is demonstrated by the fact that ancient

117

languages are taught in 79 percent of the South Asian, 59 percent of the Middle East and 49 percent of the East Asian area studies programs. Hence, in content as well as in approach, the language related and the humanities disciplines are dominated by the historical approach and the classical civilization traditions. (14)

The social sciences are a very important component in the area studies programs comprising 39.7 percent of the area specialists and 30.8 percent of the area program coursework. More specific distributive characteristics of the social sciences are presented in Table III.

Although the social sciences category includes nine different disciplines, there is a heavy concentration of area studies specialists and coursework in a few disciplines. The newer disciplines of psychology, demography, criminology and urban studies account for only 1.6 percent of the social science specialists and 0.6 percent of the coursework in area programs.

The most important social sciences are political science, anthropology and economics to which 81.9 percent of the area specialists belong and they account for 80.2 percent of the social science coursework.

Political science is the dominant social science in area studies with 44.4 percent of the social science area specialists and 38.2 percent of the social science courses. The primary focus in political science coursework by area specialists are on political institutions, processes and behavior which covers 42 percent of all political science courses. Among the broader-scope coursework, international relations represents 14.3 percent of the coursework, theory and method 7.2 percent, political instability and change 10.1 percent and general courses 22.6 percent. By contrast, the broader scope coursework in economics is far more important. Courses in economic growth and development cover 49.1 percent of the total coursework, international economics 10.2 percent and general courses 9.3 percent. The most important courses in anthropology are in the fields of social, cultural and ethnographic anthropology which represent 65.5 percent of the total.

In order to demonstrate the variation in geographic concentration in area studies coursework, Lambert introduced the concept of "areality" which is an indication of ". . . the proportion of courses in various disciplines by the unit of geographic focus." (16) For comparative purposes, Table IV presents a composite overview of coursework "areality" found in the six most important academic disciplines (language related courses are excluded).

It clearly shows that disciplines with an historical approach have the highest concentration of courses focusing on either a single region or a single country. For example, about 40 percent of the history and humanities courses deal with one country and about 40 percent focus on one

118

Table III. DISTRIBUTION OF AREA STUDIES SPECIALISTS BY SOCIAL SCIENCE DISCIPLINES AND BY WORLD AREAS IN PERCENTAGES

World Areas:	Total		Asia	Latin America	Eastern Europe	Middle East	Africa	Oceania
	Total	%	%	%	%	%	%	%
Political Science	946	44.4	48.1	28.6	54.7	45.8	37.9	9.1
Anthropology	428	19.2	18.2	19.3	3.7	21.3	27.5	81.8
Economics	408	18.3	16.1	23.6	27.2	13.0	14.1	9.1
Geography	221	9.9	8.4	12.9	8.9	11.5	10.3	–
Sociology	191	8.6	7.7	14.0	4.8	6.3	8.2	–
Psychology	21	0.9	0.8	0.6	0.7	1.6	1.5	–
Demography	10	0.5	0.5	0.8	0.0	0.0	0.5	–
Criminology	2	0.1	0.1	0.0	0.0	0.5	0.0	–
Urban Studies	2	0.1	0.1	0.2	0.0	0.0	0.0	–
Total	2,229	100.0	100.0	100.0	100.0	100.0	100.0	100.0

Source: *The Lambert Study*. See reference 15.

Table IV. DISTRIBUTION OF "AREALITY" OF AREA STUDIES COURSEWORK BY SELECTED ACADEMIC DISCIPLINES IN PERCENTAGES

"Areality": Academic Discipline:	Comparative with Disciplinary Focus %	Comparative with Topical Focus %	Comparative with Geographic Focus %	One Region %	One Country %	One Section of a Country %	Total %
History	2.4	2.1	6.9	45.2	42.6	0.8	100.0
Humanities	9.8	6.0	5.5	38.3	39.6	0.7	100.0
Anthropology	16.2	13.6	5.3	50.5	13.0	1.4	100.0
Political Science	16.5	9.7	10.8	37.9	25.0	0.1	100.0
Sociology	22.3	25.8	7.3	28.1	16.5	0.0	100.0
Economics	36.0	17.4	8.1	23.8	14.7	0.0	100.0

Source: *The Lambert Study*. See reference 17.

region. In contradistinction, the newer social science disciplines, such as sociology and economics in which there is a greater concern with general scope theories, focus predominantly on a comparative approach in their coursework. Political science ranks in the middle of these two general trends. While 37 per cent of its coursework have a comparative approach, 25 percent are focused on a single country and only 16.5 percent are conducted according to a general disciplinary comparative approach. This pivotal position of political science in the continuum of history and the humanities as the most configuratively oriented disciplines and sociology and economics as the most theoretically and comparatively oriented disciplines is characterized by Lambert in the following generalization:

> Wherever we went, whether talking to area specialists or heads of social science disciplinary departments or participating in the seemingly endless conferences on the future of area studies, we found the presumed juxtaposition between . . . "the discipline generalists" and the area specialists. Implicit in this formulation is a negative judgment of the worthwhileness of the area-oriented intellectual enterprise in what I call the rigor versus mortis debate. While the debate is holistic, that is relating to area studies as a whole, its proper domain is in the social sciences, even though most area specialists come from disciplines outside the behavioral sciences . . .
>
> . . . On a campus, the dividing line between hostile and hospitable camps usually comes in the middle of political science, with political institutionalists being in favor of area specialization and the behaviorists opposed. If a political science department as a whole is favorable to area specialists, the general area program tends to be strong, and if even sociology and economics are favorable, the soil is indeed fertile for the growth of area studies. On the other hand, if the political science department is in the midst of a "red shirt" obsolescence battle, pushing out the institutionalists, if the historians are switching from chronological and country history to topical and comparative history, and if the anthropology department is in the hands of hard line functionalists, area programs will have a very tough sledding on that campus. (18)

A third important generalization, based on Lambert's data, is that there is a variation of disciplinary emphases in area studies programs according to the geographical distribution of world areas. Asian and Middle East studies are heavily dominated by the historical, language-related and humanities disciplines. Language and literature, history and political science are the most significant disciplines in Eastern European Studies.

121

In Latin American and African studies, political science, history and economics are the most important disciplines. Oceanian studies are conducted almost exclusively by anthropologists.

From the perspective of social science coursework, 60 percent of anthropology courses in area studies programs were on Latin America and Africa. Fifty seven percent of economics courses were in Latin American and Eastern European studies and 50 percent of the political science courses were in Eastern European and East Asian studies, which indicates the Cold War concern about developments in the Communist world.

Hence, the older, established area studies on Asia and the Middle East are strongly influenced by the historical and configurationist-oriented disciplines while the relatively recent development of Latin American and African area studies are most influenced by the social sciences. Within Asian studies, South East Asian studies are more similar to African studies in this respect which reflects its relatively recent development.

This examination of the disciplinary composition of and approaches to area studies has, hopefully, helped to elucidate the sources of tension between historically oriented configurationists and behavioral science oriented discipline generalists. Although nominally very diversified by the many academic disciplines involved, area studies are dominated by the history, language and literature, and humanities disciplines and by the "institutionalist oriented" political scientists. They comprise the core of specialists and coursework in area studies programs. They represent the stronghold of the configurative approach and set the tone for area studies with their emphasis on the uniqueness of the world's many different culture groups. Since most of the area specialists do not come from a behavioral sciences background, it has been extremely difficult for the theoretically and methodologically oriented social scientists to persuade area studies specialists to adopt broad-scope analytical perspectives and comparative approaches to studying social, economic and political patterns of behavior within and among the regions of the global political system. In fact, the dominant trend in the progressive establishment of area studies programs in American universities has been in the opposite direction, moving from a broad-scope coverage of a world area to division into separate subareas and then to further fragmentation into programs on a particular country in the world area. (19) Multi-regional competences by area specialists are extremely rare and can be considered insignificant as a source of potential change in approach to area studies. (20) Furthermore, since most area studies are organized as loosely coordinated interdepartmental programs with a multi-disciplinary steering committee rather than an autonomous, degree-granting academic administrative unit, it is unrealistic to expect that students, aspiring to achieve area specializations, will be exposed to a theoretically integrated curriculum. Area studies competence is acquired through linking a multi-disciplinary, configurative specialization with the prevailing orientation within a single academic discipline. (21)

From the perspective of the social sciences, there is a significant variation in the degree to which area studies have penetrated the different academic disciplines. They have had little impact in psychology, sociology and economics, but remain part of the mainstream in anthropology and political science. From the perspective of the international relations discipline generalists, it is sobering to recognize that international relations courses involve only 14.3 percent of all the political science courses in area studies programs, 5.5 percent of all social science coursework and 1.7 percent of all area studies coursework. Proportional insignificance of such dimensions should lead to a greater recognition and understanding of the constant tension between regional international relations and area studies specialists with their different assumptions about and approaches to the search for knowledge.

Theories of regional international relations

The gulf between the area studies approach and the theoretical approach to international relations by the discipline generalists presents a serious dilemma for students of regional international relations. While the configurative approach of the former places the main emphasis on specific cultures, the major theories developed by the discipline generalists have been global in scope. For the latter area studies are viewed as research aides in their quest for verification of recurrent global patterns of behavior. Therefore, the international region as a unit of analysis imposes artificial boundaries because geographical location and particularities of cultures may not be the most important variables in explaining a pattern of behavior. Instances which confirm central tendencies of a behavior pattern may only be found in a few, or even in as many as one half, of the actors located within a particular region while a greater number of actors in another geographical location may show more clearly the behavioral characteristics which the global-scope theory is supposed to explain. From the perspective of the regional international relations specialists, the problem now becomes how to account for the attributes and behavioral characteristics of actors, located within that particular region, which do not fit into the central tendency being investigated. Should such "deviant" cases be explained as a series of unique events? Do they demand separate description and explanation based on a configurative approach? If the theory-guided regional analysts opt for the use of a multitude of theories and methodologies, to which they would be intellectually predisposed, they run the risk of spending more time on explaining to their students and readers diverse theories and methodologies than on their application to the particular region under study. (22) Furthermore, it is highly probable that they would still be faced with deviant cases within the region which they, as regional specialists, are expected to be able to account for.

Another serious problem is that many theories used by discipline generalists are only nominally global in scope. Dependency theory, for example, has been developed based on empirical research which is "Third World centered." Power theories are similarly supposedly global in scope, although their supporting empirical research has been great power biased. Interdependence and transactionalist theories have been "globalized" by postulation although the empirical references are drawn predominantly from the Western industrialized states of the "First World." Most specifically, regional integration theories were "Europocentered" in origin and have been inapplicable in other regions of the world.

Finally, some of the global-scope theories, such as theories of functionalist cooperation and the World Society, remain basically conceptual frameworks untested by comprehensive, systematic, empirical research.

Hence, the theory-guided regional analysts, in trying to adopt the major international relations theories, face a series of predicaments in which, 1) some theories are so broad in scope as to be untestable according to the rules of evidence by which they want the validity of their studies to be assessed; 2) a single, partial theory is an insufficient basis from which to provide a comprehensive description and explanation of all the actors in a particular region, which is expected of a regional specialist; 3) some of the theories are "globalized" prematurely, based on empirical research applicable only to some regions; 4) the use of multiple theories and methodologies tends to distract from a comprehensive, substantive coverage of the region under study, (23) and 5) a configurative approach is unacceptable to the analysts committed to social scientific standards.

Within the context of this general dilemma, and in spite of these predicaments, theory-building efforts in regional international relations have proceeded continuously since the end of World War II. The various theories proposed will be reviewed in this section according to the three categories of: the regionalism and world order approach, regional integration theories and regional subsystems theories.

The regionalism and world order approach

Analyses of regionalism and world order have had three major emphases: socio-cultural commonalities, political power configurations and regional institutions. (24) Common socio-cultural attributes as the unit of analysis characterized the writings of Bhoutros-Ghali and Northrop immediately after World War II. (25) The most important foundation for regional associations is sociological solidarity arising from racial and ethnic affinities, according to Bhoutros-Ghali. Upon that foundation could be built regional cooperation in settlement of national security types of disputes and in socio-economic relations. In a global perspective, Northrop identified the following seven major cultural-political units which could serve as the basis for regional associations and solidarity: Asia, the Islamic World, Sub-Saharan Africa, Continental Europe, The Soviet Communist World, Pan-America and the British Commonwealth. (26) The development of world order would be assured by these cultural-political units accommodating to each other in a concert of cultures, drawing upon the best from each of the diverse civilizations which would lead to a world philosophical synthesis. This emphasis on different philosophies springing from the world's major civilizations has not been pursued through systematic empirical investigations of the extent to which commonalities of cultural attributes have contributed to regional solidarity. The various studies of pan-regional ideologies in Latin America, Western Europe, the Middle East and Africa as a source of political mobilization within regional unification processes could be viewed as extensions of the earlier preoccupations with the role of cultural affinities in the development of world order. (27) However, the latter type of studies have not had a major impact on contemporary research in regional international politics which, in this context, seems more concerned with the reemergence of substate political movements around ethnic solidarity presenting a challenge to the existing state system. (28)

The power politics perspective, and particularly its balance of power aspects, has been applied in analyses of regional international relations. It has focused on regional-level inter-state power equilibriums. In the 1950's, George Liska developed two types of regional associations based on power configurations: the great power orbit and the small state entente. (29) The great power orbit concept is a new version of classical sphere of influence thinking. Its structure is based on the need by smaller states to accommodate to a great power within a region through formation of regional associations or formal alliances. The success of great power orbits as a source of international stability is dependent on the general foreign policy orientation of the great power involved. Within this broad conceptual framework, Liska analyzed the similarities and differences in relations between the U.S.S.R. and the Eastern European states and between the U.S. and the Latin Ameircan states. The second type of regional associations among smaller states is based on a shared perception of threatened absorption into a great power orbit dominated by an expansionist great power or by competing expansionist great powers. Liska compared the historical experiences of the Little Entente among Eastern European states in the 1930's and the Arab League in the 1950's as empirical references. He concluded that small power regional associations were not likely to become successful counter-weights in regional conflicts involving great powers.

From a world order perspective, intra-regional equilibrium, based on great power orbits, might become the basis for a world balance of power structure which would be stable and peaceful. However, such a global equilibrium also contains the potential for inter-regional competition and violent conflicts which might be less frequent, but of much larger magnitude. Hence, such a development represents an uncertain and potentially high risk approach to global cooperation.

The power politics approach is the root of the more recent conjectures about the emergence of a "pentagonal" global power structure consisting of the U.S., the U.S.S.R., China, Japan and Western Europe. The rising significance of the multi-regional OPEC and the Group of 77 in UNCTAD appear to be an important cross-current, dampening the "pentagonal thinking" so very much in vogue in the United States during the early days of the Nixon Administration.

The study of regional international institutions has been one of the main emphases for international relations specialists on regional international politics. This is because the enormous growth of such institutions represents the most tangible, empirical indicator of the increased significance of regions in global politics. (30) Many of the earliest studies have been descriptive overviews of various regional institutions, (31) but several attempts at developing taxonomies for comparative purposes were made in the early 1970's. (32) The basic variables used in establishing typologies have been geographical proximity of members and the objectives or functions of the institutions. The most important categories have been the division into military security, general political and socio-economic types of regional international institutions.

More specific studies were conducted to investigate the relationship between macro-political institutions and the United Nations Organization in the field of collective security and peace-keeping. They examined the degree to which the global and the regional institutions' roles were compatible and complementary. (33) The ability of regional security institutions – such as NATO and the Warsaw Treaty Organization – and the macro-political regional institutions – such as the Organization of American States, the Organization of African Unity and the Arab League – to prevent, resolve and control localized conflict has been analyzed by several writers. (34) While the peace-keeping and peace-making performance record of regional institutions was slightly better than that of the United Nations Organization, their role at both levels indicated severe limitations in cases of intense international conflict involving great powers as well as in cases of severe internal conflicts. From a world order perspective, however, the conflict control role of regional institutions represents an important counter-argument to the globalist collective security advocates because these regional institutions have demonstrated that there are circumstances where it is helpful to follow the policy doctrine that "peace is divisible" and there are advantages to being able to confine the scope of conflicts by the intervention and mediation by "like-minded" and familiar elites from neighboring states acting through a regional institution. Assessing the performance of regional institutions, Joseph S. Nye concluded that:

> [they] . . . have made modest contributions to the creation of islands of peace in the international system and their costs for world peace in terms of conflict creation have been less than their modest benefit to the world in conflict diversion. (35)

However, to dampen the claims for regionalism as the best road to world peace, Nye also concluded, from his systematic, comparative analysis, that, based on a comprehensive assessment such regionalist claims have been inflated. The growth of regional institutions have indeed been a remarkable development in contemporary world politics, but their capacities to control inter- and intra-state conflicts as well as to promote sustained socio-economic integration have not lived up to the expectations their number and declared intentions would suggest.

Regional integration theories

Description and analysis of the role of socio-economic micro-regional institutions have been dominated by regional integration studies. Compared to the regionalism and world order approach with its philosophical–historical orientation, loosely constructed conceptual frameworks and single case or simple comparative methodological characteristics, regional integration studies were, until the mid-1970's, heavily empirical theory oriented. In fact, theories of regional integration proliferated to the point that at least

127

four sub-groupings were identifiable by the late 1960's. They were the federalists, transactionalists, functionalists and neo-functionalists theoretical perspectives. These theoretical perspectives have been discussed in detail in an earlier chapter in this book and in several compilations of papers. (36) For the purpose of this discussion, it is important to observe that the major difference between regional integration theories and other analytical perspectives used in studying international regional cooperation is that, whereas international cooperation is assumed to develop through better adjustments in relations among states through the use of intergovernmental institutions, (37) regional integration is assumed to involve a gradual unification process whereby an authority–legitimacy transfer takes place through the political structural transformation of creating a regional scope federation that displaces the autonomy of the member states participating in the process.

The main characteristic of integration theories is that they had their origins in the Western tradition of pluralists, interest groups politics and in the theoretical assumptions about the political impact of intensified economic interdependence based on liberal capitalist international policies and practices. During the early phase of theory developments about regional political integration, the focus was almost exclusively centered on Western European experiences, especially the European Communities. (38) By the mid-1960's, the application of the pluralist, neo-functionalist model was expanded to such non-European experiences as the Latin American Free Trade Association, the Central American Common Market, the East African Community and the East European Comecon. (39) During the late 1960's and early 1970's, in an attempt to progress from such parallel descriptions and analyses of different integration experiences to more systematic, comparative research, Joseph S. Nye developed a conceptual framework with proposed measurements and indicators in which integration processes were disaggregated into their economic, social, political, institutional, policy, and attitudinal aspects which, after sufficient research findings, were then to be reaggregated into a comprehensive causal model. (40) The model has not yet been implemented and must be considered an abortive attempt. At the same time, Lindberg and Scheingold published an important collection of theory papers evaluating the state of scholarship in regional integration studies. Proceeding much more cautiously by then, Ernst B. Haas characterized the previous developments in the subfield as "pre-theories" and presented more modest empirical generalizations about the nature of the integration process. He developed an important new distinction among Western, Eastern and "Third World" integration experiences based on the recognition that "background conditions" for infegration differed so significantly among the different regions that the process characteristics as well as the outcome potentials were severely affected. In other words, the Western European centered neo-functionalist theory (or pre-theory) was not generalizable to the point where it could be applied to other regions. By the late 1970's, Haas declared regional integration theories obsolete or obsolescent even for studies of the European Communities. (41) The major theory-builders in the United States abandoned regional integration studies and turned their attention to broader-scope frameworks such as interdependence, dependency and the politics of global technology transfers. Today, regional integration studies survive predominantly in the form of specific issue-oriented and public policy-oriented analyses of the European Communities. Even this last surviving experiment in regional integration is considered to be struggling to maintain its socio-economic integrative features in the face of general economic stagnation and the pull toward global interdependence through extra-regional policy realignments caused by "external forces". (42)

Regional subsystems theories

Attempts to introduce the systems approach to the study of regional international politics have been characterized by the convergence of two different developments within the international relations discipline. In the first place, the theory-building efforts by the behavioralist discipline generalists were extended to the regional level. The international systems approach provided a suitable conceptual tool because it postulates the feasibility of decomposing complex interaction processes into different levels of analysis. It allowed for the division into a global-dominant system, regional-subordinate systems, and state-as-actor systems levels.

By the late 1960's, systems oriented international relations specialists proposed conceptual frameworks in which regional international relations could be analyzed as the intermediate unit of analysis as well as level of analysis between world politics and foreign policy analysis of single states. At a very high level of abstraction, Roger Masters postulated the feasibility of the development of a "multi-bloc model" of world politics. (43) It represented a regional application of Morton Kaplan's global-level structural reductionist modeling within which Masters demonstrated that, if it was assumed that regional political integration had developed to the point where each region would have the same decision-making characteristics as a single state actor, then the structural properties as well as the behavioral rules of Kaplan's Balance of Power Model could be applied and the same systems maintaining potential would be obtained. (44)

The advantages of a systems approach to regional studies were examined in a special issue on international subsystems in *International Studies Quarterly* in late 1969. (45) In the introductory overview article by Peter Berton, it was argued that the adoption of a "sub-macro" systems approach would reduce the number of units and the complexity of interactions and would provide a comparative framework through which the lack of data on the "newer" regions beyond Western Europe and North America could be remedied in a systemic manner. (46) The principles of a systems approach were described and its potential application to regional studies discussed by Michael Banks, who argued that treating regions as international subsystems would move analysis beyond the narrower confines of the various functionalist theories of international integration. (47) The use of a comparative conceptual framework in the study of five international subordinate systems was illustrated by Cantori and Spiegel and systems analysis of international relations in North Africa, East Asia and the Communist System were presented by other contributors to this special issue. (48)

A new conceptual framework for comparative studies of inter-regional relations among integrating regions was proposed by Karl Kaiser. (49) He criticized the integration theorists for their lack of concern about the role of external forces in the regional integration process. Expanding the scope of enquiry beyond the confined parameters of changing relations among states involved in integrative processes within a particular institutional context, he developed a typology of structures of integration and postulates and hypotheses about the effects of various types and stages of integration in one region on the integration developments in other regions.

Critical of the preoccupation with different global-level structural models by the discipline generalists, Oran Young introduced a "discontinuities model" that, he argued, would overcome the simplistic characteristics of a bipolar–multipolar dichotomy, increasingly inadequate for analyses of international relations as intensive bipolarity of the Cold War period was being displaced by more complex detente relations. (50) According to Young, congruence of global and regional issues and actors is a variable condition and world politics is moving in the direction of greater and greater discontinuity between global level and regional level issues and actors. Therefore, it was necessary to develop a model which can capture the emerging discontinuities both at the level of global politics *vis-à-vis* regional international politics and at the level of regional subsystems *vis-à-vis* each other. A conceptual framework based on multiple subsystems with different structural properties and process variables as well as variance in degree of penetration of global system features in regional international politics is the most appropriate approach and the "discontinuities model" represented an initial theoretical contribution in that direction.

Roughly concomitant with these tensions of the systems approach to regional subsystems analysis, several regional specialists presented more rigorous analytical perspectives in their studies of a particular region. (51) They, too, were critical of the global or single state perspectives of the discipline generalists and they advocated greater attention to systematic studies of regional international relations as an intermediate level of analysis. Leonard Binder, especially, was severely critical of the great power bias of the "globalists" and the inapplicability of their conceptual schemes to Middle East studies. (52) Similar to the contention by Oran Young, Binder argued that the global power's influence goes through a refraction process whereby the power of outside actors enters the regional subsystem in different, variable forms due to the intra-regional forces and interests. East Asian, South Asian, Middle Eastern and Sub-Saharan African international relations were studied by these specialists through the application of a subsystems framework which emphasized the particular region's "structural features" such as configuration of power, core and periphery inter-state relations, linkages with the dominant system and regional institutional structures as well as their "textural features" such as common cultural attributes, shared historical experiences, pan-ideologies and frequency of interaction as criteria for 1) delineation of the region, 2) degrees of distinct political attributes, and 3) relative autonomy *vis-à-vis* other regions and the global "dominant" system.

The main weakness in these attempts at becoming more theory oriented in regional international relations studies is that the new conceptual frameworks have not been followed up by construction of methodologies which would be the basis for comparative empirical research by regional specialists. In fact, even the conceptualizing has suffered from great disparity. In an excellent article by William R. Thompson, reviewing the regional theory literature, conceptual disparity was one of the glaring problems. (53) Reviewing the works by 22 international relations specialists, published between 1958 and 1971, Thompson found 21 different attributes used in defining the concept of a region. Most significant, though, was his finding that there had been practically no cumulative progress in reaching agreements among the theorists. After a matrix analysis of the 22 theorists by the 21 attributes, he found only 22 percent of the potential cells where checked and among the 22 theorists, there were ". . . only 4 of 136 nonredundant pairs showing any substantial connectivity." (54) At the completion of an explicatory analysis of the attributes, Thompson arrived at the following general definition of a regional subsystem:

. . . the necessary and sufficient conditions for a regional subsystem are as follows:

1) The actors' pattern of relations or interactions exhibit a particular degree of regularity and intensity to the extent that a change at one point in the subsystem affects other points.

2) The actors are generally proximate.

3) Internal and external observers and actors recognize the subsystem as a distinctive area or "theatre of operation."

4) The subsystem logically consists of at least two and quite probably more actors. (55)

While these characteristics remain quite general, Thompson expressed the hope that they would be the starting points in future attempts to specify the definition of a regional subsystem.

Recognizing the lack of generally accepted definition of regions, Bruce Russett undertook the task of trying to delineate regional boundaries through an inductive approach which was supposed to establish the degree to which states clustered around certain attribute and behavioral variables. (56) The variables Russett used were 1) social and cultural homogeneity — according to common religious, linguistic and ethnic identities; 2) common political attitudes and external behavior — according to uniformity of UN voting on major issues; 3) political interdependence — according to common membership in regional international institutions; 4) economic interdependence — according to foreign trade relations; and 5) geographic proximity. Through the use of factor analysis, Russett attempted to delineate regions according to the degree to which congruence were manifested by clustering of states sharing commonalities on all five variables. While his findings did allow the rejection of the null hypothesis that there would be no significant clustering, he concluded that, by his criteria, there were no clearly delineated regions in the world. In most cases, regional demarcations were not sharply distinguishable. Instead, it was a matter of continuums where one might think of certain core states within regions and then gray zones of periphery states between them which was shown by some degree of deviation from high correlation on all factors by some states.

Russett's findings showed that Eastern Europe had the highest congruence on the five variables and Latin America was also fairly distinct as a region. The Western Community and Asia were in an intermediate position as distinguishable regions. Among the rest of the states, the Middle East and Black Africa were the most distinct smaller regional groupings.

While Russett's work can be criticized on several grounds — especially

132

the adequacy and appropriateness of his criteria and the inferences he drew about the relationship between his regional groupings and probabilities of conflict and integration developments, it remains the only pre-theoretical, descriptive delineation of regions based on systematic, empirical research. Critics have been more preoccupied with ridiculing the findings of commonality on some criteria which defied the common sensical concept of geographic proximity — such as the strong commonality of Indonesia with the Middle East's Muslim identity, the Phillippines' shared Catholic culture with Latin America and Southern Europe, and Japan's high degree of economic interdependence with the Western Community — than concerned with the further development of a more refined empirical model by which to replicate Russett's efforts to overcome the established deductionist approach to delineating regions and membership by states in them. (57)

The most comprehensive conceptual framework for the comparative study of regional international relations was developed in the early 1970's by Louis Cantori and Steven Spiegel. (58) It represents a consolidation of major points made in the preceeding literature on the subject and an effort to synthesize them into a coherent analytical perspective. Thus, Cantori and Spiegel accepted the criticism made by previous regional subsystem theorists that 1) international relations theory was too preoccupied with the global-scope bipolarity versus multipolarity issues, 2) that it was great power biased, 3) that there was increasing "decoupling" between global and regional issues, and 4) that integration theories were too narrowly focused on non-coercive, cooperative relations following the assumptions of a functionalist socio-economic dynamic and ignoring power political relations as well as the role of external powers in regional international relations. Stating the rationale for an "empirical systems approach", they invoked the arguments made earlier that 1) regions constituted an important intermediate level of analysis between global politics and states' foreign policies, 2) that such analysis would reduce the number of units of analysis and the complexity of international politics, 3) that it could provide conceptual linkages between area studies specialists and political science and international relations discipline specialists, and 5) that it was necessary to recognize the particularities characterizing individual regions while establishing an encompassing analytical framework by which to compare their similarities.

Adopting a systems approach, Cantori and Spiegel defined a system as ". . . the totality of relations which exists between the autonomous units in a particular arena . . ." (59) They posited three different levels of arenas as the global-dominant system, the regional-subordinate systems and the state-internal domestic systems. Regions were defined as ". . . areas of the world which contain geographically proximate states forming, in foreign affairs, mutually interrelated units." (60) In this general context, the authors defined the subordinate system as follows:

> . . . a subordinate system consists of one state, or two or more states which have some common ethnic, linguistic, cultural, social and historical bonds, and whose sense of identity is sometimes increased by the actions and attitudes of states external to the system. (61)

Cantori and Spiegel then proceeded to delineate fifteen subordinate systems in world politics based on criteria derived from their definition such as 1) that geography is a critically important determinant, 2) that a subordinate system could exist of one state (e.g., the U.S.S.R.), 3) that every state could be a member of only one subordinate system, 4) that external powers could be important actors in defining a subordinate system, 5) that the subordinate system was shaped by the historical, political, social and economic factors indigenous to the region and 6) that delineation of subordinate systems can change over time due to volatile political and ideological factors. (62)

The fifteen subordinate systems delineated by this method were: West Europe, East Europe, the U.S.S.R., North America, Latin America, South West Pacific, East Asia, South East Asia, South Asia, the Middle East, North Africa, West Africa, East Africa, Central Africa and Southern Africa. Only five subordinate systems were selected, however, for comparative analysis. The dynamic of their conceptual framework was based on the assumption that the states constitute the independent variable, the regional-subordinate system where the dependent variable and a number of pattern variables and structural variables constituted the intervening variable. An overview of their conceptual scheme is provided in Table V. It is postulated that the pattern variables can be described and explained according to the composite attributes and behavioral characteristics of the member states in a subordinate system. Completion of that stage of the analysis, in turn, provides the basis for establishing the characteristics of the structural variables, thus identifying the states which comprise the core sector and the periphery sector as well as the intrusive states which significantly affect relations within the subordinate system. (63)

The major emphasis, when examining the pattern variables, is on mapping out the balance of power structure and the degree of conflict and cooperation as a manifestation of "the structure of relations." In this sense, the empirical systems approach to regional studies attempts to incorporate power theory and integration theory as used in international

134

Table V. OVERVIEW OF CANTORI AND SPIEGEL CONCEPTUAL FRAMEWORK

Independent Variable:	Intervening Variables: A-Pattern Variables	B-Structural Variables	Dependent Variable
The States 142 Sovereign States 16 Colonies	A 1: Nature and Level of Cohesion A 1.1: Social A 1.2: Economic A 1.3: Political A 1.4: Organizational A 2: Nature of Communication A 2.1: Personal A 2.2: Mass Media A 2.3: Elite Exchanges A 2.4: Transportation A 3: Level of Power A 3.1: Material A 3.2: Military A 3.3: Motivational A 4: Structure of Relations A 4.1: Spectrum A 4.2: Causes A 4.3: Means	B 1: Core Sector B 2: Periphery Sector B 3: Intrusive States B 3.1: Methods of Participation in the Subordinate Systems	Types of Subordinate Systems: Integrative Consolidative Cohesive Coherent

relations as well as analytical frameworks developed by comparative politics theorists. (64) Cantori and Spiegel conducted a comparative analysis of five selected subordinate systems — West Europe, Latin America, the Middle East, West Africa and South East Asia — in terms of pattern variable characteristics of their core sectors, periphery sectors and the methods of participation by intrusive states. Their analysis was interspersed with selected articles from the regional international relations literature. Adhering to their assumption that it is premature to treat subordinate systems as an independent variable until a more thorough comparative analysis of the structure and behavior of relations *within* subordinate systems has been completed, they concluded with a first cut at classifying subordinate systems according to their degree of cohesion.

From a theory-building perspective, the Cantori and Spiegel framework is a valiant and valuable experiment in formulating a comprehensive and comparative approach to the study of regional subsystems. Unfortunately, their effort went astray on methodological grounds. The basic dynamic of moving from independent through intervening to dependent variables was not followed by the authors. Instead, they turned the dynamic around by following a structural, reductionist and geographical determinist approach whereby delineation of subordinate systems boundaries and membership in the different subordinate systems is the result of the authors' evaluative judgment. The structuralist approach became the starting point for their analysis of the significance of the intervening pattern variables and the structural variables of core and periphery sectors. The intervening variables do not govern their analysis as they postulated they should. Instead, their analysis is governed by their pre-determined delineation of the fifteen subordinate systems and their core and periphery sectors. The intervening variables are not treated as autonomous units, but as qualitively determined labels for evaluative generalizations. As a result, the analysis became static and the more specific it became, the more questionable the empirical validity of the usage of the variables became. At points, the comparisons appear contrived and almost forced upon the realities of the political relations under investigation.

In the construction of their comprehensive conceptual framework, Cantori and Spiegel went to great length to identify a large number of variables to be included. A total of 88 variables were supposed to govern the delineation and structural and behavioral characteristics of subordinate systems. Yet, they bypassed the critically important methodological step of specifying by what combination of strengths, the 72 sub-variables would serve to operationalize the four pattern variables. Nor did they specify the interconnectedness of the four pattern variables, although they did suggest that cohesion, communication and level of power determined the structure of relations within a subordinate system. By what combination of pattern variables core and periphery sector membership would be established was also left unspecified. Similar to a great deal of international relations research based on the systems approach, the actors included and the relations among them are postulated to be systemic without operationalized indicators of what constitutes systemic relations. On the basis of a reasonable set of postulates, but without establishing empirical indicators beyond suggestive data in the appendices, Cantori and Spiegel proceeded to identify subordinate systems membership for 158 states and colonies in fifteen distinct subordinate systems. The selection of five of them for detailed comparative analysis was not explained in terms of the relevance of their selection to the empirical application of the proposed conceptual framework.

However, as a pioneering effort to expand the scope of conceptualizing, the Cantori and Spiegel framework provides an important challenge to further development which should not be prematurely dismissed because of methodological shortcomings in their application of the comparative approach they developed. In the process, they have identified serious flaws in the earlier, narrower-scope integration theories and they have identified a multitude of variables involved in a comprehensive and comparative empirical systems approach.

Summary and conclusion

One of the major conclusions to be drawn from this review of selected regional international relations literature is that there is a basic epistemological and methodological incompatibility between the area studies approach and the empirical theory approach to international relations studies of regional subsystems within a global political system. Area studies follow a configurative approach which prevails because of the intellectual traditions characterizing the core academic disciplines that dominate the composition of area studies programs. Students of international relations who want to pursue a regional specialization are confronted by a dilemma because the major theories are global in scope and based on the assumption that culture and geography, the key factors for area studies specialists, are treated as only two (and often not the most important) among a large number of variables considered significant in the investigation of recurrent patterns of behavior in world politics.

Nevertheless, some theorizing about regional international relations have been undertaken throughout the post World War II period. The earliest examples have been discussed under the category of the regionalism and world order approach. Applying normative and loosely constructed conceptual frameworks, it focused on cultural–political affinities, balance of power configurations and international institutions as building blocks in the development of a more peaceful world order based on stable, cooperating regions.

Beginning in the late 1950's, theory-guided regional integration studies flourished for two decades. They can be viewed as a hybrid between the regionalism and world order approach and the empirical theory approach adopted by the discipline generalists.

Since the late 1960's, attempts have been made to apply the logic of systems theory to studies of regional international relations. So far, however, this type of theorizing has, by and large, been characterized by a great deal of conceptual "dappling" for short periods of time. The main weakness is that the regional subsystems conceptual frameworks have not been sustained by the methodological follow-up necessary to make them viable models for comparative empirical research. The magnitude of such a methodological task is clearly indicated by the complexity of the conceptual framework developed by Cantori and Spiegel. (65) In addition, the 81 general propositions and hypotheses assembled from the theory literature by Thompson (66) as an inventory, organized according to eight categories of international subsystems relations, is even more indicative of the enormity of the challenge which confronts theory-building efforts.

It leads to the inevitable, final conclusion that regional specialists within the international relations discipline are faced with the need to take on the sustained, step-by-step task of consolidating and integrating the previous conceptual frameworks in order to facilitate comparative research in the future. To concentrate on improving theories of regional international relations will fill an important void both within the discipline itself and for the academic discipline specialization portion of the curriculum for future area studies specialists. It would be a worthy replacement of the current pretense that the two approaches are somehow intellectually reconcilable through the right kind of administrative bridge-building.

References

1. For a more extensive discussion of this development see Harry Eckstein, "A Perspective on Comparative Politics," in H. Eckstein and D. Apter, editors, *Comparative Politics: A Reader*, New York: The Free Press, 1965 and Raymond Platig, "International Relations as a Field of Inquiry," in J. N. Rosenau, editor, *International Politics and Foreign Policy*, New York: The Free Press, Revised Edition, 1969.
2. Platig, ibid., footnotes 2, 3, and 5.
3. Richard D. Lambert, *Language and Area Studies Review*, Philadelphia: Monograph 17 of The American Academy of Political and Social Science, October, 1973. I have drawn extensively upon the findings and discussions in this major study. Hereafter, it will be cited as *The Lambert Study*.
4. Compiled from data in Tables 3.44 (pp. 109–10); 4.2 (pp. 122–3) and 6.31 (p. 257) in *The Lambert Study*.
5. Lambert divided Asian Studies into the three sub-areas of South Asia, South East Asia and East Asia. The East Asian sub-area was by far the largest program with the South East Asian sub-area being the smallest. These three sub-areas have been aggregated by this author throughout the discussion in this section of the chapter.
6. Charles Maier, Conference Co-Chairman at the Opening Plenary Session, "Conference of Europeanists," Washington D. C., March 29–31, 1979.
7. Eckstein defines the configurative approach as ". . . the analysis of particular political systems, treated either explicitly or implicitly as unique entities." In Eckstein, op. cit., p. 11.
8. For a descriptive, general characterization of the discipline generalists in international relations, see James N. Rosenau, *International Studies and the Social Sciences: Problems, Priorities and Prospects in the United States*, Beverly Hills, California: Sage Publications, 1973. Rosenau's analysis is based on a survey of 101 leading generalists and 187 discipline generalists who responded to

Lambert's survey of area specialists. It is an interesting and useful study through which to compare the two groups of scholars.

9. *The Lambert Study*, Table 3.43, pp. 106-7.
10. Drawn up from data in Table 3.43, pp. 106-7. Ibid.
11. References to area studies courses are based on Lambert's data collected from 203 NDFL Area Programs. The general discussion of area program courses is found in ibid., Chapter III. I computed the distributions of coursework among both academic disciplines in general and the social sciences in particular drawing on data provided in Table 4.3, pp. 126-7. A comparison of the percentage distribution of area specialists and program coursework revealed only a few significant differences. The core academic disciplines were more predominant in the coursework distribution (61.8 percent) than in the specialists distribution (46.5 percent), while the social sciences were more proportionally significant among the specialists (39.7 percent) than in the coursework distribution (30.8 percent). Languages and Literature coursework represented a much larger proportion (30.2 percent) than the comparable proportion of specialists (14.1 percent); in fact, more important than the number of history courses. In terms of the distribution among world areas, there was no significant differences in the percentage distribution of coursework and area specialists, except that Eastern European history courses did not show as high a proportion as the Eastern European area specialists. The world area distribution of social science courses and area specialists were highly similar, showing only a 2-3 percent variation, except in Middle East area studies where political science area specialists were slightly higher (6.2 percent) than the coursework. Since the area specialists sample is much larger than the number of area programs on the basis of which the coursework distribution is based, it is considered the most reliable data and will, therefore, be given the heaviest emphasis in this analysis.
12. Ibid., p. 133.
13. This category comprises only the advanced language courses. The basic language skills courses (defined as the first three years of college level language courses) are excluded. If they had been included, language related coursework would have accounted for 50.8 percent of all area program courses used in the survey.
14. Lambert concluded that, ". . . Overall, one gets the impression that humanities equal historical." Ibid., p. 131.
15. Compiled from data in ibid., Table 3.44, pp. 109-10.
16. Ibid., p. 141.
17. Compiled from data in ibid., Tables 4.5, p. 132 and 4.13, p. 141.
18. Ibid., pp. 138-9.
19. Ibid., pp. 102-4.
20. Ibid., Tables 3.34 and 3.39 on pp. 100 and 102 respectively. Generally, while 21 percent of the area specialists expressed primary interest in several areas, only between 2 and 5 percent reported engaging in U.S.-based professional activity about pairs of regions. The exception was South East Asian specialists, 25.8 percent of whom also listed East Asian studies as part of their professional activities.
21. As Lambert observed, ". . . So, in reality, area studies on most campuses is a loose confederation of courses and professors with an occasional and not very heavily used interdisciplinary blueprint . . . It is the student who may be interdisciplinary in the sense that he can move cafeteria-like among the courses, all firmly rooted in one or another discipline." Ibid., p. 121.
22. An example of this is found in Kjell Goldmann's *Tension and Detente in Bipolar Europe*, Oslo: Universitetsforlaget, 1974. While this study is an excellent piece of social science research, it requires considerable advanced knowledge of European international politics and is, therefore, difficult to use as a text in a European regional course.

23. An important, related problem is that the acquisition of multi-theory and multi-methodological skills tend to be as time-consuming as acquiring area studies competence and the two often compete for the individual student's priorities.

24. The World Order approach to studies of international relations is consciously normative. Its general objectives are to examine existing conditions and situations, as well as "relevant utopias" and "preferred worlds", in order to propose actions which will minimize violence and maximize social and economic welfare, social and political justice, participation in public policy decision-making and ecological balance. Although world order studies are heavily influenced by the advocacy of "some increase in central guidance capacities at the global level," it is not dominated by dogmatism in the form of demanding the formation of a world government. In this context, the examination of regionalism in world politics is done for the purpose of establishing the degree to which it facilitates or hinders the achievement of the general objectives of the approach. See Richard A. Falk and Saul H. Mendlovitz, editors, *Regional Politics and World Order*, San Francisco: W. H. Freeman and Co., 1973, pp. 1–6. This volume is presented by the editors as an extension of their compilation of materials published in their four volume, *The Strategy of World Order*, New York: World Law Fund, 1966. For another interesting explication of regionalism theories, consult Ronald Yalem, *Regionalism and World Order*, Washington D.C.: Public Affairs Press, 1965. Also, Joseph S. Nye, Jr., editor, *International Regionalism: Readings*, Boston: Little, Brown and Co., 1968. Although this compilation of articles is generally concerned with various aspects of regionalism and world order, they are not as explicitly normative as the Falk and Memdlovitz collections.

25. Yalem's discussion of "the sociological approach" to regionalism is based on Bhoutros Ghali's theory. Ibid., pp. 18–20.

26. F. S. C. Northrop, *The Taming of the Nations: A Study of the Cultural Bases of International Policy*, New York: The Macmillan Company, 1953, pp. 277–95.

27. Basic literature on pan-regional ideologies include, 1) Samuel Guy Inman, *Problems in Pan-Americanism*, New York: George H. Doran and Co., 1925; 2) Denis de Rougemont, *The Idea of Europe*, New York: Macmillan and Company, 1966; 3) Sylvia Haim, *Arab Nationalism: An Anthology*, Berkeley, California: University of California Press, 1962; and 4) George Padmore, *Pan-Africanism: The Coming Struggle for Africa*, London: Dobson Books, 1956.

28. Consult Seyom Brown, *New Forces in World Politics*, Washington D.C.: The Brookings Institution, 1974; especially Chapter 9 and Werner Link and Werner J. Feld, editors, *The New Nationalism: Implications For Transatlantic Relations*, New York: Pergamon Press, 1979.

29. George Liska, *International Equilibrium*, Cambridge, Massachusetts: Harvard University Press, 1957.

30. Bruce Russett reported that membership in regional international institutions was one of the most important factors in delineating regions. See his study, *International Regions and the International System: A Study in Political Ecology*, Chicago: Rand McNally and Co., 1967. Joseph S. Nye showed in his study, that 100 of the 183 intergovernmental type of international institutions were regional. About three quarters of the regional institutions were established since the end of World War II and a majority of them were formed to increase socio-economic cooperation. See his study, *Peace in Parts: Integration and Conflict in Regional Organization*, Boston: Little, Brown and Co., 1971.

31. Examples are Ruth C. Lawson, editor, *International Regional Organizations: Constitutional Foundations*, New York: Praeger Publishers, 1962, and A. H. Robertson, *European Institutions: Cooperation: Integration: Unification*, London: Stevens, Third Edition, 1972.

32. See Joseph S. Nye, "Regional Institutions" in Falk and Mendlovitz, op. cit., and Lynn H. Miller, Regional Organizations and Subordinate Systems," in Louis

J. Cantori and Steven L. Spiegel, editors, *The International Politics of Regions: A Comparative Approach*, Englewood Cliffs, New Jersey, Prentice-Hall, Inc., 1970.

33. Inis L. Claude, "The OAS, the UN, and the United States," *International Conciliation*, No. 547 (March, 1964).

34. Linda B. Miller, "Regional Organization and the Regulation of Internal Conflict," *World Politics*, XIX, No. 4 (July, 1967); Lynn H. Miller, "The Prospects for Order Through Regional Security," in Falk and Mendlovitz, op. cit.; Joseph S. Nye, *Peace in Parts*, op. cit., Chapter 5, "Controlling Conflicts: The OAS, Oau, Arab League," pp. 129-72.

35. Nye, ibid., p. 182.

36. See the chapter by Paul Taylor in this book and Leon N. Lindberg and Stuart A. Scheingold, editors, *Regional Integration: Theory and Research*, Cambridge, Massachusetts: Harvard University Press, 1971; Reginald Harrison, *Europe in Question: Theories of Regional Integration*. Paul Taylor and A. J. R. Groom, editors, *International Organization: A Conceptual Approach*, London: Frances Pinter Ltd., 1978.

37. See Paul Taylor's Chapter "A Conceptual Typology of International Organization," for a detailed discussion of this distinction between cooperation and integration in Taylor and Groom, ibid.

38. Examples are Karl W. Deutsch *et al., The Political Community and the North Atlantic Area*, Princeton, New Jersey: Princeton University Press, 1957; Ernst B. Haas, *The Uniting of Europe*, Stanford, California: Stanford University Press, 1958; Leon N. Lindberg, *The Political Dynamics of European Economic Integration*, Stanford, California: Stanford University Press, 1963.

39. Ernst B. Haas and Philippe C. Schmitter, "Economics and Differential Patterns of Political Integration: Projections About Unity in Latin America," *International Organization*, XVIII (Autumn, 1964); J. S. Nye, "Central American Regional Integration," *International Conciliation*, No. 562 (March, 1967); J. S. Nye, "Patterns and Catalysts in Regional Integration," *International Organization*, XIX, No. 4 (Autumn, 1965) and Andrzei Korbonski, "The Evolution of COMECON," *International Conciliation*, No. 549 (September, 1964).

40. J. S. Nye, "Comparative Regional Integration: Concept and Measurement," *International Organization*, XXII, No. 4 (Autumn, 1968) and *Peace in Parts*, op. cit., Chapters 2 and 3.

41. Ernst B. Haas, *The Obsolescence of Regional Integration Theory*, Berkeley, California: Institute of International Studies, U.C. Berkeley Research Series No. 25, 1975 and his "Turbulent Fields and the Theory of Regional Integration," *International Organization*, XXX, No. 2 (Spring, 1976).

42. Alternative conceptual frameworks for the neo-functional pre-theory have been suggested by Paul Taylor, "The Politics of the European Communities: The Confederal Phase," *World Politics*, Vol. 27, No. 3 (April, 1975) and Gunnar P. Nielsson, "The Parallel National Action Process: Scandinavian Experiences," in Taylor and Groom, op. cit.

43. Roger D. Masters, "A Multi-Bloc Model of the International System," *American Political Science Review*, LV (December, 1961).

44. Morton Kaplan, *System and Process in International Politics*, New York: John Wiley, 1957.

45. "Special Issue on International Subsystems," *International Studies Quarterly*, Vol. 13, No. 4 (December, 1969).

46. Peter Berton, "International Subsystems — A Submacro Approach to International Studies," in ibid.

47. Michael Banks, "Systems Analysis and the Study of Regions," in ibid.

48. S. J. Cantori and Steven L. Spiegel, "International Regions: A Comparative Approach to Five Subordinate Systems," J. H. Siegler, "News Flows in the North

African International Subsystem," T. W. Robinson, "Systems Theory and the Communist System" and D. C. Hellmann, "The Emergence of an East Asian International Subsystem," all in ibid.

49. Karl Kaiser, "The Interaction of Regional Subsystems," *World Politics*, Vol. 20, No. 1 (October, 1968).

50. Oran Young, "Political Discontinuities in the International System," *World Politics*, Vol. 19, No. 3 (April, 1968).

51. Leonard Binder, "The Middle East as a Subordinate International System," *World Politics*, Vol. 10, No. 3 (April, 1958). George Modelski, "International Relations and Area Studies: The Case of South-East Asia," *International Relations*, Vol. 2 (April, 1961). Michael Brecher, "International Relations and Asian Studies: The Subordinate State System of Southern Asia," *World Politics*, Vol. 15, No. 2 (January, 1963). William Zartman, "Africa as a Subordinate System in International Relations," *International Organization*, Vol. 21, No. 3 (Summer, 1967).

52. In Binder's words, ". . . Middle Eastern patterns are relatively independent of the 'rules' regulating the dominant bipolar system," in ibid., p. 429.

53. William R. Thompson, "The Regional Subsystem: A Conceptual Explication and a Propositional Inventory," *International Studies Quarterly*, Vol. 17, No. 1 (March, 1973).

54. Ibid., p. 95.

55. Ibid., p. 101.

56. Bruce Russett, op. cit.

57. Among the most severe critics of this study, see Oran Young, "Professor Russett: Industrious Tailor to a Naked Emperor," *World Politics*, Vol. 21, No. 3 (April, 1969). By now, there seems to be greater awareness of Young's critique than familiarity with Russett's study.

58. This discussion is based on both their book, *The International Politics of Regions: A Comparative Approach*, Englewood Cliffs, New Jersey, Prentice-Hall, 1970 and their subsequent article entitled, "The Analysis of Regional International Politics: The Integration Versus the Empirical Systems Approach," *International Organization*, Vol. 27, No. 4 (Autumn, 1973).

59. Cantory and Spiegel book, ibid., p. 3.

60. Ibid., p. 1.

61. Ibid., pp. 6–7.

62. Ibid., summarized from pp. 5–6.

63. Ibid., pp. 20–2.

64. Ibid., pp. 387–9.

65. The Cantori and Spiegel approach has not become an acceptable starting point for methodological developments, but it has been used as a general analytical guideline for separate, but parallel descriptions and analyses of seven regional subsystems in the recently published introductory text edited by J. N. Rosenau, K. W. Thompson and G. Boyd, *World Politics: An Introduction*, New York: The Free Press, 1976. While the concepts of core and periphery sectors are applied as useful organizational vehicles for some of the authors, the analysis of Latin American international politics is conducted without such a structural differentiation and the discussion of the African subsystem is based on the general observation that the core, periphery differentiation is inapplicable. For all of the authors, however, the selection of core and periphery sector state members is based on the same structurally predetermined approach used by Cantori and Spiegel.

66. W. R. Thompson, op. cit.

PART II

TEACHING INTERNATIONAL RELATIONS
TO MID-CAREER STUDENTS

CHAPTER 8

The Teaching of International Relations:
A Note on the Curriculum

Randolph Kent

It will not come as a surprise to anyone who has read the first part of this work that one of the major difficulties in teaching international relations is merely choosing what to teach from the multitude of approaches and analytic levels which comprise the discipline. When the program's faculty first began to consider recording their experiences in mid-career education, one member complained that the undertaking was not only pretentious (since university lecturers were for the most part "pedagogically untutored") but the project was engendering a false divide by suggesting that what we teach mid-career graduate students is different from what we teach normal graduate students. "There is a discipline called international relations," maintained the reluctant project participant, "and I teach to whomever will listen."

As Part II makes readily apparent, what and how the faculty have chosen to teach are very much admixtures of their field interests and their sensitivities to the types of students they are teaching. While this, too, will not come to the reader as a blinding revelation, what is of interest is to see in the subsequent faculty contributions how and in what ways the inter-active process between teacher and student has influenced the selection and presentation of materials.

In this same way it is also interesting to note how the very curriculum, itself, has been adapted to the particular types of needs and demands of the program's mid-career clientele. Or, alternatively, it is also interesting to note how, despite the variety of difficulties which mid-career students face in undertaking a part-time degree program, the curriculum has been able to remain stringent and demanding and relatively coherent.

There is no doubt that when the program was first established the director and faculty assumed that for all intents and purposes a "graduate

143

program is a graduate program." The reality is, however, that a mid-career, part-time graduate program is not comparable in several fundamental ways to a full-time "conventional" graduate program catering to students in their early 20s; that indeed not only is there a difference but there also *has to be* a difference.

Furthermore, adjusting the curriculum to meet that "difference" has been a problem compounded by rapid change within the discipline of international relations. Hence, as the reader reflects upon these few thoughts on the curriculum and upon the contributions concerning teaching of fields within the discipline, it is important to bear in mind that two significant and distinct elements shape the overall approach of the mid-career program, viz., the demands and needs of a particular clientele, and the rapid evolution of the discipline. As the reader will soon be reminded, on more than one occasion the former and the latter are "diametrically opposed," or, at least too often will one find that the attempt to satisfy the demands and needs of mid-career students has not always been enhanced by the twisting and turning routes of the academic study of international relations.

In the most basic sense, the structure of USC's United Kingdom Graduate Program is probably similar to most master's degree by examination programs. In other words, to complete the degree, a student must undertake eight courses, each course being worth four credits. Generally speaking, a four credit course consists of sixteen, three hour sessions. Upon completing the eight courses, a student must take "comprehensive examinations" which consist of a four hour written portion and approximately a one hour oral portion. Of the eight courses, four are required and four are electives, but the reasons for both types of courses will be discussed below.

The curriculum: its evolution and purpose

In retrospect, one probably has to admit — but with no sense of embarrassment -- that what we as a faculty had learned about mid-career education became clearer and gained coherence at those times when outside pressures forced us to justify what we were doing. This is not to say that our thoughts on mid-career education had not matured quite steadily over time, but rather to suggest that the "stages" we had reached were rarely recognised even by ourselves until we, as a faculty, found ourselves defending our goals and approaches against those unfamiliar with the requirements of mid-career education. A case in point occurred at the end of the 1960s when upheavals throughout US universities and colleges brought

144

demands for greater students participation in developing curricula. One of the results at USC's School of International Relations in Los Angeles was the abandonment of required courses and comprehensive examinations. However, we in the English program felt strongly that not only should requirements be maintained but that comprehensive examinations should remain a standard part of the curriculum. Without required courses, at least from our perspective, we would lose the tool with which we established an "academic common denominator" in an academically heterogeneous group, and comprehensive examinations forced students, subjected to the disadvantages of disjointed, part-time studies, to put "the whole" into perspective.

While what we were learning might only have been articulated during such times of crisis, we in fact were learning, experimenting, planning and rethinking for a considerable amount of time between crises. The not infrequent changes in the program's curriculum, the amount of "fine tuning" of required courses were all evidence of this.

Reflecting upon these alternatives and adjustments of the curriculum over the past thirteen years leads us to suggest that there were probably five main "problem areas" — areas that spelled the difference between mid-career and conventional graduate education — which stimulated our experimentation and approaches.

(1) *Conceptual Rigidity* — Perhaps it there is any single theme upon which subsequent contributors focus most consistently in Part II of this work it is the means of overcoming our students' "conceptual rigidity." The term would seem to suggest an acute degree of intellectual oscification, but that generally is not what the contributors are saying. Conceptual rigidity might best be understood by describing three causes of its manifestation. The first might be regarded as a function of "age", where the student appears to lack the desire or willingness to flow with relative ease from one sort of analytical framework to another. The student works well within a fixed set of assumptions — probably the same set of assumptions with which he entered the program — but finds it difficult to move out of that one "paradigm." That this is viewed principally as a function of age is an impressionistic statement, reflecting most of the faculty's opinion that, when compared with conventional graduate students, mid-career students are far more reluctant to "think in different ways."

A second aspect of conceptual rigidity derives from "experience". It is perhaps obvious in the extreme, but it bears repeating that the accumulated life and work experience of a mid-career student represents one of the most interesting and frustrating facets of mid-career education.

Experience, on the one hand, forces the lecturer to contend with reality, to demonstrate the applicability of his theme to someone with considerable understanding of a certain view of the world. On the other hand, the experience factor can also be extremely frustrating when instructors are confronted with student "logic", "proof," and "analysis" based upon the anecdotal.

Conceptual rigidity also arises out of the prospective student's perception of the program's purpose. Mid-career students, as several contributors point out in subsequent chapters, frequently undertake the program because they feel that it will either make them better at the jobs they are doing or will prepare them for different jobs they hope to be doing. In either case, there is a sense of "practicality" which predominates, or, if that is too extreme, a sense of "knowing what one wants to know." It is relatively rare that the teacher in our sort of program finds himself with students who initially feel unsure about the general parameters, if not the very subject matter, of courses they are entering. To the same extent, this does not seem to be the case with more conventional graduate students, and, in part, it is this functional orientation of our kind of mid-career student, knowing what they want to know, which to a certain extent explains why there is an unwillingness to be conceptually more flexible and why the program can be a great disappointment, a great shock or both.

(2) *Academic Diversity* — A second problem area affecting the development of our curriculum is one which strikes at the very core of mid-career education, namely, what we call "academic diversity." By academic diversity, we mean the extraordinarily heterogeneous mix of undergraduate disciplines and academic institutions which an average class in our program represents. Because of the amount of nationalities we attract, our student-body is probably more heterogeneous than those of most similar mid-career programs; nevertheless the fact remains, more often than not, that the very nature of mid-career education requires that one contend with academic diversity as a substantial factor in curriculum design.

Mid-career students not only have a relatively pragmatic approach to education, but also frequently see such educational opportunities as part of a "change of life," as part of a chance to begin a new career. It is perhaps a self-imposed distinction that we make, yet we feel justified in suggesting that, where the normal graduate student is assumed to have at least an "undergraduate level" of knowledge about the graduate subject upon which he or she is embarking, the mid-career student — at least in the humanities or social sciences — should not be considered by that basic criterion. For the latter, "life experience" — no matter how amorphous or difficult to define such jargon might be — can in several respects compensate for the lack of relevant academic background. This appears to us readily apparent from our experience of teaching "international relations to international practitioners."

Having said this, however, the very division of this book — the divide between Part I and Part II — should quite clearly indicate that one cannot blithely assume that "life experience" will give a student a grounding in the fundamentals of the discipline. One needs to generate a certain "common denominator" of knowledge, a certain basic level which will enable instructors to cover materials of a graduate standard. Hence, within the confines of an eight course graduate program, we find ourselves "cramming in" not only a graduate degree program, but also a level of "remedial work" to set the stage for graduate work.

(3) *The Problem of Analysis* — The third problem area ironically is perhaps the most familiar to most academics and yet not frequently mentioned in Part II; that problem is the need to emphasize the art of *analysis*. It probably serves little purpose to make a distinction between mid-career and normal graduate students here; teachers always complain that their students, on whatever level, do not know how to analyse, and anyway analytical capability is a bit like virtue: one never is really sure what the right level is.

Having said this, the need to inculcate in our students the basic tools of analysis has been an important feature of our curriculum design. Students, who in many instances are extremely sophisticated and worldly, see education as a process where information is imbibed, and less as a process where the conventional is challenged, where "facts", themselves, are to be tested and retested. The exercise of being forced "to define your terms," to trace the steps taken to arrive at "your conclusion" and to take a conclusion and "now change your assumptions" is often an extremely trying experience for our kind of student. Maybe a student has not done "this kind of thing" for well over a decade; on too many occasions, students may never have been forced to go through this sort of experience as undergraduates. Nevertheless the different conceptual approaches to which students are exposed demand, not rote learning, but an ability to expose basic assumptions, to strip arguments to their very essence — perhaps the very stuff of what we academics should be able to offer.

(4) *Retooling for Research* — Clearly related to this concern for developing

or revitalizing analytical capabilities is the program's concern for research. Every graduate program in the social sciences should force students to "get their hands dirty" in research, not because of the end product *per se*, but rather for the insights which it gives about the way social science data and evidence are compiled. And yet a fourth problem area in designing the curriculum has been that research, from methodological and analytical points of view, is too often a lost art for many students. For students from Third and Fourth World countries, research is too often a totally unaccustomed art. Furthermore the concept of research is more often than not regarded by our students as epitomizing the kind of academic art solely of use to academics or those who aspire to that calling. It is not a practical undertaking; it is not "learning" in the sense that a mid-career student very often means when he or she joins the program.

However, we see research as being very much part of the "learning process." Besides providing insights into the process of the accumulation of data and evidence, research — if controlled properly — forces the student to make conceptual as well as methodological assumptions *explicit*. And it is this process of exposing, challenging, testing basic assumptions which perhaps lies at the base of mid-career education.

(5) *A Concept of Relevance* — The last problem area to which we have been sensitive in devising our mid-career curriculum has been that of "relevance." Relevance is a term frequently used and too infrequently well defined. To our students the term suggests immediate and practical utility of the subject matter to professional interests; to us, the term means how the presentation of the subject matter can relate to our students' perceptions and experiences. In this latter sense, relevance is less concerned with practicality and more concerned with the need to establish a "linkage" between "their world" and "ours." Given the importance in mid-career education of establishing such a linkage or bridge, it is disappointing to reflect how little success we have had in spanning the two worlds. We have frequently discussed the problem at length, but the result has been generally that students have been expected more often than not to wend their way to our world, rather than we to theirs or at least meeting at some compatible half-way point. However, most instructors, as will become clear in Part II, have individually experimented with ways to bridge the gap.

These five problem areas, which have affected in a significant way our general approach to the curriculum, are addressed in one form or another throughout the majority of contributions found in Part II of this work. However, before embarking upon these contributions, the reader may find

148

it useful to get some sense of how a student progresses through the program, both in terms of course sequencing and course requirements. The table below lists the types of courses — requirements and electives — offered during three phases of the program: phase one, 1969--1975; phase two, 1975-1977; phase three, 1977-1979. The lists of electives are not intended to be complete, but rather to indicate changing emphases in the curriculum.

TABLE 1

Requirements	Electives
Phase One: 1969-1975	
Theory and Methodology	Soviet Foreign Policy
Advanced Studies in International Politics	Diplomatic Issues of the Middle East and North Africa
Strategy and Arms Control	International Economic Relations
International Organization	Contemporary International Relations in Europe
U.S. Foreign Policy	Diplomatic Issues of Southeast Asia
Phase Two: 1975-1977	
Theory and Methodology	Domestic Determinants of US Foreign Policy
Advanced Studies in International Politics	Contemporary International Relations in Europe
Strategy and Arms Control	Diplomatic Issues of Africa
International Organization	Multinational Corporations in World Politics
	Science, Technology and Politics
Phase Three: 1977-1979	
Theory and Methodology	Money in the World Economy
Issues and Approaches to International Relations Methodology	International Relations of China and Japan
Processes of Conflict and Cooperation	Diplomatic Issues of the Asian Sub-continent
Research Project Course	International Security Affairs
	Aid, Trade and Development

"Sequencing", or the order in which electives and required courses are introduced, is a quite telling factor about mid-career education. In a simple sense it concerns the way a student begins the program, and even more basically whether that student begins with the required survey course on international relations theory or an elective. This very basic and seemingly trivial point, however, emphasizes the need for the academic administrator to be sensitive to the intellectual expectations and

149

capabilities of the mid-career student. A student, no longer used to the ambiguities of theoretical considerations and unused to toiling in the world of abstractions, might find a survey course on international relations theory disconcerting, a shock which could well undermine the student's morale. Frequently after a lengthy interview with a prospective student, the program director will recommend that the student begin with an elective (for example, Soviet Foreign Policy; Multinational Corporations in World Politics) to at least ease the academic immersion by giving the student something he or she will "recognize," something which is tangible.

Alternatively, after the interview, the director might feel that a student is in fact able to begin with a highly abstract overview course such as international relations theory. However, whatever the particular start, the important factor to emphasize from our experience is the need to have a curriculum sufficiently flexible to allow for different "starting speeds" without altering the standards of the eventual finishing point.

With few exceptions, our part-time, mid-career students begin with one course and end with one course. In general, the majority of students find themselves "doubling up," viz. taking two courses in at least one and more likely two semesters during their pursuit of the degree. No matter how a student's course program is organised, there are certain sequencing patterns that must be followed. A student must take the basic theory and methodology course, as described by Richard Little in Chapter Nine, no later than the third course in the program. While we do not feel that a student has to begin with the basic theory course, we do feel that we, as a faculty, should have the opportunity to assess a student's performance in such a crucial course before we recommend that the student be allowed to continue the degree program.* No other required source can be taken without this basic survey having been completed. Therefore, for example, the advanced methodology course, described by Christopher Mitchell in Chapter Ten, may be taken by a student only after the survey course.

For most of the program's history, aspects of conflict and cooperation in international relations have been separated into two distinct headings under the titles of Strategy and Arms Control and International Organization, as discussed by John Groom and Paul Taylor respectively in Chapters Eleven and Twelve. However, as John Groom has pointed out in his chapter, we are now experimenting with a course designed to probe the "commonalities" of conflict and cooperation, and have, therefore, merged

---

*A student is "screened" after he or she has completed three courses, or, in other words, his or her coursework is assessed by the Core Faculty to see whether the candidate should be allowed to continue the degree program. More often than not the screening process affords the faculty an opportunity to make recommendations to the student about ways the student's work might be improved.

the essential elements of the two required courses into one, called *Processes of Conflict and Cooperation.*

The reasons for this merger are two-fold. In the first place the intention of the strategy course and the international organization course was not to develop specialists in either area, but rather to provide students with insights into sources of conflict and cooperation. These are "lessons" applicable to all aspects of international relations, whether one is involved in aspects of international political economy or military strategy. Conflict and cooperation are closely related concepts, and the desire to explore these concepts and to stress their inter-relationship led to the merger.

A second reason is the need to limit the amount of required courses that students must take. While a good proportion of the student-body feels that even to have four required courses out of eight is too much, the faculty has consistently felt that four is a maximum only becuase of the need to satisfy the diverse reasons and interests which have prompted students to join the program. Hence, by merging two required courses into one tightly constructed unit which gets to the essential messages of both strategy and international organization, we also have "extra room" to deal with another problem that has become increasingly evident in the program.

It has become more and more apparent that the program required what has been provisionally labeled a "research project course." Mitchell in his assessment of teaching methodology has mentioned the difficulty of getting students "to get their hands dirty" in research, and particularly in research that it not derived from the traditional, single case study approach. The reasons for this stem from students' lack of backgrounds in anything but historical methods to the simple fact that to students it appears "easier" to do a research paper based upon a single historical incident than to go through the efforts of alternative studies with methodologies they only partially understand.

Therefore, the new fourth requirement, which can only be taken after the theory course and the methodology course, has three purposes. One purpose is to force students, in undertaking a research project of their own choosing, to make the theories and methodologies they use *explicit.* This sort of precision allows our students to experience the important point raised in their study of the philosophy of science that we all work from theories supported by proofs that are intrinsically linked to particular paradigmatic assumptions. Another reason for introducing a research project course is that students are forced to bridge the gap between theoretical and methodological considerations and their own conceptions of reality, the latter generaly reflected in students' choices of research topics. Lastly, the research project has been designed to afford a student

151

time to concentrate solely upon his or her project. The substance of the course is a sharing of research experiences that each student uncovers as research projects pass various stages towards completion. This sharing of experiences is important for students who, in the academic sense, are unfamiliar or have forgotten what research entails, who by the nature of their part-time status have a limited amount of time to do research; and who are generally being challenged to undertake methodologies with which they are unfamiliar.

The results of this new requirement unfortunately cannot be incorporated into Mitchell's subsequent chapter since this book will be in the press before the results of the first research project course can be assessed. However, to a significant extent, the very frustrations and problems to which Mitchell alludes have spurred on this attempt to have the lessons of theory and methodology impact upon students' research.

Elective courses, those that are not deemed to be requirements for the purposes of attaining the master's degree, also are fraught with various complications. For example, whether one is referring to courses involving international political economy or foreign policy analysis or regional area studies, there is an obligation to relate such electives to the substance of the required courses. This is not particularly easy when one considers the amount of "idiographic" or specialized knowledge which most electives have to cover and the nature of interests and education which most instructors who deal in such electives bring to their subjects. Either there is little time to devote to relating an elective to the core subjects and still do justice to the former, or there is little inclination or incentive for the instructor to take his well honed specialization into areas he or she might regard as alien or irrelevant to a particular expertise.

Furthermore, where one might more readily assume that students approach the core courses with an equal degree of "ignorance," that same assumption can by no means hold for elective courses. With our type of student, one must bear in mind that within any group there may well be individuals with more than a highly developed degree of sophistication in any particular elective, e.g. international issues in a region, or aspects of political economy. Therefore, it is often very difficult to find the right level to pitch an elective.

Given such problems, the chapters which follow by Harrod, Kent and Nielsson reflect various attempts in different types of electives to integrate what might be regarded as genotypic and phenotypic knowledge and to cope with the unevenness of students' backgrounds and levels of knowledge. The reader must bear in mind that the issue of integrating electives with what we have termed core courses is by no means a problem

152

unique to our type of program. What perhaps makes us more sensitive to the problem are the demands of our clientele who are quick to point out not only the divide between the real and the academic worlds but also between academics within the academic world. However, the point, here, is not to suggest creating a "gestalt" where there is not one, or imposing integration where differing levels of analysis would make such an exercise intellectually untenable. The real issue in integrating the core courses with electives is two-fold: in the first place, to show that aspects of theory and methodology can have utility when it comes to analyzing subjects of an idiographic or configurationalist nature, and in the second place, to emphasize that even the most sophisticated political analyses rests too often upon basic assumptions which are insufficiently challenged.

Upon completing the four core courses and four electives, a student is then eligible to take the comprehensive examinations. The written portion of these examinations require the student to answer five questions in four hours: two questions from the theory and methodology section, one question from the Processes of Cooperation section, one question from a section entitled Processes of Conflict,* and the final question from the Applied Theory section.†

Like so much of the program, the comprehensive examinations are designed to emphasize integration of course material, analytically consistent development of concepts, and application of the theoretical with "real world" material. Hence, generally speaking, comprehensive questions are broad-based, forcing the student to establish the parameters in which he or she wants to address a particular question, leaving the student to weave together the relevant and appropriate theoretical and methodological strands, and certainly leaving the student to structure his or her answer in an analytically consistent way. The Applied Theory section, in which a student is expected to answer one of a set of theoretically-based questions in terms of his or her elective, to a significant extent reflects our continuing concern with giving to our students some sense of what earlier we defined as "practicality." In other words, by asking for example, "what

*The two sections, Processes of Conflict and Processes of Cooperation, had originally been Strategy and Arms Control and International Organization. The reasons that the name of the sections had been changed are the same as those for changing the courses, reasons discussed earlier in this introduction.

†It is a reflection of the changing nature of the program as well as of the discipline that thirteen years ago, the final section of the "Comps" involved U.S. Foreign policy. In the mid-70s, this section concerned either the foreign policy of the U.S. and/or the states of Europe. Now in the late 1970s, this last section asks a student to answer one of a set of theory based questions using material from any elective course to provide examples. This again reflects our desire to make bridges between perceived reality and the world of theory.

relevance conflict analysis might have upon a particular aspect of your chosen elective," a student has an opportunity to consider the relevance of a body or theoretical and methodological literature in terms of a particular region, e.g. the Middle East, or an issue area, e.g. law of the sea, and so on.

The oral portion of the comprehensive examination is the "final check." Occurring normally one week after the written exam, the "orals" allow examiners to clear up any "misunderstandings" that might have arisen in the written examination, and also provide an opportunity for examiners to discuss the discipline of international relations with the candidate "as someone who is about to be awarded a master's degree in the discipline."

It is rare that the oral portion of the comprehensives really demonstrate the calibre of students, for no matter how senior the individual may be in his or her profession, there is only too often a demonstrable inability to articulate and communicate ideas effectively. In part this may well be the fault of the program. Students may not receive sufficient time to participate in class, becasue their uneven academic backgrounds force lecturers to emphasise lectures at the expense of a true seminar format. It also could be the "fault" of students who, as older students, are embarrassed or unnerved by exposing themselves to the give-and-take of an academic discussion, and hence come to the "orals" unpracticed in the art of discussing a discipline in which they do not feel like experts but merely advanced students.

In reflecting upon the totality of our attempts to teach international relations to mid-career, part-time students, perhaps the key to the "education process" is that of generating a "trauma." It is our view and has been our experience that the most effective learning process for mid-career students has involved building up a kind of trauma leading to experiences of sudden "breakthroughs." The process demands both repetition and a consistent challenging process in which the student is asked to argue his experience and his perception of events through alternative analytical approaches. The "breakthroughs" are of different types and happen at different times. A breakthrough might mean that, while a student sees the significance of alternative approaches strictly as of academic interest, he or she still experiences the "wholeness" and the inter-relationships of various theoretical approaches. The student can move "horizontally" and "vertically" in the world of systems, structural violence, integration theory, decision-making theory and so on, without needing to categorize in terms of what should have been learned in a particular course. Or, a breakthrough might mean a fundamental change in an individual's own perception and explanation of events and of the world. This is much rarer with our kind of student. More often than not such fundamental changes in attitudes usually go hand in hand with a turning point in an individual's life, e.g. retirement, change of career.

The breakthroughs occur also at different times, and there is not necessarily a correlation between previous training in the discipline and conceptual breakthroughs. They occur, but when — just before the comprehensive examinations . . . or just after, or after the second or third or seventh course — is generally unpredictable. Nevertheless we do believe that the creation of trauma leading to breakthroughs is in part a result of the repetition and insistence upon conceptualization which mark our approach to the educational process.

CHAPTER 9

A Paradigmatic Approach to Teaching International Relations to Mid-Career Students

Richard Little

Although there have always been mentors ready and anxious to teach princes the art of diplomacy – Kautilya and Machiavelli spring readily to mind and no doubt their peers stretch back to the dawn of man's history – the art of teaching international relations in institutions of higher education by more unassuming teachers to less elevated audiences has a much more recent history, dating from the end of the First World War.

From the inception of international relations as an independent discipline, however, there have always been very real reservations about the nature of the subject and the possibility of teaching it effectively. The easy self-confidence displayed by the mentors of princes about their own knowledge and understanding of world politics was not, unfortunately, passed on. Contemporary advocates of the discipline have been beset by a sense of insecurity about the status of international relations as an academic discipline. In the mid-fifties, for example, Harold Sprout, a major force in the development of the subject, commented on doubts about the "inherent pedagogic virtue of the discipline"; (1) and even in the early 1970s, William Fox could still identify a sense of "inferiority" among international relations teachers when their discipline compared with other social sciences. (2)

Despite these doubts expressed by members of the discipline, there has, nevertheless, been a growing interest in international relations. Nowhere has this interest been more firmly represented than amongst mid-career students. With the growth of global interdependence, an increasing number of individuals are finding that their work takes them to foreign parts. Frequently, this contact can sensitise individuals to the importance of international relations and it is, therefore, hardly surprising, that the

156

academic study of international relations proves an attractive option to many who, in their mid-careers, decide to pursue further academic studies.

In general, mid-career students have a practical orientation towards study. They are not interested in "knowledge for the sake of knowledge". The basic desire is to be given a "box of tools", concepts, in more formal language, which can be taken away and used to analyse the world. Students want to know "what is going on out there".

In the past, for a variety of reasons, not the least of which was the underlying sense of insecurity within the discipline, there was a strong desire on the part of teachers in international relations to satisfy this desire for tools which could be applied to the analysis of world events. But it is possible to raise considerable doubts about the desirability of supplying a student, particularly a mid-career student, with such a box of tools. It can be argued that such an approach not only fails to acquaint the student with some of the very real conflicts which can be found within the discipline, but it also reinforces a positivistic belief, already prevalent amongst many students, that there is a "correct" view of the world which can be identified using the right techniques. In this chapter I want to argue first that mid-career students are very prone to examine the world on the basis of a particular perspective or paradigm. I then want to examine the reasons why the study of international relations has in the past often encouraged this tendency. Finally, I want to argue that this tendency results in a distorted view of both the discipline and the world of social reality. As a consequence, it is important to develop a multi-paradigmatic approach to teaching international relations to mid-career students.

The mid-career student

Although it is impossible to provide a profile of a mid-career student which will encompass every student that falls into this category, nevertheless, it is fairly safe to suggest that most mid-career students work in large complex bureaucracies which have world-wide connections. The bureaucracy may be a bank, a branch of the military, an embassy or a multinational corporation. In all these cases, the mid-career student, by operating in these institutions, has acquired professional experience and is normally only too familiar with organisational problems which stem from size and complexity. The mid-career student, therefore, has a wide range of experience which is not normally possessed by the graduate student who has not yet taken up a profession. As a consequence, in contrast at least to some graduates, the mid-career student rarely believes that there are any easy answers to the problems thrown up by international relations.

It is obviously important for any teacher to endeavour to tap the range of experience possessed by a group of mid-career students. But at the same time, it needs to be recognised that past experience may, in fact, pose problems for the students. Harold Sprout, for example, has observed that for anyone coming to the discipline of international relations, having achieved professional competence in another area, there are "two sets of prison walls" over which the individual must endeavour to escape: "that of his own basic intellectual training or discipline and that of his national culture." (3) It is not difficult to see how both of these walls may encircle the mid-career student. Those from the military, for example, are often orientated towards security and they tend to subsume international relations under this heading, whereas students from the business world can often find the issues of security somewhat remote and they are much more familiar with ideas associated with interdependence and transnationalism. However, divergent orientations of this kind can be fairly readily accommodated. Much more difficult are the problems raised by the student with an engineering background who objects to the "pseudo-scientific" approach to the analysis of international relations, or the student with a background in the arts or languages, who longs for an historical approach to the discipline and objects to the preoccupation with abstract concepts. If such students refuse to move outside of the framework imposed by their original intellectual training, it can prove extremely difficult for them to advance their understanding of international relations.

Sprout's second prison wall, associated with national ethnocentrism, however, can prove even more difficult to contend with because its manifestations may be less overt. Much of our understanding of the world comes, in fact, not from formal education, but from an informal process of practical experience. Morgenthau has observed that:

> It is an obvious fact of experience that professional education is only one – and not necessarily the most important – among several factors that mold the mind and character of those to be educated. Family, society, the experiences of life itself are more persistent and authoritative teachers than the schools. Education to be effective must be organically tuned to the totality.

Morgenthau goes on to argue that his own views on international relations were accepted after the Second World War, therefore, not because of the force of his arguments, or the quality of his teaching. Rather it was that events in the real world had rendered individuals amenable to accepting his ideas. He puts it like this:

> The organic relationship between professional education and the totality of education experience is strikingly revealed in the field of political education. The measure of success that education in world affairs has had in the United States in recent years is primarily due not to the quality and quantity of its professional educators but to the experiences that the American people have undergone during and after the Second World War and to their interpretation by political leaders. What is being taught today in American colleges, say about the balance of power, to be accepted almost as a matter of course, was taught, however sporadically, thirty and twenty years ago, only to be dismissed as absurd. It is not professional education that has made political understanding in this respect possible. Rather it is political experience that has made the truth plausible. Professional education has proved the validity of political experience through historic example and analytic demonstration. (4)

In this instance, political experience coincided with an academic perspective, but Morgenthau was in little doubt that this was no more than a happy coincidence. He did not believe that political experience would always operate in this fashion. On the contrary, he believed that the task of the teacher of international relations was to "correct" for the biases normally absorbed through political experience. According to Morgenthau, political science:

> must adapt its emphasis to the ever changing circumstances of the times. When the times tend to depreciate the element of power, it must stress its importance. When the times incline toward a monistic conception of power in the general scheme of things, it must show its limitations . . . When the reality of power is being lost sight of over its moral and legal limitations, it must point to that reality. When law and morality are judged as nothing, it must assign them their rightful place. (5)

Morgenthau, however, is pessimistic about how far any teacher can extend the student's view of reality beyond the ethnocentric views which prevail within society. In line with Mannheim, he argues that everyone's thinking is circumscribed by the views of society and that as a consequence, the "mind of the political scientist is molded by the society which he observes". (6) Everyone's view of reality, therefore, is inevitably going to be blinkered and the individual can only hope to search for truth

159

in the area permitted by societal blinkers. But even within these limits, argues Morgenthau, in attempting to reveal this limited or partial truth there will be strong objections from society. The position and influence of the social scientists within society, therefore, will be strongly determined by his or her willingness to provide an academic justification for the prevailing view of society. Needless to say, Morgenthau strongly advocates the necessity for the academic to retain an independence of judgment.

Although some social scientists continue to insist, as does Morgenthau, that we are inevitably trapped into looking at the world in terms of a prevailing societal viewpoint, there seem to be good reasons for denying that our views are necessarily moulded by society. If this belief *were* true, then no one would know that his or her views were being moulded and it would be impossible to make, or certainly verify, the claim.

Nevertheless, as I shall show in the next section, although societal views can have a powerful effect on the orientation of a discipline, there is a lot of difference between the idea that there may be a prevailing view within a discipline and Morgenthau's assertion that the views of a discipline are dictated by society. The acrimonious disputes amongst academics tend to undermine the credibility of Morgenthau's position. As a consequence, in international relations, what the academic can offer the mid-career student is a set of competing world-views, or paradigms which may provide a ladder of escape over the prison walls built by both ethnocentrism and professional expertise.

The historical development of teaching international relations

The decision to encourage teaching and research on international relations was made after the First World War. The violence and destruction wrought by the war convinced some of the academic establishment that the subjects of war and peace should be taught and studied systematically as part of the effort to insure against the recurrence of such a disaster. There was, however, no established area of knowledge from which to create a new discipline. As Martin Wight has clearly identified, an examination of past philosophical writings about international relations reveals an "intellectual and moral poverty". (7) Political philosophy failed to provide a foundation on which to build a contemporary discipline of international relations. There was, therefore, a desire to study international relations but no intellectual heritage on which to draw. As a consequence, the institutional setting for the discipline preceded the gestation of international relations as an area of knowledge; there was a small band of academics in search of a subject.

Many of the initial doubts about the "pedagogic virtue" of the discipline stemmed from this absence of an intellectual heritage. In the first place, there was no sense of a discipline boundary which could identify and encompass its members and towards which prospective members could gravitate. The inchoate nature of the incipient discipline is clearly reflected in the letter written in 1919 offering the first chair of international politics to the University of Wales.

The new professor was to study "those related problems of law and politics, of ethics and economics, which are raised by the project of a League of Nations, and for a truer understanding of civilizations other than our own". (10) Given these terms of reference, colleagues in other disciplines could be forgiven for questioning whether international politics could be formed into a coherent discipline capable of being taught to students.

At the heart of the problem seemed to lie the amorphousness of the subject matter: how were the boundaries of the discipline to be defined? Morgenthau has pointed out that a great deal of the discussion in the proceedings of the International Institute of Intellectual Cooperation centred on this question during the period between the two world wars. He cites one speaker as saying with irony:

> One can without doubt call international any phenomenon because it belongs to all countries. Anything one wants to then becomes international. From this point of view, sea sickness is an international fact; not only does one experience it on all oceans; but there are societies against that disease, and one can conceive of an international league whose purpose it is to do research and compose the methods with which to combat the disease. Yet the question remains outside our field of inquiry until one concerns oneself with the conclusion of an international convention obligating vessels to equip themselves with certain medicines which we recognize as necessary for protection against sea sickness.
>
> I beg your pardon for having chosen that imaginary example. I wanted only to indicate the need for a narrow definition of international studies. (12)

Although the comment was meant to be ironic, from a teaching standpoint, the issue was critical. Just what was to be taught to students in this area? The question was not easily answered and in practice, during the early days of the discipline, the study of international relations devolved into an analysis of those international institutions and conventions which were designed to promote peace within the international system. The approach was practical and legalistic; this resolved the problem of content, although not in a way which was likely to generate intellectual excitement.

Criticism of the "pedagogic virtue" of the discipline have not, however, stopped at this point. Critics have also pointed to a tendency for the teaching of international relations to support prevailing national policy, so that the shape and direction of the discipline have been moulded by the flow of foreign affairs. Far from operating in an "ivory tower", removed from the hurly-burly of everyday life, academics in the field of international relations, argues this brand of critic, have been all too ready to adjust the direction of the discipline to bolster government policy.

Quincy Wright, for example, associated this tendency with a process of "indoctrination" which he believed was incompatible with a liberal theory of education. From the moment of its establishment in the United States, the teaching of international relations had, he argued in 1955, "successively and in a measure successfully guided opinion". As the policy of the United States shifted, so also did the orientation of teaching international relations. (16) But, of course, Wright was not only asserting that the discipline has followed in the wake of world events, but furthermore, that the discipline had justified the actions taken by the "home" side. Wright was not alone in these criticisms. At the end of the 1950s, C. Wright Mills observed caustically that "political scientists, especially in dealing with international relations since the Second World War certainly cannot be accused of having examined United States policy with any oppositional vigour". He went on to assert that much of the work in the discipline had been "irrelevant to understanding important realities, but not irrelevant to the scientific applauding of official policies and defaults". (11)

The sense of insecurity engendered by internal and external criticism of the "pedagogic virtue" of international relations has had a fundamental effect on the approach to teaching. In a report to UNESCO, produced in the mid-50s by Professor C. A. W. Manning, for example, the solution to the problem of how to teach international relations was stated in terms of developing a set of concepts which would deepen the students' understanding of the international *complexe* as Manning referred to activity in the international arena. (12) Since that time, the discipline has been inundated with textbooks which endeavour to perform just this function, although few manage to emulate the subtlety found in Professor Manning's own text. Until recently, most of these texts have been written from the standpoint that the discipline has in its possession a basic set of concepts which can be acquired by the diligent student and used to interpret international events.

Of course, the texts do identify debates within the discipline, but the debates are defined within the confines of the basic concepts. After reading most texts, therefore, the impression is given of an essentially unified discipline progressing in the same manner as other social sciences. However, Morgenthau has argued that this conception of unity has been deliberately fostered within the discipline and he asserts that the stress laid upon "core" courses in international relations programmes, where the concepts basic to the discipline are laid out and examined, reflects this preoccupation with unity. (13)

The preoccupation with presenting a unified front is not, however, peculiar to international relations. It is a tendency which is all too common in the social sciences. Economists schooled in the Keynesian tradition often have only the foggiest notions about Marxian economics, and, by the same token, psychologists trained in a behavioural mode eschew any serious consideration of Freudian analysis. In other words students tend to be taught a discipline within the confines of one school of thought. Alternative schools are virtually ignored.

There are inherent difficulties associated with any attempt to examine a subject from more than our perspective, but the failure of social science to tackle these difficulties has been encouraged by the somewhat positivistic views held by many social scientists. There has always been within social science a penchant for believing that observation of the world is a neutral act and that, as a consequence, by systematic observation of the world, it is possible to identify what is "really" going on. The behaviouralists, in particular, have been prone to believe that disagreements about what is happening in social reality arise only because of sloppy research methods; the behaviouralists set out from the premise that all divergences within the discipline can be reduced to empirical questions which can be answered by systematic investigation.

The unquestioning belief in the neutrality of observation in the social sciences has been largely undermined by the intrusion of the ideas of Thomas Kuhn from the philosophy and history of science. (14) Kuhn demonstrated unequivocally for most social scientists that in the natural sciences, and, by inference, in the social sciences, observation is not a neutral act; it involves interpretation and interpretation rests upon theory. It follows, therefore, that observation is a theory-laden activity: one's view of the world is dependent upon the theory held prior to observation. Failure to appreciate this fact has led to exaggerated claims for the ability of behaviouralism to allow social science to "advance". In practice, behaviouralism has not solved any of the basic disputes in the social sciences. Indeed, some social scientists, of a behavioural persuasion, are

163

coming to very radical conclusions as a consequence of Kuhnian ideas. Martin Rein, a professor of social policy in a department of Urban Studies, has argued:

> I firmly believe that reality can be constructed in different ways, that these constructions may be incompatible and that there is no final way to determine which is truer and no procedure for choosing among these constructions of reality, because they are ideologies — that is, frameworks of interpretations where knowledge, values, and ways of organizing the world are inextricably interwoven. (15)

Although anathema to many social scientists in the past, there is now a growing acceptance of the idea that because of the complex and multi-faceted nature of social reality, it is necessary to take a number of different "cuts" in order to understand what is going on. In other words, it has to be accepted that social reality, like an orange, can be sliced open in a number of different ways. And with each cut, the world looks different. Before providing the student with a set of tools to examine the world, therefore, it is necessary to convince the student that there are radically different ways of looking at the world, each generating different images. There is, therefore, no one set of tools available which can be used to examine the world; there is instead a set of conflicting tools which can provide sharply contrasting interpretations of social reality.

Accepting this line of argument, therefore, it is necessary to adopt what Rein refers to as a "multi-paradigmatic approach" to the study of international relations.

A multi-paradigmatic approach to teaching international relations

In addition to stressing the theoretical base to observation, Kuhn has also been responsible for introducing the conception of a paradigm to social scientists. The term has proved to be so elastic that before extending it yet again to embrace the idea of a multi-paradigmatic approach to international relations, it is perhaps worthwhile referring back to Kuhn's use of the term.

Natural science has made enormous strides in understanding the physical world on the basis of the assumption that physical events can be described and explained by a set of fixed and unchanging laws. According to Kuhn, within any field of knowledge in the natural sciences, there is, during periods of what he calls "normal science", universal agreement about these laws. These laws represent all that the scientists know about the world at that point in time and it is on the basis of this body of interlocking laws that scientists form a common view of how the world operates. It is this "universally recognized scientific achievement" which constitutes what Kuhn calls a paradigm.

The paradigm sets the agenda for research, because not only does it establish what is known about the world, but also because it establishes what is not known. During periods of "normal science", scientists work within the parameters set by the paradigm. Observations which fail to conform to the dictates of the paradigm are regarded as anomalies to be set to one side. So, for example, although acupuncture cannot be explained by the paradigm currently used by Western scientists, and the explanation offered by practitioners of acupuncture cannot be embraced by the paradigm, Western scientists have not been tempted to overthrow their paradigm. Acupuncture is simply an anomaly. At some future point, it is assumed that a new paradigm will be formed which will take account of all known laws and also provide an explanation of acupuncture. Kuhn depicts this shift in paradigms as a gestalt-switch, with one view of the world being replaced by another. The decision to reject one paradigm is, says Kuhn, simultaneously the decision to accept another. (16) He draws an analogy with the idea of a social revolution, arguing that "like the choice between competing political institutions, that between competing paradigms proves to be a choice between incompatible modes of community life". (17)

Having analysed how science progresses, Kuhn goes on to argue that the necessity for having universal approval for a paradigm has important pedagogical consequence. The most important is that scientists tend to be unaware of these paradigm shifts because of the way that science is taught. With every new scientific breaktrhough, and the formulation of a new paradigm, the work of earlier scientists is reinterpreted in the light of the new paradigm. The findings and interpretation of previous scientists are examined through the lens provided by the new paradigm. In this way their work is integrated into the new paradigm. Old textbooks are discarded and new ones, written from the perspective of the new paradigm, are produced. This procedure, according to Kuhn, has the effect of eliminating any historical dimension to the development of science. It has, furthermore, encouraged the belief that the development of science has been cumulative. The gestalt-shifts in science are smoothed out of the picture.

Although many philosophers of science have been very critical of Kuhn's formulation of how science progresses, social scientists have been extremely attracted by the idea that knowledge can be divided up in terms of discontinuous incompatible views of the world. It gives rise to the suggestion, for example, that Marxist and Keynesian economists are operating on the basis of different paradigms with the consequence that they are examining the same reality through two quite distinctive lenses; thus they interpret the same evidence in two quite different ways. This explains why it has not been possible to resort to empirical evidence in order to resolve the differences between these two schools. In discussion, members of the two schools talk past each other: each reinterprets what the other is saying in the light of their own paradigm, thereby distorting what the opposing party is saying. (18)

Because of the preoccupation with the unity of the discipline, together with the powerful influence exercised by contemporary events on the orientation of the discipline, there has been relatively little sense of debate within international relations until comparatively recently. Although there was some discussion when the idealist phase gave way to the realist phase, it was short-lived and realism quickly swept the field. By the same token, when the realist approach was challenged, it too was quickly superseded in general textbooks which began to draw attention to phenomena associated with interdependence and transnationalism. Generally, the impression is given in these texts that such phenomena are new and that the international system is in a condition of transformation, although there is no clear agreement amongst these writers about the future direction of international relations. In other words, these texts do not set themselves up in opposition to their realist predecessors; they tend to work from the assumption that they are providing a new and more accurate picture of contemporary international relations.

But this attitude is changing. Keohane and Nye in their discussion of interdependence, for example, have argued that throughout the 1950s, when the Cold War was at its height, thinking in international relations was dominated by issues concerned with national security. However, as the fear of military attack waned, "national security had to share its position as the prime symbol in the internationalists lexicon with interdependence. Economic relations now began to seem increasingly important." Keohane and Nye insist, however, that this change of paradigm did not come about as a consequence of changes in the real world. On the contrary, economic relations amongst states have always been important. They argue, instead, that the realist mode of analysis had "helped to codify a perspective" in which "fundamental changes in economic relations among advanced industrialized countries seemed insignificant". (19) When the post-war world is examined through the perspective advocated by Keohane and Nye, of course, these economic relations appear to be anything but insignificant.

Accepting Keohane and Nye's argument, therefore, a paradigm which took account of interdependence and transnationalism at the end of the Second World War would have been just as appropriate as the state-centric paradigm which prevailed. It is of interest to note, therefore, that such a paradigm had already been formulated during the inter-war years, although it was never adopted because members of the discipline were so imbued with the state-centric conception of the world. The paradigm was developed by the Chicago School of Politics, primarily by Charles Merriam, who recognised that the decentralised nature of the international system was not dissimilar to the decentralised nature of urban politics. In a discussion of this paradigm, Fox has argued that this school of thought "had been coming to see their task as the pluralistic study of whatever groups participated in the political process. Politics, groups, process, power, and behaviour were pushing aside states, governments, sovereignty, public law and institutions as organizing concepts of political science. 'International relations' — in reality inter-state relations — in this perspective expanded to become 'world politics'." For the pluralist, therefore, "World Politics" resembled "metropolitian politics". (20) Put in these terms, it can be seen what a radical departure the pluralists were making to the paradigm from which the idealists and the realists were operating; the latter were both operating from a state-centric view of the world whereas for the former, world politics was pluralism writ-large. It was, however, another thirty years before the discipline began to adopt the pluralist paradigm.

But it is not only the pluralist paradigm which was excluded during the early days of the discipline. Ever since the First World War, there has been a third view of international relations which has been virtually ignored by the discipline. This third paradigm arises from Marxist thought and it examines international relations not from the perspective of a set of independent states, but from the perspective of a group of states hooked into a world economy. Although Marxists have for long periods of time had no more than a desultory interest in international relations, since the Second World War, with the emergence of the third world, Marxists, or more generally, structuralists, have paid increasing attention to an explanation of international relations based on the conception of world economy.

As might be expected from historical materialists, this school of thought has paid considerable attention to the origins of the modern world system. Immanuel Wallerstein has argued, for example, that there have only been two forms of world systems: world empires and world economies. In the past he argues that world economics were highly unstable and tended either to be converted into empires or to disintegrate. The peculiarity of the modern world system is that a world economy has survived for 500 years. For Wallerstein, therefore, this modern world system is "an economic but not a political entity". (21) This line of argument cuts through both the other paradigms and provides a very distinctive conception of international relations.

There are now, therefore, a variety of paradigms which can be employed to examine international relations. (22) Each provides a very different explanation of what is going on in the world. These are not, however, just academic frameworks. They reflect differences which can be found in the real world. Policy-makers view the world in different ways, which is why policy recommendations can vary so much. Some developmentalists accept the Marxist view of the world and see the third-world countries locked into a condition of structural dependency. Only by breaking ties with the developed world, it is argued, can these third-world countries ever hope to advance. But other developmentalists, who have a more pluralistic conception of the world, argue that the only hope for development in the third world is via contact with the developed world. (23)

Conclusion

For reasons already outlined, many mid-career students approach the subject of international relations for the first time locked into a particular view of the world. Of course, this attitude of mind is not peculiar to the mid-career student. Many academics within the discipline approach the subject from a clearly defined perspective or paradigm which operates to the exclusion of other paradigms.

Hopefully, however, the academic will have reviewed the alternative paradigms and, while knowing that there are rival viewpoints, insist upon working within one paradigm. So, Morgenthau, for example, in recent editions of *Politics Among Nations* (24) acknowledges rival viewpoints, as does F. S. Northedge in *The International Political System*. But having acknowledged these viewpoints, both resolutely pursue the idea that the state represents the "irreducible basic unit of the international system". (25)

While it is the prerogative of the academic to work within one perspective, it is important that students should be aware of the very different approaches to the discipline which are available. It is necessary, therefore, to adopt a multi-paradigmatic approach to teaching. By presenting the student with a variety of paradigms, the student can be helped, first to acknowledge that there may be "prison walls" which circumscribe the thinking of us all, and second, to surmount the walls. Divergent paradigms, in other words, should help students to think in terms of multiple-realities.

The object of this exercise is not to precipitate anxiety or insecurity on the part of the student; nor is it to encourage the student to adopt a new paradigm; nor is it to push the student into a position of relativism such that "anything goes". Instead it is hoped that by examining a range of paradigms, which start from very different premises about the world, the student will come to appreciate that a view of reality is not given, but is constituted or codified, and that reality can be constituted in a variety of ways. Presenting a student with alternative paradigms should generate the kind of creative tension which anthropologists have experienced when they come to appreciate how differently other cultures "see" the world. As Dorothy Lee puts it:

> According to the conceptual framework of my culture, I perceive my own behaviour differently from the ways in which people of another cultural framework view theirs. And which of these is the true way? . . .
>
> I turn to the study of other cultures largely to answer this question. I believe that these are all different codifications of the same reality, and different responses in terms of these codifications . . .
>
> When I study other cultures, I find a different codification; I get a different glimpse of reality, from a different starting point. I find other, equally self-consistent systems of symbolization, with diametrically opposed principles of validation of experience. Thus . . . I am able to see my culture as one of many possible systems of relating the self to the universe, and to question tenets and axioms of which I had never been aware. (26)

In the same way, by teaching in terms of paradigms, mid-career students, who are often extremely knowledgeable and experienced may come to a greater awareness of the "tenets and axioms" which they employ when they examine the world, and a greater appreciation of the "tenets and axioms", employed by others.

It is important for the social scientist to insist that it is always possible to take what Allison calls a number of different "cuts" at reality. (27) That reality can be explained in a variety of different not necessarily complementary ways may tell us more about the nature of social reality than about the deficiencies of social sciences. Although it is unquestionably easier and more comfortable to view the world from a single perspective, teaching from a single perspective, in the social sciences in general and international relations in particular, can be unproductive and misleading. It can leave the student with the belief that understanding is associated with the accumulation of "facts". Given the schisms which exist within the social sciences and the uncertain state of knowledge in every field, such a belief must be considered erroneous. It is preferable to present the student with radically different views or paradigms of the world.

References

1. See C. A. W. Manning, *The University Teaching of Social Sciences: International Relations*, Paris, UNESCO, 1954.
2. W. T. R. Fox, "After International Relations, What?" in *A Design for International Relations Research*, Monograph 10, The American Academy of Political and Social Science, ed. N. D. Palmer, Philadelphia, 1970, p. 29.
3. See ref. 1, p. 21.
4. H. J. Morgenthau, "International Relations as an Academic Discipline" in *Politics in the Twentieth Century*, Chicago, UCP, 1971, p. 312.
5. "The Commitments of Political Science", ibid., p. 269.
6. Ibid., p. 258.
7. M. Wight, "Why is there no International Theory" in H. Butterfield and M. Wight (eds), *Diplomatic Investigations: Essays in the Theory of International Politics*, London, Allen & Unwin.
8. See ref. 4, pp. 300-1.
9. Ibid.
10. Q. Wright, *The Study of International Relations*, New York, Appleton-Century-Croft, 1955.
11. C. Wright Mills, *The Sociological Imagination*, Harmondsworth, Penguin Books Limited, 1959, p. 95.
12. See ref. 1.
13. Ibid., 4
14. Thomas S. Kuhn, *The Structure of Scientific Revolutions*.
15. Martin Rein, *Social Science and Public Policy*, Harmondsworth, Penguin Books Limited, 1976, p. 256.
16. See ref. 14, p. 77.
17. Ibid.
18. It is important to recognise that the application of "paradigm" to describe such a debate involves a fundamental distortion because for Kuhn, a paradigm only exists if it possesses universal acclaim. Paradigm shifts therefore, can only occur over time. However, the idea of scientists operating on the basis of different paradigms and thereby possessing incommensurable views of the world, at different points in time, compares so closely to the situation where social scientists possess, contemporaneously incommensurable views of the world that the extension of the concept appears to be helpful.
19. R. O. Keohane and J. S. Nye, *Power and Interdependence*, Boston, Little, Brown & Co., 1977, p. 7.
20. W. T. R. Fox, "Pluralism, the Science of Politics and the World System", *World Politics*, 1978, p. 597.
21. I. Wallerstein, *The Modern World-system*, New York, Academic Press, 1974, p. 15.
22. For an alternative but similar division of the disipline into paradigms, together with an excellent review of the literature, see M. H. Banks, "Ways of Analysing the World Society" in A. J. R. Groom and C. R. Mitchell, *International Relations Theory: A Bibliography*, London, Frances Pinter, 1978.
23. For a discussion of the interaction between social science "theory" and public policy "doctrines", see Robert A. Packenham, *Liberal America and the Third World*, Princeton, PUP, 1973.

24. Hans J. Morgenthau, *Politics among Nations*, 5th edition, New York, Knopf, 1973.
25. F. S. Northedge, *The International System*, London, Faber, 1976, p. 9.
26. Dorothy Lee, *Freedom and Culture*, Englewood Cliffs, Prentice Hall, 1959, p. 2.
27. G. T. Allison, *The Essence of Decision*, Boston, Little, Brown & Co., 1971.

CHAPTER 10

Methodology and Mature Students: Reflections upon Pedagogical Problems

Christopher Mitchell

In our discussion of the development of the methodological debate in international relations during the 1960s and contained in Chapter 2 we noted the emergence of a number of conflicting approaches to the "business of research", and the consequent deep divisions over both the methods and purpose of increasing knowledge in the field. As a consequence of such divisions, one of the prime difficulties of teaching any academic course on the methodology of international relations during this time has been, and remains, the vast amount of material to be included in any comprehensive course. From a pedagogical point of view, the first problem is one of selection, and of making sense out of the complex welter of issues and arguments which bedevil contemporary international studies. The USC M.A. Programme in the United Kingdom adds a further set of complex problems, which arise from possessing a clientele of mid-career students, most of whom have practical experience of at least some aspects of international relationships and behaviour, and many of whom approach their second degree in a highly practical frame of mind, implicitly asking: "What can I learn in this degree that will help me towards a better understanding of my own environment, and to carry out my own duties and functions more effectively?" The two sets of problems, of course, are linked, for while the intellectual integrity of any M.A. programme demands that the material contained in courses shall be there mainly through its intrinsic worth, the complexity of the particular subject matter and the particular needs of the student body affect to some degree what issues are raised, the manner in which they are discussed, and the method of presentation.

The choice of what to present is made more complicated by a further fundamental principle we feel should underly our particular methodology course – that students can best appreciate the substantive findings of the field when they have had, at least some practical experience of the manner in which such findings are reached. In other words, we accept the need not merely to teach in the abstract about methodology, and research techniques leading to findings; but also to provide an opportunity for students to experience the difficulties of problem selection, research design, data gathering, interpretation and writing up of findings – or as many of these processes as can, realistically, be covered during a four-month-long semester.

In other words, the problems of competing philosophies and modes of research previously discussed in Chapter 2 inevitably complicate the teaching and learning process on any course dealing with methodology in the study of international relations. We may safely say that the situation currently confronting *any* students of theory and methodology in international relations is somewhat confusing, and to any *mature*, or mid-career students transferring to a Masters degree in international relations from some other (possibly non-cognate social science) discipline, is a particularly harrowing process. We may summarise by repeating that, at its most basic, there are at least three competing methodologies, or modes of research, confronting a student of international relations at the present time. As a consequence, to understand the theoretical literature currently making up the field a student should be introduced to these three modes and able to fit different research findings into their relevant epistemological "slot":

(a) *The Classical*, which adopts a familiar historical approach to studying international relations, concentrates upon description of the past and intuitive interpretation of the present; tends to deal with single, and arguably unique situations (or at least, the unique aspects of them); and generalises – if at all – with caution and within a set of assumptions, central to which is the difference between the domestic and the international environments.

(b) *The Behavioural*, which is self-consciously "scientific" and comparative, aims at generality, rigour, and the formulation of testable propositions; tends towards the quantitative and unreadable; yet shares with the Classical mode a commitment to empiricism, and a state-centric framework of assumptions within which its problems arise and are investigated.

(c) *The Post-Behavioural* (*or Paradigmatic*), which draws support from a renewed interest in philosophy, emphasises the importance of values and shared background assumptions about the nature of "the real

173

world" in influencing research problems and findings; and thus in international relations, rejects a state-centric approach, and — in extreme formulations — the existence of international relations as a separate field of study itself.

One practical aspect of the difficulties encountered in "understanding the theoretical literature of the field" is the lack of suitable material to help in teaching a course on methodological approaches. Particularly lacking at the present moment is a solid introductory study that links together all the modes (or methodologies) we have discussed, reviews their implications for the practicalities of research itself (and the evaluation of research findings); and portrays the actual, grubby business of carrying out research in the field. There are a number of useful introductory books on the philosophical preoccupations of the social sciences (Wallace (1) and Lessnoff (2) are two of the theorists); and fewer that attack the problem of how to set about a research project (Gurr (3) is undoubtedly the most easily comprehensible of such books currently available). However, all of these approach the problems, principles of research design, and research techniques from disciplines such as sociology, social-psychology or political science. Hence, even mature students experience difficulty in making the intellectual leap from a methodology or research technique applied to another social science discipline and a set of research problems (or findings) that form the content of one aspect of international relations studies. Individual books can be used to illustrate research within the various modes, and others can be used to illuminate the actual operation of particular research techniques on specific problems. Zinnes's recent book (4) comes closest to filling a serious and long-standing gap in the international relations literature, namely a clear and comprehensive review of philosophies and methods, and their interconnection; but eventually her volume is too idiosyncratic to fulfil this particular need. The field still awaits a good textbook on methodology, while readers containing current findings that illustrate various research methods (such as Meuller's, (5) or the by now neo-classic Rosenau collections (6) tend to belong firmly to the behavioural mode of research, and to be quantitatively inclined.

The lack of a suitable, comprehensive text is, of course, a practical problem for all students undertaking courses in the methodology of international relations. Far more fundamental for mature students with little initial background in international relations are the major intellectual problems posed by what at first seems to be the highly tenuous connection between the findings of research conducted in our three "modes". A solid historical case study of the impact of British public opinion of

174

policy-making in the 1930s appears to have a remote connection with a cybernetic model of desigion-making processes, and none at all with an experimental analysis of choice in conditions of uncertainty. A second intellectual capacity is that each of the "modes" appear to possess its own implications for the method of carrying out research. These prove particularly puzzling if students must complete some original work of their own during a course, and, worse still, its own criteria for evaluating what constitutes valid research problems, and "good" research.

Thus, from our particular stance, major current problems in teaching any course in international relations methodology are firstly those of trying to explain clearly the existence and nature of the tripartite division of research philosophies currently existing within the discipline; secondly those of showing the effects of each of the three modes in the range of research work currently being undertaken within the overall field; and thirdly, of showing each mode upon the preliminary, but vital conceptual, and intellectual processes that have to be undertaken by the students themselves before they can embark upon original research work of their own even when this is merely the application of a tried and tested research technique to novel material. Two major obstacles often arise to prevent this being carried out successfully. The first is the difficulty of making remote and apparently esoteric debates about the philosophical foundations of a field of study relevant (i) to the practical business of evaluating existing research findings — what we "know" about the field, or the contents of the disciplines; and (ii) to the business of producing an original piece of research for oneself in connection with the lot of these issues. Problems about the order in which material should be introduced inevitably arise. Should one first tackle the philosophical issues — they are, after all, fairly fundamental — or should one allow students in "at the deep end" and then point up the shortcomings in their research design? Should one discuss examples of "good" and "bad" research, and then point out bases for the criteria that underlie such evaluations? Should one follow a "cook-book formula" by demonstrating the range of research techniques available and hope that some of their difficulties and shortcomings will be revealed in use? There seem to be no easy answers, but experience has revealed that many mature students, even more than undergraduates, have a desire to plunge headlong into research without being bothered by the remote and the philosophical.

Structuring a course in methodology when confronting this range of practical and intellectual problems involves an inevitable compromise — or series of compromises — between competing demands. To help mature students make some sense of the varying theories, approaches and

175

frameworks to be found in current literature, and thus appreciate the various contributions to there being different types of "knowledge" in international relations, the course should undoubtedly begin to familiarise students with the different research philosophies discussed in Chapter 2. It should introduce them to the actual process of research itself, and to the techniques available to expand knowledge in the field. And it should link up with their (often somewhat limited) familiarity with existing theory and findings in international relations gained from a previously undertaken course in international relations theory; finally, it should be presented in such a way as to seem relevant, interesting and worthwhile to an a-typical student clientele.

In our initial endeavours to shape a suitable methodology component, the issues tended to be structured so that all competing requirements were to be fulfilled through the presentation of material on philosophy, techniques and findings by the instructor; by the students' own reading (which, given the part-time nature of the degree, inevitably turned out to be inadequate, no matter how dedicated the individual student); and by the preparation of an original piece of research, which became the written requirement for the course. The material presented in classes divided into two major themes; (a) a brief review of the competing research philosophies, beginning with the Bull-Kaplan "great debate" of the mid-1960s, (7) working through the classical methods of research and the nature of scientific method in the natural and social sciences, to the problems (and pitfalls) of measurement and eventually to the place of values and fundamental assumptions affecting research; and (b) a somewhat longer discussion of the uses (and misuses) of specific research techniques, ranging from historical case studies to massive time series or cross-national analyses using aggregate data. In the event, the students' individual research projects turned out frequently to be single case studies – very much in the classical mode – of some country, region or issues within the realm of the students' personal interests. (Often these were associated with their professional background and concerns, and tended to be derivative, based upon secondary rather than primary documentary sources, and sometimes reflecting all the shortcomings of classical analysis, with none of its strengths of detail.) This reaction may also be partly attributed to the student's gradual confrontation with the increasing number of widely different (and often apparently esoteric) research techniques developed during the "behavioural decade". The sheer proliferation of basic research techniques now employed in international relations, and available for students contemplating original research themselves often, paradoxically, became a barrier to the production of anything but the most classical of descriptive case studies.

In its way, this problem for courses on methodology is quite apart from that of connections between the philosophical debate and the question of appropriate research methods for appropriately formulated research problems. A glance through any recent quarterly in the field will reveal at once the wide range of esoteric techniques being employed in various parts of the field, ranging from more or less complex forms of content analysis, through survey research, numerous events data studies, simulations, and studies based upon game theory and other formal models, to full-scale efforts to trace out the root causes of a single major international war, such as Choucri and North's recent research on the decades leading up to 1914. (8) Faced with such a proliferation, many mature students were inevitably driven back to the familiarity of a single case study, using the tried and familiar approach of documentary analysis, or to the use of a single research technique, with which they became familiar, rather than a multi-technique attack upon a problem.

After maintaining this basic structure for the methodology course for a number of semesters, various sources of feedback from the students (questionnaires, *ad hoc* comments, drop-out and incomplete rates and — most important of all — the anticipatory comments of students *about to begin* the core methodology course), it became evident that the course was failing to meet the basic needs of the students, and that a major and complex crisis had arisen. Apart from low morale, the crisis mainly consisted of: (a) a huge gap between the material previously covered by the course on methodology; and (b) an equally large gap between the research approaches and techniques discussed in the formally taught part of the course, and those used in the actual research projects undertaken individually by students. For example, given that the bulk of students were constrained by their own interests and available time to a descriptive case study, it was obvious that formal discussions of a case study approach were seen as helpful and relevant — at least in the immediate practical task of fulfilling course requirements. But the same could hardly be said of discussions of survey research, simulation studies, or analysis using large quantities of Events-Data. In rare cases, individual members of the class were aware of the use, and usefulness, of such techniques in their own areas or professions; or that — for example — the Department of Defense had both used Events-Data analysis and was interested in Threat Recognition and Analysis as an "early warning system", based upon a set of profiles of national government response patterns to previous cases or confrontations. However, these were rare instances, and for the majority of mid-career students, the most familiar mode of analysis appears to remain the written brief, rather than the graph or statistical table. Interestingly enough, students with a military background often appeared more familiar with, and sympathetic towards quantitative studies and to the idea of the development of "general" theories of international behaviour than the civilian students. Perhaps this is a legacy of McNamara!

As a result of such highly "negative" feedback, it became obvious that a major restructuring of the course had to be undertaken, and some hard thought be given to the contents of the course and what was demanded of the students. The major gap between the core course on existing theories of international relations and the core course on the nature, form and production of theories could perhaps best be bridged by taking a number of approaches, theories and frameworks already discussed in I.R. 500 (the introductory theory course) and asking the students to reappraise them as "theories" (or something else), and then as *adequately tested* theories. (Few theories have survived this latter appraisal.)

The gap between the research techniques discussed in class and those used in the students' own personal research could be closed by changing course requirements to a number of short, practical exercises giving individual experience in the intricacies of questionnaire design and administration, of content analysis of written or spoken material, or of the use of computers to coded information already gathered into a data set. The gap between apparently esoteric philosophical debates about evidence, explanation, theory building or testing, and starting assumptions or paradigms could be made more realistic, or, at least, more practically relevant, by taking some situation or event historically and often personally familiar to mid-career students and demonstrating how different explanatory schemes could produce different interpretations of the same familiar "facts", or, at least, different orderings in their relative importance. In this respect, Allison's three versions of the Cuban missile crisis have always been invaluable. (9) However, the increasing debate about the origins of the Cold War (starting with revisionists such as Alperovitz, (10) Kolkos, (11) and Williams, (12) proceeding through Maddox's assault on revisionism (13) and ending with Holsti's recent *A.P.S.R.* (14) article) has provided another way of introducing both the debate about the nature of the "classical v. behavioural" approaches, and about the manner in which paradigms affect what is studied and how it is studied. Finally, the basic research process can be successfully encapsulated in the initial planning of a personal research project (to be carried out at a later stage in the programme), a requirement that will at least introduce students to the problemation, specification and operationalisation stages of research — stages which, many academic researchers would agree, are the most intellectually taxing in the entire process.

While the structural changes outlined in the previous paragraphs may be intellectually sound and pedagogically desirable, the question still remains about whether they (and the course in methodology as now constituted) meet any of the perceived needs of mid-career students who are rarely, if ever, contemplating a future in academic research, or even the use of multiple regression analysis or survey research in the course of their present career. In many ways, this is the most difficult (and, a purist would argue) least important consideration to be kept in mind when originally planning or re-structuring a course on methodology. In miniature, it is the dilemma chronically facing scholars who have chosen the long-term task of theory-building when they are asked for immediate practical help by practitioners.

Our experience to date is that the question has only been answered in a rather negative fashion, in the sense that examining the fundamental assumptions about knowledge (and hence about conventional assumptions about the contemporary world, its structure and processes) has aided many of our mature clientele to view their environment in a new light, and help them to question things in their own historic experience that were taken as givens. This questioning takes place not in the sense of replacing one set of certainties with another, but of examining, and beginning to understand the often problematical manner in which certainties are established, and the essential tentative nature of social knowledge. Whether this is enough to justify a core course on methodology is another matter, it is certainly rarely the case that the actual research approaches and techniques are immediately seized upon as being applicable to solving a practical problem confronting a student's organisation or bureau. Indeed, many are rejected as too esoteric, or as being based upon unsound premises, or merely as representing an adverse cost–benefit ratio when compared with more conventional forms of analysis and reporting.

In the main, then, our experience has also shown that mature, mid-career students tend to be particularly unhappy with research activities carried on in both behavioural and paradigmatic modes, and to possess, almost without exception, a set of classical background assumptions and ultimately are happiest with classical approaches to research. To some degree, this should not be unexpected. We are all classicists at heart, both by inclination and experience, and are embedded in a classical mode of reasoning and argument, whether this merely be common-room discussion of the Middle East problem, media analyses of the latest riots in South Africa, or even a seminar discussion of some subject not our immediate speciality. More specifically, we all share a familiarity with the literary and historical approach to understanding aspects of our environment, and to the descriptive study which employs a narrative mode of exposition, and what Hempel has called "explanation by context". (15) Given that this is a familiar and constant mode of analysing and explaining our social environment, and that it increasingly becomes the standard means of so doing as we proceed through life, it is hardly surprising that mature students should evince impatience with efforts to introduce them to other modes of analysis, or to point to methodological shortcomings in tried and familiar methods. The result is often, therefore, a rejection of both behavioural and post-behavioural modes, or, at best, an unwilling acceptance that they "might" be of use in certain limited aspects of international relations. In their own research, our students remain happiest with single case studies, and with the problems of using (and hopefully evaluating) historical evidence of "what happened and why" through the specialist's unique knowledge, common sense, or intuition.

We should add to this the impression that our mature students, have appeared to remain far more pragmatic and prescriptive in studying theory and methodology than younger, less professionally involved students. This should be no surprise; as we have already emphasised, many of the mature students come to their courses in the hope that they will provide help with existing careers, or insights into areas of the world to which people might be posted, or with which they are already familiar. Hence, they again have a reason for being somewhat impatient with philosophical disagreements of a rarified nature, although greater interest has been often shown in the actual techniques of analysis in operation on substantive problems.

This, then, remains the situation after ten years of relative methodological confusion which, regrettably, shows no signs of any grand conjunction, or the emergence of some overarching paradigm which will subsume and unify the current diverse strands in social science and international relations technology. Hence, for some time in the future, any honestly taught course in methodology will have to reflect and deal with current philosophical confusion in the social sciences in general, and in international relations in particular. This transmitted confusion, in turn, must reflect existing uncertainty about the boundaries and contents of the field as a whole. The only alternative would seem to be choosing one research philosophy as "the right one", and teaching about the nature of research according to the criteria of that philosophy to the exclusion of others. This might be a straightforward and comfortable way out of the current dilemma, but it would be an undesirable one. Genuine differences regarding the philosophy of the social sciences do exist, and − given that international relations claims to be a laggard member of those sciences — should not be ignored. At the present stage of development within the field the temptation is to acknowledge briefly the existence of the classical and paradigmatic modes of research, often in a critical fashion, and then take advantage of the extent and diversity of research techniques and related findings within the behavioural mode by basing a course upon this approach to contemporary international relations scholarship. It is somewhat more straightforward to plunge into a discussion of research design using aggregate data and computerised analysis, particularly given the pragmatic orientation of western social science, than to embark upon an exploration of why we select certain kinds of entities, attributes and relationships for study (by implication, why we do *not* select other possible candidates) and what are the effects of our selection processes upon the possible range of findings. (We should emphasise that post-behavioural and paradigmatic methodology frequently falls into the opposite trap of discussing competing paradigms, or social-science-as-ideology without bothering with the techniques by which their selection of entities and relationships for study can be said to exist in the referent world, rather than solely as constructs within their own minds.) Our own view is that a judicious balance must be maintained, and that ultimately, even rather career-oriented mature students come to appreciate an introduction to the dimensions of the debate, and its implications for existing "knowledge" about the international environment. We may not have yet succeeded in achieving such a judicious balance within our own course on international relations methodology, but at least it is the goal towards which, gradually, we are working.

References

1. W. L. Wallace, *The Logic of Science in Sociology* (Chicago, Aldine, 1971).
2. M. Lessnoff, *The Structure of Social Science* (London, Allen & Unwin, 1974).
3. T. R. Gurr, *Politimetrics* (Englewood Cliffs, N.J., Prentice Hall, 1972).
4. D. A. Zinnes, *Contemporary Research in International Relations* (New York, Free Press, 1976).
5. J. E. Meuller (ed.), *Approaches to Measurement in International Relations* (New York, Appleton Century Crofts, 1969).
6. J. N. Rosenau (ed.), *International Politics and Foreign Policy*, 2nd edn., (New York, Free Press, 1969).
7. H. Bull, "International Relations: The Case for the Classical Approach", *World Politics*, April 1966; and M. A. Kaplan, "The New Great Debate", *World Politics*, October 1966.
8. N. Choucri and R. C. North, *Nations in Conflict* (San Francisco, Freeman, 1975).
9. G. T. Allison, *Essence of Decision* (Boston, Little Brown, 1971).
10. G. Alperovitz, *Atomic Diplomacy: Hiroshima and Potsdam* (London, Secker & Warburg, 1965).

11. G. Kolko, *The Politics of War* (New York, Random House, 1968).
12. W. A. Williams, *The Tragedy of American Diplomacy* (Cleveland, World, 1959).
13. R. J. Maddox, *The New Left and the Origins of the Cold War* (Princeton, N.J., Princeton University Press, 1973).
14. O. R. Holsti, "The Study of International Relations Makes Strange Bedfellows; Theories of the Radical Right and the Radical Left", *American Politicsl Science Review*, March 1974.
15. C. G. Hempel, "Reasons and Covering Laws in Historical Explanation" in S. Hook (ed.), *Philosophy and History: A Symposium* (New York University Press, 1963).

CHAPTER 11

Teaching Strategy to Mid-Career Students: Thoughts on a Decade's Association with USC's Programme in Britain

A. J. R. Groom

While an academic spends a good part of his professional life teaching, he is rarely promoted for teaching although its personal satisfaction and intellectual rewards are considerable. However, teaching adds little to his renown since it is essentailly a private affair — between teacher and student. A teacher rarely sits in the lecture, tutorial or seminar of a colleague through the length of a course as a non-participant observer so that teaching reputations are tenuous affairs built upon hearsay, inadequate formal student evaluations and extrapolation from other aspects of an academic's work and personality. Moreover, it is one of the inanities of the academic profession that few beginners are exposed to more than a desultory attempt to train them in teaching methods and assessment of teaching experience. My own lack of pedagogical training and accomplishments gives rise to a certain fear and trepidation in reflecting upon my experiences teaching strategy to mid-career USC students over the last decade. I can relate only personal impressions based on untutored observations. Like all my colleagues in the programme, I care greatly about my teaching and I reflect upon my experiences but perforce it is the reflections of a pedagogical ignoramous. Before I turn to a discussion of teaching the strategy course, I should like to make some comments about the general characteristics of the USC-U.K. programme.

Since the late 1960s, I have become increasingly involved in the USC programme in Britain. As a member of the core faculty consultative group I have advised students, led study trips to international organisations abroad, organised simulations, organised conferences between USC students and students from British universities and acted generally as factotum. In addition, I think that I am the only member of the group who has been responsible at one point or another for each of the four current core courses. In all this I have been fortunate in the intellectual stimulus I have received from colleagues and students alike and I have formed lasting and cherished friendships. Indeed, it is one of the heart-warming aspects of the U.K. programme that, despite the vagaries of a programme predominantly staffed by part-timers and taught to evening students, there is a real sense of academic and personal community.

The international relations network is truly transnational in personnel (teachers and students), research and literature and USC forms a major node in this network. For example, over the years we in Britain have had the pleasure of working with numerous visitors from campus who have come to teach for a semester. This has the advantage of facilitating the comparability of standards and the content of courses and of ensuring that staff and students in Britain both feel themselves to be, and indeed are, an integral part of a multinational programme and scholarly community. This also enables us to compare research experiences as well as to develop friendships. This process has been furthered by visits of British faculty to teach a semester in Los Angeles – a visit that I have had the good fortune to make.

It must be recognised, however, that there are major differences between the institutional framework of a United States and a British university, which over time have been made complementary in the USC-U.K. programme. Universities in the United States have, in comparison with British universities, a tendency to be bureaucratic in their attitude and procedures, over-administered and, if I dare to say it, over-financed. British universities have not developed an independent academic bureaucratic element to the same extent as in the United States and they are chronically underfinanced (to the point where some universities do not permit staff to make telephone calls before the cheaper rate begins in the afternoon!).

University education in the United States has become a "mass" phenomenon since the end of the Second World War. Thus, there has been a need to devise a system the principal purpose of which is to cater for the better-than-average, but not brilliant student. The course unit system, itself broken down into sub-units of programmed learning, meets this need. The student proceeds at his own pace through a well-defined programme in each course until he has jumped all the hurdles and piled up the credits necessary for a degree. At no point does he have to "put it together" and view his undergraduate or Masters work as a whole. This, however, is changing at the graduate level, at least, since comprehensive examinations seem to be playing a more significant role in the assessment process.

184

The British universities have traditionally catered for an educational élite who are given a book list, access to libraries, a tutor, facultative lectures and occasional essays in preparation for a set of comprehensive examinations in three years' time (in non-science subjects). This system is also subject to change as several British universities have introduced the course unit system in response to a growing proportion of the population attending university. Thus, there is a degree of convergence between the United States and British university systems.

The faculty in the USC-U.K. programme have been able to innovate precisely because we are not wholly in either system. Moreover, as the result of our experiences, some of the USC-U.K. innovations have been incorporated into both USC campus and British university practices. We have been most fortunate in having Directors of the U.K. programme and administrative and academic supervisors on campus who have been willing to keep the bureaucratic burden to a minimum and to support us in the development of new courses and the like. They have given us freedom and responsibility to explore and innovate especially in areas which are particularly pertinent to the special features of the USC programme in Britain.

One such special feature is that, for the most part, both faculty and students are part-time. From the point of view of faculty this means that it is only possible to teach a course if it corresponds to courses which are being or have been taught in the home institutions. Gradually, under Dr Nielsson's direction, a core faculty emerged of teachers who were prepared to teach compatible courses which had a coherence when taken together that was often lacking in similar programmes in their home institutions. Because of the condition of working in the periphery of two systems, Dr Nielsson could pick and choose his faculty and his courses to fit his masterplan. In our home institutions we cannot since we have *tabula rasa* neither in terms of faculty, courses, nor degree programme. In our "half-way-house" between campus and a British university we have been able to do things that we consider worthwhile and interesting more easily and sooner than is usually the case in home institutions which have, nevertheless, benefited from our innovations by their subsequent adoption. Thus the faculty have been able to turn their part-time status to advantage.

For students, there are fewer advantages to the part-time status since the high standards of the programme require that students devote practically all their non-professional time to the essentials of the programme. That so many reach the required standard over a sustained period of two years never ceases to astonish me and it is a tremendous tribute to their intellectual and personal qualities. While we can offer a student an intellectually challenging programme, we can only do so at the cost of much "blood, sweat and tears" and the minimum of family life. That spouses are willing to put up with the plethora of the programme's demands on their partners bears witness, in many instances, to the intellectual content and high standing of the programme.

Any part-time student misses some of the social–intellectual stimulus and fun of student life even though he more than achieves the required academic level of depth and range of knowledge. In a certain respect, this drawback is compensated for by the fact that our students are "mature students". Mature students have usually passed the more raucous stage of student life and do not have to take time off to grow up. Thus, although part-time mature students may have less time available, they tend to know what they want and to work harder and thereby to make fuller academic use of their time. On the other hand, there are several possible difficulties: they may have lost the knack of academic ways, they may have closed minds and they may not have sufficient academic "loitering time" to allow ideas to "gel".

The first problem is usually resolved by students re-learning academic techniques; their teachers are always ready to help them in this. If they fail to do this they are screened out of the programme either through the self-realisation that the academic world is not for them, or occasionally through the formal screening process.

The second problem, that of closed minds, is more serious. I think that it was Karl Deutsch who once remarked that we do not learn new modes of thinking after the age of thirty but merely become more adept at working within existing frameworks. You cannot teach an old dog new tricks, only new ways of performing old tricks! Some of our students are very set in their mental ways and it is a constant battle to get them to consider new ways. I hasten to add that they are few in number. Moreover, the purpose of the exercise is not to force them to adopt new ways, but merely to make them aware of such ways and be sufficiently open in mind and spirit as to come to a scholarly assessment, as opposed to a "gut reaction", of the merits and drawbacks of new concepts, techniques and methodologies.

The third problem of lack of time for intellectual digestion is in part compensated for by the comprehensives, the preparation for which entails the student reviewing what he has learned throughout the programme. To be successful the student must have a general competence in the field. The comprehensives are a fundamental element in the standing of the programme since, while a student may occasionally be able to scrape through in a particular course, a set of wide-ranging written examination questions and an hour's oral examination usually give a clear indication of general competence. As a programme we have not in the past given the student enough help in preparing for this ordeal. Of course, review sessions have been organised in various aspects of the field but perhaps every student's final course ought to be an overview seminar returning to the central themes of the core courses.

Until the mid-1970s, the USC–U.K. programme involved making educational adjustments for the homogenous cultural and educational background of a student body consisting of American professional (predominantly military) mid-career people undertaking a degree-programme in a British environment, taught by an Anglo-American faculty. This is now changing more towards a heterogenous pattern with students of various nationalities being attracted from international business and from embassies. In this new context, I have never experienced political or other difficulties arising from the presence of students who are nationals of states at loggerheads or engaged in hostilities. Tact, intellectual integrity, common courtesy and the superordinate goal of common academic interests have always enabled us to avoid or overcome any possible difficulties.

It is perhaps as well to remember that USC students are "deviants". Most servicemen, most diplomats, most employees of multinations have neither sufficient wit nor will to take the USC programme. Our students are an exceptional minority, anything but run-of-the-mill. For a start they tend to have an "international" orientation, that is an interest in or curiosity about "things foreign" which in part explains their presence in Britain, their careers (Join the Navy/a MNC/the Foreign Service and see the World!) and their academic interests. At the start of each course I ask each student to tell me his reasons for joining the programme. This "international" outlook often manifests itself, although it is not always formally acknowledged. Some students join because the acquisition of a Master's degree in international relations will be of direct use in their career either to qualify them for advancement or because of the application of particular skills or specific knowledge gained in the programme. Others join the programme purely out of academic interest often in search of intellectual stimulation. A further motive is the need to re-tool for a change in career, particularly into the educational system at various levels. Some students candidly avow that they need a Masters but that their choice fell on our programme because of the absence of any competitions of a similar standard and standing in other fields such as business administration. Whatever their initial motivation it is my experience that by the time a student has completed the programme he has become very committed to it — and a remarkably small number of initial candidates fall by the wayside.

But not everything in the garden is lovely. American students generally, and students with a military background in particular, have, in my experience, tended to be very task-oriented, rather than holistic in their conceptions. They want "their orders", detailed guidance and instructions of what it is they have to do. They write excellent papers of an empirical, descriptive nature that require industry and organisation rather than conceptualisation and innovation. They are much more willing than students in British universities to dabble with unfamiliar research techniques. They are relatively weaker, however, in conceptual analysis and in epistemological questions perhaps because of their previous experience of programmed "education" with its strict, clear and finite course requirements. They do not always appreciate that it is a question of general competence not specific knowledge — not that the latter is to be denigrated. In fact, it requires a considerable effort on my part before USC students are able to distinguish between a conceptual analysis and an off-the-top-of-the-head speculative, so-called, "think piece"!

I also find it hard to be a good "liberal". By "liberal" I mean the creation of a situation in which students feel at ease when expressing views contrary to those of the teacher confident that they will be assessed not so much on the conclusions they draw but on the quality of thought and research by which they arrive at their conclusions. Most students like to be able to agree with their teacher and USC students try hard to do so. This is hardly surprising in that most of them practice professions in which there is a high degree of socialisation into institutional norms and value systems. Occasionally students who feel that they cannot go along with my views seek their solace in a psychological withdrawal, but for the most part I manage to persuade the class that we share a common basis in empirical theory, scientific method and rigorous control of values and that value prescription is our own personal affair. After all, values are not subject to empirical verification and an "is" does not imply an "ought". We have thus usually learned to live with a plurality of value preferences while at the same time conducting an open scholarly dialogue.

A different battle concerns the literature in the field. USC students initially pester the teacher for a textbook. I understand their concern: they are used to such texts, they are pressed for time and want to make sure that they cover the essentials and USC encourages them to buy set books. I deplore this practice since I hope that they will become competent in the subject rather than merely in the set material. Instead, I encourage the students to take an odyssey through the literature. To this end I have prepared long annotated bibliographies for the courses that

I teach.* In short, I attempt to destroy the textbook mentality, not always with as much success as I would like.

Usually, I meet students in the strategy course when they have already taken the basic introductory courses in theory and methodology. I can only pay tribute to my colleagues, Michael Banks, Richard Little, Chris Mitchell, Dennis Sandde, and Gunnar Nielsson who have frequently taught these difficult courses in the past. In two courses they have worked wonders in giving a group of students with a diverse background a basic conceptual and methodological framework. They make the way smooth both for the students and for their colleagues and their work is an impressive vindication of the core faculty concept since the basic courses and teaching philosophies are complementary and supportive. In my view, we must constantly strive, at the Masters level, to move away from the piecemeal rigidity of the particular, task-oriented approach with which students enter the programme to a more holistic conception of the study of world society.

Elsewhere in this volume I have commented upon the evolution of strategic studies.† In the strategy course I have tried to anticipate these developments and to set the course in the context of the social sciences in general and international relations in particular.

Within the specific context of the programme, I try to relate the strategy course as much as possible to the courses on theory, methodology and international organisation and make it complementary to the course on peace research and conflict analysis and this intention goes far in explaining my choice of topics and approach to teaching the course. Indeed, I am now experimenting with a course on "conflict and co-operation" which takes endemic change as its starting point and then seeks to examine the factors that lead to a conflictual or co-operative response to change – to power politics or legitimised politics. Of course either pure "ideal" type is very rare but why particular transactions fall at a particular point on the spectrum between power politics and legitimised politics and how and why relationships veer towards one pole or oscillate is the very stuff of political analysis and the understanding of world society.

It is quite possible to teach strategy essentially from a "technical" point of view concentrating on weapons systems, the military balance, procurement and military capability. This is an approach that I abjure for several reasons. If the USC programme is to have a central core then

*These form part of a little volume covering the field of international relations theory – A. J. R. Groom and C. R. Mitchell (eds), *International Relations Theory: A Bibliography*, London, Frances Pinter (New York, Nichols), 1978.

† See Chapter 3.

courses must be related to that core. I try to cast the strategy course in such a way that it develops from the theory and methodology course. For example, I begin by exploring the conceptual paradigms of strategists, conflict researchers, and revolutionaries, not confining myself to contemporary writers but going back to Hobbes, Locke, Machiavelli, Marx and the debate between the idealists and the realists. I give much emphasis to the conceptual, methodological, epistemological aspects of strategy partly because such questions are of continued relevance and usefulness and partly because this approach makes strategy an important part of the whole. The technical side I do not give so much attention to since it is the subject of student papers. It can be "mugged up" if the fundamentals are there and it is constantly changing. It is also so extensive that it is difficult to be both coherent and comprehensive. With a more conceptual approach, it is possible to be both coherent and comprehensive. A further reason for not emphasising the technical side is that the military students are familiar with it from their Staff College and daily lot. However, they lack the conceptual framework for making good use of such information. Moreover, to relegate technical analysis to a secondary role diminishes the likelihood of an embarrassing situation in which a student might inadvertently reveal confidential information associated with his work. I always make a special point of stressing to students that a university is a free, open institution owing loyalty to nothing other than the pursuit of knowledge. Thus all contributions to the seminar are public and on the record. Students must therefore be their own censors, be they military or embassy personnel. However, I do not wish to dramatise what is more a possibility than a problem.

In laying greater stress on the conceptual as opposed to the technical side of strategy, I have not ignored other aspects of the field as it has evolved. Apart from the oral reports, written conceptual and empirical papers chosen by each student, the general background reading and the lecture–discussion part of my strategy course have moved from a concentration on the major powers a decade ago to the consideration of a wider range of issues. I have already noted that I find it helpful to start with a consideration of the conceptual world of the strategist, the conflict researcher and the revolutionary. I then try to bring the students' attention to aspects of the defence system and its context including the relationship with foreign and economic policy and to the literature on decision-making in so far as it is relevant to defence and the military–industrial complex. In the future, I intend then to spend more time than hitherto on the sociology of the military and civil–military relations. In a sense, the foregoing is preliminary to the analysis of deterrence that follows which is set in the

190

context of the manipulation of threats at various system levels. I also use the discussion of the concept of deterrence to include a mini-case study of strategic nuclear deterrence between the super powers. This is followed by a rather more extended study of the modalities of limited war, nuclear and non-nuclear, in Europe which serves both to illustrate the concept of limited war and to satisfy the particular curiosity of those students who are concerned with such eventualities in their daily work. We then descend further down the escalatory ladder to examine revolutionary warfare, guerrilla warfare and terrorism both from a political science point of view and also from the writings of practitioners (and many students have had practical experience in Vietnam). This leads me into a discussion of the arms race and of arms control and disarmament before spending a little time on peacekeeping. Finally, I touch upon British defence policy since it is a subject on which I have worked extensively and, again, a considerable number of students (both military and from embassies) have a professional interest in the topic. Clearly there is much that is left out (for example, alliances) but the students' oral reports and written papers are wide-ranging and usually bring in such subjects.

My course is unusual in that a high percentage of the participants are professionally engaged in cognate work. This is both an advantage and a drawback. It is an advantage in that there is a degree of background knowledge not always evident in other courses. However, even when such background does not exist I have always found students exhibiting sufficient motivation, goodwill and hard work for its generation. There is, on the other hand, the possible disadvantage of students professionally engaged in the domain thinking that they "know it all". Such instances are rare and are usually concerned with the empirical day-to-day aspects of the course. "If you knew what I know you would think like I do" is often the response of practitioners whose concern is with daily events and who have access to privileged information. This course, however, is not designed to provide a commentary on current events but seeks to introduce the student to the less ephemeral aspects of the subject. More frequently the flattering response has been that, while both military and other students have sometimes found the course directly useful in their work they have also found it most helpful in putting their day-to-day concerns into a wider perspective. After all, there is nothing as practical as a good theory, however short their supply may be!

CHAPTER 12

The Teaching of International Organisation

Paul Taylor

The question now arises of the approach which might be most useful in explaining the essence of international organisation as extracted from the field sketched out in Chapter 4. How does one teach satisfactorily the subject called international organisation to a group of mature students, many of whom have established careers? This is not only a question of classroom technique, but also one of deciding upon the broad lessons which the subject contains. The most important test of such lessons is probably that they involve skills which can be transferred to other, new areas of international organisation. It is also not just a question of teaching details of the theories which were mentioned in Chapter 4 but of extracting from them something "portable".

The student is being asked to look at developments which, we have argued, could be seen as part of the evolving constitution of international society. One of the things which should be taught, therefore, is the basis of international order: what could lend durability to such a constitution, however it be constructed? The answer, to this question like so many other questions in international relations, cannot be provided in full in the classroom — or here — though a start can be made in the hope that the intelligent student will acquire a sense of the missing pieces at a number of points in the course. The student should also learn that the answers involve a conceptual diversity: they should know that there are various ideas about the basis of order in international society, as there are about order within the state.

The main distinction in thinking about order in international society, as Claude has pointed out, reflects, on the one hand, the ideas of John Locke, and on the other, of Thomas Hobbes. (1) Locke's view, stated in very general terms, is that order is the product of agreement between members of a society, whilst that of Hobbes is that order is imposed by a higher power called the Leviathan. In a more modern idiom the Lockean versus the Hobbesian approach translates into *Gemeinschaft* and *Gessellschaft* respectively – community and society. Ferdinand Tönnies was responsible for producing this translation. (2) The kind of attachments found in *Gemeinschaft* involve duty, obligation, loyalty, the feelings associated with familarity, predictability and agreement about the broad ends of social action. The Lockean agreement was somewhat more limited than this, and was associated more specifically with the arrangements necessary to permit individuals to possess those goods to which they were thought to be entitled, but the direction of thought is similar. Without agreement there can be no order; agreement about the rules of the system is likely to go with feelings of loyalty and obligation; if agreement, loyalty and obligation exist, the procedures and processes by which society is governed are likely, on the whole, to be accepted and to be made permanent. The examples of this in the modern world are nations, families and churches; if they possess stability, and if they show order, they do so because of profound agreement among their members and the reinforcing emotions of loyalty and obligation, and a sense of interrelated rights and duties.

The implications of this for modern international society are that if order is to be maintained, consensus must be developed among governments and peoples. There must be a convergence of opinion about the goals which should be achieved if society is to attain those qualities and characteristics thought to be indispensable. In international law, for instance, there must be agreement about principles and this must precede the setting up of formal procedures, such as police forces, for compelling obedience. In the writings of some international organisation scholars this general view of the main supporting element of the international constitution has frequently been reflected: Karl Duetsch, according to Bruce Russett, sees stability in his security community as being maintained because of a consensus among the people who form it; (3) David Mitrany saw an international community being built by functional co-operation based upon a co-operative ethos – or consensus; Dag Hammarskjold was also very much in the tradition of John Locke when he spoke of the need to develop a "sophisticated constitutionalism" which was essentially based upon agreement among governments, which were thought by Hammarskjold to be the irreducible inhabitants of international society, and which involved the general acceptance of procedures by which potential or actual disorder in international society was to be averted. (4) It is important that students should recognise these characteristic tendencies in thinking about the basis of order and that they should also understand that they involve no necessary level of centralisation or direction.

The Hobbesian tradition is perhaps followed less directly. *Gesellschaft*, or society, attaches individuals in a much more tentative way than does community, *Gemeinschaft*. Tasks are performed because of a more limited obligation or contract. Individuals may be dismissed if they fail to fulfil their contractual commitments. There is no feeling of duty or loyalty, and a much higher level of competitiveness. In modern political science terminology one conceptual equivalent is pluralism. In international relations the views of Hans Morgenthau about international society are representative of this approach. The competitive aspects of the state are stressed, and the over-riding motivation of state behaviour is seen as self-interest. Any interests are seen as legitimate in the market-place of political interaction, but it is apparent that, though self-interest and competitiveness are central to the political philosophy of Hobbes and his input into modern pluralism is in this area recognised, there is nevertheless now no exact equivalent of the Leviathan. The modern international society has no dominant power. There is, however, an equivalent where there is stability, in the acceptance by participating entities of the rules which are to govern the competition. Competitiveness, which dominates, is restrained in the self-interest of all by the recognition that certain minimum rules are necessary if the game is to be played at all. These rules are an aspect of the Leviathan, who is now revealed in modern dress, variously disguised as "the system" or perhaps "the regime": unless its rules are followed, self-interest cannot be attained. (5)

In modern theory of international organisation there are several examples of theories built upon the idea of *Gesellschaft*. The most important is probably neo-functionalism in which it is accepted by its leading founder-scholar, Ernst Haas, and his followers, that all interests "that enter the market-place" are legitimate, and that a stable political community is made up of competing interest groups who are persuaded to accept the constitution of their group because it produces rewards. (6) Stability, it should be stressed, does not arise because of a convergence of interest, or of consensus, but because of conventional limits upon continuing disagreements. It is a *managed Gesellschaft*. In views on the development of international law the equivalent of this approach is one which gives priority to the setting up of procedures for imposing sanctions upon law breakers, above agreement about principles of law. Subjects are seen as coming to agree to those laws which they can be made to obey. An example of this is in the writing of Clark and Sohn on *World Government Through World Law*, (7) which holds in essence that effective law in international society can be expected only if backed by a power which is superior to that of likely law breakers. Law requires, in other words, a redistribution of power rather than agreement on principles of law. Unfortunately the complexities of the process by which potentially warring entities are brought to agree to a superior power in international society are not discussed in these writings, though it must be admitted that they are not very different from those involved in obtaining agreement to the minimum rules required to manage a competitive system, in that they must ultimately depend upon acceptance of a better way to obtain self-interest. It might be added that there was inevitably an unstated assumption about the general character of those principles of law which would be stressed. The "power first" approach became less fashionable when it could no longer be assumed that "Western" values would predominate!

Other aspects of the basis of order in international society which students should consider, and which therefore should be mentioned, are authority, legitimacy and sovereignty and high versus low politics. These are conveniently dealt with by the teacher as linked concepts. The nettle of sovereignty will not be grasped here, but it is widely accepted that the sovereignty of the state is bound up with the authority of the government, and that each involves the views and feelings of citizens. The distinction between high and low politics is also related to the question of whether political relationships are accepted as legitimate, as well as whether actors have authority. The idea that there are no issues which are essentially matters of low politics or high politics is particularly important to the student of international organisation. It supports the idea that whether or not something is, for instance, a matter of high politics, is a matter of circumstances and perceptions, and that these, being socially determined, may change as society changes. Questions of high politics may become questions of low politics if they become the subject of legitimized relations. (8) The consolidation of international order is the spread of networks of legitimised relations, the reduction of the range of questions of high politics insisted upon by sovereign states, and the growth of international authority, which may or may not involve the erosion of the state system and the curbing of national sovereignty.

The most important point which the student should absorb, however, is that there are a large number of forms which international order reflectted in a stable constitution can take. At one level, this is a question of knowing that theories of international organisation tend to have an implicit or explicit end situation, or related alternative end situations. Hence knowledge of the theories leads to an understanding of such concepts as international government, world government, international community, functional interdependence, and even asymmetrical functional overlap. (9) At another level, however, the student is involved in a more difficult exercise. He is learning the importance of an attitude of mind, which could be called open-mindedness, towards these outcomes, and indeed towards the assumptions and, sometimes, specific arguments of the theories themselves. The main reason for seeking and acquiring this condition is that the alternative, a closed mind, is both unwise and irresponsible. It is unwise because it leads to the misunderstanding of the extent to which individuals, including the student, are themselves influenced by unconscious forces, which may be called systemic elements. Judgments about others' responses to circumstances and about the soundness of one's own position may therefore be ill-founded: the value reference of social choice is overlooked. It is irresponsible because it is a denial of the education process: it rejects or discounts views which are not in accordance with the initial position, and therefore treats the process of study more as a mechanical learning process than as a deepening of understanding. It implies that what is studied is ultimately no concern to the student. But it seems to this writer that education in the social sciences, including, of course, international relations, also inevitably involves obtaining one's bearings in relation to the major features of society, and of making at least a tentative choice of the desirable direction of evolution of that society. And, having made that choice, the student is inevitably to some degree a participant. He may not necessarily attempt to influence decisions directly through professional or pressure groups, but nevertheless in his daily life, in the routine of social exchange, he is continuingly faced with opportunities, which he may not consciously seek, to push society in one direction or another.

Mid-career students, particularly those whose work context is directive and hierarchical, sometimes experience difficulties with keeping or acquiring an open-minded attitude towards their studies. These remarks are highly speculative, and it should be stressed that the present writer is not an educational psychologist, and that they do not apply invariably to the students in the programme. But the relatively clear-cut chain of command tends to inculcate in mature students in the middle rank the attitude that decision-making is relatively impervious to systemic forces such as long-term economic forces (it is often reflected in the attitude that although there may be conditions of scarce resources, it is still the skill of the boss which counts); or to ideological factors (expressed by the opinion that while *we* study evidence, *they* deal in prejudice); or to established habits of work (the consequence of many years of working in an environment characterised by very specific bureaucratic norms). Evidence which confirms these influences is discounted in some way. The idea that people

196

may be in some cases manipulated by circumstances is either rejected or not understood. It is also difficult for them to sympathise with the idea of long-term pressure at a number of different levels within the state effecting changes rather slowly in individuals and groups and frequently without their realisation. One example of this is a great reluctance to accept the possibility of any long-term modification of national sympathies within transnational processes or structures. This problem of student attitudes is particularly important in the subject of international organisation which very often deals in long-term changes, such as the changes in attitudes towards the nation which are discussed in functionalism, and in the less tangible systemic forces. But the decisions affecting high politics made by individuals, who battle to impose themselves on circumstances, are frequently found instantly credible, because this bears an obvious relationship to life as it is thought to exist among some mid-rank students in the model of a smoothly run bureaucracy.

Personnel in mid-career, particularly if they have been successful, tend to have a well-developed sense of what is realistic. That is seen to be concerned with direction, with power, with the immediate, and with the human virtues of persistence, determination and winning: individuals are thought to impose themselves on circumstances. It is less concerned with unconscious influences, systemic constraints, and adapting to new circumstances (though very senior officers may come to be more aware of these factors). Although empirical work is necessary to test these hypotheses, this writer's view is that the more intelligent students who are successful in their existing careers in the military and diplomatic services, and analogous professions, are more likely to find empathy with subjects such as strategy, and more power-political theories, and be less sympathetic with theories which stress system, process and environment such as are more frequently found in international organisation. Those who are less settled in their career tend to show a much more varied pattern: they may be more perceptive in their understanding of longer term or "larger" factors, and consequently somewhat cynical about the changes of politics, bureaucratic or otherwise, achieving significant change. Or they may be highly impatient with the constraints of bureaucratic norms, and attracted to ways of changing things quickly, by political means, even, perhaps, revolution: they recognise the same "reality" as the successful mid-career students, but react to it differently.

The above remarks may be a serious over-simplification of the situation in the teaching and study of international relations. It may be that courses and indeed areas within courses in the subject can be classified in a much more sophisticated way in terms of their attractiveness to certain kinds of student personality. For instance, it seems to the present writer that there are some courses, which might be called *hard*, becaue of the violence (actual or potential) to which they refer. Strategy is obviously one of these, but the traditional diplomatic history type of approach is probably also a slightly *softer* form of this course, in that it also tends to centre around competitiveness and violence. Other courses, particularly the study of co-operation between states, may be called *soft*. These tend to be concerned with rather longer term processes for the building of order. Between the two are courses which have various mixtures of hardness and softness and which appeal to students frequently because of their natural interest in scandal, in deviousness, in addition to power. One or two of these courses appeal because of their relevance to personal psychology, which again brings home to students the possibility of personal manipulation with its direct and obvious pleasures. Such courses tend to be about the psychological factors in international relations. Courses which appeal to the students' interest in scandal, fixing, and so on, are those on such questions as international business. The fascination of such courses, which tend in fact towards the *hard* side, results from the peculiar combination of scandal and power which they are able to project.

The question arises of how a course could be so constructed and taught that it encourages a greater open-mindedness and balance in the student. It is assumed that nothing much can be done about the more basic kinds of appeal which students find in courses. The answer must of course be evasive: such an attitude cannot be taught, although opportunities can be given to the student – or taken from him – to acquire it. Opportunities can be presented by being very careful about presenting theories as alternative versions of a truth, and no single theory as the only true way. In doing this great care must be given to the evaluation of theories as satisfactory or unsatisfactory in terms of scholarly standards such as scientific method. But, at the same time, students should be made aware that ways of thinking about the role of international organisation, even theories of international organisation, may be accepted as legitimate or more useful, or true, by a large number of scholars or practitioners or the general public, for reasons which are essentially social psychological, and that their social status is itself one of the reasons for trying to understand them. Functionalism, for instance, has had an impact upon the thinking of international civil servants, though they may not always be familiar with details of the theory. Neo-functionalism has certainly affected the ideas of the civil servants at Brussels working for the European Communities. And of course Dag Hammarskjold's vision of the quasi-*Gemeinschaft* character of the United Nations system had an impact upon practitioners there, and upon the shape of that organisation. Sometimes rather ill-formed attitudes of the general public are related to a particular theory. The fact that theories of international organisation may have a social status is a reflection of the possibility that assumptions on which they are based are themselves related to particular socially determined values and attitudes. For example, neo-functionalism has one of its intellectual roots in the experience of mature industrial/capitalist organisation in federal America, while transactionalism is more tied in with experiences of nation-building in Europe. To take theories back to their basic assumptions, and to demonstrate that these may themselves be socially determined, or that even in the case of the most scientific theories they may have a certain arbitrary quality, is to tempt the student to re-examine his own values.

The student is presented with a picture of theories of international organisation as a symptom of an existing level of order in international society, and as an element which is helping to shape it. Theories are seen to have a number of purposes — descriptive, explanatory and prescriptive — and to have a social status — even in scholarly communities — which does not necessarily reflect their worth in science or scholarship. They are based upon a number of different assumptions, and involve different end-situations and relationships with particular social, national experiences.

An underlying difficulty with the particular sense of the realistic which is possessed by some students is that they are reluctant to accept that international organisation has any real point or purpose, and, in particular, that it can have any significant effect upon the traditional power relations between nation-states. They find it easy to believe in the importance of studying theories of strategy or the multinational business corporation when it affects the third world because they have an effect and implications which they find credible. There is a visible impact. But this is to be expected, of course, among military and diplomatic personnel, and generally among men of action: how can international organisation be anything but fairly marginal and unimportant, they ask? There are areas of potential and actual development that have been encouraging, they acknowledge, but as yet this seems to be more theory than practice. The impact of international organisation is indeed hard to convey to students with such attitudes. Much depends upon the flair and rhetorical skills of the teacher in adding colour and a feeling of importance to the subject. But more specific steps are, first, to describe the ways in which international organisation has grown. The work of Singer and Wallace, Judge, and Skjaelsbaek is helpful here: (10) something that has grown so fast must be worth watching. Secondly, the British are singularly well placed to talk about the importance of international organisation because of the involvement of the International Monetary Fund in her economic problems in the 1970s. This at least is an instance of an organisation doing something and appearing to have power. Also of course Western Europe has a very large number of institutions which are a very rich source of material to illustrate the proposition that they can act. (11) There is also the problem of convincing students that international society has a surprising amount of order despite the continuing appearance of disorder, conflict and, in some ways, worsening problems. The assertion of order seems to ring hollow when the student is faced every day with reports of international conflict in his newspapers. Ultimately this problem of teaching is insoluble except in the sense that it is possible to accumulate instances of order and to point to the evidence discussed above. But this teacher knows no certain way of measuring levels of general international order as against disorder, and presenting this to the student. In view of this, references to specific instances of impact, peace-keeping forces, disease control, common markets and so on are very important. (12)

There is, however, an alternative need which impresses the teacher of international organisation. The requirement of helping students to obtain an open-mindedness towards the subject reinforces a tendency to stress the diversity of the subject, and perhaps an eclecticism in approach, which is less tempting in other branches of international relations. But the student also expects a rather neat package of ideas, a careful organisation, and an appearance of coherence in the material, qualities which are discouraged by his other needs. He feels happiest, in other words, if there is a fairly rigid framework. The mid-career student, especially, dislikes mysteries, loose ends, the kind of murky waters in which less mature students like to drift or into which they fall. The main reason for this is that the mature student, in a position of responsibility in a chain of command, is accustomed to receiving tight instructions, a clear mandate and to giving these himself. Any blurring of the edges makes him feel uneasy, and he tends to blame and dislike a creator of mysteries, either in a senior or subject. It is not denied that all students like courses which are carefully prepared and arranged, and it is also not denied that the mature student in this type of career may also frequently receive confusing instructions. But his ideal is a carefully considered, clear-cut mandate.

The problem of coherence is worsened by the absence, because of the changing character of the subject, as we have seen, of a satisfactory single course text. This problem has been alleviated by the present writer by using a typology of theories of international organisation which arrange the theories mentioned in Chapter 4. It should be pointed out again that although various approaches have been dominant in the four successive phases of writing in international organisation, traces of all approaches have survived into the present. International organisation has accumulated theories as it has increased in complexity. The main distinction in the typology is between the various purposes of the theory. Most writing of international organisation can be divided into three broad classes under this general heading.

Adjustment theories

These are theories about styles of inter-governmental co-operation which sees states as irreducible actors and concentrates upon the understanding of ways in which governments have tried to solve problems with which they are faced. Problems may come to them, and be tackled through international organisation, from international society or from developments within their own states. Broadly they are characteristic of the first two phases.

Integration theories

They are about fundamental changes in the context of decision-making which may be found at any one of four levels of a state: that of the people, that of organised non-governmental groups, of bureaucrats and of governments. At any one of these levels changes are detected which generate processes leading to increases in contacts, links, attachments, interdependencies and interpenetration. This type of theory is found in the last two phases.

Constitutional theories

These have one of two purposes: they may either prescribe an ideal order in international society and in this sense are similar to the classical political philosophy of the nineteenth century and earlier (Locke, Hobbes, Mill, Burke and so on); or they use a particular constitutional form such as *confederalism* or *parallel legislation* as the model which illuminates existing arrangements among a group of states, and provides a way of arranging and selecting descriptive or explanatory material. They may be found in any of the four phases.

These three broad types of theory by no means exhaust the range of writings in international organisation, but they do organise a significant percentage of it, and provide hooks on to which a number of other related writings can be hung. This is not the place for an exhaustive breakdown of the categories — the present writer has attempted this elsewhere — but it would be appropriate to give some indication of the way in which they may be used. (13) It should be remembered that the object is to give the student a sense of the coherence of the field, however arbitrary, and to give them the feeling of progress through a determinate territory.

1. *Adjustment theories* are conveniently broken down into styles of inter-governmental co-operation which are illuminated by reference to characteristic decision-making processes, in particular international institutions and types of security systems and security procedure. The styles of inter-governmental co-operation are called co-operation, harmonisation, co-ordination and supranationalism, and these are arranged so that they reflect an increasing impact upon national policy and an increasing role for the international institutions. *Co-operation* is found in limited, one-off acts of common enterprise among governments; *harmonisation* involves the consolidation of existing compatabilities in policy by international agreement sometimes expressed in treaty or convention. The impact upon policy is rather small; there is an expectation, however, of alignment and an unwillingness to endanger accidentally existing levels of agreement. There is an expectation of a convergence of interest which will increase the area of harmonisation in the future. Examples of this are the *partial agreements* of the Council of Europe. *Co-ordination* exists when states are aware of a superordinate goal, and an institution is able to manipulate national interest so that government policies are fitted into a common plan. There is an impact upon national policies, which are otherwise divergent, and, sometimes, on structures. Examples of this are the NATO Force Plan and the annual programme of the OEEC, and the various aid programmes of the UN and OECD. There are of course many other examples of co-ordination in international organisation and institutions. *Supranationalism*, the most advanced form of intergovernmental co-operation, occurs when states allow an institution to act independently in relation to groups and individuals within the state. They grant this right to the international institution because they accept that this is a way of helping them to adjust to new needs and problems; and it helps the states to survive.

The development of these themes can be adjusted to the interests and enthusiasms of a particular teacher in particular international institutions and organisations. But it is useful, as international organisation is about order, to relate them to the various "ideal" types of security system such as collective security, the concert system, and the balance of power, and to security procedures, such as those of pacific settlement, preventive diplomacy, permissive enforcement and enforcement. (14) The teacher should explore the relationships between procedures and systems and attempt to categorise the style of inter-governmental co-operation which is characteristic of each of them. For example, preventive diplomacy is associated with the style of inter-governmental co-operation called harmonisation as it depends upon a minimum consensus among the major powers — not, obviously, necessarily a positive agreement — and their recognition that involvement in a dispute could endanger existing harmony. Co-operation, on the other hand, is more related to pacific settlement procedures such as mediation, arbitration, conciliation and good offices. These comments should at least suggest the way in which a large number of writings (Claude, Burton, Haas and so on (15)) can be related to a coherent general framework. The ideas can be expanded, as has been pointed out, into detailed discussion of the working of international institutions.

2. *Integration theories* which refer to the *first* level (see p. 201 above), namely changes at the popular level, may be illustrated by reference to the ideas of Karl Deutsch and of David Mitrany. They stress the development of a feeling of community at the mass level, though they are also concerned with developments elsewhere. Transnationalism is related to the development of integration at the second level, that of non-governmental groups. Neo-functionalism concerns, particularly, bureaucrats and people in key institutional settings (the interpenetration of bureaucracies, changes in decision-making). These theories, which may be called *process federalism*, such as those of Dag Hammarskjold, concentrate on the integration of governments, in the sense that they are mainly concerned with processes by which separate governments can be increasingly involved in an international federal constitution. (16) One or two other theories, such as those about the implications of more powerful institutions for the exercise of control by governments and people, may be related to the framework, though again much depends upon the individual teacher's judgement. It may be convenient, for instance, to discuss the problems of popular control over the work of international institutions in the context of neo-functionalism, which is most explicitly concerned with the transfer of power to a new centre, and therefore by implication poses this problem in a more serious form. The control problems of governments, discussed by for instance Cox and Jacobson, may also be discussed in this specific context, and for the same reasons. The various integration theories are described briefly in Chapter 4 and it would be superfluous to discuss them again at this point.

Constitutional theories of the highly prescriptive kind are frequently dismissed as being too speculative to be worthy of discussion in the classroom context. This writer disagrees. They illustrate the problems of prescription, itself something of value, and are frequently useful indicators of thinking about features of the contemporary international system. Writings such as those of Clarence Streit, on *Union Now*, and Clark and Sohn, on *World Peace Through World Law*, are therefore well worth considering. (17) Their style of reasoning, their assumptions, their view of the world should be considered. The constitutional analogy approach is also useful as a provider of particular insights into regional politics such as the development of the European Community. The present writer has again considered this question elsewhere.

This typology has been sketched in this chapter to illustrate, however faintly, the way in which a measure of coherence can be imposed upon a rather dispersed un-unified subject. This writer has found in such a typology a way of overcoming the problems of the lack of a coherent text on international organisation which includes the theories of the sixties and seventies. (It also provides the framework of a recent general text of which the present writer was co-editor. (18)) Students in the USC programme have seemed to find in it a useful map through a rather difficult terrain.

The requirements of teaching the subject called international organisation to a group of mature mid-career students are the same in many important respects as those required to teach any group any subject. One expects to educate them, or, rather, to help them to educate themselves. And one expects them to understand the major problems of the field when they have completed the course. In the field of international organisation one expects them to be equipped also, more specifically, with the tools for evaluating any descriptive, explanatory theory about international society, and not simply to condemn it because of a lack of accord with preferred values. They should try to understand that it is part of a complex and long tradition. When the elements of this tradition are understood the first important steps have been taken towards the building of bridges between various intellectual disciplines, and towards the development of an *inter-subjective consensus*, not just among scholars but among a wider group.

References

1. Inis L. Claude Jr, *Swords into Plowshares*, loc. cit., p. 48. See also Leon N. Lindberg's comments in reply to this point made by Claude reported in Carnegie Endowment for International Peace, *Functionalism: Final Report of the Conference at Bellagio*, University of Sussex, 1969, p. 3.

2. For discussion of these concepts see Geoffrey Goodwin, "International Institutions and International Order" in Alan James (ed.), *The Bases of International Order*, London, Oxford University Press, 1973, pp. 156–87, esp. pp. 159–63; and Paul Taylor, *International Cooperation Today*, London, Elek 1971, p. 4.

3. Bruce M. Russett, *Power and Community in World Politics*, San Francisco, Freeman, 1974, p. 328.

4. See Geoffrey Goodwin in Alan James, loc. cit., p. 160.

5. For an excellent account of the pluralist view of interest see Ernst B. Haas, *Beyond the Nation State*, Stanford, Stanford University Press, 1964, pp. 30–40 and *passim*; for an excellent account of "regimes", see John Gerard Ruggie, "International Responses to Technology: Concepts and Trends", *International Organization*, Vol. 29, No. 3, Summer 1975, pp. 557–84.

6. Ernst B. Haas, *Beyond the Nation State*, loc. cit., p. 34.

7. Grenville Clark and Louis B. Sohn, *World Peace Through World Law*, Cambridge, Mass. (3rd edition), 1966.

8. For a discussion of these problems in the context of functionalism see A. J. R. Groom, "Functionalism and World Society" in A. J. R. Groom and Paul Taylor (eds), *Functionalism: Theory and Practice in International Relations*, London, University of London Press, 1975, at p. 99.

9. Ernst B. Haas, "The Study of Regional Integration: The Joys and Anguish of Pre-theorising", *International Organization*, Vol. XXIV, No. 4, Autumn 1970, p. 634.

10. See also Anthony J. N. Judge, "International Institutions: Borderline Cases, Functional Substitutes and Possible Alternatives" in Paul Taylor and A. J. R. Groom (eds), *International Organization: A Conceptual Approach*, London, Frances Pinter, 1978.

11. See Michael Palmer and John Lambert *et al.*, *European Unity: A Survey of the European Organizations*, London, Allen & Unwin, 1968.

12. One recent useful account of international institutions at work is Evan Luard, *International Agencies: the emerging framework of Interdependence*, London, Macmillan, 1977.

13. See Paul Taylor, "A Conceptual Typology of International Organizations" in Paul Taylor and A. J. R. Groom (eds), *International Organization: A Conceptual Approach*, loc. cit., pp. 118–36.

14. Ibid., pp. 124–5.

15. See, for example, John W. Burton, *Conflict and Communication*, London, Macmillan, 1969.

16. See Dag Hammarskjold, Speech at University of Chicago, 1 May 1960 in Wilder Foote (ed.), *Dag Hammarskjold — Servant of Peace*, London, The Bodley Head, 1962, p. 252.

17. See ref. 7 above.

18. See ref. 10 above.

CHAPTER 13

Approaches and Problems Arising in Mid-Career Education in International Political Economy

Jeff Harrod

Introduction

It is in the nature of teaching and the intellectual basis of any teacher's competence that each teacher may have a different philosophy of teaching, see different objectives and seek out different results. Therefore, any philosophy of teaching described here is not a normative or evangelical statement, but rather a statement of personal inclinations which need not be heeded or shared by others.

In this writer's view teaching has two basic objectives: to impart knowleged, whether it be facts or methods, and to assist in the development of awareness, that is to make connections, develop insights and see patterns which would have otherwise remained unobserved. If the objective of increased awareness is to be achieved then presentation and emphasis must change with the psychological and social base of any particular group of students, even though the body of knowledge in any subject remains the same. For this reason alone substantial differences in presentation and approach must be made between the teaching of undergraduates, graduate and mid-career students.

In any educational process the teacher enters into a dialectic with the sum total of cognitive accumulation in any individual student. Usually this process leaves with the student a residual amalgam comprised of background, perceptions, culture and values fused with the facts, ideas and insights developed in the educational process. This is not always the case; sometimes, and especially in adult education, there is a temporal and nominal displacement of existing perceptions with those of the writers in the discipline or the teacher, for the sake of exams. In other cases new ideas may be produced which overtake or add to those existing within the subject.

In undergraduate teaching there is a dialectic between the teacher and the students' high-school teacher, the homilies of parents and peers, the psychology of post-adolescence, all of which are set in a life experience, that of a pupil and student, of which the teacher has had direct experience. Particularly, perceptions and ideas of undergraduates have usually been untested by direct experience. In the teaching of mid-career students the dialectic is with the residual amalgams of past formal education, the accumulated perceptions and prejudices of mature life experience, and the tested ideas and perceptions, all these set in a framework of work and life of which the teacher has usually *not* had direct experience. These factors of a mid-career student's background can be examined in relation to the subject matter of international political economy in order to indicate the special teaching requirements and course structures for effective teaching of the subject. These factors may be grouped under three headings: (i) Background Knowledge and Attitudes; (ii) Career Position; and (iii) Academic Background.

Background knowledge and attitudes of mid-career students in international political economy

The historic events connected with the world economy which were described in Chapter 5 are part of the experience of mid-career students. They can usually remember the media presentation of all or some of these events, have felt the effects of them and sometimes experienced them at first hand. The impact of these events on the student varies and what follows is a partial summary of some of the more important attitudes and perceptions developed from such experience.

Clearly the most important overall effect of the developments in the world economy in the past ten years is heightened awareness of its existence and its importance to domestic politics and international conflict. The politics of international economic relations has begun to replace the previous widespread involvement in strategy and the issues surrounding nuclear armaments. This is, of course, the reason for the increased demand for the subject.

Another important impact on the student comes via the media. International political economy is treated at great length by the media; the most substantial change in newspaper content, for example, over the past ten years has been the increase in business and economic news of all types. The mid-career student is most often an avid consumer of media output and as a result believes that he is in possession of considerable knowledge and insights into the subject. Unfortunately, the structure of the media, the nature of the recruitment of its professionals and the need to satisfy diverse audiences mean that it presents a fairly simplistic explanation of events, usually reflecting single cause arguments which rest on a number of generally accepted myths. The media views on any particular world problem must then be taken as a given, and a base from which to start discussions.

A further complication in relation to the general background knowledge of the mid-career student results from the activities of pressure groups and organisations concerned with the problems of world poverty. These groups create a vast amount of publicity on the global maldistribution of wealth, on poor countries and on relations between rich and poor countries. This has resulted in the circulation of partial information and also assisted in the precipitation of moralist attitudes towards the problems. Such exposure often promotes two attitudes towards the structure and mechanisms of the world economy: either a resistance or irritation with any discussion which seems to disguise "the real facts" or impedes a search for a prescription to world poverty and continued emphasis on the ethics of the situation; or *an aggressiveness* towards discussions which, it is felt, will lead yet again to an amplification of the already known facts and a call for, what is now known, as a "new international economic order".

Mid-career students rarely approach a subject with an intellectual and attitudinal neutrality, and the origin and nature of the attitudes, as these last, are of great importance in the adjustment of teaching techniques. The current over-exposure of the subject in the media makes this task a little easier in international political economy because many of the attitudes are derived from this over-exposure.

Career position

International political economy is a policy subject in that the concepts, arguments and analysis are all inputs to policy-making at the highest level. Most mid-career students are not in policy-making positions and many realise that they will never be. Yet unlike other subjects, where it is realised that the subject is unlikely to have any practical application short of an increase in general awareness and knowledge, students generally expect to get more useful knowledge from international political economy.

There is, therefore, as a result of their career position, sometimes a resistance to the examination of theories or the use of abstraction because of the apparent lack of practical application. While the undergraduate may ask if theory is relevant to his future work and ambitions, the mid-career student, already in the middle of his undergraduate future, may ask if theory is relevant at all.

Such resistance is found, of course, in all subjects and there are many counters and explanations of this position but international political economy has the advantage in that the impact and results of theories and perceptions held by policy-makers, past and present, exist concretely because they affect material life. Particularly relevant to mid-career students and useful in teaching is that it can often be demonstrated that accepted views, myths, policies or fashionable ideas about the world economy have affected working lives and career patterns through absorption into organisational ideology or policy.

Finally many mid-career students have had international experience, sometimes with economic organisations. While this experience is often valuable material for the group it can also have the effect of reinforcing badly thought-out values and positions and may cause level-of-analysis problems. Part of the challenge of mid-career teaching is to be able to incorporate parochially developed attitudes and views of social reality derived from career experience into the abstractions and generalisations which are necessary for an education in the nature of world economy.

Academic background

International political economy suffers from two basic problems in relation to the academic background of mid-career students; first, the lack of any academic background in economics and secondly, the presence of any academic background in economics. Any course for mid-career students must then provide both basic economics and remedial economics at the same time

Students with economics may be apprehensive of having to deal with economists' concepts, which have in general been surrounded by an aura of complexity and difficulty, mainly to disguise their commonsense basis. For these students, economic concepts must be approached from the definition of economics as "applied common sense". Those who have had an economics background may find the looser approach to international economics a strain. Economists have been the most confident of scholars (some would say self-righteous and discipline-centred) which has left its mark on some students. These latter find it difficult to see the theories and concepts of their undergraduate work, which they believed to be neutral and scientific, as perhaps emerging from a power and historical context or being used for a political purpose.

For the mid-career student, then, the course must provide some introductory economics for those whose background has been in other social or natural sciences and remedial economics for those who had economics but not political economy.

Conclusion

On the basis of this analysis of the background of mid-career students and its relationship to the subject matter of international political economy, a variety of special teaching techniques and presentations can be developed.

Thus, for example, the importance of the media in providing information and forming attitudes meant that provision had to be made for critical use and discussion and analysis of media events and reports. Likewise, it was found that to try to provide remedial and introductory economics at the beginning of the course in a block was a clumsy method of teaching, it lost the interest of those who had economics and disappointed those who looked for the politics in the subject. One method to overcome this was to devise a course which presented the structure and operation of the world economy by major transaction — aid, trade and finance — and provided the "pure" economics of each before turning to the political economy of the transaction. This provided a continuous link between the economics and international politics and heightened the sense of interplay between theories of economics and their political origins and international political impacts.

Once the analysis of the mid-career student's background and needs in relation to any particular subject is completed, each teacher would opt for different techniques and heuristic devices according to his or her own style. What seems to be essential in mid-career teaching is that from the beginning student background is analysed and placed before the administrative or traditional undergraduate demands of the subject.

The future of international political economy in mid-career teaching

International political economy is a new subject in university course structures, or at least rehabilitated with a new content, compared with its nearest approximation, the traditional political economy as developed in the latter part of the last century. Its newness has meant that approaches, content and analysis have not yet developed into an accepted "mainstream".

The inroads made into positivist economics and the reluctance to adopt a deductive, speculative or ideological position within the subject has led to a teaching of the subject which alternates between a descriptive, analytical and prescriptive style. At present, the tendency is to adopt a descriptive approach towards the competing world views, ideologies and models involved in international political economy, a positivist approach towards testing these theories and a prescriptive approach towards the perceived current problems ("managing the world economy").

A future development may be the establishment of major texts and of positively or dialectically accepted doyens in the field. This will certainly result in a greater uniformity of approach than is currently apparent, not that this is necessarily desirable. If this does not happen three major demands are likely to be made on the subject. The first is for grander theorising as to the global origins of economic systems, of industrialisation and of the societies which it produces, and the basic international relationships which they precipitate. (1) The second is connected with the "end of growth" era, in the form of a demand for illumination of the economic linkages which have political effects and which spill over into international political relations. (2) The field is currently poorly equipped to deal with this demand and may indeed fail to meet the challenge. Finally, demands of a predictive nature will also be made on research surrounding the field. Unlike past predictive efforts the demand is more likely for broader constructed "alternative futures", than precise predictions based upon exponential projections and catastrophe theory.

These demands, if met, will help the field to keep pace with the growing sophistication and interest in the larger and more abstract problems which the late 1960s students will bring with them as mid-career students in the late 1970s and early 1980s.

References

1. As is found in the work of such authors as K. Polanyi, *The Great Transformation*, New York, 1944, and subsequent work; Barrington Moore, *Social Origins of Dictatorship and Democracy*, London, 1967; C. Kerr and Associates, *Industrialism and Industrial Man*, New York, 1960 and E. J. Hobshawn, *Industry and Empire*, Harmondsworth, 1969.
2. Some attempt is made in this respect in R. W. Cox and J. Harrod, *The Social Roots of Power* (provisional title), forthcoming, 1979.

CHAPTER 14

The Teaching of Foreign Policy Analysis

Randolph Kent

Why are we trying to make a distinction between teaching "normal" graduate students and "mid-career, part-time, graduate students"? Are we suggesting that we make academic concessions for the latter which we would not do for the former? Are we saying that, given the nature of part-time, mid-career graduate students, we impose different types of requirements and assessment procedures than we would if our students were full-time? Are we assuming that the differences between the two kinds of student bodies are indeed so distinct that the substance and presentation of our academic material must adjust significantly to meet such differences?

The answer is simple: in one sense "yes", and in another sense, "no".

From the perspective of teaching "foreign policy analysis" to mid-career students, the questions above might be answered in another way. There is a body of material within the realm of foreign policy analysis which we feel is important to transmit to those involved in a graduate programme in international relations; and while that material is a "relative constant", the way it is presented and assessed is dependent upon the strengths and weaknesses of the types of students involved.

Accepting the obvious fact that differences between types of students do make a difference, it is perhaps incumbent upon us to define what we view as the essential differences. As with any attempt at generalising, we may well be accused of "over-homogenising" our groups under focus, but here we shall just assume that our own experiences will reflect an honest attempt at an accurate, though admittedly subjective, evaluation, and that many of the gross distortions or exaggerations might be described perhaps as yet another example of a "levels of analysis" problem.

The nature of the student body

The mid-career students whom we serve — whether from the military, multinational corporations or the diplomatic corps — are involved in one way or another in what is regarded as "the real world". More often than not, they undertake the programme to enhance their understanding of the environment in which they operate. They seek in other words to expand their effectiveness within a context defined either by their professions or by what they already perceive they should know.

This factor has three consequences that might be categorized as the expectations, the organisational perspective and the preconceived notions of students in the programme, each of which must be borne in mind by the instructor of foreign policy analysis.

In my experience mid-career students approach the study of inter-national relations with strong hopes of practical insights into the mechanics of global politics. In one sense, theory courses are frequently regarded by students as rights of passage that will allow them to proceed to the substantive reality of the discipline. That reality is viewed as emanating out of either "area courses" or courses where titles and descriptions suggest practical knowledge, such as "foreign policy analysis".

Mid-career students want to know "how governments work", "how interest groups impact upon the machinery of foreign policies", and are frequently frustrated by the "pre-theoretical considerations" which such issues engender. The various psychological and cybernetic approaches that suggest a lack of responsiveness in foreign policy institutions are too often viewed as "academic frills" or as "irrelevancies" when there is a "real world" in which nation-states appear to be responding "rationally" (in the Realist sense) to actions of others.

Thus, in presenting foreign policy analysis from the perspective suggested by Chapter 6, we are immediately confronted with a gulf between the expectations of students and the ambiguity and inconclusive state of the foreign policy analysis art.

The organisational perspectives of students who generally are occupied with the day-to-day problems of large organisations are, on the other hand, a significant bonus to the foreign policy analysis instructor. Not only are students receptive to the dilemmas involved in foreign policies emerging from the labyrinth of organisational and bureaucratic politics, but they enthusiastically proffer their own experiences to sustain the potency of the bureaucratic politics "message". However, herein lies an interesting paradox; for while more than aware of the limits of organsational cap-abilities within their own institutions — governmental or non-governmental

— they often are unwilling to acknowledge that other institutions, governments, etc., might be equally as constrained. For example, for our American students the implications of bureaucratic or organisational processes upon U.S. foreign policy are clear and apparent, but that the Soviet or Israeli systems might be susceptible to the same failings is a consideration often difficult for students to incorporate into their approaches to foreign policy analysis.

In one sense, students' reluctance to apply the organisational theme to other state systems goes hand in hand with a fixed image with which most of our students view global politics, one which we described in an earlier chapter as the "billiard-ball" model. To a very significant extent, it is a view promulgated by professional demands: one which tends to stress a difference between the "real world" and a world of the classroom; one which assumes rational consistency in the vast majority of state actions; one which engenders the belief that most state actions are carefully calculated moves in a well-defined chess game. To the naval intelligence officer with responsibilities to monitor the Soviet fleet in the Mediterranean, Soviet manoeuvrings are viewed as part of holistic pursuits of national interests. Elements of Soviet bureaucratic politics or disjointed organizational processes are discounted in the intelligence officer's report, and instead such fleet movements are regarded as essentially rational and consistent ploys in the bi-polar game. (1)

The same tendency to cling to such billiard-ball assumptions seems to be characteristic of non-military students as well as those, for example, from multinational corporations or the diplomatic corps. Beyond professional reinforcements, the billiard-ball model reflects partly a generational factor and partly a fact of media reinforcement. For those students exposed directly or indirectly to the study of international politics in the early 1950s or 1960s, the prevailing orientation of their study was the world of the Realists. This conception of state actions is in turn perpetuated by the media's tendency to describe state actions as fundamentally rational, consistent and holistic. This last point is not to suggest that the perspective of the disjointed and incremental foreign policy process is indeed the right and only view, rather the point is made merely to suggest that alternatives to the rational state process view are more difficult to broach to our type of student than the conventional graduate student.

Ultimately probing the grey areas of the analytic and cybernetic decision-making processes is in some senses to challenge the competences of students' own institutions. But let me also suggest another paradox which not infrequently emerges. While on the one hand our students clearly recognise the impact of organisational processes and bureaucratic politics upon the system in which they, themselves, operate, they also tend to consider themsleves independent of such impacts. In a recent evaluation of 22 students' reactions to the consequences of the organisational/bureaucratic perspective upon their own decision-making, only two students sited the perspectives' relevance to their own work. The remainder either felt that for them the perspective was principally of "academic interest" or assumed that "I don't get caught in the trap because of the nature of my job". (2)

In the classroom context

Yes, there is a distinct difference between the conventional graduate student and our mid-career student, and the contrast is nowhere more marked than in the classroom. It is not the quality of research assignments or examination performance which reflects the difference; it is rather the diversity of knowledge, the relative intolerance of ambiguity, the attitude towards instructors, and the approaches required to motivate students — all part of the classroom environment — which seems to spell the distinction.

One of the most striking aspects of our programme, and I would imagine of any programme which deals with our diverse type of student body, is the tremendous disparity of knowledge, reflecting in part cultural and social as well as educational and professional diversity. While all students must meet the graduate school requirements of the university, the fact of the matter is that a Nigerian diplomat with an "upper second" in English from Ahmadu Bello University, Zaria, will be at a disadvantage in a U.S. foreign policy course when compared to the U.S. naval officer with a political science degree from Northwestern and experience as a White House fellow.

Looking around the classroom, the instructor teaching the politics of a region, of a specific nation-state or foreign policy analysis in general cannot but be struck by the immediate difficulty of finding the right level to pitch lectures. The issue is not a comment on students' abilities but instead is a statement about the differing background and experiences of students. This factor is also reflected in a further potential hazard, namely, the lop-sided dynamics generated in the classroom. Specialists can take over; and not necessarily for the common good. A student whose profession is banking might, for example, launch into the intricacies of Regulation X in the context of the 1971 dollar crisis, and leave the rest of the class perhaps at a loss. This potential hazard also has an opposite side, one which instead of being described as "lop-sided dynamics" might be described as no dynamics at all.

Our type of student is not only sensitive about what he does not know, but also what he does know. In other words, he or she may be very unwilling to proffer his or her own experience and add to discussions for the simple reason that the student may have too great an expertise about a particular issue and feels embarrassed about "showing off" or reluctant because of the potential confidentiality of the information he or she could offer. As opposed to classroom discussions dominated by a few individuals, this latter situation offers the uncomfortable prospect of no discussion at all.

In suggesting differences between the normal and mid-career graduate student, there is a temptation to make comparisons far more didactic and clear cut than perhaps are warranted. When one states that mid-career students are less tolerant of ambiguity than the conventional graduate student, it is not an observation universally applicable nor one which implies an extreme degree. That mature students are less tolerant of ambiguity than other graduate students is part of a "grey area" of distinctions. In dealing with mature students, it is my experience that they consistently prefer being told "what it is" than "what it might be", they prefer the instructor to proselytise (as long as it has no overt ideological commitment) rather than pose a range of possible alternatives. More often than not from the student's point of view, a successful class is one which leaves the student with a specific set of points which indicates the instructor's views, and not one in which the student has to deal with the ambiguity of counterveiling scenarios, alternative paradigmatic perspectives and contending approaches.

The instructor's views also suggests a further aspect of the classroom context, that of the relative deference to the instructor. Once "the professor" has given his views, it can on occasion be very difficult to generate discussion for the simple reason that "the issue has now been covered". Discussion too often revolves around the periphery of the subject, and direct confrontation over main issues seems to be limited once the "authority" has spoken. While our students are as outspoken as any about the value of a particular class or about the quality of an instructor, there remains in the classroom a sense of greater willingness to defer to the supposed "expert." Generally the exception to the rule arises over points of specific facts or details, when, for example, a particular re-structuring of the NATO Planning Group is misinterpreted by the lecturer, a student might well point it out. Yet, on matters of concepts, themes and most substantive issues, the student's willingness and/or feeling of the need to challenge the instructor is less apparent than in normal graduate classroom conditions.

Earlier I mentioned the natural gulf which emerges between students' expectations – given their reasons for undertaking the programme – and instructor's interests – given the theoretical approaches to the study of foreign policy. Seeking ways to bridge that gulf is in one sense fundamental to ensuring that levels of motivation in the class are maintained. While I have suggested that a degree of didacticism is preferable to academic ambiguity, there is also a very apparent need for gearing a "foreign policy analysis" course to meet in part the preconceived assumptions which students have about the purpose and substance of such a course. A course on foreign policy analysis may cover cognitive mapping, organisational and group behaviour, attribution theory and decision-making theory, and perhaps never actually explain the behaviour of China and Japan, as discussed in newspapers, magazines and the like. But, here is where the compromise or the bridge-building begins; for whatever the academic justification of maintaining a foreign policy analysis programme on a high level of abstraction, the interest and motivation of a class will deteriorate if certain kinds of preconceived expectations are not fulfilled. The point goes beyond merely offering examples to substantiate a thoretical proposition; the instructor must take his theoretical propositions and have them emerge through cases – "the real world" – with which students can identify. To trace, for example, the communications networks in the Israeli Government in 1973, in the context of the Middle East War of that year, is a more effective way to impart the message of role and cybernetic theories to our type of student than to lead with the theories and add a smattering of brief examples. I would prefer the latter because it would ensure that the theoretical propositions are well grounded; but I compromise my own inclinations in order to ensure that a workable level of motivation is maintained.

Given such factors which emerge in the classroom context, are there ways which I have found to mitigate the problems and utilise the strengths of our kind of mature student body? The answer depends, in part, on how foreign policy analysis enters the student's particular programme.

The approach outlined in an earlier chapter (Chater 6) as the fluid boundaries of the foreign policy analysis field enters a student's programme in at least two or three ways. A student is briefly exposed to aspects of decision-making theories and comparative studies of foreign policies in the introductory course entitled *Theory and Methodology in International Relations*. More often than not a student will also find that these approaches will be used in such area courses as *Contemporary*

International Relations of Europe or *Formulation of American Foreign Policy*.

Since my own experience with mid-career students stems principally from teaching either *Formulation of American Foreign Policy* or *Foreign Policy Analysis*, I shall base my observations upon these two. Naturally each poses its own set of teaching problems and each shares certain common features. Furthermore, as I have tried to suggest before, the field of foreign policy analysis is indeed multifaceted, and where and what to select from the plethora of approaches is but another fundamental concern.

United States foreign policy as a regional study in the foreign policy analysis context

The very term "regional studies" suggests regional and national uniqueness. It implies "idiographic" material which serves as explanatory bases for the actions of particular states or groups of states. The term certainly does not overtly convey a theme of general applicability, or, nomothetic knowledge, to the study of states as a specie of actor. And, yet I feel that both idiographic characteristics and general applicability can be presented in such regional area courses as U.S. foreign policy.

Given what I have termed as the gulf between expectations and the characteristics of our student body, my approach to the study of contemporary issues in U.S. foreign policy poses three demands upon me: (i) an approach which will survey the idiographic material suggested by the title of the course; (ii) a means of involving our students in the subject matter and overcoming the lack of classroom dynamics too often due to the diversity of student backgrounds; and (iii) an approach which will allow for the introduction of a foreign policy analysis theme that leaves a message more nomothetic than the course title implies.

America's ubiquitous post-war role always poses the problem of where to start. However, every instructor in this area of international politics has his or her own sense of what is important, and probably by necessity hazards the potential criticism of incompleteness by just delving in areas which the instructor finds of particular interest. In my U.S. foreign policy course, I seek to uncover in the most general sense major points of continuity and departure in America's relations with other powers. The survey of such major points is essentially contemporary history, tracing the evolution from Potsdam to the Pacific Doctrine of U.S. responses to the international environment. A more conventional historic survey is, in my view, necessarily intertwined with aspects of political economy, and, therefore, the pattern beginning with the Bretton Woods and San Francisco Conferences progresses inexorably over nine classes through the Tokyo Rounds and Pacific disengagements. Yet, the approach is not merely a review of contemporary history; instead it suggests a theme which goes well beyond a mere regurgitation of historical linkages. Slowly, over the first nine lectures, I hope to convey to students that there are patterns to the U.S. political adjustment process; that the types and degrees of such adjustments depend upon those factors which determine the capability of the United States (and perhaps nation-states in general) to be responsive to their environments. Hence, a theme begins to emerge which goes beyond the idiographic; for while one can seek explanations of the adjustment process in terms of America's particular legislative–executive relations, one can also find explanations in the context of cybernetic, cognitive and analytic paradigms as well. Take, for example, the continuity of "containment" as a leitmotif of post-war U.S. foreign policy. Despite one level of adjustment, which might be described as "tactical" (e.g. the Eisenhower Doctrine), it would appear that in the face of a global environment which had been significantly transformed during the late 1950s and 1960s, the U.S. clung to the basic tenets of a policy, formulated in the early post-war period, for more than twenty-five years. On one level, one can point to the idiographic; but on another level one can posit the question of the degree to which cognitive consistency, attribution theory and the like serve as an equally powerful level of explanation. And, in this same context, as an explanation for the demise of containment, does one merely rest with the idiographic or does one suggest such explanations as a "systems overload" in the cybernetic sense or attitude change in a Festinger sense?

These are questions to which I will return in discussing the third demand which arises in teaching our types of students a regional area course in a foreign policy context. At this stage, however, the first point is merely this: the demands for idiographic insights can be met, the gulf between expectations can be narrowed, and the pattern which leads to more nomothetic understanding can be established, when broaching such a difficult subject as U.S. foreign policy.

Clearly teaching to be effective entails student involvement. Yet, student involvement goes beyond merely generating discussion in class; more fundamentally it involves stimulating a sense of relevance of and identification with the subject on the part of the student. Given the diversity of students' backgrounds perhaps surprisingly the easiest problem to resolve is the lack of a common level of information, for in a more "informational sense" there are a variety of books, e.g. W. G. Carleton's

Revolution in American Foreign Policy, which can establish a common base.

What is far more difficult is to inculcate the individual student with a sense of identification with the subject. The problem is in part a perceptual one. How does someone from a totally different culture transpose his or her own political assumptions into the peculiarities of American concerns and objectives? How does someone who comes from a country outside the immediate realm of bi-polar struggles find relevance in such considerations? How does an American citizen integrate his understanding of American objectives and concerns with the concerns and objectives of other states, or, in other words, with the international environment in which the United States has to act and respond?

While such questions are by no means completely resolvable, or unique to my course or to courses which incorporate a wide range of "international practitioners", my response has been simply to attempt to deal with the issues of relevance and recognition through the type of course requirements which I assign. For example, a student is asked to undertake a research probject employing his or her particular expertise (e.g. military, financial, diplomatic) in analysing an aspect of my survey of U.S. foreign policy. The emphasis of the project is not to deal with the policy component as a holistic national initiative, but rather to concentrate upon a particular situation as seen from bureaucratic and interest group perspectives. A diplomat from Egypt might be asked to analyse the communication flows from various Egyptian ministries during the formation of the Baghdad Pact; or an American banker might be asked to analyse the Japanese governmental process during the 1970 demands for Japanese revaluation; or the student in the U.S. military might be asked to analyse the implications of the Multilateral Force from the British Ministry of Defence or French military perspective.

Whatever the particular subject, this type of assignment serves several functions. It makes the study of U.S. foreign policy "relevant" to the extent that it utilises a student's particular expertise in the context of the subject matter. It also aids in establishing a degree of "rapport" or familiarity with the subject as a whole to the extent that the student proceeds to the analysis of a particular U.S. foreign policy episode from a cultural perspective with which he or she is familiar. (For those from the United States, they proceed from the security of understanding more or less the American governmental process into the unknown of an aspect of America's international environment).

Furthermore, this type of assignment – by signalling that various levels of expertise and cultural diversity can be incorporated into the general subject matter — also assists in stimulating classroom dynamics. In one sense, everyone is an "expert" since each is encouraged to view the subject from the "correctness" of his or her own perspective.

On another plain, this kind of assignment has yet another benefit, stemming from the particular way the interactions of states are analysed. In analysing to the extent possible the communication flows between governments, between governments and interest groups, etc., one begins to get away from the conception of the holisticness of states' actions, including those of the United States and the states with which the United States interacts. In other words, one begins by such assignments to move away from billiard-ball conceptions into alternative "paradigmatic" explanations.

This point leads to what I feel is the third obligation imposed upon me as an instructor: an approach which will allow for the introduction of a foreign policy theme that leaves a message more nomothetic than the course title suggests. Through the first nine lectures, in outlining what I have called the idiographic content, I have begun to establish patterns of continuity and change in the foreign policy behaviour of the United States. I have sought to assess that country's responsive and adaptive capabilities over approximately a thirty-year period. In the meantime, students in working on assignments have most likely begun — consciously or unconsciously — to deal with a variety of variables (i.e. process variables) which suggest non-Realist explanations of policy behaviour. The time seems right to suggest a more universal theme.

The last four lectures of the course are spent on exploring factors which might inhibit the responsive capabilities and adaptive capacities of states. Students are given brief insights into the cognitive worlds of Holsti, Kelman and others, into the group inhibitions suggested by authors such as Janis, and into the complexities of governmental processes discussed by an ever-increasing body of writers. With this build-up, adaptive and responsive capabilities are considered in terms of the limitations imposed by the factors above; crises are viewed from the vantage points of cognitive, cybernetic and analytic levels; and ultimately the question is posed of the degree to which policy-makers in the United States, those who formulated and those who perpetuated "containment", or the policy-makers of any state, can adjust to the international environment as readily as needs, global values and critics might demand.

Foreign policy analysis as a course

The first thing which strikes me as I review the ways I have taught foreign policy analysis is the change in my approach to presenting the theoretical issues entailed in the subject. When I first undertook this subject, I felt that it was of critical importance to emphasise the theoretical under-pinnings, and leave the practical "reality", the application to filter into the subject almost tangentially. What was of ultimate importance, I felt, was to ensure that the groundwork was laid, that the theory – which, outside the classroom context, students would probably never make time to consider – was well established.

However, after a great deal of experimenting, one thing became very clear; unless one leads with the "reality", the theoretical substance is at best only partially imbibed, let alone digested. Far more so than con-ventional graduate students, our type of student is reluctant to leave the world of applicability for the more abstract and arid plain of theory.

I had initially felt that the build-up from cognitive processes through group dynamics to governmental processes along essentially theoretical lines would establish bases from which students, themselves, would be able to construct relevance. This, however, had not been the case. It had become increasingly evident that levels of abstraction were only palatable if they emerged out of analysing the "real world". Instead of my block-building of theory, I was "forced" to devise my course around case studies, case studies which were about real countries, real decision-makers, real foreign policies. In one sense, theoretical perspectives had to filter through from the case studies, and not, so to speak, vice versa.

While my instinct to ensure sound theoretical underpinnings has clearly come into conflict with my sense of the need to bridge the gulf between what I deem as fundamental and students' demands, there has emerged an unexpected benefit from the case study emphasis. Only too often, critics of foreign policy analysis have condemned the ethnocentric character of the subject as a form of Anglo-American intellectual imperial-ism which takes little account of the remainder of the globe.

In many respects the criticisms are valid, but at least the case study approach has forced me to reach beyond the Anglo-American texts to con-sciously seek applicability in non-British or American contexts. Group dynamics in Ghana's 1972 decision not to devalue, cognitive limitations of Mexican leaders in the planning of land reapportionment, Japanese bureaucratic methods of "ringisei", the organizational response of the FAO under threat from the World Food Authority, the rise of the Soviet Navy as an organisational response to Khrushchev's strategic rethinking, cognitive closure of Israel's intelligence community in October 1973, all suggest application of foreign policy models and pre-theoretical consideration that go well beyond the conventional analyses of American or British foreign policy processes. And, while a sound development of the theoretical approaches themselves probably suffers in the time-consuming case study orientation, the loss is counterbalanced by the benefits of revealing to students' general applicability of the intellectual components of the foreign policy analysis theme.

The reorientation of my teaching approach to foreign policy analysis is a fitting point on which to conclude this discussion, for it suggests a symbolic answer to the question which I posed in the beginning of this chapter: "Why are we trying to make a distinction between teaching 'normal' graduate students and 'mid-career, part-time' graduate students?" In one sense, the answer lies in the simple fact that there is tremendous pressure to sublimate the abstract for the concrete, that the "ennui" of theoretical debates can best be overcome by having theory arise from the cover of the practical and real. Although the message, itself, is not necessarily striking, students' resistance to and dislike of a more theory-laden approach is. Therein lies the seeds of at least one distinction between our type of graduate student and others.

Furthermore, I have suggested earlier in this discussion that requirements which I assign in my courses serve a purpose beyond mere individual assessment. Requirements also serve the function of "equalisers" in a culturally and academically diverse class. They help in the process of generating classroom dynamics when the lack of such dynamics is an initial hazard which is always difficult to overcome in our kind of setting. More fundamental, however, is the symbolic importance of such assignments, for ultimately they reflect the need to make certain kinds of academic concessions in order to bridge the gulf between our students' perceptions of relevance and our own sense of what is important to transmit to those involved in a graduate programme in international relations.

References

1. In a survey of students' attitudes about the relevance of the particular approach this author took to foreign policy analysis (refer to ref. 2 below), one naval student said that, even if he did accept the tenets of my approach, he would not last a day "on the watch" were his intelligence reports to move away from the "billiard-ball" interpretation of Soviet fleet movements.
2. Two groups of students during the 1977–8 academic year who were doing foreign policy analysis classes received questionnaires and were subsequently interviewed individually by myself, the instructor. The questionnaire consisted of ten open-ended questions, seeking to determine the students' opinions about the relevance

of my particular approach to the study of foreign policy to "real world" international relations and the relevance of this approach to their own lives. For all three types of students, i.e. military, diplomatic, businessmen, the bureaucratic and organisational themes found considerable favour. However, businessmen felt that such problems could be readily overcome, whereas military and diplomatic personnel found such factors "endemic in the system". Most students felt, however, that despite the "interesting approach" a considerable portion did not conform to the ways states really operated.

CHAPTER 15

The Comparative Study of Regional International Relations

Gunnar Nielsson

One of the hardest problems in the curriculum design of the United Kingdom Program has been to coordinate the regional international relations courses with the core-course structure that has dominated the program. Theory and methodology courses and the global-scope courses on strategy and conflict analysis comprise the core of the curriculum. Generally, we have succeeded in sequencing the mid-career students' course work so that theory and method courses are completed first with subsequent completion of the other global-scope analytical topic courses. The regional courses are taken along the way as additional courses when students do two courses during one semester or they have frequently been offered during summer sessions.

The final, comprehensive examinations are structured around the core course topics with an occasional exam question on a regional international relations issue. The exam review program during the last semester before the comprehensives are planned exclusively around the core course materials. The general expectation is that courses on regional international relations would provide students with opportunities to apply the general theories and methodologies discussed in the introductory core courses as well as the specific conceptual frameworks used to guide the analytical topic courses. Similarly, in preparing for the comprehensive examinations, students are expected, on their own, to integrate the regional course materials and research papers with the core course materials as substantiating evidence for the validity or weaknesses of various theoretical approaches.

With the exception of the present author and the present director of the U.K. Program, who have taught the European regional course, faculty teaching regional courses are not part of the continuing interactions and intellectual exchanges which characterize the productive relationship

225

among the core faculty who have shaped the general "teaching paradigm" that has emerged since the early 1970s. Hence, in content as well as in academic organization and administration, the role of regional international relations courses has remained of secondary importance, the "stepchild," so to speak, of the intersubjective consensus which otherwise has prevailed among the faculty teaching in the program.

Within this general context, regional courses on Asia, the Middle East and North Africa, Europe, and the Soviet Bloc have been offered at regular intervals. Due primarily to staffing problems, the Latin American international relations course has only been offered a few times throughout the many years the U.K. Program has existed.

The tension between the area studies approach and the theoretical social science approach, elaborated upon in a previous chapter, has been experienced in this program in a variety of ways. Most of the faculty teaching the regional courses have been trained as area studies specialists with academic discipline specialization in history and comparative government. Consequently, and understandably, the emphasis has been on the configurative approach with chronological, descriptive, historical reviews of particular states in a region, interspersed with interpretive analysis of particular current issues. In some cases, regional courses have had a comparative politics emphasis on "within state" political processes rather than relations across state boundaries or transnational interactions. In other cases, regional courses have been structured around a single sub-region and the analysis of specific issue areas have been greatly influenced by the instructors' active advocacy and involvement in attempts to provide solutions to conflicts in the region. With a few exceptions, the syllabus followed in regional courses have not included any of the theory-oriented literature on regional international relations reviewed in Chapter 7.

Regional Courses and the Mid-Career Student Clientele

Regional international relations courses are of great interest and particularly suitable to the intellectual predispositions and professional backgrounds of the mid-career students. In terms of backgrounds, they are widely traveled, and not just in the sense of the brief, direct observation opportunities of touring different areas of the world. Whether military or diplomatic officers or executives in multinational enterprises, this student body comprises the epitome of what can be considered "professional transnationals" who have already served in various capacities as long term residents in the various regions of the world. Furthermore, they all expect that adaptation to foreign cultures during lengthy stays to be part of their future professional qualifications and private lives. Hence, information about, and analysis of, the various regions in the world has a direct, practical application to an extent not usually found among other graduate students of international relations.

The configurative approach to area studies fits well with the initial, intellectual predispositions of the mid-career students' penchant for studies of "the real world". Descriptive analyses of specific, policy-oriented issues within the methodological context of a single-state case study are viewed as attractive extensions of the briefs and positions papers they are used to write as part of their normal professional activities. In that perspective, configurative types of studies satisfies the IR pragmatic orientation to pursuing studies which are perceived to be immediately useful for their current professional positions.

Our expectation of having the students use regional courses as "laboratory-equivalents" for the testing of specific theories and conceptual frameworks has been a constant source of tension. Upon completing some of the theory courses, students who have attempted to apply partial theories in a research design for a regional course have been greeted with indifference, lack of understanding or outright hostility by instructors educated in the area studies approach. When students seek assistance from the core faculty in the development of a social scientific methodology for a regional course research project, friction sometimes develops over course autonomy, a situation which is exacerbated because area studies faculty are not integrated with the core faculty.

Conversely, a new student who completed a regional course before taking the theory and method courses (in order to get into the right sequencing of these courses) will often react to the theoretical and methodological issues and problems with a great deal of resentment after having dealt successfully with "the real world" events in the regional course. In fact, some students end up with a bad case of "intellectual schizophrenia" wondering whether or not the core courses and the regional courses belong within the same academic discipline.

Experiences in teaching the regional course on European international relations

The following review of teaching European international relations is undertaken because it represents an attempt to ameliorate the tension between the area studies approach and the general theoretical approach by experimenting with application of partial theories in the context of a regional course. (1)

The delineation of a region's boundaries is one of the first important problems one faces when planning a regional course. In this case, since the inception of the Cold War, dividing the European region into Western and Eastern European studies has become conventional practice in mainstream international relations curricula as well as in research and professional journals. (2) In fact, Eastern European relations are sometimes treated as a secondary adjunct to analyses of Soviet foreign policy. For this course, it was decided to return to the concept of "geographic Europe" for the descriptive and analytic treatment of the attribute theme (which will be discussed below). This delineation includes all the Eastern and Western European as well as the Mediterranean European states. Delineation of boundaries always involves arbitrary decisions when it comes to the boundary states. Hence, Turkey presents a problem because most of its territory and cultural attributes are traditionally identified with asia Minor, but it was included based on its European foreign policy orientation. Similarly, it is important to acknowledge that the Soviet Union, in terms of physical as well as political characteristics, is an important regional actor both in a European and an Asian context as well as being a global superpower. The important role of the United States in Western European international relations and in terms of its and the Soviet Union's global level superpower relations have been treated analytically under the category of "intrusive states". (3) While such difficulties have to be contended with in every regional course, it has not been a major obstacle in this one.

Descriptions and analyses of European international relations are pursued according to four major themes; regional attributes, security policies, and alliance policies, East–West detente in Europe, and cooperation and integration. The attribute theme involves an attempt to bridge the gulf between the configurationist concern with remaining truthful to the complexity of specific cultural contexts as well as fitting major historical strands into a comprehensive coverage of an area and the advantages of applying conceptual frameworks as explanatory vehicles for providing a comparative, developmental perspective.

The basic thesis is that cultural identity is the important variable indicating degrees of diversity within the region while the socio-economic modernization processes are variable considered indicators of a recurrent pattern. The concepts of *Gemeinschaft* (community) and *Gesellschaft* (society) are explicated and differentiated as the analytical framework for a descriptive overview of cultural nationalist attributes and functionalists societal attributes of the 30 European states. A taxonomy of single community and multi-community societies and political systems is used to provide a developmental perspective of nation-building and state-building since the mid-nineteenth century.

The basic proposition investigated is that modernization processes lead to similar types of demands for changes in societal relations, but diverse responses occur because of differences in community attributes and societal values. Differences among political systems are viewed as a function of diverse cultural settings and various stages of modernization, according to which, political transformations have been dependent on different rates of political mobilization of the middle and working classes. This factor is considered a critical variable in comparing the differences between political systems that managed an evolutionary adaptation to changes in the societal environment caused by industrialization and states experiencing revolutionary changes because of an inability to adapt to increasing industrialization and the rise of democratic values among the new, politically mobilized movements. The effect of international conflictual interaction on the state-building process and the political systems' adaptation process is discussed through a review of the major international wars in Europe between 1815 and 1945.

With this approach, attribute patterns can be discerned sufficiently to establish a crude typology which identifies a North-Western, an Eastern and a Southern subregion. For the discussion of the three subsequent themes, these subregions are considered separate international subordinate systems within "geographic Europe."

The lectures on the attribute theme are supplemented with simple statistical material, graphs and maps which are important lecture aids in providing an overview of the specific manifestations of the variables within the thirty European states. During the period taken up with the attribute theme, each student is required to complete a short paper on the attributes and their interrelationship within a single political system. This assignment enables the student to examine and evaluate the adequacy of the theoretical framework and to explain the dynamic relationship between community groupings and demands for adaptation to modernization pressures. The single political system perspective provides the student an opportunity to gain some familiarity with, and appreciation of, specific contextual complexities.

The selection of the three specific international relations themes reflects the present author's view of a spectrum of international political behaviour spanning from extreme conflict relations to international political integration as the opposite extreme of cooperation. The extreme conflict end of the spectrum is dealt with through the security policies and alliance politics theme. The starting point of the analysis is the extensive destabilization effects of World War II. The strategic studies perspective is introduced in a discussion of the Cold War issues leading to the conflict structure of a bipolarized Europe. Capability analysis, the evolution of different strategic doctrines, and the security organization features of the North Atlantic and Warsaw Treaty Organization are used for a comparative treatment. Intra-bloc disputes and inter-bloc confrontations are discussed following a power politics theoretical framework and an options analysis of future security policy developments for both military blocs concludes this theme.

The theme on East–West detente in Europe is developed as an intermediary type of international political behavior in the conflict–cooperation spectrum. Detente is viewed as a varying process that fluctuates between tension-inducing behavior leading toward conflict relations and tension-reducing behavior leading toward formation of a security-community. (4) Focused on East–West relations in Europe since the early 1960s, the development of the detente theme proceeds from an initial conceptual distinction between tension-reducing processes as rational actor policy choices resulting in deliberate diplomatic processes and the functionalist/conflict analysis perspective on detente developments as the result of adaptation processes whereby tension-reduction policies are reflections of systemic changes within and among political systems due to increased interdependence in socio-economic relations. The early phases of detente in Europe are discussed as being a predominantly rational actor dominated process – the various treaties between the US and the USSR between 1963 and 1972 and the "treaty package" in Europe in the early 1970s are examples of deliberate detente diplomacy. (5) The current phase of detente processes are discussed in the functionalist/conflict analysis framework of adaptation processes resulting from intensified "low politics" interaction. That involves a review of changes in economic relations between East and West in Europe and an examination of the current issues of "Eurocommunism" in Western Europe as an example of increasing interpenetration of the two types of political systems. Future prospects for detente are evaluated according to two different scenarios entitled "the cooperative bipolarity" and "the functional cooperation" scenarios in which several discernible trends are conjecturally extended into logically consistent, but empirically unverified models of development.

The last theme of regional cooperation and integration is focused primarily on the European Communities. The theme is introduced by a review of particular features of the international political economy of Europe. The increasing dependence (external reliance) by the national economies on the world economy in general and the Western and Eastern

European economies specifically is discussed as an international dimension of the industrialization process introduced earlier as part of the regional attribute theme. The rise of an extensive regional institutional network since 1945 is described through the adjustment theory of international organization. The fact that these institutional networks still reflect the bipolarized conflict structure and the role of the two superpowers as "external forces" in shaping them are emphasized. A distinction is made between international political cooperation types of regional institutions — such as the Council of Europe, the OECD, EFTA and the CMEA — and the expectation of political integration based on international economic integration — as has been the case with the European Communities. With this distinction as general international "background conditions", the development of the European Communities since 1957 is examined from the federalist, transactionalist, functionalist, and neo-functionalist theoretical perspectives. The future prospects for integration of the European Communities' member states are evaluated by counterposing the neo-functionalist expectations with Paul Taylor's "confederal phase" and my "parallel national action" conceptual frameworks. (6)

In addition to the normal lecture discussion approach to teaching, we have also used simulations and field trips as learning techniques. In a more simplified form, simulation has been used several times with scenarios designed on the basis of crisis-laden issues which could be played more intensely during three day weekend exercises which were held in special conference centers in the English countryside. (7) Thus, in connection with several courses in the program, we have conducted simulation exercises designed around the Vietnam War, the various Middle Eastern wars, and European crisis situations. (8) The main emphasis has been on the international political implications of crisis resolution rather than on sophisticated war games. In a more elaborate form, we designed an exercise in which detente diplomacy in Europe by the major powers and representative minor states was simulated. It was the first time we worked with a non-crisis scenario that emphasised diplomatic conference activity. The simulation was conducted as an integral part of the course for a whole semester and resulted in a lengthy report with forecasts of developments within a six month future timeframe.

The advantages of simulations have been viewed primarily as a complementary teaching tool. Students do not gain a great deal of additional information through the use of simulations. They do provide a tool through which greater awareness of complexity in international political processes is achieved because it is possible to introduce the factor of simultaneity of events and communication flows which a specially or sequentially organized, written analysis of lecture presentation cannot so easily capture.

Field trips to international institutions in Europe have been conducted regularly because we consider it a great advantage to provide an opportunity for the interplay between ordinary classroom learning and contact with decision-making officials involved actively in the issues being studied. Thus, we have had annual field trips to the European Communities institutions in Brussels and Luxembourg, the NATO political and military headquarters in Brussels and Gasteau, and the Organization for Economic Cooperation and Development in Paris for day-long lecture and discussion sessions in connection with the European course. In connection with other coursework, we have conducted field trips to the UN institutions headquartered in Geneva and the International Court of Justice in the Hague, to Moscow for sessions on Soviet foreign policy and the CMEA, and to Egypt for sessions with Egyptian foreign office officials and representatives from the Arab League.

The simulation and field trip experiences add a dimension to international relations studies which we consider extremely valuable. They have also had an important socially integrative effect. Since part-time, mid-career students seldom have the opportunity to develop a sense of being a student body in the same way as on a campus, the weekend simulation exercises and the week-long field trips have been important social environments for both faculty and student participants which have resulted in a more open and participatory conduct of subsequent seminar discussions.

In evaluating the experiences with teaching the European regional course from an instructor's perspective, three generalizations can be made. In the first place, there is always a great interest in taking the European course. After all, everybody is in daily contact with some aspect of national political life and international relations of Europe since we all reside there. The direct observer experiences are found through private, personal contacts, daily mass media coverage and, for many of our students, professional responsibilities. Furthermore, direct familiarity with several European societies is obtained from frequent, short business and leisure trips as well as our field trips. There is, therefore, a wealth of different kinds of reference sources students and instructors can draw upon which is not normally the case in the professional study of international relations and it is of great benefit in conducting the course.

Secondly, there is a constant intellectual friction, for students and instructor alike, over the expectation that students need to ascertain command of certain historical background materials and contemporary factual data in order to grasp the significance of the various theories, models and conceptual frameworks used to guide the study of European international relations. That problem is exacerbated by the general variation in coursework background among the students in the course. Because there is no systematic sequencing in taking regional courses, some students are quite sophisticated in their familiarity with theories and methodologies while others have had no previous coursework in any of the core courses. The most successful experience I had in teaching the European regional course was when I was able to do a two semester sequencing with a lecture course during the first semester which followed the thematic approach discussed above followed by a research seminar which focused on the detente theme and with students who had completed both the previous lecture course and the theory and methods courses. In my judgement, those students produced some of the best research papers I read during my six years with the UK Program.

Finally, the efforts to inter-relate the four themes have not yet been very successful. It requires such a high level of abstraction that it is extremely difficult to integrate the empirical references drawn upon during the coverage of each of the themes. Students seem most capable of conceptualizing about the conflictual and cooperative types of behaviour by perceiving them in a clearly separable, dichotomous fashion. The difficulties are, therefore, particularly acute when it comes to fitting in the competing theories used to analyze and evaluate detente processes. The perception of international political behavior as an admixture of cooperative and conflictual relations, depending on the issue area, *among the same actors* is very hard to convey adequately because of the complexity it involves, even at the theoretical level. (9) I have tried to reverse the sequencing of the detente and cooperation themes in experimenting with the effect of presenting conflict and cooperation behavior in a contrasting dichotomous manner and then developing the "gray zones" of detente behavior by drawing on the differences between conflict and cooperation. However, the effect of alternating sequencing does not seem to greatly improve the understanding of the inter-relations among the three themes, judging from the final exams and papers by the students involved.

Moving toward a comparative approach to regional international relations studies

The problem of better integration of regional international relations courses into the general curriculum was taken up during the recent revision of the graduate curriculum. It became an important part of the two year process of reviewing and rethinking about the curriculum structure which took place between 1976 and 1978. While the revision efforts were concentrated on the campus program, both the German Program and the UK Program faculties were consulted throughout the deliberative phases and the final implementation of the revised curriculum. (10) In regard to the position of regional courses, it was agreed that, presently, the *international relations* of a region are not the most significant aspect in the training of an area studies specialist and, furthermore, that graduates of area studies programs seldom know much about regions of the world outside the specific area of concentration. It was also agreed that courses with a regional or national area focus are a worthwhile part of a graduate education in international relations. Recognizing that the university did not have comprehensive or intensive area studies programs with which the international relations coursework could be coordinated, the way out of the predicament was to concentrate on a comparative approach to regional studies. It was felt that graduates, who had been trained through a comparative approach which concentrated on international relations of various regions, would have important teaching and research qualifications making them attractive specialists to both area programs – where they could cover several regions as far as international relations were concerned – and to the international relations discipline in general – where the comparative approach would be valuable. Furthermore, a comparative regional specialization would be an important skill in policy research and application by the international relations practitioners in terms of the greater scope of the empirical reference world it entails. This is especially significant for mid-career students' educational objectives for whom the direct practical implications are of immediate concern.

As a result of this line of rethinking, a new field of specialization entitled Comparative Analysis of Regional International Relations has been introduced as part of the revised graduate program on campus. A new core course with the same title as the field was introduced and taught for the first time in the fall semester of 1978. Ph.D. students who wish to specialize in the field must complete the core course as a prerequisite. Then, they are expected to designate a major and a minor regional specialization in which they completed research seminars and they must subsequently complete a research project comparing regional international relations in the two selected regions – the latter is conducted as a tutorial research course. Masters level students are expected to complete the core course, one regional research seminar and at least one other regional course as part of their field concentration for their comprehensive examinations.

According to the original plan for the comparative regional field, it was expected that it would cover all six regions included in the old curriculum. However, it was not possible to reach agreement among all the faculty members involved. As a consequence, there are now three different approaches to regional international relations within the campus graduate curriculum. Middle East and North African studies are developing into a multi-disciplinary area studies center and it remains a separate field. Asian and International Communism studies, which also remain separate fields of concentration, have retained the practice of requiring graduate students to complete certain undergraduate lecture courses as prerequisites for regional research seminars. (11) African, European and Latin American studies are conducted within the comparative approach adopted for the new field.

This field of concentration is still in its early, formative stage. The new core course has only been taught once so far. The syllabus consisted of three parts. In Part One, the area studies approach was reviewed, the problem of defining and delineating regions was discussed, the conceptual framework of regional subsystems was introduced and compared to the regionalism and world order approach and theories of regional integration. Part Two, which was team-taught, consisted of two sessions on each of the three regions covering the main background literature, theoretical approaches and current issues in African, Latin American and European international relations. Thematic reviews of general background literature on two regions were presented as student reports during Part Three of the course. (12)

The next step in the development of this field will be the coordination of research temes for the three regional research seminars. Among the broad themes presently considered are: 1) international security and regional patterns of conflict; 2) regional institutions and cooperation; and 3) dependency, dependence and interdependence within and among the African, Latin American and European international political economies.

It will, obviously, be several years before this experiment with a comparative approach will settle down to the point where careful evaluation and significant generalizations about its effect can be made. The preliminary literature review and the brief teaching experience suggest to me, as coordinator of this field, that both faculty and students have a great deal to learn before them, but it will be pursued by a sustained effort in the belief that such an approach represents a worthwhile educational objective. (13)

Acknowledging the constraints within which the European graduate programs operate, there are, in my opinion, several opportunities for improving on the existing uncoordinated status of regional courses in the UK Program. At a minimum, a policy of sequencing regional courses could be instituted. An overview lecture course on a particular region could be offered first, followed by a research seminar on the same region. The selection of specific regions could be changed for each center on an academic year basis. That approach would allow the students time to satisfy the expectations of familiarity with historical background materials and introductory familiarity with specific contemporary issues in the region. The follow-up research seminar would allow for more in-depth analyses of particular issue areas as well as experiences with applying various conceptual frameworks and specific methodologies.

At a maximum, the comparative regional core course could be introduced as part of the core course structure of the program curriculum. It could be taught regularly by a core faculty member who could assist the director in planning a course program that assured more systematic coordination and sequencing of all the regional international relations courses. In consideration of the substantial number of courses presently taken up by the core courses, for comprehensive examination purposes the comparative regional course could be substituted as an option instead of one of the existing global-level, analytical topic courses.

Whatever the solution may be, there can be little doubt about the need to reconsider the long-standing problem of fitting the regional courses into the general curriculum structure of the UK Program.

References

1. Dr. Randolph Kent and I have been in the fortunate position of teaching theory and methodology, international organization and foreign policy analysis predominantly and then we have been able to experiment with applying theoretical perspectives to the European regional course and the course on U.S. Foreign Policy.
2. That this division remains a current practice is demonstrated in the generally excellent, but separate chapters on European international politics in a recently published basic text edited by Rosenau, Thompson and Boyd, entitled, *World Politics: An Introduction*. New York: The Free Press, 1976. See chapters 19 and 20.
3. See Louis Cantori and Steven Spiegel, *The International Politics of Regions: A Comparative Approach*, Englewood Cliffs, New Jersey: Prentice-Hall, 1970, Chapter 1. This leads to the two-dimensional distinction of the physical location of the United States outside of Europe and the analytical distinction of the Soviet Union's role as both a superpower and a European regional power.
4. The most impressive analysis of detente processes, based on a specified empirical theory, is provided by Kjell Goldmann, *Tension and Detente in Bipolar Europe*. Oslo: Universitetsforlaget, 1974.
5. The analysis of the "treaty package" by Birnbaum is an excellent example of the rational actor model and detente diplomacy. See Karl Birnbaum, *East and*

West Germany: A Modus Vivendi, Lexington, Massachusetts: D. C. Heath and Co., 1973.

6. See Paul Taylor, "The Politics of the European Communities: The Confederal Phase", *World Politics*, Vol. 27, No. 3 (April, 1975) and Gunnar P. Nielsson, "The Parallel National Action Process: Scandinavian Experiences", in Paul Taylor and A. J. R. Groom, editors, *International Organization: A Conceptual Approach*, London: Frances Pinter Ltd., 1978.

7. The policy issue area type of simulation has been discussed in Lincoln P. Bloomfield and Barton Whaley, "The Political-Military Exercise: A Progress Report", in J. N. Rosenau, editor, *International Politics and Foreign Policy*, New York, The Free Press, Revised Edition, 1969.

8. The weekend simulation exercises involved the coordination of several classes. The Methodology course students worked on the scenario design and became the control team during the actual conduct of the simulation and then wrote research papers about the use of simulation. The Middle East courses and the European courses would hold several sessions about the initial scenario and various instructors would observe the exercise, often serving as "advisors" to particular national teams.

9. Rummel has suggested that the admixture of cooperative and conflictful relations be accepted as a general behavioral pattern conditioning most of international relations and, therefore, change should be studied in terms of the "structure of expectations" particular types of relations have created and the degree to which such expectations have been fulfilled. See R. J. Rummel, *Peace Endangered: The Reality of Detente*, Beverly Hills, California: Sage Publication, 1976.

10. As Chairperson of the School's Graduate Studies Committee, I was in constant contact with both program directors in Europe, forwarding preliminary planning papers and interim committee reports. In addition, I conducted three lengthy faculty meetings on the issues in person during business trips to Europe between February and June, 1977. A number of European program faculty members submitted written responses to proposals for revision within their particular fields of concentration. These responses were incorporated into the final report by the Graduate Studies Committee. The School's Director of Special Programs, the Assistant Director of the School and I formed an *ad hoc* subcommittee which worked out proposals on how both European programs could be adapted to fit within the generally revised campus curriculum. Generally, both programs have maintained identity with the major provisions of the new graduate program. That separate curricula structures should be avoided has been an extremely important point throughout the years the School has conducted its programs overseas. The German and the United Kingdom programs are considered an integral part of the School's graduate program and faculty as well as students freely interchange between European and campus courses. Within this general policy framework, certain adaptations have been made to suit the combination of faculty competences and the mid-career student clientele in Europe. The specific adaptations made by the UK Program to the revised graduate curriculum are discussed by the editors elsewhere in this book. The details of the revision proposals are found in Gunnar P. Nielsson, Patrick J. McGowan, Robert Bowen, Connie Lynch and Luda Spilewski, "A Review of the Graduate Program with Proposals for Revision", Final Report presented to the Faculty by the Graduate Studies Committee, School of International Relations, University of Southern California, Los Angeles, California, June, 1977. Mimeographed.

11. Asian international relations courses are linked into a campus graduate certificate program on east Asian studies that involves International Relations, Political Science and several cognate field courses.

12. Some examples of student paper topics were:
    1. "Delineating Regions by Issue Areas: A Comparative Study of Africa and Latin America."
    2. "A Comparative Study of International Security: Europe and Africa."
    3. "An Annotated Bibliography on Seven Regional International Institutions."
    4. "An Overview and Analysis of Pan-Africanism and Pan-Americanism in the Regional Subsystems of Africa and Latin America."
    5. "Economic Bases for Regional Cooperation in Europe and Africa."
    6. "North American Multinational Enterprises and Regional Responses in Western Europe and Latin America."
13. At the conclusion of his comprehensive review of the area studies approach, Lambert also concluded that a comparative approach would be a much needed improvement. As he stated it:

> Much of the sometimes rancorous legitimacy debate which emphasizes this gap . . . [between the comparativists and the area specialists] . . . would be disarmed or even made productive if further salvos could be enjoined until both sides acquired a professional competence in at least two of the areas or countries to be compared. On the comparativists' side, the tendency to contentless scholastic formalism might be eased, and on the language and area side, a march toward parochalism might also be halted and genuine, inductive comparative work carried a step forward.

Richard D. Lambert, *Language and Area Studies Review*, Philadelphia: Monograph 17 of the American Academy of Politics and Social Science, October, 1973, p. 404.

PART III

LEARNING INTERNATIONAL RELATIONS AS MID-CAREER STUDENTS

CHAPTER 16

Student Perspectives on the U.K. Program: A Profile of Responses to a General Survey

Gunnar Nielsson

Introduction

In planning this book, a survey of student perspectives on the U.K. Program as a whole was considered an important contribution to the general review of the program's attributes and developments. While student evaluations of individual courses were introduced in the early 1970s, an assessment of the entire experience of participating in the program had not been undertaken before. Consequently, the editors of this book designed a six page questionnaire about various aspects of the program (the text of it is found in the appendix) and mailed it to nearly all the graduates since 1967. The result of that venture is the subject of this chapter.

In writing up this profile of evaluations by program graduates, the author has tried to confine his role to that of organizing the data and of reporting the results through a descriptive analysis of the distribution of scores on the various aspects of the program the survey intended to measure. While the questionnaire design and the organization of responses quite clearly have influenced the outcome, interpreting the implications of the rankings has, to the greatest possible extent, been avoided. Explanations of program policies and practices have been provided where they are felt necessary as background settings for the respondents' evaluations. Keeping to the reporting role, the chapter finishes with a brief, general summary rather than a lengthy interpretative conclusion.

The discussion of the survey results which follows is organized into five sections. The first section is about general background characteristics of the respondents. An evaluation of the program's teaching approach is the subject of the second section. The third section covers an assessment of the program curriculum structure and the administration of the program

239

is discussed in the fourth sections. The last section consists of an account of the extent to which completion of the program has had an impact on subsequent career developments.

A background profile of the program graduates

This introductory overview of the backgrounds of the graduates who responded to the survey is presented in order to provide a general context for the subsequent discussion concerning their evaluation of various aspects of the U.K. Program. It covers the topics of how representative the sample is of the survey's total universe, the educational backgrounds of the respondents and their motivation for joining the program.

Representativeness of the sample of respondents

The total universe for this survey is all the graduates of the U.K. Program from August 1967 to August 1977. From the records, a total of 218 graduates were identified. The initial working assumption was that it would be possible to locate about one half of the graduates and, in turn, half of those located would respond, resulting in a 25 percent response rate.

The problem of locating the graduates represented somewhat of a detective job because this particular student clientele is extremely geographically mobile, staying in one location on the average of a three year assisgnment. We managed to get addresses on 215 of the 218 graduates. Thirty five questionnaires were returned with incorrect addresses, leaving our reduced universe at 180 graduates. Of the 180 who were contacted by mail, 87 responded. (1) That represents a response rate of 39.9 percent of the total universe and 48.3 per cent of the reduced universe of graduates contacted. Our initial working assumption was thus exceeded by 15 percent and it must be considered a very good response rate given the difficulties involved.

The eleven year time span of program graduates from 1967 to 1977 represents 31 graduating periods because students can complete their program in January, June and August of each year. There are respondents from 28 of the 31 graduating periods and the three missing graduating periods are from the earliest years in the conduct of the program.

Aggregating the graduating periods on an annual basis, there are respondents from each of the eleven years involved. However, as could be expected, the earliest years are underrepresented and the most recent years are overrepresented.

As can be observed from the overview data presented in Table 1, the

Table 1. NUMBER OF UKIR PROGRAM GRADUATES AND REPRESENTATIVENESS OF THE SAMPLE OF RESPONDENTS, 1967–77

	1967	1968	1969	1970	1971	1972	1973	1974	1975	1976	1977	Total
Graduates	16	17	23	30	15	13	21	18	26	16	23	218
Percentage	7.3	7.8	10.5	13.9	6.9	6.0	9.6	8.3	11.9	7.3	10.5	100.0
Graduates contacted	11	12	17	26	13	8	17	17	21	15	23	180
Percentage	6.1	6.6	9.5	14.4	7.2	4.4	9.5	9.5	11.7	8.3	12.8	100.0
Graduates responding	1	2	8	11	4	3	9	8	15	11	15	87
Percentage	1.1	2.3	9.2	12.7	4.6	3.5	10.3	9.2	17.2	12.7	17.2	100.0
Respondents as percentage of all graduates, by year	6.3	11.8	34.8	36.7	26.7	23.1	42.9	44.4	57.7	68.8	65.2	39.9
Respondents as percentage of graduates contacted, by year	9.1	16.7	47.1	42.3	30.8	37.5	52.9	47.1	71.4	73.3	65.2	48.3
Percentage of respondents from the Air Force, by year	0.0	0.0	75.0	63.6	100.0	0.0	44.5	50.0	33.3	27.3	60.0	48.3
Percentage of respondents from the Navy, by year	100.0	100.0	0.0	18.2	0.0	66.7	22.2	25.0	26.7	18.2	13.3	21.8
Percentage of respondents from the Army, by year	0.0	0.0	25.0	0.0	0.0	0.0	11.1	25.0	0.0	9.1	0.0	5.8
Percentage of respondents civilian U.S. Government employees, by year	0.0	0.0	25.0	9.1	0.0	0.0	11.1	0.0	26.7	45.4	6.7	14.9
Percentage of respondents other civilians, by year	0.0	0.0	0.0	9.1	0.0	33.3	11.1	0.0	13.3	0.0	20.0	9.2

respondents who graduated between 1967 and 1969 represent only 12.6 percent of the total while those who graduated during the last three years of the survey period, 1975-1977, represent 47.2 percent of the respondents. The middle-year graduates, 1970-1974, represent 39.3 percent of the total respondents. This skewing in time of the sample must be kept in mind throughout the subsequent analysis.

In terms of the occupational distribution of the respondents at the time of completing the program, 75.9 percent were American military personnel stationed in Britain, 14.9 percent were civilian employees of the U.S. Government and 9.2 percent were other civilians. While the composition of the student body has been changing significantly in recent years (2) it is a very accurate reflection of the occupational distribution of all the graduates from the eleven year period surveyed.

Among the military personnel, (3) Air Force personnel were the most numerous. They accounted for 42.7 percent of all graduates and 4.83 percent of the respondents. Navy personnel accounted for 27.1 percent of all graduates and 21.8 percent of the respondents while the graduates from the Army (we have included two graduates from the Marine Corps in this category) represent only 4.6 percent of all graduates and 5.8 percent of the sample.

The civilian U.S. Government employees among the graduates came from a number of different occupations and governmental agencies spanning from Foreign Service Officers stationed in the London Embassy to teachers in schools for dependents functioning on the military bases. From 1973 to 1976, the U.K. Program established a teaching center for U.S. Government civilian employees at a communications center near Harrogate in Yorkshire and this group represents a large proportion of the 1975 and 1976 graduate respondents in this occupational category. In general, 13.8 percent of all graduates and 14.9 percent of the respondents were civilian U.S. Government employees. The other civilian students came from a variety of occupational backgrounds, such as American businesses operating in Britain as well as U.S.C. graduate students from the Los Angeles campus. They accounted for 11.9 percent of the total graduates and 9.2 percent of the sample. Thus, in general, the occupational backgrounds of the respondents are very representative of the entire group of graduates with a slight overrepresentation of Air Force personnel and underrepresentation of Navy personnel. However, the distortions represents only about five percent.

Over time, the proportion of respondents from the Air Force have been fairly even since 1969 and from the Navy since 1970, while Army, U.S. Government civilians and other civilians are very unevenly distributed.

This is shown in particular in 1975 and 1976 when the Harrogate U.S. Government civilian employees account for a significant share of the graduates.

Academic backgrounds of the respondents

One of the most important differences between a mid-career student clientele and the conventional student body in a graduate program is the great diversity in educational backgrounds among mid-career students. There were 26 different undergraduate majors among the 87 respondents in this survey and very few had majors in international relations.

These diverse undergraduate backgrounds have been classified into four major categories, as shown in Table 2. A little over one third of the students (37.6 percent) had undergraduate majors in the social sciences which is the general category most closely related to a discipline concentration in international relations. Within this category, only 8.6 percent

Table 2. UNDERGRADUATE BACKGROUNDS OF THE PROGRAM GRADUATES

	Percentage:	*Percentage:*
Social Science Majors:		37.6
International Relations	8.6	
Political Science	17.2	
Other Social Sciences	11.8	
Professional Degrees:		30.1
Engineering	12.9	
Business Administration	9.7	
Speech, Communication and Journalism	4.3	
Military Science	3.2	
History and Humanities:		23.7
History, Philosophy and Theology	20.5	
English, French and Spanish Literature	3.2	
Natural Sciences:		8.6
Total	100.0	100.0

had completed an undergraduate degree in international relations while 17.2 percent had political science degrees. Hence only one out of four students had undergraduate backgrounds directly relevant to the graduate study of international relations. The remaining 11.8 percent of the social science majors involved degrees in general social science, economics, sociology, psychology and criminology.

Nearly a third of the graduates (30.1 percent) entered the U.K. Program with undergraduate specializations in various professional degrees. Engineering and business administration degrees were the predominant specializations, accounting for 22.6 percent of the graduates and 75.0 percent of this category of undergraduate majors.

Graduates with history and humanities academic backgrounds represented nearly one fourth (23.7 percent) of the student body. Degrees in history, philosophy and theology account for 20.5 percent of all graduates and 83.4 percent within this category.

Degrees in the natural sciences include pre-medical, chemistry, geology and biology undergraduate majors. This category is the smallest with only 8.6 percent of the total respondents.

This great disparity in undergraduate backgrounds is compensated for, to a considerable degree, by subsequent career experiences. Almost one half (44.8 percent) of the graduates had had professional work experiences directly related to international activities. Nevertheless, the unusually high diversity of academic backgrounds among mid-career students and the fact that a large majority of them hold degrees outside the social sciences are very good reasons for maintaining introductory core courses through which students can become familiarized with a common body of academic literature in the field. It will help in leveling out their preparation for more advanced courses in international relations studies.

Reasons for joining the program

In an attempt to gauge the motivations for joining the U.K. Program, five major reasons were given in the questionnaire and the graduates were asked to rank them, on a scale of one to five, according to the least to most accurate suggested response. The reasons listed were: 1) that a graduate degree was required for career progression; 2) that the respondent's job was directly related to international relations and there was thus a special professional interest in the field; 3) personal interest in international relations; 4) a combination of professional and personal interests in the field; and 5) that the respondents had a desire to continue their education and this particular graduate program was the only one available in the geographical area where they were stationed.

As shown in Table 3, nearly one half of the graduates (48.3 percent) ranked the combination of professional and personal interest in international relations as the most accurate reason for joining the program and personal interest in the subject was a very important reason given by 43.7 percent of the graduates. (4) That is probably one of the most important factors in explaining the students' strong commitment to academic achievement which the faculty has observed over the years.

The responses also demonstrated that about one third (34.5 percent) had joined the program primarily because it was the only graduate

Table 3. REASONS FOR JOINING THE PROGRAM
In percentage

	Least Accurate 1	2	3	4	Most Accurate 5	No Answer	Total
Required for career progression	23.0	25.3	13.8	13.8	6.9	17.2	100.0
International relations directly job related	14.9	23.0	25.4	11.5	8.0	17.2	100.0
Personal interest in international relations	8.0	9.2	21.9	28.8	14.9	17.2	100.0
Combination of personal and professional interest	8.0	10.3	14.9	17.2	31.1	18.5	100.0
Only graduate program available in the area	28.8	13.8	3.4	11.5	23.0	19.5	100.0

program available in their geographical area. Furthermore, there was a core of one fifth (20.7 percent) who had joined the program because career progression required a masters degree. Interestingly, there was practically no correlation between the last two reasons of career promotion and being the only program available in the area. Only 5.7 percent ranked these two reasons together as highly accurate reasons for joining the program.

In summary, it has been established that the sample of respondents is very representative of the composition of the student group during the eleven year period covered in this survey. The student clientele was predominantly drawn from military personnel with Air Force students comprising about half of the student body. Most of the civilian students were employees of the U.S. Government from various agencies. Undergraduate backgrounds were very diverse with a large majority of students entering the program without academic specializations in even the social sciences. Beyond a small core of students, who entered the program because it is a requirement for career progression, most of the students joined because of personal and professional interest in international relations.

Evaluation of the teaching approach

When asked to suggest the strongest and weakest features of the program, the high quality of instruction was ranked by the respondents as the strongest feature of the program. (5) Most of the comments simply stated that the standard of teaching was excellent, but many specifically mentioned the transnational composition of the faculty, the variety of viewpoints represented by the faculty and the personal concern about each student's academic progress shown by the faculty as key, positive features. Among the suggested weaknesses in the quality of instruction, respondents thought that the faculty was too demanding because they did not appreciate the problems of part-time students, that the instructors often were too prejudiced to their own point of view and that there was too little contact with the faculty outside the classroom. In this section, the evaluation of instruction will be discussed according to three different dimensions of the teaching approach: the conduct of classes, special projects and the comprehensive examination.

The conduct of courses

The first aspect of the conduct of courses concerns the contributions the various course requirements made to each individual's learning process. The graduates were asked to rank, on a scale of one to seven, how effective research papers, book reports and essays, examinations and oral

246

reports had been as a part of their learning process.

The results, presented in Table 4, show that the highest significance was given to research papers and the least effective learning experience for the individual was the preparation of oral reports to seminar participants. Essays and book reports as well as examinations were given medium rankings in terms of effective learning experiences. Nearly two thirds of the graduates stated that they were very satisfied with the balance among the assignments of oral reports and the various written requirements. It is a general practice in the program to plan a coursework progression for each student whereby the first courses involve a combination of book reports, essays and examinations after which the students move on to courses requiring a research paper and this seems to have been achieved in most cases, based on the responses concerning a blaance of course requirements.

A second aspect of the conduct of classes involves student participation as a group learning process. The basic approach by the instructors have been to engage in more extensive lecturing in the introductory core courses and during the early part of the semester in most other courses (usually spending the last half of each session on either student reports or general group discussion) ending up with predominantly discussion sessions in advanced research seminars. According to the rankings shown in Table 4, 60.7 percent of the graduates judged that there had been a very satisfactory balance between lecturing and discussion sessions and only 3.4 percent considered it unsatisfactory. However, only 30.2 percent thought that student participation had contributed greatly to group learning, 8.1 percent did not think it had contributed at all and 61.7 percent gave medium ranking to student participation. The graduates were even more critical in their assessment of the contribution to group learning by student reports. Only 14.2 percent believed such reports had contributed greatly, 15.3 percent did not consider them a contribution at all, with 71.1 percent giving medium rankings to student reports. Hence, preparation of oral reports about the students' individual research projects and student reports on general reading materials are considered the least significant aspect of both individual and group learning processes. It is the aspects of the teaching approach of which the graduates were most critical.

A third aspect of the teaching approach is the availability of, and access to, instructors for individual consultations about their coursework. Considering the program's governing conditions of part time students who are generally not free during day-time working hours, the geographical dispersion of the teaching centers and that many of the instructors teach courses as "add-on" to home campus teaching loads, it must be viewed as a

Table 4. EVALUATION OF TEACHING APPROACH, CONDUCT OF COURSES

In percentage

	Low 1	2	3	4	5	6	High 7	No Answer	Total
Role of research papers in individual learning									
Not effective . . . very effective	1.2	1.2	0.0	1.2	9.2	41.4	48.2	0.0	100.0
Role of book reports and essays in individual learning									
Not effective . . . very effective	1.7	4.6	5.7	13.2	22.4	28.3	13.2	10.9	100.0
Role of examinations in individual learning									
Not effective . . . very effective	4.6	4.6	8.0	15.9	27.3	30.7	9.1	0.0	100.0
Role of oral reports in individual learning									
Not effective . . . very effective	1.2	4.8	6.0	15.7	32.5	24.1	14.5	1.2	100.0

Balance among oral reports and various written assignments Unrealistic . . . very realistic	1.2	0.0	1.2	6.9	26.4	46.0	18.4	0.0	100.0
Balance between lecturing and discussion sessions Unsatisfactory . . . very satisfactory	1.1	2.3	2.3	6.7	27.0	40.5	20.2	0.0	100.0
Contribution of student participation to group learning None . . . greatly	2.3	5.8	10.5	17.4	33.7	25.6	4.6	0.0	100.0
Contribution of student reports to group learning None . . . greatly	2.3	13.0	13.0	30.2	27.9	10.5	3.5	0.0	100.0
Access to instructors for consultations Unsatisfactory . . . very satisfactory	2.3	1.2	8.1	8.1	18.4	25.3	35.6	1.2	100.0
Grading process Unfair . . . very fair	1.2	0.0	1.2	1.2	17.2	42.5	36.8	0.0	100.0

tribute to the faculty that 60.9 percent of their former students were very satisfied with the availability of the faculty for consultations and only 3.5 percent ranked this aspect as highly unsatisfactory. Finally, an overwhelming majority of the graduates (79.3 percent) believed that the grading process had been very fair.

Special projects

Four different special projects have developed over the years and have become regular features of the program's teaching approach. First, simulation exercises have been held fairly regularly since 1967. They have been baed mostly on crisis-oriented scenarios with an emphasis on political interactions rather than military-oriented war games, although the outbreak of war has been maintained as policy options for the decision-making teams. The simulation exercises have usually involved coordination of preparatory activities among several classes with students in the methodology course being responsible for scenario designs and comprising the control team. Most of the simulations have been conducted as weekend-long exercises held in various conference centers (and, on occasion, in officer clubs in the English countryside).

Second, field trips have been conducted to various international institutions and seats of government in Continental Western Europe, the Soviet Union and Egypt. They have been organized as five days to week-long visits according to various themes relevant to particular coursework, although they are open to participation by everybody in the program. Thus, there have been regular field trips to U.N. institutions in Geneva in connection with the study of international institutions, to NATO headquarters and European Common Market institutions in Belgium and Luxembourg in connection with strategic studies, international regional integration and European international politics.

Weekend conferences began as one day conferences between U.S.C. and British international relations students in the London area and expanded into regular, annual conferences for the program students during three day weekend periods and held at Cumberland Lodge in Great Windsor Park. These conferences have served two purposes: 1) the entire core faculty would hold review sessions for the students coming up for comprehensive exams, and 2) special topic sessions would be given by guest speakers for all conference participants.

Special Graduate Seminars were initially designed to bring senior academicians together with students who had almost completed the program, in order that the latter could test their developing academic tools in discussions on subjects of general academic interest. However, given the nature of some of the subjects as well as the eminence of some of the discussion leaders, it became increasingly difficult to limit the audience, and increasingly special graduate seminars "degenerated" into small lecture sessions. However, at least, such sessions seemed to enhance to some extent the academic experiences that our part-time students were receiving.

An overview of the level of participation in these four types of special projects and an assessment by those who participated of the relevance of such projects to the students' overall coursework is found in Table 5. Simulations have had the most active participation while field trips have had the least among the four types of special projects. However, this is somewhat misleading because simulations have been conducted on a regular basis throughout the survey period. Even then, simulations were stressed more in the early years of the program. Among the graduates who completed the program before 1974, 92.3 percent had participated while 60.4 percent of the subsequent graduates had participated in simulations. Weekend conferences at Cumberland Lodge have been held regularly since 1972 and 71.9 percent of the graduates since then have participated in them. Field trips were also introduced as a regular special project in 1972 and 46.9 percent of the respondents who graduated since then have participated. Special Graduate Seminars began in 1975 and 65 percent of the most recent graduates have attended them. Generally, participation in some kind of special project has been widespread. Only one respondent had not participated in any special project while 13.8 percent had participated in all four types. Most commonly, 34.5 percent had participated in two out of four special projects, 25.3 percent participated in three out of four and the same proportion participated in only one type of special project.

In the judgement of two thirds of those respondents who participated, all the special projects were considered greatly relevant to their coursework and only one percent thought they were of no relevance whatsoever. The weekend conferences and the special graduate seminars were ranked as the most relevant, but slightly more than half of the respondents believed that simulations and field trips were also highly relevant. Due to the difficulties of getting off from work and the increasing costs involved in travel, graduates found it more and more difficult to participate as extensively in field trips as they would like. Several respondents suggested that they should be confined to sites in Continental Western Europe in the future — especially Belgium and Switzerland — because they demand less time off from work and are less costly. It was also suggested that opportunities for sessions with international institutions officials and

Table 5. EVALUATION OF TEACHING APPROACH, SPECIAL PROJECTS

In percentage

| | Participated | | Low | | | | | | High | No | |
	No	Yes	1	2	3	4	5	6	7	Answer	Total
Simulations Not at all . . greatly relevant	25.3	74.7	1.5	0.0	9.2	7.7	29.2	24.6	27.7	0.0	100.0
Field Trips Not at all . . greatly relevant	62.1	37.9	0.0	0.0	9.1	6.1	24.2	27.3	30.3	3.0	100.0
Weekend Conferences Not at all . . greatly relevant	37.5	62.5	1.9	0.0	0.0	5.6	16.7	33.3	42.5	0.0	100.0
Special Seminars Not at all . . greatly relevant	51.7	48.3	0.0	0.0	2.4	7.1	16.7	35.7	38.1	0.0	100.0

foreign policy officials in the London area should be explored in the future.

In general, the survey data clearly indicate that the special projects are very valuable features in the program's teaching approach and they should be given continuous, strong emphasis in the future conduct of the program.

Comprehensive examinations

The last dimension in the evaluation of the teaching approach is the review for, and conduct of, the comprehensive examination. At the tend of the semester during which students are completing the eighth course, they take a comprehensive exam consisting of a four hour written and a one hour oral part. The School's Director of Special Programs sits as examiner on all students' orals as does the resident director while the third member of the exam committee is drawn from the various British core faculty members. The written part of the exam is composed jointly by the core faculty and is structured according to the core courses with a theory and methodology section and sections of questions on strategy and conflict analysis, foreign policy analysis and international law, institutions and integration.

In addition to normal coursework, an extensive review program is conducted during the M.A. candidate's last semester of coursework. The resident director gives an initial session during which exam procedures and how to organize the review of completed coursework materials are discussed. Subsequently, each of the core faculty members gives a review session on their respective subjects and, for the June and August examinations, the review program finishes up at the weekend conference late in the spring semester.

Table 6 demonstrates the graduates' assessment of the comprehensive examination process. Generally, 81.5 percent thought that the faculty's assessment of their performance was made in a fair manner. The review program was considered extremely useful by two thirds of the former students and only 2.4 percent found it of no use in their exam preparations.

The important point of having the written part of the comprehensives structured around the core courses was confirmed as highly successful by nearly three quarters of the graduates (72.4 percent) who viewed it as very closely corresponding with their core coursework.

The oral examination was considered a very effective final assessment of the work each individual had done in the program by slightly less than half of the respondents. Although only 5 percent thought the oral exam

253

Table 6. EVALUATION OF TEACHING APPROACH, COMPREHENSIVE EXAMS

In percentage

	Low 1	2	3	4	5	6	High 7	No Answer	Total
Review Sessions Useless . . . extremely useful	1.2	1.2	0.0	6.9	12.6	31.0	37.9	9.2	100.0
Relationship between written comps. and program coursework No correspondence . . . close correspondence	1.2	0.0	2.3	2.3	17.2	28.7	43.7	4.6	100.0
Oral part was an effective final assessment Ineffective . . . very effective	1.2	3.5	3.5	21.8	17.2	23.0	25.3	4.6	100.0
Was comprehensive exam conducted in a fair manner? Unfair . . . very fair	1.2	0.0	1.2	3.5	6.9	21.7	59.8	4.6	100.0
Totals on teaching approach:	1.6	2.7	4.6	10.4	21.3	29.9	26.7	2.8	100.0
Conduct of Courses	1.9	3.8	5.6	11.7	24.0	31.2	19.6	2.2	100.0
Special Projects	1.0	0.0	5.2	6.7	22.2	29.9	34.5	0.5	100.0
Comprehensive examination	1.1	1.1	1.7	8.6	13.5	26.5	41.8	5.7	100.0

was an ineffective assessment, it was the part of the exam process deemed least successful. Whether or not this is a reflection of the conduct of the exam by the faculty or the performance by the candidates is impossible to tell from responses to this questionnaire, but it would be an important follow-up question to pursue in any future survey and it might be beneficial to reexamine the conduct and the role of the oral part of the comprehensive examination. Among the open-ended comments, several respondents stressed the importance of having the campus Director of Special Programs participate as examiner which they viewed very positively as an indication of the significance placed on keeping the performance standards equal to those maintained in the campus M.A. program.

Since all the questions concerning the program's teaching approach have involved ranking the various aspects on a scale of one to seven, it seems appropriate to aggregate the rankings as a rough indicator of the general assessment of instructional quality. The results are shown in the bottom half of Table 6. More than half of the graduates (56.6 percent) ranked the quality of instruction very high and only 4.3 percent ranked it very low. In fact, for both the grand total and each of the three subsections, the top three rankings accounted for between 75 and 80 percent of the responses. This is indeed a strong confirmation of the graduates' judgement that the quality of teaching is one of the strongest features of the U.K. Program.

Program curriculum structure

The graduates were divided almost evenly in their identification of the curriculum structure as one of the strong or weak features of the program by their responses to open-ended questions. It was identified as one of the strong features in 23.6 percent and as a weak feature in 21.0 percent of the responses.

In support of the curriculum structure as a strong feature, the following specific points were made: 1) that it was comprehensive in scope, yet it maintained a core to it; 2) that it represented a good balance between theoretical and practical aspects of international relations; 3) that it gave the students exposure to different perspectives within the academic discipline; 4) that it stressed development of research and writing skills; and 5) that responsibility was given to the students for independent research.

Criticisms of the curriculum structure included the following specific points: 1) that there was a lack of variety of course offerings which

255

restricted the students' choice of coursework in a particular semester; 2) that there was too great an emphasis on theory; 3) that there was an inadequate coverage of "conservative" (traditionalist) international relations theory; 4) that there was not enough international history taught in the program; 5) that there was too great an emphasis on the research paper in the methodology course; and 6) that, while the option to write a thesis in lieu of the comprehensive exam was nominally open to the mid-career students, it was not a practicable choice given the conditions of part time studies. It should also be recorded that graduates from the first three years of the program's existence complained that there did not seem to be any structure to the curriculum at all, neither were there any satisfactory general-scope courses. It was graduates from subsequent years who felt that the curriculum had become too tightly structured to allow for diversity of course offerings. With these specific, different evaluative comments as background, we shall proceed in this section to review the responses to the "closed" questions concerning several aspects of the curriculum structure as well as impressions of the various specific courses.

The program curriculum structure has been described in detail in Chapter 8 in this book. Suffice it to repeat briefly here that it consists of three different types of courses: 1) general introductory courses in international relations theory and methodology; 2) global-scope, analytical topics courses in strategy and conflict analysis, foreign policy analysis, international law, institutions and integration plus international economics — which in recent years have been taught with an international political economy approach; and 3) regional international relations courses on Europe, the Soviet Bloc, the Middle East and North Africa, East and Southeast Asia, and Sub-Saharan Africa. Whereas every student normally will complete coursework in the first two categories, the experience with regional courses vary considerably among the students by the time they take final comprehensive examinations.

In the general evaluation of the curriculum structure, the graduates were asked to rank on a scale of one to seven (as expressive of "not at all" to "very much so") the extent to which the three types of courses provided a comprehensive and coherent approach to international relations studies, were intellectually stimulating, provided an understanding of international relations as an academic discipline and provided an understanding of practical problems in international relations.

A consolidated overview of rankings on these four aspects of the curriculum structure is presented in Table 7. The first observation to be made is that an overwhelming majority (three quarters of the graduates) ranked the curriculum very high in regard to providing both a comprehensive

Table 7. PROGRAM CURRICULUM STRUCTURE: EVALUATION OF THE THREE TYPES OF COURSES
In percentage

	Low 1	2	3	4	5	6	High 7	No Answer	Total
Provided comprehensive and coherent approach	1.2	1.2	1.2	1.2	20.7	40.1	34.4	0.0	100.0
How intellectually stimulating									
Theory and methodology	3.5	1.2	8.1	11.6	19.8	27.9	27.9	0.0	100.0
Global, analytical topics	0.0	1.1	1.1	5.7	25.0	36.4	30.7	0.0	100.0
Regional courses	1.2	0.0	9.4	10.6	23.5	31.8	23.5	0.0	100.0
Understanding international relations as an academic discipline									
Theory and methodology	3.5	0.0	4.6	11.5	18.4	25.3	36.8	0.0	100.0
Global, analytical topics	0.0	1.1	5.7	11.4	21.6	40.5	26.1	0.0	100.0
Regional courses	0.0	4.6	14.9	20.7	23.0	25.3	10.3	1.2	100.0
Understanding practical problems in international relations									
Theory and methodology	2.3	11.6	15.1	29.1	19.8	12.8	9.3	0.0	100.0
Global, analytical topics	1.2	2.3	3.5	4.7	8.1	52.3	27.9	0.0	100.0
Regional courses	1.2	0.0	3.5	7.0	31.4	34.8	20.9	1.2	100.0

and coherent approach to international relations studies. Secondly, the respondents found most of the coursework intellectually stimulating; in fact, less than five percent of the responses ranked all three types of courses very low in this respect. The global-scope, analytical topic courses were considered the most intellectually stimulating, but more than half of the respondents ranked the theory and methodology and the regional courses highly stimulating as well. The analytical topic courses and the theory and methodology courses were considered the most important for an understanding of international relations as an academic discipline. The lower ranking of the regional courses in this respect is probably a general comment which reflects the lack of integration of this type of course into the core of the curriculum structure, a problem discussed in greater detail in Chapter 15. Surprisingly perhaps, the global-scope, analytical topic courses, rather than the regional courses, were ranked as the most important in providing an understanding of practical problems in international relations. As shown in subsequent discussion, the strategy and conflict analysis course is considered particularly relevant in this regard. However, regional courses were also ranked highly by more than half of the respondents while, not so surprisingly, theory and methods courses were considered important as a source of understanding the world's practical problems by only one fifth of the graduates. The assumption that "there is nothing as practical as a good theory" has won adherence by only a small minority or, more probably, a good theory of international relations does not exist!

Turning to an evaluation of the individual courses, the graduates were asked to list the three courses they had found most and least difficult, most and least relevant to their perception of "the real world", and most and least enjoyable. The responses included identification of 19 different courses which were regrouped into eight categories. Five categories consist of single courses. They are: theory, methodology, strategy and conflict analysis, international economics, and directed research. International law, institutions and integration as a category consists of two different courses offered regularly. The foreign policy analysis category consists of three courses which have been offered regularly. The regional courses category consists of five courses offered at various centers, but fairly regularly. That category will be discussed in greater detail later. The justification for grouping so many courses together at this point is that the students' experiences with them vary considerably compared to the core course experiences where there is a much greater uniformity among the graduates' course experience. The category of "other" courses consists of subjects which have not been offered frequently during the eleven year survey period. It includes courses on peace research, comparative politics of advanced societies, and the Cold War. Except for the last category, all the courses have been taught by several faculty members at the same or different teaching centers of the U.K. Program. Hence, although the individuality of each instructor undoubtedly has played a role in these evaluations, the rankings represent neither accolades nor severe criticism of any single faculty member who has taught or is teaching in the program.

The results of the individual course assessments are provided in Table 8. Before discussing the distributions in detail, it is important to observe the relatively high proportion of "no answer" to the questions. The major reason is that most respondents listed only two courses instead of three in each category. In addition, a large number of respondents did not list any courses in the negative categories of least difficult, relevant and enjoyable resulting in no answer rates of 37.4, 47.1 and 36.4 percent respectively. This less discriminating response does tend to skew the results in a more positive direction than would otherwise have been the case.

The distribution of evaluations shows that theory and methodology courses were considered the most difficult, strategy and conflict analysis (as a single course) and regional courses the most relevant to the graduates' perception of "the real world" as well as the most enjoyable. Conversely, regional courses and international law, institutions and integration were ranked as the least difficult; theory, international law, institutions and integration and methodology as the least revelent; and methodology, international law institutions and integration and international economics as the least enjoyable courses.

When the positive "most" is checked against the negative "least", the composite score ("most" minus "least") of the top three courses in each of the six categories are as follows:

Most difficult:

1 methodology +14.2
2 theory +10.7
3 international economics + 3.1

Least difficult:

1 regional courses −17.3
2 international law, institutions and integration − 5.5
3 strategy and conflict analysis − 1.2

Most relevant:

1 strategy and conflict analysis +15.5
2 regional courses +11.1
3 foreign policy analysis + 9.9

Least relevant:

1 methodology − 6.2
2 international law, institutions and integration − 4.6
3 theory − 4.5

259

Table 8. PROGRAM CURRICULUM STRUCTURE: EVALUATION OF INDIVIDUAL COURSES
In percentage

	Most difficult	Least difficult	Most relevant	Least relevant	Most enjoyable	Least enjoyable
Theory	15.7	5.0	7.7	12.2	13.1	8.1
Methodology	15.7	1.5	3.8	10.0	5.0	13.4
Strategy and Conflict Analysis	7.7	8.9	18.8	3.5	18.1	0.4
International Law Institutions and Integration	5.7	11.2	6.9	11.5	8.1	13.4
Foreign Policy Analysis	6.5	5.8	12.6	2.7	9.6	8.8
International Economics	4.6	1.5	0.8	2.7	3.5	5.0
Regional Courses	10.3	27.6	20.2	9.1	20.7	11.1
Directed Research	2.3	1.1	0.0	0.4	2.3	0.4
Other	2.7	0.0	0.0	0.8	1.2	0.8
No Answer	28.7	37.4	22.3	47.1	18.4	36.4
Total	100.0	100.0	100.0	100.0	100.0	100.0

Most enjoyable:		Least enjoyable:	
1 strategy and conflict analysis	+17.7	1 methodology	−8.4
2 regional courses	+ 9.6	2 international law, institutions and integration	−5.3
3 theory	+ 5.0	3 international economics	−1.5

The most clearly distinguishable profiles which emerge are those of the methodology course being the most difficult and least relevant to "the real world" as well as the least enjoyable; the strategy and conflict analysis course being the most relevant and enjoyable; the international law, institutions and integration courses being the second ranked in all three negative rankings; and the regional courses being the least difficult and second most relevant and enjoyable.

A more detailed review of the rankings of the regional courses are presented in Table 9. The category of "area studies in general" was listed in less than five percent of the total responses and it will, therefore, be excluded from detailed discussion here. Treating the category of regional courses as a whole, i.e. the total listing of regional courses represents 100.0 percent in Table 9, the courses on European Diplomacy and the Soviet Bloc were ranked as the most difficult, relevant and enjoyable while the courses on East and Southeast Asia and Sub-Saharan Africa were listed as the least difficult, relevant and enjoyable while the course on the Middle East and North Africa was ranked in the middle position.

Similar to the previous general course ranking, when the positive "most" is checked against the negative "least" in the six categories, the top two courses were as follows:

Most difficult:		Least difficult:	
1 Europe	+20.8	1 East and Southeast Asia	−27.3
2 Soviet Bloc	+12.5	2 Sub-Saharan Africa	− 1.4

Most relevant:		Least relevant:	
1 Europe	+21.9	1 East and Southeast Asia	−28.3
2 Soviet Bloc	+13.5	2 Sub-Saharan Africa	−17.5

Most enjoyable:		Least enjoyable:	
1 Soviet Bloc	+20.9	1 East and Southeast Asia	−19.4
2 Middle East and North Africa	+10.0	2 Sub-Saharan Africa	−13.3

Combined with the high positive ranking of the strategy and conflict analysis course, these evaluations demonstrate clearly that students in the program have been far more interested in the focus on the East–West dimension in global political relations than in the North–South issues and

Table 9. PROGRAM CURRICULUM STRUCTURE: EVALUATION OF INDIVIDUAL REGIONAL COURSES
In percentage

	Most difficult	Least difficult	Most relevant	Least relevant	Most enjoyable	Least enjoyable
European Diplomacy	33.3	12.5	30.2	8.3	22.2	17.2
Soviet Bloc	33.3	20.8	30.2	16.7	27.8	6.9
Middle East and North Africa	14.9	15.3	11.3	4.2	20.4	10.4
East and Southeast Asia	7.4	34.7	13.3	41.6	18.5	37.9
Africa	11.1	12.5	7.5	25.0	7.4	20.7
Area Studies Generally	0.0	4.2	7.5	4.2	3.7	6.9
Total Regional Courses	100.0	100.0	100.0	100.0	100.0	100.0

relations within "Third World" regions in the world.

To sum up, the assessment of the curriculum structure indicates that it is a disputed issue dividing the graduates evenly in considering it both a strong and a weak feature of the program. After the first four years' existence in Britain, a definite core program emerged as a key factor in the curriculum structure and the subsequent graduates agreed, by an overwhelming majority, that it provides both a comprehensive and a coherent approach to international relations studies.

The global-scope, analytical topics courses were considered the most significant in regard to relevance in the respondents' perception of "the real world" as well as being the most enjoyable, with the strategy and conflict analysis course ranked particularly highly, the foreign policy analysis courses ranked in the middle and international law, institutions and integration courses ranked lowest. The theory and methodology courses were considered the most difficult and, although it was considered unpopular and largely irrelevant to understanding practical problems in international relations, the methodological training was cited very often in the open-ended responses as having provided a valuable skill whose significance has lasted far beyond the formal study of international relations. Hence, the evaluation of the theory and methodology courses could be interpreted to indicate that they were difficult, but necessary stepping stones to subsequent advanced research seminars.

The theory and methodology courses plus the analytical topics courses were judged to be very significant as keys to understanding international realtions as an academic discipline and to be the most intellectually stimulating courses while the courses on strategy and conflict analysis, European Diplomacy, the Soviet Bloc and foreign policy analysis were considered the most "real world" relevant in the curriculum structure.

The lack of integration into the core program of the regional courses is demonstrated by the responses and it seems clear that the "Third World" regions are considered the least interesting.

In regard to certain specific aspects of the curriculum, there is no doubt that these evaluations have provided important food for thought in the future conduct of the program, but the assessments also seem to give a general endorsement to continue most of the basic features of the program curriculum structure.

Administration of the program and maintaining academic standards

The administrative demands on the resident director and the staff of an overseas program designed for part-time, mid-career students are extremely taxing and, yet, not very highly appreciated by people on the main campuses of universities which offer such programs. The U.K. Program has maintained the sound practice of having teaching academics as resident directors which assures a high level of professional standards in the field compared to other programs which are headed by university administrators who often do not have academic specializations in the subject matter of the specific program they administer. However, in addition to staying professionally up-dated in the field in order to maintain a high quality of teaching, the consequence for the academic head of the program is that he or she must devote extraordinary attention to administrative issues and problems normally handled by a great number of specialized administrators on the university's home campus. (6) Although the size of the student clientele is relatively small, the director and the small administrative staff are responsible for every aspect of administrative support and services, from processing of the initial application for admission, through counseling, providing texts and access to libraries, to conducting the final commencement ceremony annually. Hence, the scope and diversity of administrative tasks call for extraordinary skills and commitment not normally expected of a single faculty member in a university. Additionally, the fact that the various teaching centers have been geographically dispersed in two or three different locations requiring extensive travel adds another demanding dimension to the administrative working conditions involved in conducting the U.K. Program. (7) These general comments are made in order to provide an introductory setting for the discussion of the graduates' evaluation of the program's administration which are presented in Table 10. It is divided into two parts. The first part concerns general managerial activities as these affect the students. The second part involves specific aspects of maintaining high academic standards and this section will be concluded with a discussion of the graduates' general assessment of academic standards of the program.

The first two measures in this evaluation consist of an assessment of the effectiveness of the initial orientation about the program which also includes a careful explanation of the admissions requirements. Normally, the program administrative coordinator conducts the first interview with potential students at the different teaching centers. At that point, the applicants' qualification for admission are reviewed and the requirements of the program are outlined. The resident director conducts a follow-up interview of each applicant before a decision on admissibility is made. Most of the respondents ranked these initial contacts very highly. Similarly, 73.6 percent were very satisfied with the continuous advisement about course scheduling and each student's coursework progression. Due

264

Table 10. EVALUATION OF THE PROGRAM'S ACADEMIC ADMINISTRATION
In percentages

	Low 1	2	3	4	5	6	High 7	No Answer	Total
Managerial Aspects:									
Admission requirements clearly explained									
Unclear . . . very clear	2.3	1.2	1.2	2.3	9.2	17.2	65.5	1.2	100.0
Initial orientation									
Ineffective . . . very effective	1.2	3.4	1.2	6.9	16.1	36.7	27.6	6.9	100.0
Continuous advisement									
Unsatisfactory . . . very satisfactory	2.3	0.0	2.3	2.3	12.6	32.2	41.4	6.9	100.0
Informed through student memos and newsletters									
Uninformed . . . very well informed	4.6	2.3	0.0	10.3	14.9	25.4	35.6	6.9	100.0
Academic Standard-Keeping:									
Admission standards adhered to									
Not very . . . extremely stringently	1.2	1.2	1.2	10.3	26.4	33.3	18.4	8.1	100.0
Self screening									
Ineffective . . . very effective	1.2	2.3	5.8	11.5	29.9	25.3	17.2	6.9	100.0
Formal screening									
Ineffective . . . very effective	3.5	2.3	6.9	20.7	18.4	10.3	13.8	24.1	100.0
Access to texts and general reading materials									
Unsatisfactory . . . very satisfactory	4.6	6.9	9.2	18.4	17.2	24.1	17.2	2.3	100.0
Guidance and access to libraries									
Unsatisfactory . . . very satisfactory	3.5	4.6	11.5	8.1	24.0	17.2	29.9	1.2	100.0
Total Academic Administration	2.7	2.7	4.3	10.1	18.8	24.6	29.6	7.2	100.0

to the geographical dispersion and odd work hours, it has been difficult to keep all the students continuously informed about program activities. Therefore, newsletters and student memoes are issued regularly and 61 percent of the respondents stated that they had been kept very well informed throughout their participation in the program. However, it has been somewhat difficult to assure a continuous communication flow for students located outside the London area. Generally, nearly three quarters of the graduates (70.0 percent) ranked the performance of such managerial services very highly.

The academic standard-keeping functions were evaluated in terms of the screening process and providing resource services in regard to access to texts, general reading materials and research materials in libraries. The argument often heard about overseas graduate programs, that anybody who is interested is admitted, has gained very little support among the graduates of this program. Only 2.4 percent were of the opinion that admission standards were not kept high while slightly more than half of the respondents (51.7 percent) believed that admission standards were maintained very stringently. Because of the mid-career students' diverse undergraduate backgrounds, it has been a practice of allowing about ten percent of new students to join in special admission status according to which they are screened into full graduate student status upon satisfactory performance in the first three courses.

Over the years, it has been our experience that there is an extensive self-screening process at work whereby new students withdraw after completing a few courses; for some because of the difficulty of keeping up with both work and study pressures, but for many because they do not perform satisfactorily in their coursework. In an analysis of this problem for students during the first eight years of the program in Britain, we found that only about 40 percent of the students who entered the program successfully completed it. Among the respondents, 42.5 percent confirmed that self-screening was a very effective practice in the program and only 3.5 percent did not think it took place at all.

A formal screening process was instituted in 1970. It involves an assessment of each student half-way through the coursework. It is conducted at the end of each semester during a special meeting between the resident director and the core faculty members. It is interesting to note that this formal screening process does not have as high a credibility with the students as is generally believed among the faculty. Compared to the much stronger confirmation of a self-screening process, only 24.1 percent of the graduates ranked the formal screening process as a highly effective method of maintaining academic standards. It was the measure which received the lowest scores on the administrative aspects of the program.

Providing students with access to the tools of learning has been one of the most difficult problems in the administration of the program. In response to the governing condition that students work during normal, day-time opening hours of libraries, the use of assigned texts has been adopted more extensively in all the courses than is normally the case in graduate courses. Hence, the London office has had to operate a university book store function made very difficult because of the overseas location and the constantly changing usage of required texts even for the same courses over time (which is a positive reflection of an adaptive faculty working in an academic discipline without a set textbook tradition and focused on current events). In addition, the program has purchased for each teaching center a collection of core reference materials. While it has been least successful in the Cambridge center, where students commute to one location from three different Air Force bases, more than five hundred volumes were collected in the Harrogate center library and, more impressive, the London office now houses a collection of nearly one thousand volumes as general reading materials. In regard to access to research facilities, arrangements have been made which give students users status in nearby university libraries. But a major problem has been that most students can not work in these libraries during working hours and most of the British universities and research institutes are not kept open late into the evening and during weekends as is common practice in American universities. Furthermore, in order to protect scarce resources, most libraries do not grant borrowing privileges to students outside their university. In this respect, the London area students are the best supported. Since the mid-1970s, the program has worked out a special arrangement which grants its students full use, including borrowing privileges, of the Royal Institute of International Affairs' extensive collection of international relations materials. In addition, the program directors have conducted lengthy searches of research facilities located near the teaching centers which have been written up as overview pamphlets on the availability of, and access to, research facilities in international relations.

Nevertheless, access to texts, general reading materials and research facilities remain one of the major problems in conducting the program, especially for students outside the London area. In the graduates' open-ended responses, it was cited as a weak feature in 14.2 percent of their responses in this category, making it the second-most significant problem identified. However, given the special conditions of study mentioned above, the specific assessments presented in Table 10 speaks highly of the continuous efforts to provide solutions to this problem. Only about

10 percent expressed extreme dissatisfaction while more than 40 percent were highly satisfied with the provision of access to texts, general reading materials and libraries. That can be considered quite an achievement for this type of program.

Maintaining academic standards is given very serious attention by the director, faculty and administrative staff and is highly appreciated by the students. A large number of the graduates who responded to this survey referred to the high academic standards as one of the strongest features of the program. They pointed out the advantage of small classes as well as commending the faculty and staff for maintaining tough academic requirements and for the personal concern shown to each student in his or her progression through the courses. Several graduates stated that the program had achieved an excellent adaptation to part-time student conditions and, yet, managed to maintain a high degree of integrity.

Table 11 shows more specifically the graduates' over-all assessment of the program when they were asked to rank its degree of difficulty. Sixty percent of the respondents ranked the U.K. Program to be as difficult as a conventional full-time M.A. program and only 22.3 percent believed that it was easier. As a program for part-time, mid-career students, nearly two thirds thought that this one was more difficult than other similar programs and that it was as difficult as it ought to be. An overwhelming majority (82.9 percent) did not consider the program too difficult. The last two measures should be put in the context of their constant urging that the high academic standards should be kept up because that was what had made the program meaningful and worthwhile to them. Typical of this reaction is the following comment by one respondent:

[It is] an absolutely superior program. Resist any temptation to "commercialize" it or make it less strenuous. The kind of people you want in the program will *make time* to do the work.

Impact on career development

One of the questions which intrigues those of us engaged in educating mid-career students is whether or not the completion of an advanced degree has a direct impact on subsequent career developments for the graduates. We shall conclude this survey with a description of the answers the graduates provided to a set of questions concerning this important issue. The open-ended responses to the questions were carefully reviewed before they were placed into seven categories of responses. The distribution of the aggregated answers are presented in Table 12.

Table 11. GENERAL ASSESSMENT OF THE PROGRAM: DEGREE OF DIFFICULTY
In percentage

	Low 1	2	3	4	High 5	No Answer	Total
As difficult as a full time M.A. program	9.5	11.9	15.5	15.5	44.0	3.6	100.0
Probably easier than a full time M.A. program	45.9	15.3	14.1	9.4	12.9	2.4	100.0
Too difficult as a part time M.A. program	45.1	37.8	7.3	3.7	2.4	3.7	100.0
As difficult as an M.A. program ought to be	2.3	9.2	23.0	21.8	41.4	2.3	100.0
More difficult than other part time M.A. programs	7.2	3.6	24.1	31.4	31.4	2.3	100.0

Table 12. GENERAL ASSESSMENT OF THE PROGRAM: IMPACT ON CAREER DEVELOPMENT
In percentage

	No	Not yet, but expects it to	Not sure, did not help nor hurt	Yes, marginally	Yes, but only indirectly	Yes, generally	Yes, very much and directly	No Answer	Total
Was completion of program relevant to performance in your present job?	23.0	8.1	14.9	4.6	8.1	19.5	17.2	4.6	100.0
Was completion of program instrumental in subsequent career advancement?	24.1	24.1	4.6	13.8	6.9	12.6	10.3	3.5	100.0
Was completion of program instrumental in subsequent change of career?	51.7	–	11.5	–	–	16.1	13.8	6.9	100.0
Did participation in the program affect your process of thinking and method of evaluating information in general?	3.4	–	2.3	2.3	–	13.8	72.5	5.7	100.0

The first question asked was whether or not completion of the program was relevant to performance of the respondents' present job. In other words, had there been an immediate, direct correspondence between doing advanced academic work and the daily professional activities the students were responsible for? For almost a quarter of the graduates (23.0 percent), the program was not relevant at all in their present jobs. For 20.8 percent of the graduates, completing the program was thought to be indirectly or marginally relevant or it was expected to become relevant in the future, but it was too early to tell, while 14.9 percent thought it had neither helped nor hurt. But for more than one third of the graduates, completion of the program was judged to have been directly relevant and 17.2 percent of that group expressed the view that the program work had extreme relevance to their present jobs. Impressions of the various ways in which the program had been relevant are presented through the following statements:

Definitely yes, I was selected for my present job largely because I have a dual background with two M.A. degrees — one in civil engineering and one in international relations. I am directly responsible for negotiating with the Government of Japan for a $1.1 billion construction program for the American military.

Absolutely — I am now assigned as Air Force Staff Representative to the National Security Council Strategic Warning Staff. My work requires constant reference to the days when I was working on this M.A. Program and, without it, I would have difficulties.

Yes — I am currently assigned to the U.S. Defense Intelligence Agency, writing the Defense Department estimates of Soviet and Warsaw Pact air force strengths. Central to this task is the identification and analysis of the military-political variables affecting Soviet threat perception and military force development. Without my U.S.C. training I would be unable to perform this task.

The program has been very relevant to both my past position when I conducted analysis of intelligence at the national level and presently when I am teaching American Government and National Security as well as general international relations courses at the U.S. Military Academy.

Yes — as a consultant in development of Forest and Agri-Industries, it has helped interpret the socio-political context of many projects

271

in the U.S., Mexico and the Honduras. Predicting political change abroad has helped save money and projects.

Very much so, I am writing my Ph.D. dissertation and doing research on defense and foreign affairs for a (British) Member of Parliament.

Not presently, but it was relevant to performances in previous jobs as McGovern's presidential campaign speech writer and, later Congressional Aide, specializing in foreign policy and national security.

The second question asked whether or not completion of the program had been instrumental in subsequent career advancement. Again, for about one quarter of the graduates (24.1 percent), it had not been instrumental at all. Another quarter of the respondents expected it to be instrumental in the future (being the most recent graduates, it was too early to tell at the time of the survey). Only 4.6 percent thought that completing the program had neither helped nor hurt while 20.7 percent thought it had been somewhat instrumental in career advancement. However, the advanced degree was considered definitely to have been significant in career promotion by 22.9 percent of the graduates.

The third question concerned the more dramatic impact of whether or not completing the program had resulted in a subsequent change of career. In the cases of slightly more than half of the graduates, it had not had such an impact. For 30 percent of them, on the other hand, their engagement in the U.K. Program had been so significant as to lead to a change of career. The following quoted statements from the top 13.8 percent within this group illustrate the variety of ways in which career changes had taken place:

As a result of the program, I decided to start a career in development work for Less Developed Countries. I have completed a Ph.D. in Natural Resource Planning in Colorado State University and I now work for a public foundation that is developing international aid programs related to livestock production systems.

Yes — I was a Catholic Chaplain at the time I completed the program. I left the priesthood shortly afterwards and became Executive Director of the Planned Parenthood Association of San Mateo County, California, for seven years. I subsequently returned to U.S.C. for a Masters in Public Administration and I am now working for the U.S. Department of Health, Education and Welfare.

It was extremely important as a negotiating vehicle when I retired from the Navy and sought civilian employment. It was worth roughly $3,000 in my asking price over an individual with similar experience, but no advanced degree.

Yes, it reinforced an interest in pursuit of further graduate study and preparation for work in higher education as a teacher and administrator.

Finally, from a general educational perspective, the respondents were asked if participation in the program had affected their process of thinking and methods of evaluating information in general; i.e., including, but not just about international relations. This question drew an amazingly high degree of positive responses. The program had had a significant impact in this respect in 86.3 percent of the cases with 72.5 percent responding that it had affected their general intellectual orientation very much. A few representative statements are cited to illustrate the responses:

I give more time to alternatives and work for more objectivity in my work. It is, hopefully, easier to understand or at least tolerate opposing points of view.

It has made me slower to judge because I am less sure of any particular position perhaps because of a more realistic appraisal of the complexity of most systems.

At the age of 40, I finally learned how to write a decent paper and conduct the rigorous research necessary to support it. I became much more sceptical about absolute positions (and answers), but I have not become a relativist. The program really changed my whole outlook on life.

The program in general was a good refresher in assimilating and organizing huge amounts of unfamiliar materials. "Revisionist writers" also provided good counterpoints for a rethink of long-time, comfortable opinions which was useful for stimulating one's analytical faculties.

The process of thinking I was exposed to has helped me in my approach to the business world. It is incredible how much business relies on rumor, half-information and just plain guessing. A little

273

methodical research and the ability to do it is worth its weight in gold.

It convinced me that most liberal arts courses are conceived by wooly-minded theoreticians trying to codify and quantify something that does not lend itself to either.

Most assuredly, it contributed to critical thinking. More importantly, it offered exposure to and participation in the varieties of methods for critical evaluation and thought within a social scientific process. The rigors of intellectual thought require procedures which differ substantially from everyday evaluative processes.

The program has increased my understanding of the complexity of political problems in general. I am now also aware that problems in the business world are primarily political in nature.

Absolutely! In a program like this, the emphasis must be on teaching students competent scholarship, evidence before judgment, and how to prepare coherent research reports. The Navy needs literate officers — ones with a world view and a facility to undertake independent research. They must learn how to *conceptualize* in the abstract.

I had lost the art of thinking which my undergraduate days had helped give me. My approach to just about every daily situation has been affected. I now avoid snap decisions and try to find out the full meaning of relevant events each day. I have a new slant on current events and am now able to read and discuss current global happenings with a degree of expertise.

A mid-career student clientele is an especially interesting group to query about the impact of graduate education on their careers because they are in positions to convert additional educational achievements more immediately into career pursuits than the conventional type of M.A. student who begins the first career upon graduation. Although a more systematic follow-up survey in this fascinating subject area is necessary (and would be extremely illuminating), this first cut at systematic investigation of the career impact of completing the program has revealed a certain pattern of responses. In the perspective of general educational development, the program has had a major impact on nearly every participant. In the narrower-scope context of direct, functional payoffs, between one quarter and one third of the graduates stated that completing the program had been very instrumental in subsequent career developments and another quarter expected it to be so in the future. Conversely, it had had no direct impact on the careers of about one quarter of the graduate respondents.

General summary

This account of survey results began by establishing that those who responded comprised a representative sample of all the program graduates between 1967 and 1977. Most of the students join the program because of strong personal as well as professional interest in the subject of international relations. In their judgment, the excellent quality of teaching is the strongest feature of the program. The graduate respondents gave a general endorsement to the program's present curriculum structure which they viewed as a comprehensive and coherent approach to the study of international relations.

The great diversity of undergraduate backgrounds, which characterizes this mid-career student clientele, underscores the necessity for general-scope, introductory core courses that serve to establish parity in preparation for more advanced coursework. The theory and methodology courses were viewed as such stepping stones; very difficult, but necessary for a systematic progression through the curriculum. The global-scope, analytical topic courses as a general category, and the strategy and conflict analysis course in particular, were viewed as the most relevant to the "real world" and the most enjoyable while some of the regional courses were given strong second rankings. Special projects were considered very valuable aspects of the teaching approach.

The managerial administrative activities were performed to most of the graduates' satisfaction and there was a persistent urging that every effort be made to maintain the program's reputation for high academic standards.

In this context, most of the respondents believed the U.K. Program was as difficult as a full-time conventional masters program and as difficult as it ought to be. Participation in the program had made a major intellectual impact on nearly all the graduates and, for one third of them, completing the program had been very directly instrumental in subsequent career developments.

The most significant criticisms concerned the lack of diversity of course offerings each semester and the difficulties of access to research facilities. Although they should not be dismissed and every effort should be made to alleviate them, these are endemic problems for this type of program.

However, the point that the curriculum is tending to become too tightly structured should be treated as an important caveat. The more specific criticisms of the ineffective role of student reports in the conduct of classes, the dissatisfaction with the oral part of the comprehensive examination, and the low credibility of the formal screening process as an effective method of maintaining academic standards ought to be taken up for review as important issues in the future conduct of the program.

The summary review of all the evaluative responses discussed in this chapter indicates general support for continuing the general features of the program.

This survey should be considered a first effort to conduct regular, systematic reviews of student perspectives on the program as a whole. We will quickly concede that there may have been flaws in the questionnaire design and that this account of responses could be considerably improved through more complex correlational analysis. But this survey does at least represent a beginning in moving beyond citing particular incidences of a few students' opinions and providing student feedback broader in scope than the individual course assessments which have been conducted regularly over the last decade.

Appendix

The following is a condensed version of a six page questionnaire which formed the basis of the survey. In order to abbreviate the questionnaire only the questions have been presented; scales, etc. are not included in the format below.

(A) *General Background Information*

1. What motivated you to enter the program?
2. What was your academic and professional background upon entering the program?

(B) *The Curriculum Structure of the Program*

1. To what extent did the three types of courses (i.e. (1) core courses, (2) analytical topic courses, (3) area study courses) provide a coherent and comprehensive approach to I.R. studies?
2. To what extent did the types of courses listed in question B/1 provide you with an understanding of the academic discipline of I.R.?
3. To what extent did the type of courses listed in question B/1 provide you with an understanding of the practical problems of I.R.?
4. How intellectually stimulating were the types of courses listed in B/1?

5. What three courses did you consider (a) the most enjoyable, (b) the least enjoyable, (c) the most difficult, (d) the least difficult, (e) the most relevant to your conception of the "real world", (f) the least relevant to your conception of the "real world"?

(C) *The Teaching Approach of the Program*

1. Given your overall experience in classes, was there a satisfactory balance between lecturing and discussion sessions?
2. To what extent did student participation in class discussions contribute to your learning experience?
3. To what extent did students' reports in class contribute to your learning experience?
4. Taken as a whole, to what extent were the program's course requirements an effective part of your learning process: (1) research papers, (2) examinations, (3) oral reports, (4) essays, (5) book reports?
5. Did the program maintain a realistic balance in the assignment of research papers, essays, book reports, oral reports and examinations as you progressed through the courses?
6. On balance, was the grading process conducted in a fair manner?
7. Considering the conditions of part-time studies and evening courses, was access to instructors for consultation satisfactory?
8. Considering the conditions of part-time studies during the evenings and on weekends, was access to texts and general reading materials satisfactory?
9. How satisfactory was the assistance the program could provide in terms of guidance and access to libraries?
10. Did you participate in any of the following special teaching activities: (1) simulation exercises, (2) field trips, (3) weekend conferences, (4) special graduate seminars?
11. If your response to any of the activities listed in C/10 was "yes," to what extent was it/were they relevant to your overall coursework?
12. Were the comprehensive examination review sessions useful?
13. Did the content and structure of the written comprehensive examinations correspond with the coursework you had completed?
14. Did you find the oral part of the comprehensive examination to be an effective final assessment of the work you had done in the program?
15. Was the assessment of your comprehensive examination performance conducted in a fair manner?

(D) *The Academic Administration of the Program*

1. Were the admission requirements clearly explained to you before you

entered the program?

2. From your contact with other students, how stringently were the admission standards adhered to?

3. To what extent did you observe a "self-screening" process whereby your fellow students dropped out of the program after a few courses?

4. Was the formal screening process half-way through the program effective?

5. Was the initial orientation about the program as a whole effectively presented?

6. Was the continuous advisement about the course schedules satisfactory?

7. Did the student memos and newsletters keep you well informed about the various activities undertaken in the program?

(E) *General Assessment of the Program*

1. You perhaps have discussed post-graduate (M.A.) programs with other colleagues, friends, etc., or may have participated in other M.A. programs since you were with U.S.C. Based upon your impressions, please rank the following statements as they reflect your assessment of the USC I.R. program: (1) As difficult as a full-time M.A. program, (2) Probably easier than a full-time M.A. program, (3) Too difficult as a part-time M.A. program, (4) As difficult as a part-time M.A. program ought to be, (5) more difficult than other part-time M.A. programs.

2. Was the program relevant to your performance in your present job?

3. Was completion of the program instrumental in subsequent career advancement?

4. Was completion of the program instrumental in a subsequent change of career?

5. What three aspects of the program would you suggest are its strongest features?

6. What three aspects of the program would you suggest are its weakest features?

7. Beyond learning about international relations, did participation in the program affect your process of thinking and your methods of evaluating information in general?

8. What recommendations do you wish to make for improvements of the program?

9. Any additional comments?

References

1. The author wishes to acknowledge with great appreciation the assistance provided by Ms. Nancy Fahy in managing the coding, mail distribution and collating of responses through the U.S.C. London office. The questionnaire was designed in September 1977 and mailed in October and November 1977. Responses were collected until early Spring, 1978.
2. This distribution has changed significantly since the mid-1970s. About half of the present student body are either Americans employed by U.S. multinational enterprises or non-American diplomatic personnel working in more than forty different embassies and consulates in London.
3. Students from the military are predominantly officers although the program is open to anybody who qualifies academically.
4. Rankings of 4 and 5 have been aggregated as expressions of highly accurate responses.
5. Respondents were asked, in two separate, open-ended questions to suggest three aspects of the program which they thought were the strongest and the weakest features of the program. All the different responses were recorded on a master sheet and then categorized into six general groupings: quality of instruction, program curriculum structure, academic standards, administration, library and research facilities, and characteristics of the student body. The quality of instruction category accounted for 28.6 percent of the strongest features and 11.1 percent of the weakest features suggested by the respondents. Instead of presenting a separate overview, all the open-ended responses will be used to augment the discussion of various assessments given in the "closed questions" ranking responses described throughout this chapter.
6. The result of satisfying these extraordinary, time-consuming administrative demands necessary to maintain a high quality program is that the director normally has to sacrifice time for research and writing expected for academic promotion in his or her field of specialization. The tension between satisfying administrative demands and progressing in one's own professional field of specialization was fittingly summed up in the following saw recited by one of U.S.C.'s vice presidents:

   The first year one gives up reading the specialized professional journals and research reports. The second year, one gives up reading in the academic field altogether. And the third year one begins to write a book about education.

   Perhaps the decision to produce this book, made by two program directors, exemplifies the validity of the saw.
7. During two of the six years I was resident director of the U.K. Program, a teaching center was established in Harrogate, Yorkshire. Teaching there once a week required train travel over an academic year equivalent to one and a third time around the world at the Equator!

CHAPTER 17

Inter-state Relations or World Society Transactions? One Student's Perspective on the U.K. Program

Karl Pieragostini

Although the following discussion is based on my experiences for the better part of the three years 1973-1975 as a student in the U.K. Program, it in no way presumes to be a representative picture of the 'typical' student reaction. However, I think it safe to suppose that my experience is not unique. There are most likely elements of my overall view which are the result of common threads found throughout the experiences of my fellow students. Therefore, an examination of one student's perceptions of what "knowledge" he gained from the endeavor leading to a masters degree in international relations and how he gained whatever that "knowledge" was, may prove useful when compared with the intentions and aspirations of those who attempted to act as our "facilitators". Rather than reviewing specific courses, the account which follows will focus on the basic theoretical and methodological issues of the field which are, after all, the guiding core of the program.

My initial, general reaction when first embarking upon the study of IR was one of great surprise and some bewilderment. My undergraduate training as an engineer, and my several years experience in the US Navy prior to entering the program may partially explain the decided lack of orientation I felt. Purely idiosyncratic features of my experience could have provided all elements of the explanation if it were not for the fact that I sensed a similar experience occurring in those around me. And as supporting evidence, much more recently I have witnessed the identical feeling of bewilderment and disorientation among a multi-national group of full-time masters degree students at University College, London. (1)

In the majority of cases, this feeling of unease and disorientation was expressed amongst the students in mutually supportive cynical comments on the program's irrelevancy. These common defensive tactics set the stage early for what was to be a continually crucial factor in student–professor interactions: the burden, as far as we students were concerned, lay totally with the professor to prove the relevancy of our studies. The scientific study of international relations was irrelevant until proven otherwise. This may be stating the case a bit too strongly, but it is a vitally important point, for much of the success or failure of a program such as this depends upon each professor accepting the intellectual obstacle expressed in the doubting Thomas nature of his students.

The science of international relations

In my case, this feeling of unease had its roots in an ignorance of what the study of international relations was all about. My vague notion of diplomatic history, linked in some way with the study of current "relevant problems", was immediately shattered by the introduction of "our field" (a euphemism commonly used to accommodate the vastly divergent views on what the objective of the field should be) as an aspiring social science. The need to "go scientific" was of paramount importance, we were told, if the current practices of diplomacy and strategy were to be exposed as the "quackery" it was perceived to be. (2)

As a social science, our field was declared to be behavioral, and Easton's eight tenets of behavioralism were provided as a useful foundation upon which we could build. The last of these, "integration", was given special emphasis, for if our field was to move anywhere, it had to be part of a wider interdisciplinary movement. We were urged to use the findings of sociologists, psychologists, anthropologists and others, and implored to plunder the social scientific "chest of ideas, constructs, and schema . . .". (3)

While interdisciplinary communication provided the foundation for behavioral studies, scientific method gave us the tools with which a meaningful structure of social knowledge could be built. The writings on scientific method most often cited as seminal were those of Popper (4) and Kuhn; (5) the emphasis being on Popper's notion of falsification, and Kuhn's description of normal science. Additionally, the scientific caveat, explicit in Popper and implicit in Kuhn, that all knowledge is tentative was given special attention. Continually before the student was the image of researchers rigorously testing their hypotheses against the real world of social interaction.

While I have come to see that Popper's warnings of the tentative nature of all scientific work are well founded and supremely important in guiding research, I also recognize the debilitating effect such pronouncements can have on the fledgeling social scientist. The tenets of Popperian science can seem to the recently initiated a philosophy of hopelessness; an advocation of muddling through. The statement of such warnings by a professor are undeniably necessary and he would be intellectually dishonest if he avoided them. However, they can be over-emphasised, resulting in more student alienation and judgments of irrelevancy. In defense of these caveats of tentativeness, professors argued that even in the natural sciences the most entrenched theories have been overthrown. This argument was simply not credible, especially to anyone who had even the most casual awareness of Newtonian physics. Einstein overthrew Newton it is true, and Newton's theories were shown to be less than totally accurate. However, they had also amply demonstrated their usefulness, and for that matter remain the cornerstone of applied physics. Where is the Newton of international relations or of the social sciences in general? Arguments that the social sciences are really no different than the natural sciences may have merit, but if they are too often called upon to defend the relevancy of international relations such arguments become strained and incredible to the student. Because the social sciences aspire to utilize a "scientific method" similar to that of the natural sciences does not automatically equate the two in the student's mind.

However, as one was exposed to the work of Singer, Russett and McClelland, the phrase "scientific method" came to be identified more and more with the gathering and processing of data. Quantification was the key to knowledge; in fact, knowledge "cannot be said to exist – and certainly cannot be codified or accumulated – without data". (6) The systematic collection of information was seen to be vital. An explicit and replicable system of procedures for observing and classifying information was deemed necessary if we were to "convert interesting – but theoretically useless – facts into data . . .". (7)

It became obvious to the student that this collection of data required a framework within which the researcher could comfortably operate. It was suggested that the framework most suitable for a scientific, interdisciplinary approach was "the system". Systems analysis was offered as the means by which our interdisciplinary research was to be made orderly and replicable. The exact "system" that was of specific interest in our field was defined in various ways: ranging from a complex arrangement of relationships and interactions between states, (6) to the more general notion of any "patterned interaction of variables in which discontinuities of transactions . . . form the boundary between the system and its environment". (8) Putting aside for a moment the sharp differences one could discern in these various definitions, the student nevertheless could not mistake the important emphasis that was being placed upon concepts such as "input", "process", "output", "feedback" and "environment". Of course, no discussion of such concepts would be complete without thorough consideration being given to the important work of Karl Deutsch. (9) The cybernetic model of units interacting with their environment was seen to be vital for any scientific inquiry into social behavior. But at the same time, as we students were presented with this fact of behavioral life, it became apparent that hot disputes were underway in the field as to how broadly or narrowly the concepts "unit" and "environment" were to be defined.

It should be noted here that at no time was it suggested to us that the behavioral revolution had completely overthrown or miraculously converted the advocates of a more traditional approach. In fact, the works of Morgenthau, Swartzenberger, Bull, Claude, Kennan and others were seen to be very important. However, this importance lay not so much in their ability to adequately explain or describe the world's plight, but rather in the fact that traditional analysis (even with its demonstrated failure in providing acceptable answers to vital questions) still dominated the thinking of the world's political practitioners. It was argued that our field desperately needed to become scientific if it was to prove useful in providing solutions to problems of the thermonuclear era. But at the same time, all the demonstrated academic expertise in the universe would be useless if practitioners were not lured away from their accustomed traditional approach.

While it was accepted by students that the paradigm of traditional thought produced results which fell far short of expectations and was therefore in need of revision (if not succession), it was felt that this paradigm deserved far more attention by professors than it received. Traditional thinking was seen by the students to govern the actions of those world political practitioners they read about each day in the press. However, it seemed that the traditional approach was often dismissed by lecturers *a priori* as incorrect and they chose instead to discuss the nuances of the intra-behavioral squabble. This dismissal instilled in some students the belief that they were being cheated, in that such a demonstrably important school of thought was being given only cursory attention. It also caused some to question how well the behavioralist school actually understood the thinking of their traditional colleagues.

A behavioral house divided

The student's introduction to this new, social scientific discipline was not the orderly and compelling indoctrination my commentary may have thus far suggested. In fact, concurrent with our becoming increasingly aware of the general inclinations which identified the behavioral approach to the field, we also came to see more and more clearly the disagreements and schisms which abound within the behavioral ranks. From my perspective as a student in the program, the schism of utmost importance for the study of international social behavior seemed to be the one still dividing the American school of state-centric empiricists from the London school of world society analysts. Some would argue that the importance of this cleavage is exaggerated, and that the world society approach is no more than a temporary aberration of little consequence. However, the evidence does not support such an argument, for it clearly can be seen how much influence the "cobweb" model of interaction has had on the more state-centric conscious IR scholars. Professor Singer's recent preference for the term "global" rather than "international" (11) may be, in part, a result of this influence.

The student very quickly finds it convenient, when considering the two sides which are separated by this schism over the most basic of assumptions, to label the approaches as "billiard ball" and "cobweb" thinking. In discussions, these two notions were continually referred to as models, but in fact they most often seemed to be used as heuristic metaphors meant to neatly summarise two very different ways of viewing international behavior.

It becomes increasingly clear to me that while the "billiard ball" and "cobweb" analysts both agree that traditional political reliance upon experience, intuition and general worldliness has led us nowhere, the former see the basic framework of inquiry as unchanged; that is, the interaction of states, and principally state governments, remains the most important subject of study. What was new in their approach was the rigorous application of scientific method, especially the gathering and collating of data, to the traditional, state-centric system. In 1961, Professor Singer neatly separated the myriad of everyday interactions into those which occurred at the systemic level (the inter-state system) and those which made up the sub-systemic level (the intra-state system), (12) arguing that our choice was to either study the billiard ball system (my metaphor, not his) as a whole or to restrict oneself to the analysis of the internal workings of a single billiard ball. He opined that, in describing international relations, the systemic level was preferred; in explaining them, the sub-systemic level would prove more fruitful; while in predicting them, both orientations offer promise. (12) The title of Professor Rosenau's anthology, *International Politics and Foreign Policy*, aptly summarises the systemic and sub-systemic dichotomy.

This dichotomy was criticised by the advocates of a world society approach as being unrealistic in our world of rapid and pervasive mass communication and transportation. However, the point which was often overlooked by the student, as he either dutifully accepted this criticism or rejected it out of hand, was that the systemic, sub-systemic construction was a product of 1961 and by 1969 (14) Professors Singer and Rosenau had acknowledged the importance of the transnational connection and were probing ways of explaining the demonstrated permeability of the billiard ball shell. The neat dichotomy of 1961 was deemed too restricting and unyielding, and the notion of linkages emerged. The extension of this changing conceptual perspective by the American school of analysts toward greater emphasis on non-governmental, transnational interactions was most recently reflected in an address by Professor Rosenau when he declared that in today's world, affairs are as much transnational as they are international. (15)

Confusion would be avoided and the student would in turn be better equipped to intelligently analyse for himself the various approaches, if the chronological order of ideas, models and opinions was always kept clearly in view. Here the construction of a course's planned progression is important, especially in the more theory oriented subjects. If the study of international relations theory was approached from a more historical point of view, this would prove useful to the student in two ways. First, there would be some order in what is usually seen as a collection of unrelated hypotheses and propositions proposed by thinkers who never listened to each other. It would be most helpful to the student if a chronological connection could be shown to exist where one set of hypotheses succeeded another rather than being created in a vacuum. For example, this approach could be very beneficial in showing the progression of thinking about decision making. Secondly, such an historical perspective would satisfy the felt need of students to give greater attention to the traditional approach. If for no other reason than that behavioral thinking grew out of a displeasure with the results of traditional assumptions, using a "history of thought" perspective would necessitate the open discussion of those traditional assumptions.

In a relatively new and continuously evolving academic discipline, one must continually be aware of the most recent developments in that which one is attempting to evaluate. There is little use in criticising as too simple a model which has already been subsumed by a more complex and possibly more useful one (be it either a traditional or behavioral model).

As I saw it, however, what the cobweb theorists were criticising in the approach used by scholars such as Singer was not that their models lacked complexity, but rather that they all sprang from the assumption that, for analytic purposes, the world was best seen as a system of interacting states whose actions are in some way different from, and usually more important than, all other global interactions. Professor Russett's move into a behaviorist (12a) study of the stimulus and response of states in his macroscopic view of UN voting (16) can be seen as evidence that the basic assumptions of the billiard ball analogy have not changed.

In their simplest terms, the arguments by advocates of the world society perspective, seemed to be based upon a rejection of the stimulus/response, input/output analyses of Singer, Russett, *et al*. That type of behaviorist treatment of interactions admittedly appeared more amenable to quantification, but it was suggested that what this type of analysis ignored were the "black-boxed" processes of motivation. It was argued that true behavioral research must examine the inner workings of motivational factors which account for a specific output in response to a given input. Mere recording of the output was insufficient.

Our introduction to the cobweb analogy invited the student to expand his field of vision and inquiry to encompass the entire expanse of intertwining, overlapping global transactions with "concentrations of interactions at some points, and linkages across national boundaries, sometimes clustered, sometimes infrequent". (17) For the student, this relegation of inter-state relations to just one cluster or system among many to be considered was unexpected, and led some to suspect that they had been grossly misled by the program's name. It was quite unsettling to enter a post graduate program in *international* relations and immediately be confronted with detailed criticism of the type of research, one had previously believed was the entire substance of the field: i.e., the study of interstate governmental transactions.

Levels or units of analysis?

In trying to better define for myself the exact differences in approach of each behavioral school, I began to see that a major disagreement revolved around the idea of several levels of analysis and the transferring of findings from one level to another. In his important paper of 1967, David Easton suggested that behavioral research techniques had not been developed for any units of analysis other than small groups, organisations and some

well-defined communities. (18) The efforts of the state-centric analyst
could be seen then as an attempt at replacing the individual actors in these
small group interactions with the anthropomorphised state government as
actor. Conversely, the intent of the world society approach was to show
that these small group, organisation and community actors were in fact the
substance of all world society, and that the artificialities viewed necessary
by some, because of a shift in levels of analysis, were in fact a hindrance.

What Burton, Groom and the others in the London school seemed to
be saying was that there is no level of analysis problem at all. The concern
with remaining at a certain level of analysis and the resulting grave
warnings issued to those attempting to cut across levels were viewed as
unnecessary, misleading and stifling. It was suggested that, instead of
seeing ourselves as being faced with a *level of analysis* problem, it would
prove more fruitful if we viewed our task as partly one of solving *unit of
analysis* problems. Rather than formulating artificial means of crossing
artificial barriers between interstate, intrastate, intergroup, interpersonal,
and other levels, we would find it more useful to probe systems of interactions at or across any of these levels. (19) The organising notion should
be "unit" and not "level", and the unit used must be a system of
patterned interactions, without regard to the level boundaries this system
might cross. An often quoted example of this type of behavioral system is
that which existed as a result of the Cyprus conflict. At one point, actors
as diverse as Greek and Turkish Cypriot community leaders, Greek
colonels, and the NATO Council of Ministries can be seen linked in a
system of transactions. The organising framework in our probe of trans-
level interactions was to be the system; that is, a system of patterned transactions whose boundaries are defined by qualitative or quantitative discontinuities in the transactions.

Is power the problem?

Another area of disagreement between the state-centrist and world society
analysts surrounded the themes or problems which it was felt would be
the most productive to investigate. The state-centrist analysts seemed
intent upon continuing their attempts at operationally defining the
concept of "power" and the problems associated with it. In E. Raymond
Platig's words, "as a field of inquiry international relations studies the distribution of power on a global scale and the interplay between and among
power centers." (20) Platig's concept of power was not limited to military
or economic strength, but rather was meant to "encompass the entire
range of man's influence and control over his fellow man. (21) For the

state-centrist school then, the organising framework was the single system of inter-state transactions, and the problems of utmost interest were those of power.

The Burtonian approach was distinctive in its willingness to consider any system, rather than being restricted to one, the inter-state system. Additionally, the problems, issues, or themes of greatest concern were not those revolving around the concept of power, but instead were those concerning a whole new range of other notions, including authority, legitimisation, participation, value, role, and need, to name several. Also, it became clear that the underlying hypothesis which provided the driving force of the approach was the belief that social behavior was not essentially different at industrial, small group, communal, inter-state and other levels. (22) The task was to find purely systemic attributes or features which could help explain conflict and co-operation at every level, be it in the international arena or in the classroom. The traditionalists, as well as the state-centric behavioralists, seemed content with the concept of power acting in an inter-state framework, while, in contrast, the world society approach attempted to find those stable, fundamental units of analysis (23) necessary if the myriad of social scientific research was to be integrated into a comprehensive study of society.

The world society alternative to the traditional and state-centric "scientific" reliance upon power as an organising concept was quite refreshing to the large majority of students in the program. However, the world society case for concentration on factors other than power tended to be overstated at times, and as a result alienated some in the program, especially those who had experience as international practitioners in various fields. Again, the more traditional concept of "power" was dismissed *a priori* as irrelevant to our studies. More helpful in establishing credibility for a scientific and world society-inclined approach would have been a clear recognition of the prevalence of power modeling both in and outside the academic world, followed by a detailed critique of such modeling. One suspects that the requirement for such a detailed, convincing critique would have been as useful for world society advocates as for their students.

Induction v. deduction

To this student it became quite apparent, quite early on in the program, that the vantage point of the London school of world society approach provided an exciting, new way of seeing the world; seeing it as a network of overlapping and intertwining cobwebs instead of a group of colliding billiard balls. It also allowed one to contemplate a multi-level inquiry free from the restricting notions of power politics. But this is not where the schism between the cobweb and billiard ball schools ended; it also split them over the question of empirical work and theory building. Both wings of what Easton had identified as the dual revolution in political science (24) were strongly represented. Singer, Russett and others seemed to have opted for concentrated empirical, correlational research, while Burton and those of similar views maintained that empirical work must follow, not precede extensive hypothesis formation and proposition deduction. And in any event, the research undertaken must be to seek causes and not correlations.

An excellent example of the correlational, behaviorist research found wanting by world society analysts is that of Bruce Russett in his macroscopic view of politics. (25) While Russett accepts the fact that variable selection must be guided by assumptions of "inchoate theory" of some kind, this semi-inductive process seeks to provide prediction without the necessity of understanding. Using his collection of stimulus-response data, Russett maintains that he can predict "more than 80 per cent of the variance in states' voting [in the UN General Assembly] by knowing their past behavior . . . [and] without knowing anything about changing conditions or decision-processes within individual governments." (26) This type of research is interested in predicting a political outcome as a continuation of past patterns of outcomes, without any consideration given to the process which effected each outcome. The most severe limitation, and one which Russett readily admits, is that behaviorist, correlational prediction without consideration of causation or motivation can never foresee sudden systemic change. The capability of this type of research to warn us of new patterns of behavior is nil, while its capacity to help perpetuate past patterns of behavior through the action of self fulfilling prophecy may be great.

In addition to a rejection of the method of extrapolation from past behavior, Burtonian criticism of Russett-type empiricism challenged the validity of the data base itself. The application of quantification techniques to historical data bases was falacious, for the data were originally gathered under different conditions using hypotheses no longer relevant. (27) It was also argued that the accidental accessibility to masses of quantifiable data, and the availability of sophisticated quantifying techniques all too often were predominant in deciding what was to be studied, rather than the relevance of the research to the important problems of society.

Here the world society advocates were echoing the concern expressed by students for more "relevant" research. Many found the data-mongering of Singer and Russett far removed from the international problems the world now faces, and so welcomed the Burtonian critique of such work. However, where the London approach failed for many of them was in not providing a clear, concise alternative strategy for research, just as it appeared to offer no clear alternative strategy of action to replace power modeling for the practitioner.

Description, prescription, or both?

I wish to note a final element in the rift between the two sides of the intra-behavioral schism, as I see it; namely, that concerned with the descriptive and prescriptive nature of the science. The student just setting out upon a study of international relations has some basic idea of the ultimate goal of the field he has entered, be it the narrowly defined protection of state interest and maximisation of state security, or the more general aim of world-wide reduction in wars and their consequences. The social science of international relations is envisaged by the new student as leading the way toward such goals, first through accurate description, then on to explanation and prediction, and finally ending in prescription some many years hence. The world society critique of the American school of research rudely jolted us from this comfortable assumption of an orderly progression for our science.

The views of Professors Singer and McClelland epitomise the attitude of their school of research. Singer cautioned that ". . . we are decades away from the kind of diagnostic and prescriptive base (of knowledge) that would be necessary", and he adds, ". . . the best we can do is explain in terms of tendencies, and predict in terms of odds." (28) Clearly Professor Singer was calling for more scientifically culled data on which to build descriptions and probabilistic predictions which could be used as a basis for prescription much later this century or maybe in the next. Professor McClelland seemed of the same mind when he likened his efforts to those of the meteorologist. (29) The time was for describing and predicting which way the wind was blowing and not, as yet, for contemplating the control of nature.

To our surprise, the world society analysts attacked this seemingly reasonable approach as being self-deceiving and self-defeating. It was argued that the research efforts of Singer, Russett and others were based upon assumptions similar if not identical to those of the non-scientific, traditional school: the world is a billiard table; man inherently lusts for power; conflicts are zero-sum; confrontation and bargaining are the keys to social order; institutions are the reflection of man's values and therefore must be preserved, and so forth. It was argued that these assumptions carefully guided the search for supporting evidence in any available data. The data used could have been newly collected through the assumption's filters, or could be old data gathered under very similar theoretical restraints. This selected data, posing as description, neatly fit the matrix supplied by the assumptions, and was seen as reinforcement for the initial assumptions. When a recalcitrant bit of information did not comply with the assumptions, it could always be described as a disguised version of the "real thing". This self-fulfilled prophecy of description was then available to the policy makers for their action. As traditional, historical characterisation had misled practitioners in the past, the new wave of "scientifically" induced description was poised to mislead the decision makers of the present. Policies were deduced from what was thought to be a valid description of the world, the policies were implemented, clashed with what was in fact reality and failed. As the "scientifically" based definition of world arrangements could again and again be reinforced through select data searches, the problem was thought to lie in the application of the policy-cure and not in the cure itself, resulting usually in more and more of the same. As an example, Thomas Schelling's views on a diplomacy of violence (30) were cited as of the type which led to America's self-defeating policies in Vietnam.

The world society alternative to this process of self-fulfilling research leading to self-defeating policies was fundamentally based in a Popperian concern with falsification. Only if all propositions were stated in falsifiable terms and honest, vigorous attempts made to find the falsifying instance, could we hope to break the hold of the self-fulfilling prophecies of power modeling.

It was also argued that our concern with falsification must not end with our research findings, but must be carried on into the process of policy formation and implementation. A recognition of the tentative nature of our knowledge and the undogmatic use of it would be the hallmarks of more successful policies. Once implemented, a policy based on other than power concerns (on functional concerns, for instance) could help transform the image of other policy making elites, and we could, in a way, have the mechanism of self-fulfilling prophecy working in our favor, and in favor of a world less disrupted by power-mesmerised elites.

The Burtonian approach was seen as one concerned not with pure description, but one with a firm basis in prescriptive notions, the argument being that pure description, like pure induction, is impossible. This call for a break in the self-prophetic and self-defeating processes of research and

291

policy making was accompanied by a keen awareness of the tenacious hold the dogmas of power thinking had on policy makers. Leaders were simply afraid to alter their ways so fundamentally. The consequences of playing the game by new rules were seen as too drastic to contemplate, both for the state and for the individual politician. The only answer which the world society approach could offer was the hope that a long term process of education would eventually mean that all elites viewed the world political game in a new way, as one played by functional rules rather than power ones. The shorter term hope was for an exercise in unilateralism by one state or group which would spark a process of self-fulfilling prophecy in the direction of conflict resolution. Both these long and short term hopes were viewed by many students as naively idealistic. Left unsatisfied was the student's desire to be presented with a credible scenario leading to such a transformation in elite thinking.

The criticism of Singer, Russett and the others by the world society school was mounted on two fronts. Firstly, it was argued that billiard ball, power modeling was simply not an adequate explanation of behavior; and secondly, that "power theory seems to justify or sanctify the use of power, and therefore to support non-learning, non-adjustment and resistance to change." (31) The first complaint was one of methodology, the second was a more normative one. Rather than the simple reduction of overt violence, the Burtonian goal for the study of world society was the facilitation of man's natural development, through a process of change free from the disruption of unnecessary conflict. The way to achieve this was through research and policy formation which consciously subordinated institutional or structural values to the more fundamental human ones.

This seemed clearly to be a case of subjective prescription rather than objective description, and should have been stated strongly in those terms. Unfortunately, the desire to remain "scientific" appeared to preclude such a clear stand; a stand which would have been a welcomed bit of clarity and simplicity in a murky sea of over-qualification.

World society and the USC program

The world society perspective was not simply one in a long list of approaches to which we were introduced, but rather it seemed to provide the basic criteria which governed the actual structure of specific courses in the UK program. This is not to say that the student felt a central committee was somehow dictating what was and what was not to be discussed in each seminar. However, one could sense the general impact the Burtonian school of thought was having on the way in which seminars were planned and conducted. The world society approach was new, provocative, and challenging to the students and sparked much interest. It certainly found a great deal lacking in the traditional school, but much more interestingly it found the American empirical school wanting as well; and it is this latter critique which seemed to guarantee its serious consideration in all seminars, even those whose professors had serious doubts about its contribution to the field.

The schisms dividing the approaches of the world society and American schools are both obvious and important, and will no doubt have much to do with the direction in which the field progresses. Will it be towards a satisfaction of the hunger "for data, lots of data", as Charles McClelland put it (32) and the intensified search for increasingly more sophisticated techniques of handling it? Or will researchers become disillusioned as they find themselves inundated with data which provide little evidence, forcing them to better articulate their hypotheses and enrich them through an adisciplinary exercise in thought? It is most probable that, for a while at least, both forks in the road will be heavily trodden, further separating the work of the two schools. The question remains open whether or not the two approaches can be reconciled in future. The disagreements appear very basic and seem to be leading toward either a clear subdivision within the discipline of international relations, or the establishment by world society advocates of a new, adisciplinary movement. USC's UK program has provided a forum for the world society approach, and in so doing has helped to form and foster it. Whether the program can continue to do so in the face of changing administration, faculty and student body remains to be seen.

References

1. Upon leaving the Navy in late 1976 I began research toward a Ph.D. at University College, London. As part of our program the Ph.D. candidates would have joint meetings with UCL's M.Sc. students in International Relations. These students, both Ph.D. and M.Sc., came from North and South America, East and West Europe, Africa and Asia. At this time the UCL International Relations department was headed by John Burton and had John Groom as one of the lecturers. As a result the World Society approach was dominant.
1a. J. David Singer, "The Behavioral Science Approach to International Relations: Payoff and Prospects", p. 69, in James N. Rosenau (ed.), *International Politics and Foreign Policy* (New York, the Free Press, 1969).
2. David Easton, "The Current Meaning of 'Behavioralism' ", p. 16, in James C. Charlesworth (ed.), *Contemporary Political Analysis* (New York, The Free Press, 1967).
3. Singer, op. cit., p. 67.
4. Karl Popper, *The Poverty of Historicism* (London, Routledge & Kegan Paul, 1961).

5. Thomas S. Kunn, *The Structure of Scientific Revolutions* (Chicago, University of Chicago Press, 1970).
6. Ibid., p. 65. Bryan Magee, *Popper* (London; Fontana/Collins, 1973).
7. Ibid., p. 66.
8. Charles A. McClelland, *Theory and the International System* (New York, The MacMillan Company, 1966), chapter 4.
9. J. W. Burton, A. J. R. Groom, C. R. Mitchell, A. V. S. De Reuk, "The Study of World Society: A London Perspective", International Studies Occasional Paper No. 1 (Pittsburg, International Studies Association, 1974), p. 61.
10. Karl W. Deutsch, *The Nerves of Government* (New York, The Free Press, 1966), in toto.
11. Charles A. McClelland, "On the Fourth Wave: Past and Future in The Study of International Systems", p. 17, in James N. Rosenau, Vincent Davis, Maurice A. East (eds.), *The Analaysis of International Politics* (New York, The Free Press, 1972).
12. Singer, "The Level of Analysis Problem in International Relations", in Rosenau, op. cit.
13. Ibid., p. 28.
14. James N. Rosenau, *Linkage Politics.*
15. James N. Rosenau, address to members of SPIR on September 30, 1976, printed in "SIRCH & PROBE", USC School of International Relations newspaper, November 1, 1976.
16. Bruce M. Russett, "A Macroscopic View of International Politics", p. 113, in Rosenau, Davis, East, op. cit.
17. Burton, Groom, Mitchell, De Reuk, op. cit., p. 6.
18. Easton, op. cit., p. 15.
19. Burton, *et al.*, op. cit., p. 33.
20. E. Raymond Platig, "International Relations as a Field of Inquiry", p. 13, in Rosenau, op. cit.
21. Ibid.
22. Burton, *et al.*, op. cit., p. 57.
23. Easton, op cit., pp. 22–23.
24. Ibid., p. 26.
25. Russett, op. cit., pp. 109–124, in Rosenau, *et al.*, op. cit.
26. Ibid., p. 114.
27. Burton, *et al.*, op. cit., p. 56.
28. Singer, "The Behavioral Science Approach . . ." p. 69, in Rosenau, op. cit.
29. McClelland, "International Relations: Wisdom or Science?", p. 4, in Rosenau, op. cit.
30. Thomas C. Schelling, "The Diplomacy of Violence", pp. 64–84, in John Garnett (ed.), *Theories of Peace and Security* (London, MacMillan and Co. Ltd., 1970).
31. Burton, *et al.*, op. cit., p. 42.
32. McClelland, "On the Fourth Wave . . .", p. 36, in Rosenau, *et al.*, op. cit.

CHAPTER 18

Changing Perceptions: An Approach to Teaching International Relations and its Impact on the Attitudes of Mid-Career Students

Dennis Sandole

Introduction

In this chapter I am concerned with examining and assessing the impact of my approach to teaching about international relations on the attitudes of mid-career students who were themselves international actors; i.e. whose professional lives concerned and contributed, in various ways, to the very subject-matter which students of international relations purport to study.

Why Assessment?

According to a wide-ranging discussion of assessment in the field of international relations by James Rosenau, we assess in order to generate feedback. We explore "where we have been and where we are in order to determine whether we are still on course, whether we still want to be, and whether it is possible to introduce corrections that will more unerringly steer us toward desired ends." (1) We can, in principle, assess the products of educational programs, the products of research projects, and the advice offered to governments and governed alike. In practice, however, while quite a good deal of assessment has been done of the products of research (though not very systematically), very little assessment has been done of policy recommendations and the products of various educational programs. (2) I agree with Rosenau that these other areas should be subjected to assessment as well, and that "assessment ought not to be confined to research activities." (3)

Author's Note: Thanks and gratitude are acknowledged to Ingrid Sandole-Staroste and Jack Segal for assistance in data-processing, and to Ingrid Sandole-Staroste for typing this manuscript.

The assessment study reported here is concerned with one of these neglected areas, namely, the products of educational programs. Consequently, the study is a partial response to the gap noted by Rosenau in international relations assessment.

The study, however, is meant to do more than partially fill a vacuum. I have conducted the study in order to determine to what extent, if any, I have fulfilled my major teaching objective, which is to sensitize students, particularly students who are themselves international actors, to images of international relations other than those associated with one particular philosophy, political realism.

Political realism: a pervasive and self-fulfilling framework

Anatol Rapoport tells us that "what people think, say, or write about conflict, particularly large-scale conflicts, is an important component of the man-made (semantic) environment and, hence, a determinant of the conflicts generated by it." (4) One of the oldest bases of what people think, say, or write about conflict, particularly conflict between states, and seemingly itself a source of conflict, is political realism.

Political realism — or as it is often called, power-politics theory — has been a guide to the *practice* of international relations for centuries, dating back to the fifth century B.C. in Greece. (5) In addition, it seems to have had a profound influence on the *teaching* of international relations. Assuming an intimate connection between the study and the practice of something, this is not particularly surprising. In any case, Trevor Taylor tells us that the field of international relations

> has developed a wealth of approaches and methods of study as well as a good many propositions about specific types of action, but general theory remains scarce. To an extent, power-politics theory has survived in the evolution of international relations because no new theory has appeared to displace it. (6)

Hence, whether because of intellectual bankruptcy or preference, political realism seems to have the status in international relations of what Thomas Kuhn has called a "paradigm" — i.e., it constitutes the dominant set of beliefs and values in terms of which the majority of international relations scholars view and theorize about their subject-matter. (7) Indeed, one study has suggested that political realism — or as the authors labelled it, the "Morgenthau paradigm" — has dominated not only the non-quantitative but also the quantitative study of international relations. (8) What is political realism?

Basically, realists tend to see the inter-state system as something approaching Thomas Hobbes' conception of the state of nature – i.e., a system devoid of central authority in which all men "are in that condition which is called Warre . . . of every man, against every man"; in effect, an anarchic situation in which life is "solitary, poore, nasty, brutish, and short." (9) Writing before Hobbes, Niccolo Machiavelli prescribed a program for state rulers which was meant to facilitate their survival in such a system: "A prince ought to have no other aim or thought, nor select anything else for his study, than war [because] when princes have thought more of ease than of arms they have lost their states." (10) State rulers should behave in accordance with such prescriptions even if such behaviour leads to the violation of certain moral principles -- the survival of their states dominates all other considerations. (11)

This Hobbesian–Machiavellian portrait of human behaviour may appear archaic, simplistic, or extreme. Yet it seems to be compatible with the contemporary realist view of the world within which we live – i.e., the inter-state system is always a potential, and often an actual battlefield, and the most effective way for states to survive is to be constantly prepared to do battle. This latter element does not always come across as an explicit prescription (as it does in the case of Machiavelli). It is sometimes inferred from descriptions of what states actually do: "If that's the way the world is, and if that's what states do in order to survive, *then states must do that in order to survive!*"

Perhaps the leading contemporary description of International Relations in Realist terms is Hans J. Morgenthau's *Politics among Nations: the Struggle for Power and Peace*, which has been through five editions since its initial publication in 1948 and which, as suggested above, has become the dominant set of lenses through which the subject-matter of international relations is defined and viewed. (12) Morgenthau's description is prefaced by certain assumptions, such as "politics, like society in general, is governed by objective laws that have their roots in human nature", laws whose operation are "impervious to our preferences" and which manifest themselves "in terms of interest defined as power." (13) Realist-defined, or power-political behaviour, then, seems to be biologically determined. In other words, we are more or less stuck with a certain state of affairs which is the environmental expression of our own immutable nature.

What is "wrong" with political realism? Why should students of international relations, particularly students who are themselves international actors, be exposed to alternative views?

At any point in time, *descriptive* realism, i.e., the view that the inter-state system is always a potential, and often an actual battlefield, may be difficult to challenge. However, *explanatory* realism, i.e., the view that this state of affairs is the result of biological determinism, can be challenged. In this regard, no deterministic thesis on the causation of social, political, or economic behaviour — whether biological or otherwise — has ever been verified empirically in a systematic manner, though there are many who are convinced and who have argued that they have observed such verification. Deterministic theses, therefore, seem to be sustained more by faith — as well as by the seductive temptation to reduce complexity to conceptual manageability — than by systematic empirical proof.

Explanatory realism is particularly noxious because it facilitates the translation of descriptive realism into *prescriptive* realism, i.e., the view that states must prepare to do battle, or must be in a constant and improving state of battle readiness in order to survive internationally: "If we are stuck with such a world, what else can we do?" Here we get into an interesting dynamic which, probably more than any other factor, sustains state decision-makers in their Realist perceptions and behaviours — the dynamic of the self-fulfilling prophecy.

Consider the following scenario: American decision-makers, schooled in realist principles, decide to improve a particular weapon in order to enhance their capability to defend American interests. Implicit in the American action are deterrence signals to potential aggressors; e.g., "If you perpetrate certain acts against our interests, we will respond, somehow in terms of these weapons, by acting against your interests!" Soviet decision-makers, also schooled in realist principles, define the American action as a provocative threat to their national interests and as a confirmation of their realist view of the world. So, they decide to make improvements in certain of their weapons systems. The Soviet action, in turn, confirms the American decision-makers in their realist definition of the world and stimulates them to make further improvements in their strategic armouries, etc., ad infinitum.

Biological determinism, then, does not appear to be the principal culprit behind international conflict and war; instead, it seems to be political realism itself. In other words, political realism seems to be a self-generating and maintaining system of conflict images and behaviour. This is what is "wrong" with realism. And this is why students of international relations, particularly those who are themselves international practitioners, should be exposed to alternative images.

What was the particular challenge to realism that I put to my students?

Challenging political realism: an approach to the teaching of international relations

I put my challenge to students in the form of a certain approach to the teaching of international relations. This approach was comprised of both static and dynamic components. The static component involved my approach to the study of international relations and the dynamic component involved the communication of this study approach to the students.

On the static component, i.e., my approach to the study of international relations, it is useful, in the interests of clarity, to look at this in terms of four categories suggested by Kuhn's work on paradigms – i.e., the metaphysical, theoretical, instrumental, and methodological dimensions of paradigms. (14) The *metaphysical* concerns the definition of one's subject-matter. In my case, the subject-matter of international relations is comprised of multiple actors, who may or may not represent state authorities (e.g., individuals, groups, organizations), and the interactions within and between them which may influence inter- or trans-societal/national developments and trends. (15) Because it involves actors other than states, this image constitutes one challenge to political realism in that realism tends to view states as the only actors in international relations. (Hence, political realism has often been referred to as a state-centric paradigm.)

The theoretical dimension is concerned, firstly, with the identification and formulation of research problems in need of solution and, secondly, with the conceptual settings within which attempts to solve these problems may be located. In relation to problems in need of solution, which are not always easy to identify, I emphasize that, in principle, these are solvable through systematic investigation. This constitutes a second challenge to political realism in that realism is a philosophy which can lead to the fatalistic conclusion that, except for certain limited actions, (16) there is not much that we can do. In relation to the conceptual settings, I put forward the idea that there are concepts, hypotheses, models, theories, and empirical findings which exist outside the realist or power framework which may be relevant to particular research problems. In effect, I present an argument on behalf of an interdisciplinary conceptual approach to problem-solving. This constitutes a challenge to political realism only to the extent that realism is viewed by its proponents as already possessing all of the assumptions (e.g., biological determinism) and concepts (e.g. power) it needs for an accurate picture of the world.

The *instrumental* dimension is concerned with the operational techniques in terms of which one attempts to solve a selected problem – i.e., techniques of generating, collecting, processing, and analyzing data.

Here I also argue in favour of an interdisciplinary approach and emphasize the relevance of techniques which might be associated with other disciplines. This constitutes a challenge to realism only to the extent that realism is equated by its proponents with non-quantitative or non-statistical techniques.

Finally, the *methodological* dimension is concerned with standards of problem-solving — i.e., the researcher's approach to validation and his/her view on the role of values in the research process. On the validation of hypotheses and theories, I encourage the students to look for disconfirmatory as well as confirmatory evidence. This is a challenge to political realism in that most interpretations of realism tend to be so broad as to preclude the possibility of disconfirmation. On values, I argue the point that these impact upon the research process from beginning to end. It is not just the researcher's formulation of a conclusion, but also the selection of problems in need of solution, conceptual settings, operational techniques, etc., which reflect his/her values. This is a challenge to realism in that realists claim to be observing the world as it really is and, therefore, that they are value-free or, in Morgenthau's words, "disinterested observers". (17)

The degree to which the above approach to the study of international relations was transmitted to students depended upon the particular course involved. In this regard, I have taught in four distinct course areas — (1) International Relations Theory, (2) Methodology of International Relations Research, (3) Conflict Analysis and Peace Research, and (4) International Bargaining Processes. The Theory course was concerned with paradigms and theories of international relations, approaches to the study of international relations, and the findings generated by empirical research projects. The methodology course was concerned with philosophy of science, sociology of knowledge, identification of problems in need of solution, and the design of research projects to study those problems. The Conflict course was concerned with theory and research on the sources, causes, and correlates of conflict, particularly aggressive conflict, at all levels but especially at the international level. And the Bargaining course was concerned with how actors, particularly societal/national actors, behave toward each other once a conflict between them becomes manifest.

My approach to the study of international relations has probably received its most comprehensive and intense expression in the Methodology course, followed by the Theory course, and then by the Conflict and Bargaining courses.

On the dynamic component of my approach to teaching international relations, i.e., the means by which I attempted to communicate my approach to the study of international relations, I made use of syllabuses, lectures, readings, examinations, essays, and end-of-course reviews — all rather conventional ingredients of teaching approaches. Sometimes, when circumstances and course-relevance permitted, I made use of a gaming-simulation as an opportunity for students to experience and "feel" some of the concepts which they read about and discussed in class.

Having discussed the nature of my attempted challenge to political realism, the next logical step is to discuss just what that challenge was meant to impact on — i.e., the aspects or dimensions of my students which were meant to be the targets of that challenge.

The Dependent Variables

(i) *Problems of Conceptualization*

The title of this chapter as well as the introduction indicate that this is a study of the impact of a certain approach to the teaching of international relations on the *attitudes* of mid-career students. In addition to attitudes, I could have said belief systems, beliefs, values, and other concepts. Just what is it that I wanted to talk about?

There is a fundamental problem in attempting to answer this question because, in the field of social psychology, which is probably the discipline most relevant to the study reported here, there is little consensus on the meanings of the above concepts. According to Milton Rokeach, these terms tend to be used "arbitrarily and inter-changeably, thus leading us into what Donald Campbell has aptly called a 'terminological forest'." (18) Even when scholars do settle on one of these terms, they have difficulty settling on one definition of it. In relation to the concept of attitude, which would seem to be our primary concern here, Peter Suedfeld points out that, for many scholars,

> the concept has three components: cognition, affect, and behavior. Some writers restrict this term to the first two dimensions, and view behavior as an independent dimension. . . . Still others use "attitude" to mean only emotional reactions, and refer to cognitive responses as "beliefs". (19)

And still others, such as Fishbein and Ajzen, use attitude to mean evaluative reactions. (20)

Hence, to do research on what I have referred to as "attitudes" is to open up a Pandora's box of terms with no clear, agreed-upon distinctions between them, each of which is defined in various, often contradictory ways. How have I attempted to extricate myself from this "terminological forest"?

By virtue of my selection for this study of certain dependent variables, i.e., Personal Cynicism/*Machtpolitik* and Political Efficacy (Powerlessness), which I will discuss below, I decided that I was looking principally at attitudes. After examining quite a few competing definitions, I also decided that Rokeach's definition of attitude came closest to what I wanted to talk about: "a relatively enduring organization of beliefs around an object or situation predisposing one to respond in some preferential manner." (21) And because of the nature of my remaining dependent variable, Dogmatism, I decided that I was also talking about an aspect of belief systems. A belief system, according to Rokeach, "represents the total universe of a person's beliefs about the physical world, the social world, and the self." (22)

In view of the above, I am looking at belief systems as well as attitudes. And because belief systems and attitudes are comprised of the same constituent parts, I am, by implication, looking at beliefs. Indeed, because there is an evaluative (as well as a cognitive, affective, and behavioral) dimension to beliefs, I am also looking at values. Hence, it is relatively easy to see how these terms could be used interchangeably. Though they are intimately inter-related, however, they do not mean exactly the same thing.

I have used "attitude" in the title, introduction, and elsewhere in this chapter because most of my variables are attitudes, and as a shorthand symbol of what were meant to be the targets of my challenge to political realism.

To recapitulate briefly, I am looking at the impact of my approach to teaching international relations, primarily on the attitudes but also on other aspects of the total cognitive systems of mid-career students. Now on to the specifics of the dependent variables.

(ii) *Definitions*

Two questionnaires have been used in the present study. One of these, Questionnaire A, was instrumental in providing data on three variables: Dogmatism, Personal Cynicism, and Political Efficacy. The other, Questionnaire B, was instrumental in providing data on three related variables, again Dogmatism, then *Machtpolitik*, and Powerlessness. As already mentioned, Dogmatism concerns an aspect of belief systems, while the remaining variables are attitudes.

Dogmatism has been defined, after Rokeach, as "an authoritarian outlook, an intolerance of those with opposing beliefs, and a sufferance of those with similar beliefs." (23) In contrast to right-wing authoritarianism, or fascism, dogmatism (or general authoritarianism) is concerned with the extent to which total belief systems are closed and resist change: "The emphasis is on structure rather than content – how a person believes rather than what he believes." (24)

The Dogmatism variable in Questionnaire A has been measured in terms of 18 items from Rokeach's 40 item Form-E rendition of his Dogmatism Scale. (25) (See Appendix A.) Dogmatism in Questionnaire B has been measured in terms of 5 items from John Ray's Dogmatism Scale. (26) (See Appendix B.)

The Personal Cynicism variable of Questionnaire A and the *Machtpolitik* (power politics) variable of Questionnaire B are conceptually similar. Personal Cynicism has been defined as a contemptuous distrust of people in general, as a negative view of human nature. (27) It has been measured in terms of the four-item Personal Cynicism Scale developed by Agger, *et al.* (28) (See Appendix A.) *Machtpolitik* has been defined as a preoccupation with power, particularly military power, as the means by which nations can succeed and survive in their relations with other nations. It has been measured in terms of a five-item scale developed by one of my students from his reading of Morgenthau's *Politics among Nations.* (29) (See Appendix B.)

The Political Efficacy variable of Questionnaire A and the Powerlessness variable of Questionnaire B are also conceptually similar, though the general meaning of one is the complete reverse of the meaning of the other. Political Efficacy has been defined as the view that political and social change is possible and that one can participate in effecting such change. (30) It has been measured in terms of the four-item Political Efficacy Scale developed by Campbell, *et al.* (31) (See Appendix A.) Powerlessness has been defined as the view that one cannot, in general, control events. It has been measured in terms of five items from the Powerlessness component of Dean's Alienation Scale. (32) (See Appendix B.)

Why have I selected these particular dependent variables? In view of the above definitions, it seems that changes in the students' levels of Personal Cynicism/*Machtpolitik* would indicate changes in the extent to which they held realist beliefs. Changes in the levels of their Dogmatism would indicate changes in the extent to which they were committed to maintain their belief systems, including whatever realist beliefs they held. And changes in their levels of Political Efficacy (Powerlessness) would indicate changes in the extent of their feeling that they could control events – and perhaps also indicate changes in the extent of their tendency to be active in controlling events — in accordance with their beliefs, including whatever realist beliefs they held.

Accordingly, I have selected these particular dependent variables because, particularly when viewed together, they appear to be substantively relevant barometers of the impact of any challenge to political realism.

We will now discuss one further aspect of the study before getting into the results; namely, how, where and with whom the study was carried out.

The conduct of the study

(i) *The subjects and spatial-temporal dimensions of the study*

All of the courses which feature in this study have been conducted for the University of Southern California, School of International Relations, Overseas Programs (which exist in the United Kingdom and in the Federal Republic of Germany). As already mentioned, four distinct courses were involved: Theory, Methodology, Conflict, and Bargaining. Because some of these were given more than once, the total number of courses involved in this study exceeds four. For instance I conducted one Theory course in London (with 10 students); two Methodology courses in Frankfurt (with 10 and 6 students); five Conflict courses — two in Frankfurt (13 and 14 students), one in Goeppingen (with 9 students), one in Munich (with 8 students), and one in London (with 11 students); and one Bargaining course in London (with 9 students). Hence, I have conducted nine courses, involving 90 students.

The students in the German component of USC's Overseas Programs tended to be male American Army officers. The students in the United Kingdom component, on the other hand, tended to include females as well as males, but with the latter outnumbering the former; and tended to include non-Americans as well as Americans, and civilians as well as military personnel. The military in the UK component were always outnumbered by the civilians, who tended to be drawn from the professional fields of diplomacy and international business, and sometimes the Americans were outnumbered by the non-Americans.

All of the courses were conducted in the evening, for approximately 16 three-hour sessions. All but the London Conflict course met over a four to five-month period (one session per week); the London Conflict course met twice a week during an eight-week Summer period.

(ii) *Before–After Design*

A before–after design was employed in this study — i.e., questionnaires were administered to the students on the first and last evenings of each course. In any given course, either Questionnaire A or B (but not both) was administered. In the administration of the before-questionnaire, the students were asked to complete it, with the proviso that they would be informed later of the reasons for it. In the administration of the after-questionnaire (which sometimes, due to time constraints, the students were asked to complete at home), the students were informed that the reason for completing the same questionnaire twice would soon be made known to them. Upon completion of the (in-class) after-questionnaire, the students were informed that the reason was, simply, to see if the course had had any effect on their attitudes.

Because I did not have easy access to other groups of people who may have matched my students in terms of certain characteristics, I have forgone the option of comparing the before–after scores of my students, the experimental groups, with the scores of corresponding control groups.

As already mentioned, two distinct questionnaires have been employed in this study. These were employed for two reasons: (1) to provide students who took more than one of my courses with some variety and, more importantly, (2) to explore whether similar before–after patterns for conceptually similar but operationally different variables (e.g. Political Cynicism and *Machtpolitik*) would obtain for different groups of students taking the same course (e.g., Conflict).

(iii) *Processing the responses to the questionnaires*

The students responded to the items comprising the operational definition of each variable in terms of a one-to-five Likert scale: 1 = Strongly Agree, 2 = Agree, 3 = Mixed Feelings, 4 = Disagree, and 5 = Strongly Disagree. For positively-worded items, i.e., those worded in such a way that agreement with them meant possession of the attribute being measured, this scheme was reversed so that the lower numbers represented disagreement while the higher numbers represented agreement – i.e., 1 = Strongly Disagree, . . . , 5 = Strongly Agree. For negatively-worded items, i.e. those worded so that *disagreement* with them meant possession of the attribute being measured, the original response scheme was left intact. Hence, looking at both the positively-worded items, with the reversed response scheme, and the negatively-worded items, with the original response scheme, the higher the score achieved by an individual on a given variable, the more he/she would be moving in the direction of possessing the attribute being measured by the variable.

The responses of each student to the items on each variable were summed and, dividing the sum for each variable by the total number of corresponding items, mean scores were obtained.

(iv) *Exploring Before–After Patterns*

Following on from the concluding discussion in the section on the dependent variables (i.e., the discussion on the connections between the dependent variables and political realism) Table 1 provides a typological framework in terms of which before–after changes in the values of the dependent variables could begin to be relevantly assessed.

Table 1. TYPES OF IMPACT OF AN APPROACH TO TEACHING
INTERNATIONAL RELATIONS ON THE ATTITUDES OF STUDENTS

Trends toward:	Before–After Changes in the Values of Dependent Variables*		
	Dogmatism	*Personal Cynicism/* Machtpolitik	*Political Efficacy (Powerlessness)*†
1. Committed Active Realism	+	+	+ (–)
2. Committed Passive Realism	+	+	– (+)
3. Uncommitted Active Realism	–	+	+ (–)
4. Uncommitted Passive Realism	–	+	– (+)
5. Uncommitted Passive Non-Realism	–	–	– (+)
6. Uncommitted Active Non-Realism	–	–	+ (–)
7. Committed Passive Non-Realism	+	–	– (+)
8. Committed Active Non-Realism	+	–	+ (–)

* '+' indicates an increase while '–' indicates a decrease in the value of each variable.

† The signs outside parentheses refer to Political Efficacy and the signs inside parentheses refer to Powerlessness.

For instance, a before–after increase in Dogmatism, decrease in Personal Cynicism, and increase in Political Efficacy would be defined as movement in the direction of Committed Active Non-Realism (i.e. Trend No. 8). But how would I determine whether or not this movement was due to my teaching approach – my challenge to Political Realism?

(v) *Exploring the significance of before–after differences*

In the absence of control groups, it would be difficult to say whether or not before–after differences in the values of a particular variable, or configuration of variables, were due to my experimental intervention into the classroom, i.e., due to my approach to teaching international relations *qua* challenge to political realism. Nevertheless, I could still attempt to determine which, if any, of the before–after differences were important by testing for statistical significance. Such tests would enable me to determine to what extent the before–after scores on any given variable were due to chance. The greater the role played by chance in before–after differences, *ipso facto*, the less likely it would be that the differences were brought about by the experimental intervention. In the social sciences, the minimum level of statistical significance at which it is normally considered worthwhile to talk about differences is the .05 level. If the before–after differences on any variable were significant at the .05 level, this would mean that the differences were due to chance in one out of 20 cases $(1/20 = .05)$ – alternatively, that they were not due to chance in 19 out of 20 cases.

The test of statistical significance used in this study is the Wilcoxon Matched-Pairs Signed-Ranks Test. (33)

Another way to compensate for the absence of control groups would be to explore whether consistent or similar before–after patterns emerged, especially for conceptually similar but operationally different variables, across different courses or different groups of students taking the same course. If such differences did emerge, they would be suggestive of a link between the experimental intervention and the differences, even if the differences were not reflective of statistical significance. As Hubert Blalock has said, "Statistical significance should not be confused with practical significance." (34) I would add that, in the event consistent before–after differences across different courses or groups did emerge, the absence of statistical significance should not be confused with the absence of practical significance.

Results

The before–after scores and differences for the nine courses appear in Appendices C (Theory), D.1-D.2 (Methodology), E.1-E.5 (Conflict), and F (Bargaining). The first point which must be made is that only one set of before–after differences proved to be statistically significant at the minimum level of .05 – the differences for *Machtpolitik* for the Conflict course given in London during the Summer of 1977 (Appendix E.5). This means that, in terms of the results of the Wilcoxon test, most of the before–after differences are not important. There were, however, some problems which may have adversely affected the results of the statistical tests – i.e., a combination in some cases of small samples and large numbers of tied difference-ranks which may have introduced considerable error into the calculations. (35)

As already mentioned, even if before–after differences are not statistically significant, if consistent or similar patterns or trends occur across different courses, then the findings may be reflective of some degree of practical significance. To facilitate examining whether such patterns have

Table 2. MEAN BEFORE–AFTER SCORES AND NET DIFFERENCES

Course	Dogmatism			Personal Cynicism/ Machtpolitik			Political Efficacy (Powerlessness)*			Trend toward
	Pre	Post	Dif.	Pre	Post	Dif.	Pre	Post	Dif.	
Theory (London, Spring 1979)	2.80	2.70	–.10	3.18	3.40	+.22	2.44	2.62	(+.18)	Uncommitted Passive Realism
Methodology (Frankfurt, Fall 1975)	2.69	2.66	–.03	2.72	2.52	–.20	3.72	3.92	+.20	Uncommitted Active Non-Realism
Methodology (Frankfurt, Fall 1976)	2.65	2.49	–.16	2.87	2.58	–.29	3.92	3.75	–.17	Uncommitted Passive Non-Realism
Conflict (Frankfurt, Spring 1975)	2.57	2.65	+.08	2.56	2.44	–.12	3.52	3.56	+.04	Committed Active Non-Realism

Conflict (Goeppingen, Spring 1975)	2.68	2.84	+.16	2.69	2.83	+.14	3.47	3.61	+.14	Committed Active Realism
Conflict (Munich, Spring 1975)	2.68	2.57	-.11	2.56	2.56	.00	3.94	3.72	-.22	Uncommitted & Passive
Conflict (Frankfurt, Spring 1976)	2.43	2.43	.00	2.96	3.31	+.35	2.39	2.54	(+.15)	Passive Realism
Conflict (London, Summer 1977)	2.45	2.56	+.11	3.06	3.42	+.36	2.65	2.74	(+.09)	Committed Passive Realism
Bargaining (London, Fall 1978)	2.72	2.80	+.08	2.83	2.53	-.30	3.47	3.44	-.03	Committed Passive Non-Realism

*The scores in parentheses refer to Powerlessness. Those outside parentheses refer to Political Efficacy.

occurred, the *mean* before–after scores and differences for the dependent variables (which are given as the final items of Appendices C–F) have been assembled in Table 2.

Looking at Table 2, against the typological background provided by Table 1, we can see that the one Theory course is associated with Uncommitted Passive Realism, the two Methodology courses are associated with Uncommitted Non-Realism, the five Conflict courses are associated with Commitment, Passivity, and Realism; and the Bargaining course is associated with Committed Passive Non-Realism. In terms of similarities across courses, then, the Methodology and Bargaining courses are associated with Non-Realism and the Theory and Conflict courses are associated with Realism.

Why these particular patterns? I have already mentioned that my approach to the study of international relations enjoyed its most comprehensive communication to students in the Methodology course. Perhaps this – coupled with the emphasis in this course that all problems were researchable and, in principle, solvable – is relevant to Methodology emerging as one of two courses associated with Non-Realism. But why also Bargaining?

I have also mentioned that, depending upon course-relevance and other circumstances, a gaming-simulation was operated in order to provide a dynamic setting within which students could experience and feel some of the concepts they read about and discussed in class. Since gaming-simulations can replicate a variety of relationships, including conflictual ones, and since Bargaining was concerned with what people do once they become involved in conflict relationships, simulation seemed particularly relevant to the Bargaining course. Hence, I operated a gaming-simulation, called the Prisoners Dilemma Simulation, (36) one hour each week for ten weeks during the running of the one Bargaining course.

Two points should be noted here. First, although I had run the simulation before, in the Conflict courses in Germany, the Bargaining course represented an exception to a rule – it was the first time that I had operated the simulation over a relatively long period of time, and not just for one day. Secondly, this relatively constant opportunity to experience and feel what they were reading about and discussing in class, especially about the self-defeating nature of many decisions taken by foreign policy-makers, may account for the observation that most of the students were determined to avoid "war" in their simulate-world. This determination was indexed by their agreements not to arm, and by their formulations and active consideration of strategies for international wealth-sharing and integration. According to one student, the simulation taught me to appreciate that even a simple, almost primitive framework, could serve to elicit the words and deeds that mattered in real negotiations. [It] taught me the stupidity of the concepts of victory and defeat when applied to true and lasting negotiations and compromises.

It is conceivable, therefore, that the relatively long-term running of the simulation is relevant to the association between the Bargaining course and Non-Realism (and, in contrast to the Uncommitted Non-Realism of the Methodology courses, to *Committed* Non-Realism as well). The extent of the movement toward Non-Realism in the Bargaining course is indicated by the observation that the negative differences between the before and after scores on Personal Cynicism are nearly significant at the .05 level. (37)

The Theory course may be associated with Realism for a variety of reasons. First of all, Theory tends to be the first course taken by a large proportion of students entering the USC Overseas Programs in International Relations. Consequently, it is not surprising that most of the students in my Theory course were taking their first course with USC. What this means is that this may have been the first time that the students were exposed to my kind of challenge to political realism. Keeping in mind that most of the students came to the course as international practitioners of various sorts, perhaps with relatively firm Realist views (which is suggested by their relatively high scores on *Machtpolitik*), if my challenge to political realism threatened those views, the students may have rejected my approach to the study of international relations and emerged from the course with their original views not only intact but strengthened. As Harry Triandis says, "Some kinds of audience ward off information that is inconsistent with their existing values and attitudes." (38)

Another reason for the association between the Theory course and realism may be that students in this course were exposed to a variety of schools of thought, approaches, theories, models, concepts, and empirical findings. Coupled with this may have been students feeling that all of those aspects of the field did not add up to a coherent picture, that the field was in disarray, that, after years of expensive and sophisticated empirical research, academic researchers knew very little about anything in international relations. This combination of overload, confusion, and futility, coupled with anxiety about surviving one's first course, may have had the same effects on the students that crises in general have upon people – a tendency to rely on stereotypes which become strengthened, or more rigid, under stress. As Thomas Milburn puts it, "Thought processes which are overly simplistic and concrete tend to occur among individuals experiencing crisis, and lead to thinking about the outcome of the situation in zero-sum terms." Also, "Crises increase a tendency toward rigidity of perception and thought." (39) The result of all this may have been a strengthening of whatever realist assumptions the students held.

The conflict courses may be associated with realism also because of overload, confusion, and futility. These courses covered competing definitions, concepts, and empirical findings which, as in the Theory course, may not have added up to a coherent picture for the students. Moreover, since the Conflict courses focused directly on what realism is all about, i.e., the sources of human conflict and aggression and what to do about them, it is conceivable that much of the information discussed in the readings and in class — e.g., biological, physiological, and frustration/deprivation theories of aggression — may have been defined by the students as consistent with, and therefore served to strengthen, already existing realist assumptions.

Whatever the reasons, the only statistically significant finding to have emerged from this study, one which applies to positive differences between before and after scores on *Machtpolitik*, occurred for a Conflict course — the course given in London during the Summer of 1977. (See Appendix E.5. These differences even transcended the .05 minimum level, as they are significant at the .02 level.) The fact that this course was the only one of the nine courses to be conducted twice a week over a two-month period may have played a role in the magnitude of these differences. However, another Conflict course, one which met once a week over the normal four to five-month period, generated positive differences between the before and after scores on *Machtpolitik* which were nearly significant at the .05 level — the course run in Frankfurt during the Spring of 1976 (Appendix E.4). (40)

One particular cross-course pattern that is obvious from a scanning of the results in Table 2 is that six of the nine courses (1 Theory, 1 Methodology, 3 Conflict, and 1 Bargaining) are associated with decreases in Political Efficacy (or increases in Powerlessness). Clearly, this suggests support for the aphorism that "The more you know, the more you know what you don't know". Conceivably, the courses tended to suggest to students that the world was a bit more complex than they may have thought, a suggestion which may have made them more conservative and cautious in their assessment of their capability to control events in that world.

In sum, two of the four distinct courses, Methodology and Bargaining, are associated with Non-Realism and the remaining two, Theory and Conflict, are associated with Realism. Also, six of the nine total courses are

312

associated with passivity or decreases in the feeling of students that they could control events in their environment. These cross-course patterns are not reflective of statistical significance, but they are patterns nevertheless.

Conclusion

To what extent have I been successful in fulfilling my major teaching objective? This objective, it will be recalled, was to sensitize students, particularly those who were themselves international actors, to images of international relations other than those associated with political realism.

If we were to assume that moving students in the direction of committed active non-realism was the most preferred outcome of a challenge to political realism, then I have not done well. This particular result has been achieved in only one course – the Conflict course given in Frankfurt during the Spring of 1975. On the other hand, if we were to assume that any kind of movement in the direction of non-realism constituted success, then I have done better. In addition to the Conflict course mentioned above, the Bargaining course given in London during the Fall of 1978 and the Methodology courses given in Frankfurt during the Fall of 1975 and the Fall of 1976 are associated with non-realism. Four successes out of nine courses is not bad, particularly when we take into account some of the possible explanations, discussed in the previous section, for the lack of success in the remaining five courses.

Hence, under certain circumstances, there would seem to be a link between my approach to the teaching of international relations, as a challenge to political realism, and the movement of students in the direction of non-realism. But, given the absence of control groups in my research design and the absence of statistical significance in my findings, I have not been able to demonstrate clearly that link. This applies as well to the link implied by the observed movement of students in the directions of passivity and realism. In future research, therefore, I will have to be more strenuous in my attempts to locate suitable control groups. Otherwise, whatever evidence I may generate will, as in the present study, remain largely impressionistic.

Once I have succeeded in demonstrating any kind of link between my challenge to political realism and changes in students' attitudes, I should also attempt to be more precise in the specification of independent variables. That is, in addition to spelling out the message I attempted to communicate and how I attempted to communicate it, I should also say something about the source of the message, namely myself, and say much more than I have here about the target of the message, the students. As

Triandis says, "In analyzing the attitude-change process we must consider the effect of *who* says *what, how*, to *whom*. . . ." (41) Then, in attempting to account for attitudinal changes in terms of these independent variables, I should attempt to bring into the explanation relevant aspects of attitude-change theory. (42)

In addition to increasing the rigour and sophistication of future research designs, I can also experiment with the conditions under which I present my challenge to political realism. For instance, I could vary the time when the after-questionnaire is administered. Rather than administer it on the last day of class, when pre-final examination insecurity might be running high, I could administer it after the final examination and after grades have been submitted (or after the final examination, but before grades have been submitted). Also, given the apparent different effects of my challenge in the different courses, I could counsel students to take certain sequences of courses in the degree program — e.g., one or two courses of relatively limited conceptual complexity, followed by Theory, then some more courses of limited complexity, then Methodology, then Conflict, and finally, Bargaining (with simulation).

In conclusion, as long as I remain convinced that the world is more complex than political realism would have us believe, and that, in such a world, political realism is dangerously self-fulfilling, I will continue to challenge that particular philosophy. As David Easton has said, "Is it not incumbent on us to take account of changing conditions and to be ready and willing to reconsider old images and modify them to the extent deemed necessary?" (43)

Appendix A
Selected items from Questionnaire A

Dogmatism Scale

1. In a heated discussion, I generally become so absorbed in what I am going to say that I forget to listen to what others are saying.
2. A group which tolerates too much difference of opinion among its own members cannot exist for long.
3. In times like these it is often necessary to be more on guard against ideas put out by people or groups in one's own camp than by those in the opposing camp.
4. It is often desirable to reserve judgement about what is going on until one has a chance to hear the opinions of those he respects.
5. In this history of mankind there have probably been just a handful of really great thinkers.

6. If given the chance I would do something of great benefit to the world.
7. It is only when a person devotes himself to an ideal or cause that life becomes meaningful.
8. The present is often full of unhappiness. It is only the future that counts.
9. It is better to be a dead hero than to be a live coward.
10. To compromise with our political opponents is to be guilty of appeasement.
11. There is so much to be done and so little time to do it.
12. In this complicated world of ours the only way we can know what's going on is to rely on leaders or experts who can be trusted.
13. If a man is to accomplish his mission in life, it is sometimes necessary to gamble "all or nothing at all".
14. Of all the different philosophies which exist in this world there is probably only one which is correct.
15. Most people just don't know what's good for them.
16. There are two kinds of people in this world: those who are for the truth and those who are against it.
17. Man on his own is a helpless and miserable creature.
18. Fundamentally, the world we live in is a pretty lonesome place.

Personal Cynicism Scale

1. Barnum was wrong when he said there's a sucker born every minute.*
2. Generally speaking, men won't work very hard unless they are forced to do so.
3. It is safest to assume that all people have a vicious streak and it will come out when they are given a chance.
4. The biggest difference between most criminals and other people is that the criminals are stupid enough to get caught.

Political Efficacy Scale

1. Voting is the only way that people like me can have any say about how the government runs things.*
2. I don't think public officials care much about what people like me think.*
3. People like me don't have any say about what the government does.*
4. Sometimes politics and government seem so complicated that a person like me can't really understand what is going on.*

*Negatively worded: disagreement with these items means some degree of possession of the attribute being measured. All other items are positively worded.

Appendix B
Selected items from Questionnaire B

Dogmatism Scale   *Scale*

1. In the long run the best way to live is to pick friends and associates whose tastes and beliefs are the same as one's own.
2. A person who is extremely tolerant of widely different and even conflicting viewpoints probably has few opinions of his own.
3. It is only natural that a person will have a better acquaintance with ideas he believes in than the ideas he opposes.
4. Our thinking would be a lot better if we could just forget about words like 'probably', 'approximately', and 'perhaps'.
5. For most questions there is only one right answer once a person is able to get all the facts.

Machtpolitik Scale

1. International politics is a struggle for power.
2. The main concern of the military leader is how to win victories as cheaply and as quickly as possible and how to avoid defeat.
3. Armed strength is the most important factor making for the political power of a nation.
4. The drive to dominate is common to all men.
5. Power pursued in the name, and for the benefit, of the nation is something for which all citizens must strive.

Powerlessness Scale

1. It is frightening to be responsible for the development of a little child.
2. There is little or nothing I can do towards preventing a major 'shooting' war.
3. There is little chance for promotion on the job unless a person is lucky.
4. The future looks very dismal.
5. We are so regimented today that there is not much room for choice even in personal matters.

NB: All of the above items are reflective of positive wording.

Appendix C. BEFORE–AFTER SCORES AND DIFFERENCES
International Relations Theory – London, Spring 1979

Students	Dogmatism			Machtpolitik			Powerlessness		
	Pre	Post	Dif.	Pre	Post	Dif.	Pre	Post	Dif.
1.	3.80	3.40	− .40	4.60	4.20	− .40	3.20	3.00	− .20
2.	2.40	2.40	.00	2.00	2.20	+ .20	2.60	2.80	+ .20
3.	2.40	2.00	− .40	3.00	2.80	− .20	2.40	2.80	+ .40
4.	2.40	3.40	+1.00	3.00	4.40	+1.40	2.80	3.40	+ .60
5.	2.20	2.80	+ .60	2.60	2.80	+ .20	2.40	2.60	+ .20
6.	3.00	2.00	−1.00	3.60	3.20	− .40	2.40	2.00	− .40
7.	3.20	3.20	.00	4.20	4.20	.00	2.00	2.00	.00
8.	4.20	2.80	−1.40	4.00	4.20	+ .20	1.80	2.60	+ .80
9.	2.60	2.20	− .40	2.60	2.80	+ .20	2.00	2.20	+ .20
10.	1.80	2.80	+1.00	2.20	3.20	+1.00	2.80	2.80	.00
Sum	28.00	27.00	−1.00	31.80	34.00	+2.20	24.40	26.20	+1.80
Mean	2.80	2.70	− .10	3.18	3.40	+ .22	2.44	2.62	+ .18

Appendix D.1. BEFORE–AFTER SCORES AND DIFFERENCES
Methodology of International Relations Research – Frankfurt, Fall 1975

Students	Dogmatism			Personal Cynicism			Political Efficacy		
	Pre	Post	Dif.	Pre	Post	Dif.	Pre	Post	Dif.
1.	2.17	2.33	+ .16	3.50	2.75	– .75	4.00	4.50	+ .50
2.	2.39	2.39	.00	3.75	2.75	–1.00	2.75	3.75	+1.00
3.	2.33	2.28	– .05	1.00	1.00	.00	4.50	4.75	+ .25
4.	2.78	2.89	+ .11	3.00	2.50	– .50	3.75	4.00	+ .25
5.	2.33	2.39	+ .06	2.00	1.00	–1.00	5.00	5.00	.00
6.	2.94	2.72	– .22	2.50	2.75	+ .25	4.00	3.50	– .50
7.	3.11	3.00	– .11	3.00	3.50	+ .50	2.50	2.75	+ .25
8.	3.55	3.61	+ .06	3.25	2.75	– .50	3.75	3.50	– .25
9.	2.44	1.94	– .50	2.75	3.00	+ .25	3.75	4.00	+ .25
10.	2.83	3.05	+ .22	2.50	3.25	+ .75	3.25	3.50	+ .25
Sum	26.87	26.60	– .27	27.25	25.25	–2.00	37.25	39.25	+2.00
Mean	2.69	2.66	– .03	2.72	2.52	– .20	3.72	3.92	+ .20

Appendix D.2. BEFORE–AFTER SCORES AND DIFFERENCES
Methodology of International Relations Research — Frankfurt, Fall 1976

Students	Dogmatism			Personal Cynicism			Political Efficacy		
	Pre	Post	Dif.	Pre	Post	Dif.	Pre	Post	Dif.
1.	2.72	2.78	+ .06	3.25	3.00	– .25	3.75	3.25	– .50
2.	2.61	2.55	– .06	2.50	2.75	+ .25	4.00	4.00	.00
3.	2.72	2.33	– .39	3.00	2.75	– .25	4.50	4.75	+ .25
4.	2.61	1.89	– .72	3.00	1.75	–1.25	4.25	3.75	– .50
5.	2.72	2.89	+ .17	2.50	2.25	– .25	3.75	3.25	– .50
6.	2.50	2.50	.00	3.00	3.00	.00	3.25	3.50	+ .25
Sum	15.88	14.94	– .94	17.25	15.50	–1.75	23.50	22.50	–1.00
Mean	2.65	2.49	– .16	2.87	2.58	– .29	3.92	3.75	– .17

Appendix E.1. BEFORE-AFTER SCORES AND DIFFERENCES
Conflict Analysis and Peace Research — Frankfurt, Spring 1975

Students	Dogmatism			Personal Cynicism			Political Efficacy		
	Pre	Post	Dif.	Pre	Post	Dif.	Pre	Post	Dif.
1.	2.44	2.72	+ .28	3.25	3.00	− .25	2.75	3.00	+ .25
2.	2.89	2.61	− .28	3.25	3.00	− .25	4.25	4.00	− .25
3.	2.39	2.44	+ .05	3.00	2.25	− .75	4.00	4.00	.00
4.	2.44	2.44	.00	1.75	2.50	+ .75	3.50	2.50	−1.00
5.	3.17	2.72	− .45	3.00	1.75	−1.25	3.25	4.00	+ .75
6.	2.89	2.94	+ .05	3.50	3.25	− .25	2.50	2.75	+ .25
7.	2.89	2.89	.00	2.50	2.50	.00	2.50	3.25	+ .75
8.	2.61	2.72	+ .11	2.50	2.25	− .25	3.75	3.50	− .25
9.	2.28	2.22	− .06	1.50	1.50	.00	4.75	5.00	+ .25
10.	2.55	2.72	+ .17	1.75	2.00	+ .25	4.50	5.00	+ .50
11.	2.17	3.11	+ .94	2.75	3.00	+ .25	2.75	2.50	− .25
12.	2.33	2.55	+ .22	2.50	2.50	.00	3.50	2.50	−1.00
13.	2.33	2.39	+ .06	2.00	2.25	+ .25	3.75	4.25	+ .50
Sum	33.38	34.47	+1.09	33.25	31.75	−1.50	45.75	46.25	+ .50
Mean	2.57	2.65	+ .08	2.56	2.44	− .12	3.52	3.56	+ .04

Appendix E.2. BEFORE-AFTER SCORES AND DIFFERENCES
Conflict Analysis and Peace Research — Goeppingen, Spring 1975

Students	Dogmatism			Personal Cynicism			Political Efficacy		
	Pre	Post	Dif.	Pre	Post	Dif.	Pre	Post	Dif.
1.	3.17	3.17	.00	2.75	3.75	+1.00	3.50	3.50	.00
2.	2.83	2.78	− .05	2.75	2.00	− .75	4.25	3.50	− .75
3.	3.11	3.11	.00	3.00	2.75	− .25	2.00	3.75	+1.75
4.	3.11	2.89	− .22	2.75	2.50	− .25	4.00	3.75	− .25
5.	2.39	2.94	+ .55	3.00	3.00	.00	3.75	2.75	−1.00
6.	2.50	3.05	+ .55	1.75	2.00	+ .25	4.00	4.00	.00
7.	2.17	2.39	+ .22	2.75	2.50	− .25	2.75	4.00	+1.25
8.	2.22	2.44	+ .22	2.25	2.25	.00	4.00	4.00	.00
9.	2.67	2.83	+ .16	3.25	4.75	+1.50	3.00	3.25	+ .25
Sum	24.17	25.60	+1.43	24.25	25.50	+1.25	31.25	32.50	+1.25
Mean	2.68	2.84	+ .16	2.69	2.83	+ .14	3.47	3.61	+ .14

321

Appendix E.3. BEFORE-AFTER SCORES AND DIFFERENCES
Conflict Analysis and Peace Research — Munich, Spring 1975

Students	Dogmatism			Personal Cynicism			Political Efficacy		
	Pre	Post	Dif.	Pre	Post	Dif.	Pre	Post	Dif.
1.	2.55	2.17	− .38	2.25	2.25	.00	4.00	4.75	+ .75
2.	2.78	3.17	+ .39	3.50	3.25	− .25	4.25	3.50	− .75
3.	1.83	1.50	− .33	1.75	1.50	− .25	4.75	4.25	− .50
4.	2.83	2.61	− .22	1.75	1.75	.00	4.25	3.75	− .50
5.	2.83	2.61	− .22	2.25	2.25	.00	4.00	3.50	− .50
6.	2.78	2.89	+ .11	2.50	3.00	+ .50	2.75	2.75	.00
7.	2.50	2.78	+ .28	3.25	3.00	− .25	4.25	3.50	− .75
8.	3.33	2.83	− .50	3.25	3.50	+ .25	3.25	3.75	+ .50
Sum	21.43	20.56	− .87	20.50	20.50	.00	31.50	29.75	−1.75
Mean	2.68	2.57	− .11	2.56	2.56	.00	3.94	3.72	− .22

322

Appendix E.4. BEFORE-AFTER SCORES AND DIFFERENCES
Conflict Analysis and Peace Research – Frankfurt, Spring 1976

Students	Dogmatism			Machtpolitik			Powerlessness		
	Pre	Post	Dif.	Pre	Post	Dif.	Pre	Post	Dif.
1.	3.60	3.20	– .40	3.20	3.60	+ .40	2.40	3.60	+ 1.20
2.	2.40	1.80	– .60	2.20	2.60	+ .40	1.80	2.60	+ .80
3.	2.60	3.60	+1.00	2.80	2.80	.00	1.80	1.40	– .40
4.	3.20	3.00	– .20	3.80	3.00	– .80	3.40	4.40	+1.00
5.	2.60	2.60	.00	3.80	3.80	.00	3.00	3.00	.00
6.	2.80	2.60	– .20	3.20	3.40	+ .20	1.20	1.20	.00
7.	3.00	2.80	– .20	3.20	4.20	+1.00	3.60	3.20	– .40
8.	2.40	2.40	.00	3.00	3.60	+ .60	2.40	2.80	+ .40
9.	1.40	1.20	– .20	2.00	2.40	+ .40	1.40	1.20	– .20
10.	2.60	2.80	+ .20	3.80	3.00	– .80	2.40	2.40	.00
11.	2.00	2.20	+ .20	2.20	2.60	+ .40	3.20	2.40	– .80
12.	1.80	2.00	+ .20	3.00	3.20	+ .20	2.80	2.60	– .20
13.	1.40	1.80	+ .40	2.40	4.60	+2.20	1.60	2.00	+ .40
14.	2.20	2.00	– .20	2.80	3.60	+ .80	2.40	2.80	+ .40
Sum	34.00	34.00	.00	41.40	46.40	+5.00	33.40	35.60	+2.20
Mean	2.43	2.43	.00	2.96	3.31	+ .35	2.39	2.54	+ .15

Appendix E.5. BEFORE-AFTER SCORES AND DIFFERENCES
Conflict Analysis and Peace Research – London, Summer 1977

Students	Dogmatism			Machtpolitik			Powerlessness		
	Pre	Post	Dif.	Pre	Post	Dif.*	Pre	Post	Dif.
1.	2.60	2.80	+ .20	3.00	3.20	+ .20	2.80	2.80	.00
2.	2.80	2.80	.00	3.80	4.00	+ .20	2.40	2.80	+ .40
3.	2.00	1.60	− .40	3.40	3.40	.00	2.40	2.20	− .20
4.	1.40	2.80	+1.40	2.40	3.00	+ .60	2.40	2.40	.00
5.	1.60	1.80	+ .20	2.80	2.80	.00	2.80	2.80	.00
6.	2.40	2.40	.00	2.80	3.40	+ .60	2.60	2.80	+ .20
7.	2.40	2.40	.00	2.40	2.20	− .20	3.00	2.80	− .20
8.	3.20	3.20	.00	3.20	4.00	+ .80	1.80	2.60	+ .80
9.	3.40	3.20	− .20	4.60	4.80	+ .20	2.60	3.20	+ .60
10.	2.00	2.40	+ .40	2.60	2.80	+ .20	3.00	3.00	.00
11.	3.20	2.80	− .60	2.60	4.00	+1.40	3.40	2.80	− .60
Sum	27.00	28.20	+1.20	33.60	37.60	+4.00	29.20	30.20	1.00
Mean	2.45	2.56	+ .11	3.06	3.42	+ .36	2.65	2.74	+ .09

*These differences are significant at the .02 level.

Appendix F. BEFORE-AFTER SCORES AND DIFFERENCES
International Bargaining Processes – London, Fall 1978

Students	Dogmatism			Personal Cynicism			Political Efficacy		
	Pre	Post	Dif.	Pre	Post	Dif.	Pre	Post	Dif.
1.	2.72	2.55	– .17	1.75	2.00	+ .25	4.00	3.75	– .25
2.	2.72	2.72	.00	3.50	3.50	.00	3.50	3.50	.00
3.	2.72	2.72	.00	2.50	2.00	– .50	3.00	3.25	+ .25
4.	3.05	3.39	+ .34	3.25	3.25	.00	3.75	2.75	–1.00
5.	2.89	3.00	+ .11	2.75	3.00	+ .25	3.50	3.25	– .25
6.	2.61	2.72	+ .11	2.75	2.25	– .50	3.00	3.25	+ .25
7.	3.00	2.89	– .11	3.50	2.50	–1.00	4.00	3.75	– .25
8.	2.17	2.33	+ .16	2.50	1.75	– .75	3.50	4.25	+ .75
9.	2.61	2.89	+ .28	3.00	2.50	– .50	3.00	3.25	+ .25
Sum	24.49	25.21	+ .72	25.50	22.75	–2.75	31.25	31.00	– .25
Mean	2.72	2.80	+ .08	2.83	2.53	– .30	3.47	3.44	– .03

References

1. James N. Rosenau, "Assessment in International Studies: Ego Trip or Feedback?", *International Studies Quarterly*, 18.3 (September 1974), p. 347.
2. Ibid., p. 351.
3. Ibid., p. 348.
4. Anatol Rapoport, *Conflict in Man-Made Environment* (Harmondsworth, Middlesex: Penguin Books, 1974), p. 134.
5. See Robert Purnell, "Theoretical Approaches to International Relations: The Contribution of the Graeco-Romano World", in Trevor Taylor (Ed.), *Approaches and Theory in International Relations* (London & N.Y.: Longman, 1978), pp. 23–24.
6. Trevor Taylor, "Power Politics", in Taylor, 1978, op. cit., p. 124.
7. Thomas S. Kuhn, *The Structure of Scientific Revolutions*, 2nd Edition (Chicago: University of Chicago Press, 1970).
8. See John R. Handelman, J. A. Vasquez, M. K. O'Leary, and W. D. Coplin, *Color it Morgenthau: A Data-Based Assessment of Quantitative International Relations Research*, Prince Research Studies Paper Number 11, International Relations Program, Maxwell School, Syracuse University. Prepared for presentation at the International Studies Association National Convention, 1973.
9. Thomas Hobbes, *Leviathan* (London: Dent; N.Y.: Dutton, 1950), pp. 103–4.
10. Niccolo Machiavelli, *The Prince*, translated by W. K. Marriott (London: Dent; N.Y.: Dutton, 1958), p. 79.
11. See ibid., Chapters XVI–XVII.
12. Hans J. Morgenthau, *Politics Among Nations: The Struggle for Power and Peace*, 5th Edition (N.Y.: Knopf, 1973).
13. Ibid., pp. 4–5.
14. Kuhn, 1970, op. cit., pp. 40–2.
15. This particular image is compatible with John Burton's "cobweb model of World Society". See his *World Society* (London: Cambridge University Press, 1972), pp. 35–45 and *passim.*
16. Morgenthau, for instance, advocates a return to traditional secret diplomacy and, seemingly, to the "Golden Age" of the 18th Century Balance of Power. See *Politics Among Nations*, Chaps. 31–2 and pp. 189–90.
17. Ibid., p. 5.
18. Milton Rokeach, *Beliefs, Attitudes, and Values: A Theory of Organization and Change* (San Francisco & London: Jossey-Bass, 1968), p. x.
19. Peter Suedfeld, "Models of Attitude Change: Theories That Pass in the Night", in Suedfeld (Ed.), *Attitude Change: The Competing Views* (Chicago: Aldine-Atherton, 1971), pp. 3–4.
20. Martin Fishbein and Icek Ajzen, *Belief, Attitude, Intention and Behavior: An Introduction to Theory and Research* (Reading, Mass.: Addison-Wesley, 1975), p. 12.
21. Rokeach, 1968, op. cit., p. 112.
22. Ibid., p. 123.
23. Milton Rokeach, *The Open and Closed Mind* (N.Y.: Basic Books, 1960), p. 4.
24. Fred Kerlinger and Milton Rokeach, "The Factorial Nature of the F and D Scales", *Journal of Personality and Social Psychology*, 4.4 (1966), p. 391, and Milton Rokeach and Benjamin Fruchter, "A Factorial Study of Dogmatism and Related Concepts", *Journal of Abnormal and Social Psychology*, 53.1 (1956), p. 356.
25. Rokeach, 1960, op. cit., pp. 73–80.
26. John J. Ray, "Militarism, Authoritarianism, Neuroticism, and Anti-social Behavior, *Journal of Conflict Resolution*, XVI.3 (September 1972), p. 338.

27. See Robert E. Agger, M. N. Goldstein, and S. A. Pearl, "Political Cynicism: Measurement and Meaning", *Journal of Politics*, 23.3 (August 1961), p. 490.
28. Ibid., p. 489. These items are also components of one rendition of the Machiavellianism Scale developed by Christie. See Richard Christie and Florence L. Geis, *Studies in Machiavellianism* (N.Y. and London: Academic Press, 1970), pp. 10-34.
29. Jack Melton, "U.S. Army Decision-Making Elite: Empirical Evidence for a Questionnaire." Essay submitted in partial fulfilment of IR 501, Methodology of International Relations Research, USC, SIR, German Graduate Program, Frankfurt, 6 January 1975.
30. See Agger, *et al.*, 1961, op. cit., p. 493.
31. Cited in ibid., pp. 492-493.
32. Dwight G. Dean, "Alienation: Its Meaning and Measurement", *American Sociological Review*, 26 (October 1961), pp. 753-758.
33. See Hubert M. Blalock, *Social Statistics* (N.Y. and London: McGraw-Hill, 1960), pp. 206-9, and William L. Hays, *Statistics* (N.Y. and London: Holt, Rinehart and Winston, 1963), pp. 635-7. (In addition to spelling Wilcoxon's name differently, Blalock and Hays also specify slightly different routines for the computation in T, the Wilcoxon test statistic. I have used both routines in the statistical tests.) Because I am not testing hypotheses in this study, I have made use of two-tailed renditions of the Wilcoxon Test.
34. Blalock, 1960, op. cit., p. 126.
35. In this regard, see Hays, 1963, op. cit., p. 637.
36. On the Prisoner's Dilemma Simulation (PDS), see Charles A. Powell, "Simulation: The Anatomy of a Fad", *Acta Politica* (April 1969), pp. 299-330, and Dennis J. D. Sandole, "Economic Conditions and Conflict Processes: Deterministic, Primary, Contributory, or Chimerical?", in Paul Whiteley (Ed.), *Models of Political Economy* (Beverley Hills and London: Sage, 1979).
37. With an N of 9, a T of 6 or less was required for significance at the .05 level. In this particular case, a T of 8.5 was obtained.
38. Harry C. Triandis, *Attitude and Attitude Change* (N.Y.: Wiley, 1971), p. 157.
39. Thomas W. Milburn, "The Management of Crisis", in Charles F. Hermann (Ed.), *International Crises: Insights from Behavioral Research* (N.Y.: Free Press; London: Collier-Macmillan, 1972), pp. 274-5.
40. With an N of 14, a T of 21 or less was required for significance at the .05 level. In this particular case, a T of 23.5 was obtained.
41. Triandis, 1971, op. cit., p. 145.
42. There seems to be as much, if not more, conceptual confusion about attitude-change theory as there is about definitions of basic terms. For instance, one survey has counted 34 distinguishable models or theories of attitude change. See T. M. Ostrom, "The Emergence of Attitude Theory: 1930-1950", in A. G. Greenwald, *et al.* (Eds.), *Psychological Foundations of Attitudes* (N.Y. and London: Academic Press, 1968). Also see Suedfeld, in Suedfeld, 1971, op. cit.
43. David Easton, "The New Revolution in Political Science", *American Political Science Review*, 63 (1969) and reprinted in Michael Haas and Henry S. Kariel (Eds.), *Approaches to the Study of Political Science* (Scranton, Pa: Chandler, 1970), p. 515.

CHAPTER 19

Future Prospects

Randolph Kent and Gunnar Nielsson

Introduction

Throughout this work we have focused our attention upon the ways a certain conception of the discipline of international relations is broached to a particular type of student body. The purpose of this work is not to treat either the discipline or the teaching of the discipline in isolation, but rather to show the types of conceptual, assessment and presentation approaches we have taken to deal with our kind of "mid-career" students. By looking into the future, we are not diverging from our original theme. In one sense to look into the future is to seek prescriptions for some of the weaknesses which have emerged in the past. Equally as fundamental is to ask whether or not we as scholars, given the types of directions our own individual field specialities might take, will be able to continue to work within the broad-scope "teaching paradigm" that has lent conceptual coherence to our programme to date. A further question – one which is critical for our type of programme – is whether or not our own academic conceptions of the discipline will be seen as relevant to our kind of students; for it might well be argued that in general a gap has emerged between international relations practitioners and those scholars who have questioned the utility of the intuitive perspective towards which our students automatically gravitate, e.g. the power politics, realist paradigm.

Therefore, in looking towards the future, we are posing three fundamental problems. In the first place, in assessing the past, what modifications and changes should we make to enhance the effectiveness of our kind of programme in the future? Secondly, we have imposed a certain conceptual coherence upon a discipline both disparate and amorphous by proceeding from a set of common assumptions found in what loosely might be described as the "world society" paradigm. Can we as scholars, individually, presume that we will remain comfortable in that paradigm, and, if not, will the alternative of competing paradigms be viewed by our student clientele as incoherence. Lastly, we cannot avoid the issue of relevance; it is demanded of us. Yet, relevance emerges in many forms; a Marxist or Neo-Marxist perspective is as relevant to a significant portion of the international intellectual community as is the liberal–orthodox perspective. However, the more attuned we might become to the international spectrum of alternative approaches, the more irrelevant we might become to the type of student who is motivated to take a part-time, mid-career programme with an American university.

Relevance also implies that we, as academics, stay attuned to developments within the relatively new and constantly evolving academic discipline of interational relations and that we should not shape our intellectual interests predominantly to the demands of our clientele. Alternatively, relevance might suggest a compromise, a compromise in which we actually seek to relate our alternative paradigms and perspectives to the types of students to whom we cater. Relevance, here, might suggest that, while we may not know the "truth", we are merely seeking to get our students to think about their lives and worlds in a variety of different ways.

With these three major problems as guidelines, we have organized our discussion about future prospects according to each of the specific fields of concentration dealt with in the preceding chapters.*

Theory and methodology

It is an appropriate start to begin our assessment of the future by considering the broad issue of theory and methodology. As courses, theory and methodology provide a critical, analytical and intellectual awakening for our students. They offer conceptual frameworks, challenge conventional assumptions, and open up the inter-disciplinary complexities of international relations. Beyond the courses, *per se*, they are also vehicles of integration. They provide an aspect of coherence to the remaining "core courses" and in many respects to students' electives as well. They are the catalysts against which alternative approaches to various sub-fields within the discipline are tested. Ultimately, the term – theory and methodology – is what the programme is principally concerned with; for while the ideographic details of certain regions or sub-fields may quickly be forgotten,

*For many of the main points raised in this chapter, the editors have drawn upon typescripts of two special colloquia held by the core faculty and various meetings concerning the recently completed curriculum revision.

what we hope to leave with our students are contending analytical frameworks and a willingness to pose different kinds of questions about global politics.

Yet, in stressing the importance to the programme of our concentration upon theory and methodology, we are immediately faced with the fact that we are exposing our students to an intellectual paradigm which is grounded in the assumptions of an essentially Western philosophy. Furthermore, we sense that even that "Western philosophy" faces growing cleavages as European and particularly Third World problems and approaches begin to diverge from the dominance of US international relations studies.

What form and what consequences these diverging approaches might have are difficult to anticipate. Certainly one area of divergence could be the differences in assumptions about hierarchies, and we may well find ourselves portraying, for example, approaches to State development and State actions — in terms of human values and needs, in terms of organisational analyses, in terms of alternative global structures — which for all intents and purposes have little relevance to a significant portion of non-Americans.

This problem, alone, highlights a dilemma for our particular kind of programme. While we may benefit and indeed consider it an advantage to work with students who are involved in one way or another with practical aspects of "international affairs", we have always had to cope with the unevenness of their intellectual backgrounds. Beyond merely a lack of formal political science education, a good portion of our students have little sense of history prior to the Second World War. In other words, we have no basis upon which to anchor our efforts at "forecasting". While we recognize that the academic discipline of history has as many epistemological and methodological problems as do the social sciences, the fact remains that the general lack of adequate historical backgrounds may well become more acutely felt as we try to understand and to explain paradigmatic alternatives evolving in non-US and non-Western scholarship.

This problem closely relates to another, namely the need to concentrate more intently upon cultures and ideologies "globally". We broach this issue not because we feel that ideographic differences will force us to abandon our efforts to seek global patterns or to pursue general theories about the global system. Rather we feel that greater historical, cultural and ideological depth will enable the fallacies and strengths of our present approaches and the alternatives which we might present to be better understood.

Having said this, many of us still feel that what has been referred to in previous sections of the work as the "world society"* approach will have increased relevance in understanding global relations in the future. To some, that approach in fact *is* the future, an approach that has been too under-utilized to date. Yet even the present emphasis presents a certain degree of risk.

One of the important problems with this global approach is that such a systems theory-dominated approach runs the risk of creating the impression that the international relations discipline is far more advanced in confirmation of general theories than is actually the case. But, on the other hand, the contrasting low level abstraction, issue specific approach tends to lead to the impression that we know a lot less about the general global situation — and that it is less knowable — than is the case.

Despite the intellectual appeal of the world society approach for many of us and despite the coherence it lends to the programme, it also generates two further inter-related "problems": one of our own purpose and the other of relevance.

In presenting the world society approach, we often find ourselves as proselytizers of prescription, of normative approaches which deal with what should be rather than what is. Both "should be" and "what is" are in themselves value-laden terms; and while we accept this, we also must recognize that in suggesting solutions, we are risking alienating students who generally proceed from assumptions that, while there are a variety of well intentioned academic prescriptions, there also is a real world that can be explained.

The trend in international relations studies, however, as Little has discussed earlier, is increasingly less concerned with the dominant model or contending approaches. More and more there is a general acceptance that alternative conceptual approaches to the discipline can readily co-exist. Neo-Marxist, power politics, and world society models, for example, can all provide satisfying exploratory routes to understandings of the discipline. And, yet, where does such academic "open-mindedness" leave the student. Generally speaking, the answer is: in turmoil!

To some extent, such turmoil for students in the programme has been resolved in a Gordian-Knot manner. Most enter the programme, with their various professional experiences, as "realists", "power politicians", and most leave the programme as "realists" and "power politicians". What they have imbibed from their exposure to international relations theory is that there is indeed an alternative way of explaining the international system and that way is the "world society" approach. But the world society approach is regarded by students as a stark alternative, as a

*Refer to Little, Chapter I.

331

contending and competitive philosophy to the way one conventionally views international politics. They rarely accept the subtlety that different conceptual approaches can be intellectually compatible. And to some extent the "stark alternative" result is the product of instructors' attempts to deal with the rigidity of mid-career students who have evolved firm and committed attitudes about the supposed real world. The "stark alternative" emerges out of an attempt to strip the pre-conceived notions to their essentials and to challenge the conventional assumptions which sustain those notions. "How does one define power?" "How can one reconcile bureaucratic politics models with the assumptions of rationality of the realists?" These are the challenges which, once made, suggest correctly that there are indeed other means of explication, but also incorrectly suggest — consciously or unconsciously — that there is an irreconcilable and incompatible divide amongst the various approaches. It is a problem, the bases and possible solutions of which, are not dissimilar to that found in methodology.*

In regard to methodology, one set of major issues seems to be how much, at what point in the programme, and with what perspective should methodology be taught in the programme. There is an active disagreement over whether or not to engage students in a sophisticated review of the philosophy of science disputes before they have had experiences in systematic investigations of "real world problems". The latter approach presumes that there are specific things we need to know about the world. The students should become thoroughly familiarized with the require-ments involved in conducting a systematic testing of a well formulated theoretical proposition about a relationship before they are taken through the finer points of epistemological criticisms of behavioural approaches to "knowledge building", the argument goes. The opposite position main-tains that, early on in the programme, students need a careful overview of philosophy of science issues because it teaches understanding of processes of change and evaluating the different perspectives on the nature of seek-ing the truth and "building knowledge". The demand for early exposure to the practical application of "scientific method" is based on predeter-mined characteristics of "the dependent variable"; that we, in other words, already know what it is we need to know. Recent developments of a criti-cal philosophy of science literature challenges the canons of positivist theory by arguing that "scientific method" is nothing more than a ration-alization of the *status quo* and that "truths" and "findings" based upon

*In this same vein, it is probably relevant to mention the difficulty many of our students have with the "levels of analysis" issue, mentioned in Chapter VI by Randolph Kent.

332

it are no more than plausible propositions.

Hence, one important issue in regard to methodology is what to teach students, as the mainstream American and British positivist, behaviouralist, empiricist approaches lose their coherence in the face of challenges on philosophical grounds by Continental European and Third World critics and by traditionalist, historically oriented scholars in the Western world. The compounding effect of such challenges could lead to changes in epistemology which would have an important effect on how we study international relations in the future. The questioning of the basic assumptions behind a behavioural, positivist philosophy of science could lead to a resurrection of traditional historical approaches as a result of increasing scepticism about such "reductionist fallacies" as "bivariate testing" or the pretentiousness and incomprehension of mathematical multi-model simulation of world societal relations. The attack on "positive scientism" could also lead, concurrently, to a new emphasis upon normative approaches and activist engagement by Neo-Marxist scholars who see science, not as a systematic method of verifying theory, but as a "bourgeois ideology" serving the ruling class and the liberal, capitalist dominated *status quo*.

The result could well be three very different, but equally well developed competing paradigms about which students should be familiar very early in their progression through the programme because it makes a fundamental difference in all subsequent studies that students are aware of the strengths and weaknesses of each of these paradigms. This issue around the role of methodology in teaching international relations may well be the most significant and most difficult problem with which to come to terms in the future.

Ironically, the very developments which have intensified the complexities of the methodological issue might pose some solution, from a teaching pespective, to dealing with the competitive approaches both in theory and methodology. From students' perspectives, there can be little doubt that the required methodology course has been and continues to be viewed generally as a tedious labour presenting Augean stables of irrelevance. Of the course's two components — philosophy of science and methodological techniques — the former is generally regarded as a "how many angels on the head of a pin" debate, ultimately attempting to re-enforce the world society model which was introduced in the theory course while the latter component is regarded as an attempt to thrust positivistic techniques down students' throats "to make them behaviouralists".

To some extent both impressions are not wholly unjustified. The Kuhnian or Popperian views of knowledge building are frequently interpreted by students as a further means of breaking down conceptual resistance to that "alternative paradigm", viz. the world society. Certainly the world society model has been frequently proffered by instructors as an example of the consequences to one's analysis of international politics of moving according to alternative sets of assumptions (whether they can be strictly considered a paradigmatic shift or not).

The impression that the programme has been trying to "make students behaviouralists" has been created by the instructors' general determination to provide a programme which is abreast of the discipline; and how else could one stay abreast without having some idea of the methodological techniques which have marked the whole behaviouralist movement. As Mitchell has mentioned in Chapter X, students have been intimidated by the "scientific method", have too often lost the larger perspective because of their general reluctance to get embroiled "in mathematics".

Yet, to a significant extent, both the faculty's agonies over the "methodology" hurdle and the trends of the discipline would suggest that the future holds a reasonable compromise. The contending approaches of the 1960s which suggested harsh dichotomies in theoretical and methodological issues are increasingly greeted with ennui. The question of commitment, the "right" direction, the superiority of one approach over another is regarded far more as a question of individual academic integrity and interests. What Feyerabend has referred to as the positive disorder in the accumulation of knowledge is as relevant to the discipline of international relations as it is to other natural and social sciences.*

The principle of positive disorder does not address one practical problem of teaching "the philosophy of science" to our pragmatic clientele: we still will be faced with the question of "what relevance does this have to international relations?" Nevertheless, the increasing motivation of the social sciences and our own discipline – perhaps reflected in Feyerabend – establishes a principle which is important for our students. Students, and particularly mid-career students, are perplexed about how one evaluates contending philosophies: which one is right, which one is wrong. The evolution of the philosophy of science, as increasingly reflected in our own minds, provides an answer, well summarized by Professor Richard Beal: "My only way to reconcile that kind of problem is to tell the student to glean from a particular work the standards which the author attempted to set in terms of that author's framework, and then ask whether the student can or cannot accept that framework. There just is no "truth" out there with a capital T."

This same controlled disorder also applies to the methodological content

*Refer to Chapter I.

of our theoretical approaches. It is increasingly important that we portray the behaviouralist approaches, less as the direction upon which our discipline is embarked, and more as one among several approaches to gaining knowledge. The "traditional" historical method and the development of quantitative approaches should not be presented as poles in a chronological spectrum of international relations development. The potential compatibility of alternative approaches should be made more explicit. The fact that a multiplicity of techniques – be they historical or behavioural – may generate useful hypotheses, inquiries and new analytical referents is the critical message.

Where, however, in an already clogged curriculum do we have room to present an effective case for such a message? The answer might well be that there is no further room, that – as one instructor said after a review of all the options – ultimately our students are already numbed by "philosophical and methodological debates", that few have the time and even fewer have the background to grasp the necessary essentials to bring them to even the brink of methodological sophistication.

In seeking a solution we have come to realize that one fundamental point of compromise is to force students to sort out the methodological problem on their own terms. As part of the recent curriculum revision, students are now asked, in the context of a "research project" course, to deal with their own areas of interest (most frequently associated with some aspect of their professional work), with the only requirement that their research projects explicitly and overtly identify both theoretical and methodological assumptions. At this point in time, research project testing is too new to suggest whether or not the innovation will be successful. However our purpose is – beyond merely forcing students to come to terms with methodology – one founded upon certain important assumptions which span not only theory and methodology but the programme as a whole. The first assumption is two-fold: (1) that mid-career students appear particularly reluctant to acknowledge that there are both theoretical and methodological frameworks in all human activities, be they professional or academic; (2) that mid-career students find it particularly difficult to bridge the potential relevance of theory and their perception of "the real-world". A research project which does not impose theoretical or methodological constraints, but merely requires that the students make their own theoretical and methodological assumptions will sensitize them to the nature of theory, will probably make them reflect upon other theoretical approaches to test their theoretical intuitions against academic theorists, and ultimately – it is hoped – begin to force the students to bridge that supposed divide of the "real" and the "theoretical". The second assumption is that, particularly for people who are already trained in their professions, to dictate methodological techniques generates a peculiar kind of resistance. The imposition of such techniques generates an attitude of "forced labour", e.g. "academic techniques" that really have no relevance. However, by merely pointing a student to a problem – a problem that he or she has chosen by selecting a particular research project – and by only requiring that the student make explicit the methodological approach to resolving the problem, the student is forced to measure his own intuitive methodological approach with the methodology required to deal with the research problem.

However, in preparing ourselves for the future and in seeking to present to our students an accurate portrayal of the dynamics of the discipline, it might well be argued that the paradigmatic unity of our theoretical and methodological approach, which has been a consistent feature of the programme, will be under siege.

Strategy

The world of theory and methodology is uncertain, ambiguous, and often frustrating in its complexity. But "strategy" is clear and straightforward; it is about the military extension of international politics; it is about the potentials and constraints of violence in the international system; it is concerned with throw-weights and force postures, arms limitations and geo-political alignments. Or is it?

The subject of strategy in the context of our programme straddles uncomfortably between the conventional orientation of strategy and a more fundamental concern about the nature of conflict and violence. For mid-career students, the former is preferable. MBRF, SALT, geo-politics and von Clausewitz represent the types of issues which concern many of them. Professional military officers who might well understand the technical aspects of highly sophisticated weapons systems or even policy planners from the Department of Defense have sought, within the strategy course, the "big picture" which their day-to-day activities might well blur.

That "big-picture" sought by our students is only too often merely a more sophisticated version of students' own conceptions of geopolitics, a version which might modify certain views (as revisionist historians might have modified assessments of the Cold War's origins), but really does not strike at the core issues of "why strategy?"

The "why strategy?" is a question which has increasingly embroiled us in attempts to explain the sources of conflict and methods of resolution. In introducing this concern into a "core course", we have engendered the difficult balance, mentioned above, between the conventional areas of strategic concern and questions which broach issues of political sociology. As so often has happened in our mid-career educational efforts, we find ourselves torn three ways. There is a body of material which a particular kind of student-body wants, namely, the conventional study of strategic issues. Can we afford to ignore this demand? Secondly, there are profound issues which should be broached, which we shall call "political sociology", that might well prove to provide greater intellectual challenges in the long run. But do we find ourselves again imposing a particular paradigmatic view that will be seen as a stark academic alternative to the realities of our students' world? Thirdly, to hold a master's degree in international relations, there are certain general aspects of international politics involving geo-political developments — such as capabilities, military technologies, force postures — which our students should know. Do we ignore these substantive issues and instead lead our practically-oriented students through the maze and vagaries of additional levels of abstraction concerning the nature and sources of conflict?

As we look towards the future, the answer to all three questions is increasingly "yes". And this affirmative answer is underpinned by four reasons. Despite the desires of our students for the "big picture", the fact of the matter is that our mid-career students are generally more "au fait" with the general terminology and trends of conventional strategic issues than are the conventional graduate students. Furthermore, the conventional assumptions of strategy abound in an ever-increasing amount of literature; it is accessible to our students, where perhaps less orthodox or conventional approaches are not. A second reason for our move away from conventional strategy to a political sociology orientation lies in the assumptions about what the "big picture" really is. There is little evidence that threat systems, deterrence and the like cannot be explained as readily in terms of structural violence, military–industrial complexes and communications networks as they can in terms of power politics. Thirdly, strategy in the post-war world had meant for over two decades primarily the relations between the two super powers. Yet, it can be argued that the particular superpower relationship fails to explain either the growth or function of the military or the causes of conflict and violence on a broader global scale. In other words, we are seeking to uncover global patterns which might well provide insights into conflictual relations, including those of the superpowers, but which the traditional assumption of the superpower relations may well not explain. A fourth and closely related reason which is pointing us in the political sociology direction is that we feel that the increased anarchy within the international system

337

needs to be explained, that to explain it, one needs to penetrate the myriad levels of discontent to find the critical variables that might indicate common elements of conflict. Having said this, we feel that there is a prescriptive element which we should also posit, namely the ways that conflict might be settled or resolved.

Essentially what is emerging in our approach to "strategy" is an entirely new concept of the course, as John Groom has described in Chapter XI. The course now is focused upon "endemic change" in which the spectrum of legitimized and non-legitimized relations within societies are explored. The newly-introduced course, *Processses of Conflict and Cooperation*, has been designed to achieve two objectives: (1) to tie approaches to conflict and cooperation more closely into the core courses concerning theory and methodology; and (2) to probe the essence of what strategy is about, namely potential or actual conflict and violence.

The assumption is that to understand "change" one must understand the decision-making process, the role of perception and organizational factors in that process, the relationship of elites to their societies and vice versa, the manners in which institutions seek to maintain and re-enforce control, and the needs and values which lead to harmonious as opposed to conflictual relationships. Within this realm of exploration lies strategy — not directly in the conventional, Clausewitzian sense, but in the questioning of whether conflict need be an immutable fact of the international system.

International organisation

As with our view of strategy, so, too, have our views of international organization, as a "core subject", altered considerably over the years. Like "strategy", international organisation was introduced as a core course because of assumptions about world politics rooted in the 1950s and 1960s. Paul Taylor has explained in Chapters IV and XII the evolution of this portion of the discipline and the approaches which he presents to our mid-career clientele. Yet, in reflecting upon the possible transformations of the international system as well as the possible lessons which the past might have suggested, we feel that our conceptions and approaches to the subject of international organization — that mainstay of international relations studies — will alter too.

When we say "alter", we really are suggesting two things. On the one hand, we are suggesting that the substance of that aspect of the discipline might need to be refocussed. On the other hand, we are asking whether or not the underlying "message" of what international organisation concerns, viz. adaptation and cooperation, can be more effectively presented in our mid-career program.

Traditionally the major thrust of international organisation involved cooperative developments in the international system through formal institutions, generally consisting of routinized intergovernmental representatives' interaction among states. A significant portion of the lessons we have tried to gleen from formal international structures emanated from "Western experiences" with the League of Nations, the United Nations and certainly from that "European experiment": the emergence and development of the European Communities. What we have too often failed to do is to compare such experiences with those of organisations such as the Organisation of African Unity or ASEAN or the Latin American Free Trade Association. These latter groupings may well provide a litmus test for the general relevance of our assumptions about the genesis, durability and effectiveness of formal international institutions.

On another level, our approach to international organisations might also require us to look more carefully into the "techniques" of international organisations. Instead of concentrating upon the institutional elements of organisational structures, there is increasing evidence to suggest that we look at the more informal elements which affect the workings of international organisations. For example, it is important to recognize that the inability of UNCLOS to resolve the "regime issue" of the seas has led delegates to embark upon innovative negotiating techniques which by-pass the prescribed operating procedures of the Law of the Sea Conference. Or, it is equally as important to view the functioning of international organisations from the perspective of trans-national elites, as it is from the holistic perspective of state interests.

Furthermore, we should also concentrate more upon international non-governmental actors than we have in the past. The roles of multinational corporations, for example, may not only provide clues to some of our functionalist assumptions, but they also might provide insights into the ways international organisations, such as UNCTAD or OPEC, are affected by special, non-state actors. For that matter, scores of examples abound, e.g. Friends of the Earth, Amnesty International, which suggest that the patterns of influences which affect international organisations such as the European Commission on Human Rights or Intelsat, cannot be fully understood from the traditional nation-state perspective.

On the other hand, the questioning of the directions of our course on international organisation generates the same issue which underlies this entire work, namely, what do we feel are the essential elements to provide to our particular type of students? We increasingly have felt that, while international organisation — even with such revisions as indicated above — is an important part of the international relations discipline, it does not reflect the essence of the discipline which justifies the label, "core course". Stripped of its wrappings, we view the essential theme of international organization, as one of adaptation, or *change* and *cooperation.*

It should not surprise the reader to find that the same motif was introduced in our discussion on strategy; for ultimately we see both conflict and cooperation along the same continuum, with change being the critical independent variable. In the final analysis we view the theme of "international organisation" as part of the process by which adaptation in global politics occurs. The response to change can either result from legitimized or non-legitimized authority, as Groom has discussed in Chapter III. Certain members of the United Nations, no matter how lofty their motives, can participate in causes suggesting change without legitimized bases of support. In this instance authority is imposed, and the consequence for stability or peaceful transition is determined by the perpetration of power and the overt or covert force that such imposition would suggest.

The point is that cooperation, as with conflict, is dependent upon one's assumptions about *gemeinschaft* or *gesellschaft*; it is dependent upon one's assumptions about human needs and values; it rests upon the distinctions made between Mitrany's conceptions of functionalism and Morgenthau's view of global politics; it entails the same issues of perception, communications and organisational theory that are so clearly part of conflict. It has been this very continuum, underpinned by a concern for the processes of change, which has led us away from the "core course" of international organisation to that of the new core course, mentioned above, called the *Processes of Conflict and Cooperation.* For those students who wish to concentrate on "international organisation", the course remains, but as an elective. International Organisation may or may not comprise the elements which we feel reflect the changing international system, but we hope that the students who take the course will approach it with the fundamental conceptual message we have suggested here.

International political economy

The last decade has witnessed an explosion of interest in the area of international political economy. Jeffrey Harrod has described the reasons for this academic groundswell in Chapter V and has discussed in Chapter XIII the problems he has confronted when teaching mid-career students who he finds too often have fixed conceptions about this aspect of the discipline. In trying to forecast where international political economy will fit into our curriculum in the future, we are struck by a fundamental paradox. The underlying theme of the re-emergence of international political economy is that economic theories and models have failed to cope adequately with the very issues with which they were designed to deal, that the answers to the issues raised by economists in many instances would be more effectively sought in the arena of political models and theories. If this fairly represents the bedrock upon which IPE has been developed over the past decade, we find ourselves forced to ask whether or not there is sufficient substance in international political economy to warrant its designation as an autonomous sub-field within the international relations discipline. Given the orientation of our views on theoretical approaches to the discipline in general and our particular concentration upon what we have termed earlier as "the processes of conflict and cooperation", we feel obliged to ask whether IPE is in fact but a body of evidence which serves to sustain more critical aspects of the discipline. This in no sense is to deny the valuable contribution which the orientation provided by the re-emergence of IPE has given to the discipline. Clearly what we have called the "underlying theme" has been an added impetus to challenge the assumptions of "positivism" which have dominated much of the Anglo-American approach to international relations, and certainly IPE's far ranging search for more global explanations of distribution, institutional unresponsiveness, and motivations has forced the discipline in many instances to move beyond conventional, liberal-orthodox prescriptions. And yet, to the extent that the roots of IPE are part of a much larger concern encompassing the development of societies, human needs and values, motivations, they provide tangible focii and evidence for our considerations, but do not pose core conceptual considerations of the discipline.

If the U.K. Programme can succeed in adapting the international political economy focus into its world society analytical framework, it may achieve a more balanced development in the near future than is the case in most international relations programmes in the United States. Since the mid-1970s, the awakened interest in IPE issues is approaching the development of a fad by which claims for a major reorientation of the whole discipline has become a common cause for activist "dependistas", peace researchers, Wallersteinian "world system" adherents, liberal interdependence theorists and the younger generation of international relations scholars in general who are defecting intellectually from the Cold War-based mainstream thinking by "the Establishment" within the American international relations profession.

Whatever epistemological debate the role of IPE might trigger, the subject for mid-career students is encumbered with certain problems that deserve mentioning here. Perhaps nowhere in a graduate curriculum in international relations, with the possible exception of strategy, do discrepancies amongst backgrounds and the rigidity of mature students come out more clearly than in the teaching of international political economy. We find ourselves dealing with a serious predicament. The minority of students who have been trained in economics find it extremely difficult to adjust to the political dimensions of the subject; and the majority who have received little or no training in economics shy away from the economic dimensions of the subject. In either case, there is an underlying unwillingness to compromise. The former, because of their training, see a proven tangible in the scientific rigour of economies, *per se*; and the latter, because of their lack of training, are ill-equipped to understand the economic issues which have to be brought into the political arena. Since part-time, mid-career programmes are too often forced to circumvent remedial training, the only available solution has been to use the backgrounds and personal experiences of the students to make them understand and "live" a political-economy orientation. And, even then, one is faced with the added dilemma that attempts to use the background experiences of students in order to "link" IPE issues tend to re-enforce students' justification in maintaining the *status quo*. The more their own needs and values are brought into the subject, the greater is their attempt to justify the political–economic system in which they operate. This is true, despite the fact that our students have ranged from over forty different countries, from East as well as West, from Third and Fourth worlds as well as developed American and Western European worlds. The reason for this general impression might stem from the common denominator of "transnational elites" and from the possibility that only certain types with certain orientations would join an American graduate programme in the first place.

Yet, as our own thinking has evolved, new orientations have emerged, which, while never sufficient to compensate for lack of adequate training, may help us to overcome the kinds of problems we have faced. An example of the type of orientation we are suggesting is a "focus on distribution", where a motivation of labour typology would reflect views on the ways different societies envisage their own purposes and functions and the strengths and weaknesses of these societies' assumptions. Such a typology might be separated into inspirational motivation which reflects distribution within the Soviet Union of the 1930s or within modern Tanzania; the coercive which reflects much of the state corporate system of

342

today's Latin America; and the remunerative/materialist incentive system of capitalist Western economies and societies.

This example, merely illustrative, at least suggests the types of approach which meet the interests of mid-career students since it can be described as reflecting practical problems, viz, the motivation of labour, and puts a range of alternative conceptual perspectives before the student without demanding a sophisticated understanding of economics.

Foreign policy analysis

Foreign policy analysis has maintained its separate identity in our programme because of its principal concentration upon two aspects of the discipline: the decision-making process and the comparative approach to foreign policy analysis. Each has a certain degree of universality, and to that extent, each can be broached in a way that suggests the dilemmas of state actors, as a specie, in the international system. The problem, however, with our present approaches, as described by Randolph Kent in Chapters VI and XIV, is not so much whether or not we are proceeding from assumptions that seek to apply an irrelevant Western approach to a large portion of non-Western states as it is whether or not there are themes within the context of foreign policy analysis that might be more helpful to our students.

In one sense, our students emerge from the programme without having very clear thoughts on what a nation-state really is, its origins or its dynamics. Earlier we referred to the general lack of developed historical backgrounds that is common to most of our students; and, in terms of foreign policy analysis, what a nation-state is or what the forces are which have led to its development demands a degree of sensitivity to history. Without such an understanding, the nation-state appears to be a permanent and immutable fact of international relations. It becomes a stolid feature of the global system; and the evolution, the organising concepts, the transition from one type of societal structure to another are devoid of meaning to a student who is unable to view the transitory nature — or at least the brief 300 year development — of the concept of the "nation-state".

While we may decry this lack of historical perspective, it is a fact of life which our kind of programme must endure. But is there a way out? Although we cannot engender the degree of historical awareness we believe students should have and still achieve the overall purpose of the international relations degree, we feel that there are ways to design the foreign policy analysis course which will at least mitigate the problem.

The starting point may begin with attempts to generalize about the development of societies, to utilize various perspectives which pose questions about human needs and values and social structure. We are not so foolish as to assume that a lack of historical depth would now be mitigated by a profound understanding of sociology. We are, as so often happens in this sort of mid-career education, merely planting ideas, hinting at themes which will reside in the students' minds as "intriguing". In a course dealing with foreign policy analysis, there is not the time to dwell extensively upon the societal development theme nor can we assume that our purposes would be better achieved by doing so. What we seek to implant is a sense of societal dynamics so that students might have the minimum amount of tools to focus upon issues such as pluralism, nationalism, and legitimacy.

Employed in a course which concentrates upon decision-making and the comparative study of foreign policies, these few tools would lead to understanding about such issues as state systems "converging" along the lines of bureaucratized polities, the dilemma for state decision-makers, whether in an autocratic or pluralistic regime, of dealing with contending interest groups, and the impact of non-state actors and transnational actors upon the state structures when conventional state institutions cannot adequately contend with the complexities of the international system.

Each of these issues, in turn, forces one back into the realm of how decisions are actually made. The responsive capabilities of states are dependent upon the psychological, organizational and governmental milieu which must confront complexity. Out of this might also emerge a most interesting basis for comparative study as well; for it would seem increasingly evident that the general "Western" theories of the decision-making process are by no means as parochial as we had feared. Increasingly plausible to suggest is that the characteristics of state institutions, as discussed in Chapter VI, are as pervasive in Third and Fourth world countries as they are in developed countries, with one fundamental difference, viz. that developed countries are moving away from the "Weberian" organizational/governmental syndrome while lesser developed countries remain in its midst. In other words, certain "management techniques", e.g. task force management, might change the responsive capabilities of developed governments while lesser developed countries remain ensnared in Weber's vertical hierarchies and organizational permanence.

The consequence of all of this returns us to the need to explore social dynamics. The need to understand change underlines our thoughts about the future of foreign policy as it underlines our thoughts on developments in the field of strategy and international organization. If there is any single message which we hope to have filter through the minds of our students in studying foreign policies, it is that permanence and stability in the international system can be correlated with institutions' abilities to be sensitive and adaptive to change, an endemic and consistent feature of the global political system.

Regional international relations

The study of regional international relations has come to pose a problem for us as the UK Program developed its theoretical and methodological emphasis over the last decade. According to Nielsson's review of approaches to regional international relations studies in Chapter VII, the differences between the configurative approach, which characterizes area studies, and a social science theory-guided approach are so fundamental and so intensely maintained that it seems nearly impossible to find solutions which could lead to a higher degree of integration of the regional courses into the core of the curriculum.

Traditional area studies specialists, who teach regional courses, have been trained in academic programmes with an interdisciplinary composition, but dominated by such core academic disciplines as history, languages and the humanities with only a small proportion of formal coursework devoted to the study of international relations within a particular region. The theory–oriented international relations specialists have been trained in social science theory and methodology which have been global in scope where geography and culture have often been considered artificial barriers to systematic enquiries searching for verification of patterns of behaviour.

The theory-oriented literature on regional international relations has reflected both the normative and the power political trends characteristic of various phases of the development of international relations as an academic discipline. The most recent literature appears to indicate a trend toward a comparative approach; especially the regional subsystem analytical frameworks, but they suffer from a lack of sound methodological underpinnings.

In the U.K. Program, the core faculty is in agreement that the global-scope, theoretical perspectives should have priority over the more ideographic interests emphasized in area studies. Students should be given a sense of the emergence of global patterns. Differences and similarities among political entities should be assessed on the basis of a global context which should constitute the reference points in analyses of manifestations of diversity in different parts of the globe.

But that position may well result in tension because it imposes a particular set of values upon the mid-career students most of whom show a strong interest in regional courses – whether motivated by the experiences of previous professional responsibilities or by personal interest in a particular region. There is, then, the problem of how much the program should be responsive to student demand for configurative detail while maintaining the stress on stimulating interest in the global context.

The resulting predicaments must be addressed and some kind of compromise found in the future. In Chapter XV, Nielsson has presented his experiences in trying to develop a theory-guided approach to the study of European international politics. With all the difficulties and limitations such an approach entails, it may be worthwhile to encourage existing core faculty and new instructors to teach regional courses based on a theoretical approach. For the conduct of the programme as a whole it would be important to try a more careful sequencing of regional courses over an entire academic year period in order to expose students to the more historical and configurative overview first and then follow up with a research seminar in which a theory-guided approach could be adopted by the instructors.

The experiment with developing a comparative approach to regional studies as a separate field of concentration, begun on campus this year, bears watching over the next few years. While it must be recognized that it requires considerable "retooling" and experimentation by the faculty involved, it might be possible to draw upon the experiences gained in order to better integrate regional courses with the rest of the curriculum.

In the meantime, efforts must be made to establish a closer relationship between the existing core faculty and the regional specialists who have taught continuously for the U.K. Programme.

Given the existing dilemmas involved for the entire international relations discipline, however, it is to be expected that the differences between student expectations, the currently prevailing approaches to teaching regional courses and the core faculty's stress on global-scope theories will remain a constant source of tension for some time to come.

Conclusion

Our major concern in this book has been with graduate level teaching and learning about international relations. Such an emphasis is justifiable because the characteristics and developments of an academic discipline are identifiable by its programmes of study as much as by its major research projects. In fact, the curricula can be considered indicators of solidification of trends exposed initially through the publication of innovative research. The reviews of various fields of concentration show that, while international relations studies have not reached a stage of paradigmatic stability characterizing "normal science" sustained by a textbook tradition in the Kuhnian sense, the discipline has matured to the point of consistent, albeit often contending approaches and focii, each with a core reference literature.

To develop a teaching program which is both comprehensive in scope and intellectually coherent requires, not uniformity, but the careful balancing act of adequately representing the major, different approaches and the consequences of adopting one or the other for analyses of issues. What to the uninitiated, new graduate student appears to be anarchy, can be portrayed as a positive disorder which more realistically reflects the nature of enquiries about the complexities of human behavior. This condition of positive, but controlled, disorder is well captured and presented in the theory and methodology core courses as they are presently taught. The ramifications of different conceptual and methodological approaches are not yet as well developed when it comes to applying them in the other core courses on conflict and cooperation. How to incorporate the burgeoning international political economy literature, provide a wider developmental perspective to foreign policy analysis and integrate the regional courses with the rest of the curriculum remain unresolved, but clearly identified and articulated issues for the future conduct of the U.K Programme.

The representation of developments in the various fields of concentration reflects important variations in emphasis, but, taken as a whole, there is a discernible over-arching concensus about the general approach of conceptualizing according to the world society framework. Maintaining coherence in the form of careful balancing of diversity requires special efforts to keep a faculty integrated around a common "teaching paradigm". It requires constant interaction about such tasks as joint review of the literature when composing core reference bibliographies, a process which forces a faculty to come to an agreement on priority ranking of key reference sources, jointly composed examinations and periodic review of the teaching approaches and the curriculum structure as a whole. In writing this book, we have engaged in an introspective process which has made us all more keenly aware of both the substance of the epistemological issues in international relations studies and the integrative processes the core faculty has been engaged in while developing the curriculum presently characterizing the U.K. Programme.

It has been with considerable uneasiness, if not outright trepidation, that we have made a first attempt to articulate our experiences about teaching mid-career students as a special type of educational endeavour. For it remains a paradox in academia that the pedagogical aspects of our activities is a subject which is woefully neglected in preparing for a career that involves teaching at the university level. With the greatest emphasis placed on the ability to do research and publish about it, teaching skills are expected to be obtained by osmosis after being "thrown to the wolves" in the first direct classroom experience. The acquisition of good teaching skills still constitutes the equivalent of Adam Smith's "invisible hand" element in the world of higher education. For us as a group, the pedagogical issues in teaching mid-career students involve an even more extreme version of what can appropriately be labelled an "unconscious experiment". It is a term we do not use in a self-deprecatory manner nor in any way to belittle the seriousness and commitment we have made in our efforts to teach a mid-career student clientele. The term is used to suggest that, all the while we consciously sought to provide an education of high quality, we found ourselves dealing with problems we had never originally anticipated and with needs and interest which, in many important respects, were distinctly different from experiences gained in teaching conventional graduate students. While we may not have made path-breaking points in respect to the pedagogical aspects of teaching mid-career students, articulating our experiences individually and in several special faculty colloquia has served an important clarifying function for us which we modestly hope might be useful for other academicians who are engaged in this type of programme. The most important generalization to be made in this context is that the instructor must be prepared to engage in a dialogue with practitioners who will bring into the classroom empirical experiential references, the incorporation of which into the formal classroom learning process represents a different challenging dimension.

While the quest for relevance demands that we must be responsive to student interests and expectations, it must not be forgotten that, in the educational environment of the dialogue between academicians and practitioners, the two groups have different roles to perform. They have different attitudinal predispositions and pursue different goals in their respective activities. As we view it, the academician's role is not that of training the practitioners in the specifics of their professions. In that respect, the mid-career students can teach the academicians. On the other hand, we do not seek the opposite goal of making the practitioners academicians, although some of them do change careers in that direction as a result of their experiences in our program.

The primary objective is to get the practitioners, who operate within a particular organizational milieu, to raise their horizons, so to speak; to widen the scope of their thinking about particular issues. Success comes when the mid-career students view their professional activities in a more holistic theoretical perspective and subject their decisional activities to the analytical test of alternative explanations, and their potential consequences for different courses of action, depending on which fundamental assumptions about the world are accepted as points of departure in analysing an issue. In other words, the primary purpose of the mid-career programme is one of shaking off the frequently stale view of accumulated experiences and regenerating the ability to pose questions differently and seek answers through more complex evaluation processes. We are not so naive as to assume that our approaches will fundamentally change the views of the majority of our military officers, our diplomats and our corporate executives. Furthermore, the intent is not to impose our view because we "know what is right", that would be indoctrination and not education, but rather to present such alternative approaches to reasoning and explanation that we have suggested throughout this book.

Author Index

Subject Index

355

356

Notes on Contributors

A. J. R. GROOM — Reader in International Relations at the University of Kent. Dr. Groom's works include *British Thinking about Nuclear Weapons* and, with Paul Taylor, *Functionalism* and *International Organisation: A Conceptual Analysis*.

JEFFREY HARROD — Formerly with the International Labor Organisation, Dr. Harrod is now a freelance writer and lecturer. His works include *Trade Union Foreign Policy* and a variety of major articles in the *Year Book of World Affairs*.

RANDOLPH C. KENT — Dr. Kent was director of the United Kingdom Graduate Program of the School of International Relations, University of Southern California, from 1975 to 1979.

RICHARD LITTLE — Dr. Little rejoined the University of Lancaster as a lecturer in International Relations after two years with the Open University. He is the author of *Intervention: External Involvement in Civil Wars*, and has contributed to a variety of journals and edited works.

CHRISTOPHER MITCHELL — Dr. Mitchell is a lecturer at the City University, London. He has published articles in a number of journals, including *International Studies Quarterly* and the *Journal of Peace Research*, and has co-edited, with A. J. R. Groom, *International Relations Theory: A Bibliography*.

GUNNAR NIELSSON — Dr. Nielsson is Assistant Professor in International Relations at the University of Southern California in Los Angeles and for six years the Director of the United Kingdom Graduate Program of the School of International Relations, University of Southern California. Contributions include "The Parallel National Action Process: Scandinavian Experiences" in *International Organisation: A Conceptual Approach.*

KARL PIERAGOSTINI — Graduated with distinction from the United Kingdom Graduate Program of the School of International Relations, University of Southern California. While completing his Ph.D., Mr. Pieragostini is also acting as a research assistant at the House of Commons and as London director of Educational Programmes Abroad.

DENNIS SANDOLE — Dr. Sandole has taught for many years with the University of Southern California's overseas programs. Dr. Sandole's other works include "Economic Conditions and Conflict Processes: Deterministic, Primary, Contributory or Chimerical", in Paul Whitely's *Models of Political Economy.*

PAUL TAYLOR — Lecturer in International Relations at the London School of Economics and Political Science. He is the author of *International Cooperation Today* and, with A. J. R. Groom, co-editor of *Functionalism: Theory and Practice in International Relations* and *International Organisation: A Conceptual Approach.*